RIDDLES IN STONE

The Sanctuary at Avebury, drawn by William Stukeley in 1723

Riddles in Stone

Myths, Archaeology and the Ancient Britons

RICHARD HAYMAN

THE HAMBLEDON PRESS
LONDON AND RIO GRANDE

Published by The Hambledon Press 1997

102 Gloucester Avenue, London NW1 8HX (UK)
PO Box 162, Rio Grande, Ohio 45674 (USA)

ISBN 1 85285 139 2

A description of this book is available from
the British Library and from the Library of Congress

Typeset by Carnegie Publishing, 18 Maynard St, Preston
Printed on acid-free paper and and bound in Great Britain
by Cambridge University Press

Contents

Illustrations

Illustration Acknowledgements

The author and publisher are grateful to the following for permission to reproduce illustrations: Alexander Keiller Museum, Avebury 80, 92, 93; Ashmolean Museum 25; Bodleian Library, 26, 27, 29; British Library 21, 34, 50; British Museum 41, 69; English Heritage Photographic Library 95, 96; Fortean Picture Library 13, 113, 115, 121; John Hedges 129; Audrey Henshall 87; Hereford and Worcester County Libraries 114; Historic Scotland 20, 75, 91, 109, 125, 130; Institute of Archaeology, University College, London 82; Gwil Owen 84; Pitt Rivers Museum 73; Reading Museum 83, 88; Royal Commission on the Ancient and Historical Monuments of Scotland 97, 131; Royal Institution of Cornwall 42; Salisbury and South Wiltshire Museum 51; Society of Antiquaries of London 90.

The following illustrations are by the author: 1, 2, 4, 5, 6, 7, 8, 9, 10, 11, 12, 14, 15, 16, 17, 18, 19, 22, 23, 47, 48, 53, 54, 56, 85, 86, 89, 92, 94, 98, 100, 101, 102, 103, 104, 105, 106, 107, 108, 110, 116, 117, 118, 119, 120, 122, 123, 124, 126, 127, 128, 132, 133, 134.

Preface

This is a book about places and people: prehistoric monuments and the people who have interpreted them over the past 500 years. Most of the interpreters have been archaeologists, who are the professionals concerned to explain 'what the monuments were for'. I hope to show, to the general reader as much as to the professional archaeologist, that archaeology can never quite demystify the monuments, and that archaeologists need to rewrite their subject from one generation to the next in the same way that outlooks and opinions change in any other aspect of our culture. This is not a weakness but a necessary operation to refresh the mind. The book was also written partly for archaeologists, who have too little regard for the endeavours of their predecessors, and generally none for the theories of people who do not speak the same insular language as they. A thriving alternative scene continues to produce challenging interpretations of the monuments, and archaeologists should take them more seriously than they do.

Like many other students who studied archaeology in the late seventies, my first contact with the subject was through ley hunting which, alongside astronomy, was at that time at the height of its popularity. Although I quickly rejected anything I considered to be a non-intellectual notion of the past, an interest in leys stayed with me, partly because to many of my friends they were the only thing they knew or thought relevant about prehistory. This dual interest in orthodox and fringe viewpoints subsequently taught me that no special interest group can claim ownership of the past, and that one thing that every competing ideology has in common is a desire to make the past meaningful to the present. This is no less true for the previous than for the present generation of writers.

The history of the enquiries presented here is a microcosm of the way that the British have conceived themselves in the history of the world. It is also an engaging subject in its own right. It is perfectly legitimate to enjoy William Stukeley, John Michell or Gordon Childe for their own sake, without having to agree with them. Such pleasure is analogous to the pleasure of ruins, without which this book would never have been written.

Many people have helped me in the course of writing this book, especially Julia and John Brookes. The bulk of the research was undertaken at the libraries of the Somerset Archaeological and Natural History Society, in Taunton, and the University College of Wales, Cardiff. For information, encouragement and the loan of books I also thank my parents, Wendy Horton, Paul Devereux, Rob Cole, Martin Gillham, Marion Blockley, Kevin Littlewood, Jane Orrom, Rick Pool and Rhian James. The extract from 'Archaeology' by W. H. Auden is reproduced by permission of Faber and Faber Ltd; 'Wessex Harvest' is reproduced by permission of Professor Stuart Piggott.

The archaeologist's spade
delves into dwellings
vacancied long ago,

unearthing evidence
of life-ways no one
would dream of leading now,

concerning which he has not much
to say that he can prove:
the lucky man!

W. H. Auden, from 'Archaeology' (1972)

I

Monuments in the Landscape

Archaeology can never be a science in the strict definition of the term, because nothing the archaeologist says can ever be proved wrong. Archaeologists characterise their subject as a discipline, but their study is always vulnerable to the inroads of others, in particular to those who conceive the study of the ancient world as a romantic pursuit. Thus the past can be understood in different ways. Romanticism in archaeology is based on the self-evident truth that the present is very different from the past, and that the past is 'shrouded in mystery', or 'lost in the mists of time'. In the antique grandeur of ancient monuments, or the heroic feats of mythical individuals, is the raw material for re-discovering great, lost civilisations. In Britain the elusive King Arthur has long preoccupied those of a romantic persuasion, but nothing has combined better the intellectual and romantic aspects of archaeology than the study of prehistoric monuments.

The stone circles at Arbor Low in the Peak district or Castlerigg near Keswick, and even relatively minor monuments such as the huge monolith in the churchyard at Rudston in Yorkshire, are all powerful evocations of a past seemingly beyond the reach of understanding. Such monuments, remote and strange as they are, have invited and continue to invite diverse speculation. This book is a history of those speculations: it tries to explain why and how our understanding of the monuments has changed over time.

At one time they were known as 'rude stone monuments', but now they have been classified under the generic term 'megalith', meaning large stones. As a group they constitute the oldest ruins in our landscape. In the current reckoning the earliest were erected over 6000 years ago, while the latest are a mere 3500 years old. Prehistoric monuments exist in many shapes, and have been ascribed many names, as much the product of local culture as the less colourful language of archaeology. The most basic form is the single stone known as a standing stone, a menhir or (rarely now) a longstone. Sometimes they exist in pairs, or in lines, whence the term stone rows, sometimes as stone circles. Where megaliths were used in a more architectural sense to create stone-built chambers they are known prosaically as chambered tombs, and more evocatively as quoits, cromlechs or dolmens. Many of these are still covered by mounds, which in turn are called barrows or tumuli if the mounds are of earth, cairns (or knowes in Scotland) if they are made up of stones. All of these terms are used liberally throughout this book because they are part of the megalithic literary culture.

Modern archaeological techniques have identified other forms of prehistoric engineering — earthworks which are now barely recognisable or have vanished from the

FIGURE 1. The Men-an-tol in west Cornwall is an unusual monument with an unusual list of interpretations: a cure for rickets, an initiation device used by the Druids and an astronomical sighting device are among the less outlandish.

surface of the land, and evidence for wooden posts erected in a similar fashion to stones. But I am not writing a history of archaeology as such, which would also have to encompass artefacts, because my main concern is with monuments that have visibly survived. This is for two reasons. Their conspicuousness has ensured that they have attracted attention over a long period of time. The study of prehistory began with the study of monuments; subsequently monuments have spawned a literary culture all their own. Secondly, they are our primary contact with the remote past because other forms of archaeological evidence are encountered in an entirely artificial context: either as artefacts in museums; or as plans, photographs and written descriptions of features below ground.

These factors have had another consequence. Archaeology is a specialised discipline. Laws exist to prevent anyone but a recognised archaeologist gaining access to primary archaeological evidence in the ground. Such evidence is presented to the public, usually in the form of museum exhibits, solely on the archaeologists' terms. But with monuments in the landscape the archaeologist is unable to exercise this same degree of control, because access to them is unrestricted. The consequences of this have been shown in recent years by the theories of astronomers and ley hunters. Monuments are there to be interpreted by anyone.

Dr Samuel Johnson once said, and there are probably people, especially bored children, who agree with him, that a rude stone monument has 'neither art nor power in it, and seeing one is quite enough'. Conversely there are those of us for whom a solitary standing stone in a muddy field is not only worth seeing, but is actually worth the effort of *going to see*. The latter point was taken up by the sculptor Richard Long, who in 1978 created a sculpture entitled 'A Day's Walk Past the Standing Stones of Penwith

FIGURE 2. The interior of the West Kennet chambered tomb near Avebury. The monument's restoration in the 1950s involved the removal of the human remains that made it a tomb.

Peninsula', trailing past eight stones in the landscape of west Cornwall. Many people less self-consciously cover the same territory, hurrying by car between stone circles like the Merry Maidens and Boscawen-un, the great stone burial chambers like Chun Quoit and Lanyon Quoit, and the holed stone known as Men-an-tol. The highlight is Men-an-tol, so inscrutably weird that it positively demands suggestions (fig. 1). People stand by it and make jokes about the original ring doughnut. The Cornish poet D. M. Thomas called it 'the wind's vagina', although this has never stopped people poking their heads through it to have their photograph taken. Indeed I would go so far as to say that scrambling through the hole is the decent thing to do.

Our perceptions of these places differ, and are conditioned by the context in which we view them. A visit to the long barrow at West Kennet in Wiltshire, together with a little knowledge of its recent history, will demonstrate how a single place can be reinvented in different ways. To the archaeologist West Kennet is a chambered tomb, perhaps the most impressive in southern England. At one end of a long earthen mound is a stone-built passage giving access to five chambers (fig. 2). However, in 1860, Dr John Thurnam, the medical superintendent of Devizes asylum, excavated one of the chambers, not realising that there were four others waiting to be discovered. In the 1950s, when the Ministry of Works planned to restore what had become a somewhat dilapidated structure, a new series of excavations was undertaken by Stuart Piggott and Richard Atkinson of Edinburgh University. Piggott and Atkinson excavated the remaining four chambers. They were able to show that the tomb originally had a forecourt, and that the chambers and the entrance to the passage were sealed off when the tomb went out of use.

Today West Kennet is a tourist attraction. As we walk inside, breathe the earthy atmosphere, run our fingers over the cold stones, and wonder how people with such a primitive technology could have raised such gargantuan stones (hard work!), few of us consider that we are in a place that we are not supposed to be. The tomb was deliberately blocked up to keep people out and the dead in. The disarticulated remains of about forty-six people have been taken away, an act that has changed, and arguably diminished, the monument's meaning. West Kennet is a tomb no more, it has become a sanitised cultural commodity, exploited to that effect. Its builders and users would not have welcomed its appropriation by anyone and everyone, but modern egalitarian society will not make allowance for that. It has become everybody's history. Even archaeologists can now only understand it by reference to the literature and artefacts accompanying its excavation. To them it is a partially dissected remnant of an extinct society, while to modern pagans it is still a living entity. The winter solstice is celebrated here, and afterwards you can witness the archaeology of pagan life − fires lit in the passage, candles ranged around the chambers, and offerings of fruit left against the chamber walls. Such practices would not have been possible even fifty years ago. West

Kennet has become something else, a reinterpretation structured around mutually exclusive understandings of its past.

This has always been the case, both within and between different generations of enquirers. In little over a hundred years between the seventeenth and eighteenth centuries, five separate surveys were made of Stonehenge, by Inigo Jones, John Wood, John Aubrey, William Stukeley and John Smith (two architects, a scholar and two doctors), and each drew a different configuration of stones, and offered correspondingly different interpretations (fig. 3). The intellectual roots of archaeology go back to the seventeenth century with the discovery and study of Avebury by John Aubrey, although the romantic conception of ancient monuments is even older. Since Aubrey's day our knowledge of the monuments and the people who built them has grown exponentially, giving the impression that archaeology is slowly but surely revealing the truth about prehistory. However, it has become clear to archaeologists that linear progress is not axiomatic. In the late 1960s science was able to provide a far more accurate method of dating these monuments than had hitherto been possible. The results shattered so many preconceptions that archaeologists were forced to reflect inwards and ask to what extent our preconceptions and prejudices colour our interpretations of prehistory. In this context David Clarke was able to write in 1972:

> Archaeological interpretation changes generation by generation, and we are accustomed to interpret this succession as 'progress'. But is it? There is an uncomfortable suspicion that much of this change is directionless and that the changes we may wish to see as cumulative progress towards more exact knowledge are little more than a succession of contemporary mythologies.[1]

This was my point of departure in writing this book, to write a history of ideas as a sequence of myths about the monuments. But Clarke's view cannot be accepted without qualification. There is certainly such a thing as progress. Ever since the 1830s, when the Stone, Bronze and Iron Ages were first postulated, prehistorians have been sorting their evidence into a chronological sequence, and in this they have been increasingly successful. It is when we move to the deeper level of the meanings and actions associated with the monuments that we are writing about our own ancestry, and so perhaps bring our current world views to bear. Eighteenth-century antiquaries accepted the chronology of world history given in the Bible, and that Britain had been peopled after the Flood by the sons of Noah. This structured the way that they interpreted the monuments, but it was wholly different to the view of later nineteenth-century archaeologists who believed that the human race descended from apes, and gradually progressed from savagery to civilisation. In post-imperialist Britain this latter view is itself no longer tenable, and once the word 'progress' is replaced by 'change' the monument builders are seen in an entirely different perspective.

FIGURE 3. These four surveys of Stonehenge were made in a little over one hundred years between the seventeenth and eighteenth centuries. Each surveyor saw a different configuration of stones.

We are informed enough to know now that the eighteenth-century antiquaries were wrong, but I intend to avoid a simple right or wrong dichotomy, and accept that current theories are just as much myths as their predecessors. The word myth is not used to demean the ideas of those who promote them. Theories are an attempt to make the past meaningful, or at least comprehensible, and we need conceptual frameworks in order to function mentally. This is what I mean by myths, which have nothing to do with being true or false. One of the dogmas that science has espoused is that an objective, detached viewpoint is the only possible way of arriving at the 'truth'. Yet there is never a single truth. Ask a white man to explain the history of the British Empire and you will have one version, but ask a black woman and you will have another. There is no such thing as a neutral, detached viewpoint. We know the past by knowing ourselves, and if we could escape from ourselves the past would become pointless. The past only has meaning because it involves us.

Each archaeology is of its time, which is one of the themes of this book. However, there is one important exception to this rule of thumb: that is popular culture, which seems to have persisted for long periods with little change, and to which we usually confine the term 'myth'. While folklore has contributed much to the romanticisation of the megaliths, viewed in its own right it reveals a more intimate relationship with the past than the modern archaeologist can hope to achieve, given that it belonged to people for whom the past was present in their own landscapes. It is to folklore that we first turn.

2

Pagan Traditions

We begin at the beginning, with a creation myth, and the story of how the Cornish quoit got its name. In Mounts Bay, at Penzance in Cornwall, is the island known as St Michael's Mount. Its Cornish name is 'Carreg-luz-en-kuz', meaning the white rock in the wood, from a local belief (now proved by geologists) that the sea around Penzance was once low-lying woodland. It was here in this wood that Cormoran the giant decided to build his home. But he did not want a house in the woods; like all giants he wanted his house raised up above the trees so he could survey the surrounding countryside. Cormoran selected some huge cubical masses of granite from some distance away. His wife Cormelian then got the job of dragging them to the required spot, and piling them one above the other to create their giant-made mount.

None of the other Cornish giants had to go to quite so much trouble to build their homes. In west Cornwall, known as Penwith, they all lived on high vantage-points, in what are now prosaically called Iron Age cliff castles and hillforts. Maen Castle, near Land's End, was the home of Trebiggan (can you really have a giant with 'biggan' in his name?), Trencrom the home of Trecrobben, Chun Castle of Jack the Hammer. A later occupant of St Michael's Mount was called Carreg Cowse (a corruption of Carreg-luz-en-kuz).

A little further east, near Redruth, is the granite peak of Carn Brea, on which various outcrops had names like the Giant's Head and Hand, Giant's Coffin and Giant's Cradle. Back in Penwith there were outcrops known as Giant's Frying Pans, Dinner Plates, and Chairs. The giants certainly left us with plenty of archaeology, most of which is the debris of their fun and games. On the slopes of St Michael's Mount are loose slabs of granite called 'buttons', from a game known as bob-button, the aim of which was to throw a stone at a target and knock it off its perch. But the favourite game of the giants was throwing quoits, the name attached to all of Cornwall's chambered tombs because of their flat capstones (fig. 4). The giants put some of these quoits to other uses: the ruined Carwynnen Quoit was the Giant's Frying Pan; Trethevy Quoit was the Giant's House; and Lanyon Quoit, with its horizontal eighteen feet by nine feet capstone, was used as a dinner table.

The folklore of giants crops up in other parts of Britain and, as in Cornwall, most of it is connected with fun and games. Quoit is a common alternative name for cromlech or dolmen in west Wales. Another giant-flung monolith is the Busta Stone in Orkney, a ten feet high standing stone thrown by the giant of Papa Stour at the giant of Mavis

Grind. On a stickier note, Robin Hood's Butts, a group of round barrows in Somerset, were said to be clods of mud thrown by a couple of giants in a mud-slinging contest.[1]

The Dwarfie Stane on Hoy in Orkney is an unusual rock-cut tomb said to have been a giant's house, which given its size must have been like a hermit's cell. Following up the domestic theme are two chambered cairns in North Wales, one of them in Anglesey, called Barclodiad y Gawres, meaning the Giantess's Apronful. The name comes from a story repeated often in folklore. A giantess is travelling to some place and a weary traveller coming in the opposite direction is carrying a sack of shoes, saying 'Look – I've worn out all these shoes coming from the place you're going', whereupon the giantess gives up, drops her apronful of stones and returns home.

Legends attributed to giants can equally well be attributed to King Arthur or the Devil. Arthur's Stone at Dorstone in Herefordshire was the place where Arthur slew a giant (fig. 5). There is a stone beside the tomb where the giant fell, leaving the impression of his elbows in the rock. The capstone was a quoit thrown by Arthur, and

FIGURE 4. Mulfra Quoit, like most Cornish chambered tombs, takes its name from its flat capstone, said to be have been flung by a giant.

FIGURE 5.
Arthur's Stone in
Herefordshire was
the place where
Arthur slew a
giant.

if you know where to look you can see the indentations of his thumb and fingers in
the rock. Arthur's Stone in Gower, whose several tons of capstone were said to have
been a stone stuck in Arthur's shoe, makes Arthur himself look like a giant. In fact
this is how he appears in early Welsh folk tales, like 'Culhwch and Olwen', where
Arthur is a beneficent giant grappling with other giants, witches and monsters.

Apart from the interchangeability of characters, the folklore connected with giants
shows that when we talk of the folklore of prehistoric monuments we are talking about
the folklore of the landscape. This is its context, and it remains true for just about every
legend, tradition, ritual or superstition connected with these sites. They invariably
correspond to the folklore of natural features such as rock outcrops or trees, later
archaeological features such as Iron Age fortifications, Christian places like churches
and especially wells, and even secular buildings like houses.

Such folklore was not just oral culture. It was made up of stories, beliefs, rituals and
festivals passed on by word of mouth from one generation to the next. When this
chain of knowledge was rapidly dwindling in the nineteenth century, conscientious
middle-class fieldworkers went out patiently collecting and cleaning up the culture of
the lower classes before it vanished in the name of progress. In its most quaint form
folklore has long since been hijacked by the Merrie England brigade. One look at a
maypole dance, a church fete, or a fairy story for children, and it becomes obvious that
folklore is in need of rescuing from what E. P. Thompson described as 'the enormous
condescension of posterity'.

Folklore is Culture, not Arcadia, and the standing stones and burial mounds of
prehistory had their special place in local culture, often through their sheer physical
presence. Avebury, in the middle ages a small village growing up in the shadow of the
gargantuan stones, is a good example. Here the villagers, presumably at the instigation

of the church, went to the extreme of trying to eliminate the stones, and all the cult and cultural baggage that went with them, by burying them. At the same time a gathering, where local people 'made merry' with cakes and ale, took place on Silbury Hill every Palm Sunday.

Plenty of other prehistoric sites were used for assemblies of various sorts. The use of stones in the inauguration of kings has its origin in Scotland, where Pictish kings were inaugurated at the Grenish stone circle in Inverness. Another circle, Huntly in Aberdeenshire, was used for courts of assembly in the middle ages. In 1349 a court was held at the Old Rayne circle in Aberdeenshire to settle a dispute between William of St Michael and the Bishop of Aberdeen over the ownership of certain lands in the district.

Moots were held at barrows and hillforts, a use that can be traced back at least to Saxon times. On North Ronaldsay it was customary to assemble at the Holland standing stone at Hogmanay. A different sort of gathering, known as the Ram Feast, took place at a standing stone near Holne on Dartmoor. On May Day, before sunrise, the men of the village would gather there and proceed to the moor where they selected a ram lamb; after running it down they brought it back and tied it to the stone. Its throat was ritually cut, then the lamb was roasted whole. At midday the men fought manfully against each other for the first slice of meat, then the afternoon and evening were spent in a customary bout of dancing, wrestling and cider drinking.

The ultimate origin of these customs is impossible to trace, but there is no reason to suppose that such gatherings have not been taking place ever since the stones were raised. The Victorians may have embellished, and occasionally fabricated, their evidence, but much genuine folklore is essentially timeless. Although we can be confident that most folk beliefs have roots extending deep into the prehistoric past, some of them refer to events we can place in time. The most obvious of these historical contexts is Arthurian. Arthurian lore is widespread in western Britain and Brittany, but associations with megalithic monuments are most common in Wales, where you find many a Coetan Arthur (Arthur's Quoit), and in Carmarthenshire a Coetan Myrddin and Carreg Fyrddin (Merlin's Quoit and Merlin's Stone). Arthur's Stone at Dorstone in Herefordshire is the exception in these Arthurian associations, because elsewhere Arthur never actually did anything at the places he gave his name to. He became patron of the stones, just as saints became patrons of churches and royalty patrons of public institutions.

Robin Hood is the equivalent English folk hero, and his folklore stretches far beyond Sherwood Forest. Groups of round barrows known as Robin Hood's Butts can be found on the Blackdown Hills in Somerset, Bromfield in Shropshire and Verwood in Dorset; meanwhile in Derbyshire a group of cairns is known as Robin Hood's Pricks. Two standing stones near Alawalton in Northamptonshire are petrified arrows fired by

Robin Hood and Little John, but now I'm scraping the barrel – tales of Robin Hood do not easily lend themselves to landmarks in the countryside.

By contrast the Dark Age invasions of the British Isles, and the ensuing bloody battles, lend themselves perfectly to legends of place. The Danes crop up in grave sites in Wessex, and in the area of the Danelaw – East Anglia to Humberside. There is also a Danish King's Grave, a standing stone in Argyll, but the name is deceptive because it refers to the mythology of Norse invasions. It was erected over the grave of a Norse prince killed in the Battle of Sluggan. Another Norse chieftain, Kolbein Hruga, became the popular Orkney giant known in Scots as Cubbie Roo. He was so big he could cross from one island to another in a single step but, like all his fellow giants, he hated getting his feet wet and so spent his time building bridges. One day he gathered up all the stones he would need to build a bridge but was so absent-minded he forgot where he had put them. The pile of stones, instead of being called the Giant's Apronful, is the cairn known as Cubbie Roo's Burden.

The Norse invaders of historic times brought their mythology with them, especially to Orkney and Shetland, which were a Norwegian province until the late fifteenth century. Another foreign import was the Teutonic metalworker Wayland who appears quite unexpectedly in southern England. Wayland's Smithy is the chambered long barrow on the Ridgeway in Oxfordshire where, in exchange for a silver groat left on the capstone, the invisible blacksmith shod the horse of anyone passing by. The barrow has been known by that name since at least the tenth century, when it is mentioned in a land charter of Compton Beauchamp.

The Saxon invasion of Cornwall provides the most complete story in the mythology of conquest. In about AD 930 the Saxon King Athelstan defeated the Cornish King Hywel and his army at a place called Boleigh (meaning the field of slaughter), and a stone circle (now known as the Merry Maidens) was erected as a trophy to commemorate the victory. Nearby are two tall standing stones, now known as the Pipers, which were said to mark the positions of the opposing leaders when they met to discuss peace terms.

According to tradition, kings and heroic warriors took their worldly goods with them when they died, or failing that they were buried in luxurious golden coffins. Stories of buried treasure concealed in barrows and hillforts are common, from Cornwall to Kent to Scotland. The large barrow at Veryan Beacon, overlooking Gerrans Bay in Cornwall, goes one better. It was said to be the burial place of the mythical Cornish King Gerennius. His body had been conveyed across the bay in a golden boat with silver oars, which was then dragged to the top of the beacon and covered by an earthen mound.[2] Alas, excavation there in 1855 ruined a good story: all it yielded was a standard cist burial.

Excavation of barrows has sometimes given credibility to buried treasure stories, but none has unearthed the remains of the giants said to be buried in them. Even so there must have been many rumours because Giant's Grave is a common name for barrows and chambered tombs. A crofter at Tigharry on North Uist found a skull from a barrow which was so big that when he placed it on his head it covered his shoulders. Just as unlikely is the story of a barrow opening at Trevegean near Land's End in the sixteenth century. The diggers found the bones of an 'excessive big carcase', which apparently confirmed the etymology of the name, as it means 'town of the giant's grave'.

Apart from being the abode of a giant the Dwarfie Stane in Orkney was, as its name suggests, also reputed to be the home of a troll or trowe. Only in folklore could two such contradictory legends happily coexist. Fairy knowes and sitheans (meaning fairy knowe) are common names for barrows and cairns in Scotland, and there are some trowie knowes in Shetland. Fairies play music, gorge themselves at feasts and sometimes dance wildly around their barrow hideaways. And if you pass one of their knowes at night be sure to wear a hat – some of these fairies can make your hair stand on end.

Few people were able to catch sight of these diminutive creatures, and a meeting with them was a portent of good or ill – there was no in-between. A man was passing the stone circle near Machuinn in Perthshire, which used to be known as Lawers Sithean, when he heard music. He stepped into the ring, unaware that it was a fairy dwelling, and on leaving was presented with a white horse of lightning speed. He had no idea why luck was so kind to him, just like the ploughman who was working near the Beedon barrow on the Ridgeway in Berkshire. When his ploughshare broke he walked off home to fetch his tools, but when he returned he found his ploughshare already mended by the fairies.

Others were not so lucky, like the two people who peered into the Greflabbas Knowe in Shetland to watch the dancing in celebration of a fairy child. They brought a keg of buttermilk as an offering, but because they had not been invited they were turned to stone. Food offerings were commonly made to placate the fairies, especially at wells, otherwise they would wreak a terrible vengeance. In Scotland milk or beer was poured into the hollows of stones, or through the aperture of holed stones, to propitiate the spirit brownie, guardian of cattle.

The fairies, it seems, were running the world's first protection racket, and they dispensed their own form of justice. One night a feast was in progress on top of the Fairy Hill near Kirk Malew on the Isle of Man, when an unsuspecting passer-by was offered a drink from a silver cup. He looked at the strange liquid in the cup, but instead of trusting the fairies he refused to drink it. When he emptied the contents to the ground the fairies vanished instantly. Not sure what to do with his strange acquisition he asked the advice of the parson, who promptly commandeered it for use as a communion chalice. But soon the celebrants had to stop using it: those who drank from it went mad.

A species of fairy called spriggans, grotesque looking creatures with spine-chillingly hideous laughs, sometimes acted as the guardians of buried treasure. But they would not reveal themselves until the treasure-hunter was on the verge of discovering his booty, when their ugly bodies would emerge from the rocks and frighten the grave robber, who invariably dropped his spade, ran back home as fast as he could go, and locked all the doors.[3] Only the lucky ones didn't go mad. Finding buried treasure was the ultimate way to get rich quick, but life never turned out to be quite that simple. It is said that Coetan Arthur near Llanenddwyn in Merioneth will only reveal its treasure when the end of a rainbow rests on the capstone, as will the self-explanatory Crock of Gold, a cairn on Dartmoor. Elsewhere you have to dig for it.

If the treasure was not guarded by spriggans, there were invariably some other nasty surprises in store. Talk of buried treasure under the Balegreggan standing stone near Campbeltown was too much for one opportunist, but as he was digging under the stone it suddenly leaned towards him. Sensing a warning he left well alone, although the stone is still leaning today. The same thing happened when a treasure-hunter was digging under the Carreg Fyrddin near Abergwili, but he ignored it and kept on digging. Then the stone fell and crushed him to death, which served him right. It took the pulling power of five horses to lift the stone upright again. The man who dug under the Tristan Stone in Cornwall received another kind of omen. As is the wont of treasure-hunters, he chose a clear moonlit night to help him work by, but the sky blackened with gathering clouds and, just as he was about to strike lucky, a ferocious thunder-storm sent him running for dear life.[4]

Thunder-storms feature again in stories of attempts to remove stones. Grave robbing was one form of desecration, plundering stones for domestic or farm use another, a taboo reinforced in the number of stories of failed attempts to destroy stone circles and barrows – ironic given the number of stones that were removed and barrows ploughed out in recent centuries. When gunpowder was packed around the stones of Long Meg and her Daughters in Cumbria the only loud bang came from the heavens, followed by a shower of hailstones, at which point the workers scattered in all directions. When barrow digging became a fashionable pursuit in the nineteenth century reports of excavation work being preceded by violent thunder-storms were commonplace. In 1815 excavation of the Beedon barrow in Berkshire ended in farce when the labourers swore never to return after a thunder-storm had scared them away.

Many a farmer has successfully removed stones and, after great labours transporting and erecting them for their new use, found he had not quite got away with it. A farmer who noticed that two of the stones from the Mains of Hatton circle in Aberdeenshire would be ideal as gateposts discovered that as soon as they were erected his horses refused to go through the gate. Forced to admit his wrongdoing he transported the stones back to the circle and reerected them. But whereas it took two horses to drag the stones down the hill to the farm, it took only one horse to drag them uphill again. Much the same story was told of the farmer who removed the tallest stone of the King's Men at Rollright to make a bridge over a stream – four horses were needed to pull it downhill, but one horse could pull it back up.

Farmers who were able to make amends by replacing stones were the lucky ones. When the stones of the Cairnfauld stone circle in Kincardineshire were removed, the farmer found his cattle suddenly inflicted with disease. Worse happened to the farmer who ploughed out the earthen mound covering West Lanyon Quoit in Cornwall, in the process of which the structure of the stone chamber collapsed. His cattle died, his crops failed and he died in poverty.

The destruction of barrows was hardly any less blasphemous. If any of the contents were removed, which they often were, it was unlucky to keep any of the bones or an urn inside the house. The hapless treasure-hunter who dug into the Torlin Cairn on Arran provides the perfect cautionary tale. He returned home without any treasure, but with a skull; as soon as he entered the house with it the walls began to shake, as if being subjected to an earthquake. He soon realised that some supernatural force was punishing him for grave-robbing, so he rushed back to the cairn and reburied all the bones. But from that day on he was a nervous wreck, continually looking over his shoulder. His misery came to an end when he was mysteriously thrown from his horse at just the wrong place – he was sent flying over a steep embankment and his splattered remains were found on the rocks below.

Several farmers have found the presence of the Beedon barrow in Berkshire a nuisance, and have tried to plough it out to make sowing, ploughing and harvesting in the field easier. This is typical of why farmers were predisposed to get rid of these monuments. But no matter how many times they drew the plough through it the barrow retained its size and shape. An attempt was made to move the three monoliths known as the Harold Stones at Trellech in Monmouthshire (fig. 6), and the Longstone at East Worlington on Exmoor, but in both cases the stones refused to budge, even when a team of horses were used. A farmer employed oxen to try and drag away the Merry Maidens in Cornwall. But with no luck. Even 'all the King's horses and all the King's men' could not shift the Whistlestone in Gloucestershire. They used oxen and horses to try and dismantle the Devil's Den near Avebury and the Hoar Stone in Gloucestershire, but each time the chains broke.

Another tradition said that even if you did manage to move the Hoar Stone it would return to its original site overnight. The same was true of Zennor Quoit in Cornwall. The stones, seemingly with a life of their own, would return to their original formation. The ultimate insult to the exhausted workhorses and their masters was that as soon as their backs were turned the stones would uproot themselves, dance around the fields, do a twirl, or nip off for a drink, then return to their original places as though nothing had happened.

This kind of folklore is especially common in Brittany and Cornwall, where all kinds of things such as natural rockpiles (the most famous being the Cheesewring on Bodmin Moor), submarine rocks, gateposts and roof tiles would do a little turn at a specific time and while no one was looking. The cue for these megalithic revels was usually when they heard the clock strike midnight. Whether a particular stone is in hearing distance of the local church clock, or even whether the church has a clock, is not the point. The Long Stone at Minchinhampton, superglued to its spot by day, suddenly takes an exercise run around the field; the Diamond Stone, in the great circle at Avebury, prefers just a gentle stroll across the road and back; the Wimblestone in Somerset uproots itself and takes a wander over the Mendip Hills, exposing a pot of gold glistening in the moonlight; the Rollright Stones in Oxfordshire head off to a nearby stream for a drink; the Nine Stones in Derbyshire break into dance.

Sunrise and cock-crow had just the same effect. Cock-crow signals Maen Llia, a standing stone in the Brecon Beacons, to go for a drink at the stream (fig. 7); at sunrise the stones of the Grey Wethers on Dartmoor revolve once. Other stones only move once a year. On midsummer's night the St Lythans dolmen near Cardiff whirls around

FIGURE 6. The Harold Stones at Trellech in Monmouthshire. No amount of human effort can move the stones an inch. Another story is that they are stones thrown by the Devil at the nearby church.

three times, then the structure – three uprights and a capstone – becomes limbs and body to go and drink at the stream. Meanwhile Arthur's Stone in Gower goes down to the sea for a midnight swim, which is a fair trek of three miles (fig. 8). Finally, every Hogmanay the Quoybune Stone in Orkney walks to the Loch of Boardhouse for a drink. Watching the stone move through the darkness was definitely not recommended, as those who thought they were man enough to survive the ordeal were all found either dead or delirious at daybreak. A more common tradition is that none of these animated stones would move if anyone was watching them, a joke played on children to test their credulity.

But the joke is merely the degeneration of an earlier belief. In Norse folklore trolls and giants were creatures who roamed the lonely mountains at night, but as soon as the sun rose they were turned to stone. In this trancelike state they remained trapped until darkness fell, when they came to life once more. Haltadans – meaning the limping dance – is a perfect illustration of this. The cairn, on Fetlar in Shetland, is so denuded that only its kerb of large stones is now visible, said to be trolls dancing who were turned to stone when the sun rose over the horizon. Given the equally strong Nordic flavour of Orkney folklore, the Quoybune Stone is probably another Norse giant trapped by the sun, but there are so many stories of stones coming to life, found in all parts of the country, that they must surely have a similar native origin, being complemented by stories of flesh and blood being turned to stone.

Most petrification legends concern punishment for misdemeanours, as in the story of Long Meg, told to Celia Fiennes in 1698. Long Meg, or 'Great Mag', is the tall

FIGURE 7. When the cock crows, Maen Llia standing stone in the Brecon Beacons saunters to the nearby stream for a drink.

FIGURE 8. On midsummer's night Arthur's Stone, in the Gower peninsula near Swansea, goes down to the sea for a midnight swim, a distance of three miles.

FIGURE 9.
Long Meg and
her Daughters in
Cumbria. In 1698
Celia Fiennes was
told that the
daughters were
petrified for solicit-
ing Meg 'to an
unlawfull love by
an enchantment'.

FIGURE 10.
The chambered
tomb at Rollright
is known as the
Whispering
Knights: a group
of conspiring
soldiers huddled
together.

stone standing apart from the circle of stones, her daughters, all sixty-eight of them
(fig. 9): 'the story is that these soliciting her to an unlawfull love by an enchantment
are turned with her into stone; the stone in the middle which is called Mag is much
bigger and have some forme like a statue or figure of a body but the rest are soe many
craggy stones'.[5] Who turned them into stone nobody knows. Another tradition says
that they are all petrified witches, and that Meg is Meg Meldon, who was tried for
witchcraft in the seventeenth century.

The most famous of the non-Christian petrification legends is the story of the Rollright
Stones, and this time it was a witch who cast the spell. It is the story of a King, or

would-be King, travelling across country with his army. At Rollright he met a witch who said to him:

> Seven Long Strides shalt thou take,
> And, if Long Compton thou canst see,
> King of England thou shalt be.

What could be easier, he thought, as Long Compton was just down below in the valley. But as soon as he took his seventh stride a mound (long barrow) suddenly appeared before him, blocking his view. The gleeful witch then intoned:

> As Long Compton thou canst not see,
> King of England thou shalt not be.
> Rise up, stick, and stand still, stone,
> For King of England thou shalt be none,
> Thou and thy men hoar stones shall be,
> While I myself an eldern tree.

So the king was turned to stone – the King Stone. So were a group of knights who were at that moment huddled together and whispering as they conspired against him – the dolmen known as the Whispering Knights (fig. 10). Meanwhile the circle of stones are his ugly-looking soldiers (fig. 11). The story goes on to say that the king and his

FIGURE 11. The circle forming the Rollright Stones is known as the King's Men. In the eighteenth century William Stukeley described the stones as 'corroded like worm-eaten wood by the harsh jaws of time'.

army are only held there in a trance – no wonder they need to go off for a drink sometimes – and that one day they will return to life and the king will claim his crown. As for the eldern witch she has been variously located, because when one tree dies another grows up. It is said that (like all elders which were supposed to be witches or fairy trees) at midsummer when she is in flower she will bleed when cut. On midsummer eve there used to be a local gathering at Rollright where the people formed a ring around the King Stone while one man cut the eldern witch. As she bled the king momentarily moved his head.

Witches are not very often associated with stones in the landscape. In folklore there was a distinction between white and black witchcraft, the origin of which had nothing to do with Christianity. The white witch, sometimes also called a wise woman or charmer, had an accepted place in the communities of rural Britain. She (some men also had these powers) could cure diseases, divine the future and interpret omens, as well as exorcise the 'ill-wishes' of black witches. It was the malevolent black witches who were occasionally said to have used standing stones as meeting places.

It is a black witch who appears in 'Milking the Dun Cow', a popular folk tale collected by William Stukeley when he visited Middleton-in-Chirbury in Shropshire in 1753. The story was invoked to account for the nearby Mitchell's Fold stone circle. The stone ring was the place where a cow gave milk to all the honest people, who were trusted to take no more than a pail each. But then a witch came along and cunningly milked the cow into a sieve, whereupon the cow disappeared, never to return, and the witch was turned to stone. She was the stone that once stood in the centre of the ring.

The kinds of services offered by the white witches were also available through a myriad of popular folk charms. Some of them involved pilgrimages to certain places, usually wells, where patients were ducked, or 'bowssenned', in the water. People also resorted to wells for divination where they threw pins into the water. But these practices were also carried out at some stones, especially holed stones. The Men-an-tol in west Cornwall is Britain's best-known holed stone, a place where various rites of natural magic were performed. At dawn, usually on the first three Sunday mornings in May, children suffering from a variety of ailments, such as rickets, scrofula and rheumatism, were taken to the stone by their parents. The children were stripped naked and then passed nine times through the hole widdershins (against the sun). If it was a boy he was passed from the woman to the man, if a girl from man to woman. The children were then drawn on the grass three times against the sun.[6]

Adults suffering from rheumatism and sciatica used to crawl nine times around the stone, and if thin enough squeezed themselves through the hole. Similar rites were performed at Cornwall's other large holed stone, the Tolven Stone near Gweek, where, when the children had been passed through the hole, they were put to sleep on a grassy mound beside the stone. There were many natural rock apertures scattered over the Cornish landscape thought to be a sovereign cure for back pains, as long as you could get through the hole without touching the sides. Whooping cough was cured by passing a child under the belly and over the back of a donkey, or better still a piebald horse.[7] Other conditions were cured by dragging children through holes in hedges and clefts in ash trees. Even so none of them was as effective as the Men-an-tol, except perhaps the holy wells. There were three wells within a five-mile radius of Men-an-tol which could cure rickets, involving a similar ritual of ducking the children nine times then putting them to sleep on a grassy patch nearby.

Whooping cough and rickets were also cured by passing children through the Long Stone at Minchinhampton (fig. 12). The Toothie Stane is one of the portal stones of the Carraig an Talaidh chambered cairn in Argyll. Toothache sufferers were supposed to drive a nail into the stone at midnight, thus curing themselves by passing the pain into the stone. At Rollright women rubbed their breasts against the stones to induce fertility. Geoffrey of Monmouth, writing in the twelfth century, talks of libations poured on to the stones of Stonehenge, again part of a healing ritual, claiming 'there is not a single stone among them which hasn't some medicinal virtue'. Whenever they fell ill the giants who had erected Stonehenge poured water over the stones, which was then collected into baths which had been prepared at the foot

FIGURE 12. The Longstone, near Minchinhampton in Gloucestershire. Whooping cough and rickets could be cured by passing afflicted children through the hole. At other times, when no one is looking, the stone takes a run around the field.

of each stone. By mixing the medicinally charged water with herbal concoctions the giants were able to heal their wounds. These medicinal virtues were still preached in the eighteenth century, according to the Reverend James Brome in his *Travels over England* of 1707: 'if the Stones be rubbed, or scraped, and Water thrown upon the Scrapings, they will heal any green Wound, or old Sore'.[8]

In Orkney mothers used to visit the well at Bigswell before going to the Stone of Odin. There they passed their young babies through the hole, as it ensured that they would never shake with palsy in old age (fig. 13). It was also visited in a kind of engagement ceremony where lovers clasped hands through the hole and swore fidelity, as well as the intention of marrying when economic circumstances allowed it. This sounds rather picturesque, but a Mr Ker was told in 1780 that as soon as they had sworn undying love 'they proceeded to Consummation without further Ceremony'. The veneration in which the Stone of Odin was held was thrown into sharp focus in 1814 when the tenant farmer, Captain W. Mackay, broke it up and then started on breaking up the nearby Stones of Stenness. There was a public outcry – the Procurator Fiscal issued a court order restraining him from destroying any more stones. Mackay, who was not a native Orcadian, was subsequently the victim of two arson attempts.

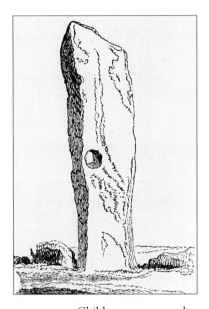

It had been customary to leave an offering of bread, cheese, a piece of rag or a pebble at the Stone of Odin, and offerings were usually left at stones with powers of divination. Cakes made of barley and honey were left at Arthur's Stone in the Gower by women anxious to be assured of the fidelity of their lovers. Divination with brass pins was carried out at the Men-an-tol. The pins were laid crossways on top of the stone, and the enquirer could then ask it any question of future events. When he or she returned to the stone the answer was read according to the changed positions of the pins, or whether they had gone altogether.[9]

FIGURE 13. Children were passed through the Odin Stone, at Stenness in Orkney, to ensure they would never shake with palsy in old age. The stone was destroyed in 1814 by an improving farmer. (*Fortean Picture Library*)

Charms usually rely on the performance of a rite three or nine times. At Stenness you had to walk around the stones three times to receive a cure, and three or seven times around Arthur's Stone in Gower. At a barrow near Newport Pagnell the fairies appeared if you ran around the barrow nine times without stopping. There is divinity in odd numbers. Stone circles in the south west of England are likely to be called Nine Maidens or Nine Stones – near Altarnun in Cornwall is a stone circle which the farmer restored with nine stones because he assumed it to be the correct number. The Spinster's Rock, near Drewsteignton in Devon, was reputedly built by three spinsters (fig. 14). Across the country you find Nine Barrows and Seven Barrows where the number makes no sense in terms of quantity.

But numbering the stones of stone circles is notoriously difficult. The tradition that the stones cannot be counted belongs to many of Britain's best known circles: Stanton Drew, the Hurlers in Cornwall, the Rollright Stones, Swinside in Cumbria, Long Meg and her Daughters, Callanish and Stonehenge. Correctly numbering the stones of Stonehenge was supposed to invite misfortune, though Charles II claimed to have been

FIGURE 14. The Spinsters' Rock, near Drewsteignton in Devon, was reputedly built by three sisters.

man enough to tempt fate and win. Meanwhile anyone who could count the Rollright Stones three times and come to the same number each time would be granted a wish. At Stonehenge, the Hurlers and Rollright the only reliable method of counting was for a baker to place a loaf on each stone, and then to compute the number of stones by counting how many loaves were left in his basket. A baker tried this at Rollright, but found that once he had gone all the way round the ring the first loaves he had placed had mysteriously vanished. Seeing this as a portent he leapt back into his cart and drove away, resolved never to try again.

No folk belief contributes more to the mystery of stone circles than this widespread numbering superstition. Does this superstitious dread of counting the stones belong with the original use of the circles, or is it merely the culture of people who do not understand them? If the tradition came after the event then why does the same story of the baker's loaves occur as far apart as Cornwall and Oxfordshire? This is one of the imponderables that confronts any attempt to see in folklore vestiges of the beliefs and practices of the stone circle builders. There are examples, however, of archaeological interpretations which confirm local tradition. Perhaps the best comes from the chambered cairns of Orkney, all of which at one time had their hogboy or hogboon. This was the guardian spirit of the family or farm, in effect the ancestor who had founded it, and in whose honour the mound was raised. The hogboy had a powerful hold on the fortunes of the living, which meant sacrifices had to be made to him. These included milk and ale, and the slaughtering of cocks or cattle. As late as 1909 a farmer on Voss declared that when his father died the family killed a heifer in honour of the mound dweller. Archaeologists would reject this evidence as a valid way of reconstructing the past – for a start, the hogboy clearly descends from the Norwegian *haug-bui*, and so is less than 2000 years old in Orkney. Nevertheless in the 1970s, when Colin Renfrew made his study of the chambered cairns of Orkney, he concluded that each cairn was a territorial marker and was a shrine to an ancestor cult, more or less what the folklore had been telling us.

Other examples are less clear-cut. The midsummer gathering at Rollright is an obvious candidate for study, as are the fire festivals that took place throughout Europe on midsummer night. In Norwich it was the custom to roll a wheel through the streets, then set fire to it and roll it down a hill. Interpretation of this flaming wheel is fraught with uncertainty. It could symbolise the decline of the sun during the latter half of the year, or it could just be people having a good time. In Penzance in the 1860s the festival was certainly a boisterous event, with torchlight processions weaving in and out of blazing tar barrels. Beacon fires were lit all along the coast from Penzance, and yet the area's wealth of megalithic sites had no part in the proceedings.

If it is established that midsummer was important to the stone circle builders then the folklore is only telling archaeologists what they already know. In this case folklore is enriching archaeology less than archaeology is enriching folklore, because it is implying that the midsummer fire festival may be 4000 years old. Archaeology can show that other customs have a similar vintage. Folklore tells us that pins and other objects were thrown into wells and springs in divination rites, and we know that votive offerings were thrown into rivers, streams and bogs as early as the Bronze Age. Inside the bank at Stonehenge are fifty-six pits, known as the Aubrey Holes, into which archaeologists have suggested that prophylactic libations were poured. This immediately calls to mind the custom of pouring milk into the hollows of stones to propitiate the fairies. However, as soon as the scope is widened, hopes of making similar connections quickly evaporate. Archaeology is as yet unable to shed any light on petrification legends, animated stones or fairy revels.

The use of folklore as folk memory obviously has serious limitations, but folk beliefs can be interpreted in another way that arguably gives them more meaning. Giants are a race of beings long extinct. Their 'archaeology', and the stories woven around them, are part of a disjointed and mythical narrative about the creation of the landscape. Buried treasure, and the taboo against grave-robbing, establishes veneration of the ancients, as does the belief that certain stones should not be moved. They are part of the unchanging world of nature. Meanwhile the little people, stones that dance and elder trees that bleed come together to create an informal, sometimes contradictory, set of beliefs, the legends complementing the landscape and making it spiritually alive. The spiritual life of nature is unlocked when rites of natural magic are performed, the magic power of the stones curing children of rickets, and endowing kings with the wisdom to rule or the courage to fight. Nature becomes a deity, a pagan view of the world that was absorbed and redefined by the strange brew of medieval Christianity.

3

The Church and the Devil

Even by a generous estimate the newest of the stone monuments of prehistory were at least 1500 years old when the Christian missionaries came to proselytise the British. The oldest monuments were nearer 4000 years old. But because they ceased to be built it does not follow that the stones ceased to be used, or at least visited, although this is not an argument for cultural continuity. Given the long passage of time, it is inherently more likely that the monuments were forgotten and subsequently rediscovered.

One of the enigmas of Stonehenge is how such a well-constructed temple could have ended up in such a ruinous condition, with several of its large sarsen stones completely missing. Part of the answer appears to be deliberate destruction; and the first phase of iconoclasm at Stonehenge seems to have taken place during the early period of Roman rule, between AD 43 and 410, before Christianity became established. Excavation at Stonehenge also unearthed a Romano-British burial inside the monument.

When General Pitt Rivers excavated Wor Barrow, a long barrow in Dorset, in 1893 he discovered eight Neolithic burials, but in the top of the mound and in the ditches he found seventeen burials of the Romano-British period, identifiable by their accompanying pottery and coins. Roman coins have regularly been found during the excavation of long barrows in southern England and have long since ceased to raise any eyebrows. Explaining them is more difficult. In 1955 Stuart Piggott and Richard Atkinson found six coins buried around the façade of the West Kennet long barrow near Avebury, all but one of them minted in the fourth century. Piggott dismissed the idea that they were dropped accidentally by casual visitors. The only alternative explanation is that this and other long barrows were not forgotten and ignored, but had become objects of some new age cult.

The occasional use of ancient mounds for burial continued into pagan Saxon times. There is a Celtic equivalent in Cornwall and Wales where numerous standing stones have Latin inscriptions carved on them. A typical example is Men Scryfa, only a few hundred yards from the Men-an-tol in west Cornwall, which bears the Latin inscription RIALOBRAN CUNOVAL FILI meaning 'Ryalvran son of Cunouallos'.[1] The menhir was appropriated and converted into a pagan memorial stone.

Other standing stones were Christianised. An episode in the Life of St Sampson tells us that sometimes stones were the focus of pagan cults. Sampson was born in 486 and was a pupil at the Celtic monastery of Llantwit Major, where he was ordained as a priest, later becoming a Bishop. In 521 he sailed to the north Cornish coast, then sometime later travelled over the moors to the south coast, with a cart carrying his holy vessels and books. At a place called Trigg he encountered a group of pagans worshipping an 'abominable image', either a stone or a stone with an image draped over it. Sampson interrupted them and fearlessly preached the word of God, after which the pagans were baptised, while on the stone itself he carved a cross. No one knows where this stone is, or was, but the meaning is clear enough. There are other stones that illustrate the same point. The Longstone at East Worlington on Exmoor has five crosses on it, while Lilla Howe, in north Yorkshire, is a round barrow surmounted by a standing stone reworked into a cross. Ty Illtud is a chambered cairn in Breconshire, meaning the 'house of St Illtud'. Inside the chamber a variety of designs are carved on the walls, of which crosses are predominant.[2]

The Emperor Constantine adopted Christianity as the official religion of the Roman Empire in 313, but in Britain it had to compete with the many native cults that flourished during this period, which is where the renewed interest in the long barrows appears to fit into place. Some of these native cults were later absorbed by the church, others were condemned. When Theodore of Tarsus was appointed Archbishop of Canterbury in 668 he embarked on a tour of England, then tried to regulate the dioceses and bring Christian practices into line with those of Rome. Evidently displeased with some of the goings-on he had encountered, he declared in his Penitentials 'no one shall go to trees, or wells or stones, or enclosures, or anywhere else except to God's church'. Canute became King in 1016, the first Danish King of England, and again had to familiarise himself with the habits of his new subjects. In 1018 he declared that 'it is heathen practice if one worships idols, namely, if one worships heathen gods to the sun or moon, fire or flood, wells or stones or any kind of forest trees, or if one practises witchcraft'. Alfred, King of Wessex from 871 to 899, had denounced *anfitheatra* as being centres of Devil worship. What exactly was he referring to? Surely nothing as rare as Roman amphitheatres, but rather earthwork enclosures and perhaps even stone circles.

In other respects Christian and pagan practices blended together nicely. Childless Breton women used to rub their bellies against the menhirs to induce fertility; now they were rubbing up against stone images of saints. Nor was the church always consistent in what it condemned. In Saxon England laws were passed to prevent holed stones being used to perform charms, but in Ireland they were carved with crosses and given a patron saint. The one cult acquired wholesale for Christian purposes was well worship: the proximity of sacred waters clearly influenced the siting of a number of churches.

There is a famous passage from a letter written by Pope Gregory I to Abbot Mellitus in 601 as the latter was about to embark on a mission to England. The manuscript does not survive, so we have to rely on a quotation given by the Venerable Bede over a century later:

> We have been giving careful thought to the affairs of the English, and have come to the conclusion that the temples of the idols among that people should on no account be destroyed. The idols are to be destroyed, but the temples themselves are to be aspersed with holy water, altars set up in them, and relics deposited there. For if these temples are well-built, they must be purified from the worship of demons and dedicated to the service of the true God.

This is the kind of historical source that promises much but in the end delivers very little. The was nothing new in the Pope's instructions. In an attempt to rid the Empire of paganism once and for all, Theodosius, from 392 to 395 the last Emperor of the unified Roman Empire, decreed that pagan temples should be converted to Christian churches. His successor as Emperor in Rome, Honorius, issued a similar edict in 408. Such statements prove nothing because they are only declarations of intent, while the Pope could hardly claim to have a grass-roots knowledge of English pagan practices, or even temples. However, some pagan places *were* appropriated for Christian worship.

The problem of the Christianisation of Britain and the building of churches is that the two did not happen simultaneously. Very few existing parish churches in Britain were founded before the ninth or tenth century at the earliest; most are later. The earliest churches in Saxon England were minster or monastic churches. Minsters were staffed by priests whose mission was to convert the populace at large. There is no reason why their churches should occupy ancient sites but they often do. A good example is Wells Cathedral, founded as a minster church about 700 on land owned by Ine, the newly-converted king of Wessex. The building was sited beside the sacred wells and excavations beneath the tenth-century Saxon cathedral have revealed a pagan Roman mausoleum of the later fourth century.

A large proportion of the pagan places adopted by Christianity were Roman – most of the old Roman towns had a monastery or cathedral in the middle ages – but the sites were not necessarily religious. St Peter and St Michael on Cornhill, and St Dionis Backchurch, were all built on the site of the basilica and forum of Roman London. The Romans had embraced well culture just as the Christians would do, and the joint connection influenced the site of Winchester, Wells and Exeter cathedrals, and of course Bath Abbey. Churches were also sited on natural features, usually hilltops. There are a number of churches or chapels built on such hills in south-west England, including Glastonbury Tor, Brentor, Burrow Mump, Roche rock, and St Michael's Mount. Finally, we come to a handful of churches which are visibly, or known otherwise to be, linked to prehistoric monuments.

The church at Knowlton in Dorset was founded in the twelfth century but never stood in the centre of the village. It stands inside a late Neolithic henge, or circular enclosure, which never contained a stone circle. The churches of Coldred and Kenardington in Kent also stand within ancient earthworks, and many others are built either on or near barrows, including Taplow in Buckinghamshire, Fimber in Humberside and Ogbourne St Andrew in Wiltshire. At Ludlow in Shropshire when the church was being extended in 1199 a long barrow had to be removed to make way for it. A contemporary account mentions 'tria mausolea lapidia' (three stone tombs), so it was probably a megalithic chambered barrow. Clearance of the site uncovered three skeletons which were promptly dusted down and hailed as three Irish saints. They were buried inside the church and were expected to perform miracles and attract pilgrims, whose offerings would enrich the church.

In the churchyard at Llangernyw, Denbighshire, are four standing stones, two of which have crosses marked on them. In the churchyard of Kilchoman is a cup-marked stone with a Celtic cross above it. Stone circles occupy part of the churchyard at Midmar in Aberdeenshire and Ysbyty Cynfyn in Cardiganshire, where three stones are incorporated into the churchyard wall. In 1890 a stone was found beneath the pulpit of Llandysiliogogo church in Cardiganshire. The tallest standing stone in Britain stands in the churchyard at Rudston in Yorkshire (fig. 15).

There may also be a link between the stones and church at Avebury. The church was founded after 900 and, according to Domesday, stood on *Terra Regis* (the King's land). It stood away from the Saxon village, which was to the south west of the great circle, and although the church is conspicuously *outside* the circle it is very conspicuously *at* Avebury. In 1114 a Benedictine priory was founded next to the church, on the site of the present Avebury Manor, so for a while Christianity was well represented here.

Dunino church in Fife was said to have been built using the stones of a stone circle, which may or may not have been on the site of the present church. The stones were apparently Christianised by having crosses carved on them. This story may be true, but it is legend, unverifiable. So is the story of Athelstan, giving thanks for his victory over the Cornish in 930, founding a monastery at St Buryan on the site of another stone

FIGURE 15. The standing stone in the churchyard at Rudston in Yorkshire. Rudston means 'rood stone', rood being the Saxon word for cross, but any crosses that were carved on it have now weathered away.

circle. There is even folklore which suggests that some places were deliberately avoided. The aptly named Chapel o' Sink is a stone circle in Aberdeenshire where, so the story goes, all attempts to build a chapel were thwarted because every night the walls mysteriously sank into the ground. The builders got so tired of having to renew their work that they gave up.

The relationship between churches and stones, wells and trees, does not mean that there was a great conflict in the middle ages between Christianity and paganism. A few examples from sites in Scotland show how the stones continued to play a part in local culture, but not necessarily in a religious sense. The people of Lewis never lost their respect for the stones of Callanish, which were called Tursachan, possibly meaning the place of pilgrimage, and where people gathered on May Day and midsummer morning. A popular expression in Scotland, 'Are you going to the stones?', used to enquire whether your neighbour was going to church. Indeed some stone circles are known by the name Kirk – in 1784 the Stenness circle was referred to as the Kirk of Stainhouse – and some were traditionally places of sanctuary. The right of sanctuary was possessed by churches and churchyards until it was abolished in 1624. The alternative name for Cnoc Mhic Eoghainn, a standing stone on North Uist, was the Sanctuary Stone; the Carraig an Talaidh chambered cairn in Argyll was likewise also known as the Sanctuary Stones. Two standing stones at Knocklearoch on Islay only needed to be touched to secure immunity from arrest, but in direct contradiction they also were traditionally the place where two priests were hanged. Another stone on North Uist, Clach Mhor A' Che, standing near Kirkibost church, was used to tie up miscreants during divine service.

None of this necessarily means very much. However, the church could act against pagan practices when it felt the need. A stone circle on Iona was destroyed in 1560 because offerings were still being made there. The sheer scale of Avebury made it much more difficult to destroy but, probably at the behest of the priory, the church did its best. An edict issued by the Council of Nantes as early as 658 had required 'Bishops and their servants to dig up and remove and hide to places where they cannot be found, those stones which in remote and woody places are still worshipped and where vows are still made'. Nantes is in north-west France, a country littered with big stone monuments, but ironically nobody seemed to take much notice there. In Brittany Christianisation of stones was commonplace. Avebury can consider itself unlucky.

The felling and burying of stones at Avebury had begun by about 1300, as a worn silver penny minted in the reign of Henry III (1216–72) was found under one of the stones in the Kennet Avenue. The smaller stones suffered most because they were the easiest to bury, but the irony is that had they not been buried they would almost certainly have been broken up for building stone in the eighteenth century. During one of these fellings an itinerant barber-surgeon had joined the working party, but when the stone accidentally fell on him he lay trapped until archaeologists extricated

FIGURE 16.
The Hurlers, on
Bodmin Moor in
Cornwall, have
been known as
petrified hurlers
since at least the
sixteenth century.

him 600 years later. In exchange for his freedom he handed over a leather pouch containing three silver coins, from the condition of which the archaeologists dated his misfortune to the 1320s.[3]

The other thing medieval Christianity gave to the stones was folklore. The trio of circles on Bodmin Moor known as the Hurlers were supposed to be men turned to stone for playing hurling on a Sunday (fig. 16). Hurling was a cross between football and rugby, the only rule of the game being to get the ball in the opponents' goal. The story of the Hurlers was told to Richard Carew when he was writing his *Survey of Cornwall* in the 1580s. It reminded him of something he had heard elsewhere: 'the like whereof I remember to have read touching some in Germany, who for a resemblable profanation with dancing, through a priest's accursing continued on a whole year together'.[4] This is a reference to an exemplum known as the Dancers of Colbeck. An exemplum, a kind of allegorical tale, was a style of sermon used in the middle ages by preaching friars. The people of Colbeck had assembled at the church at Christmas and were performing a ceremony known in Britain as church-clipping. This originated as a pagan spring festival, and required the people to join hands and dance around the church in a ring. However, as there was a time for dancing and a time for worship, the priest of Colbeck made his feelings known by condemning his parishioners to dance for a whole year without stopping. Holding hands in a ring they literally danced themselves into the ground until they were buried up to their waists. This exemplum was well known in Britain – it was first mentioned by William of Malmesbury in the twelfth century and Carew knew about it three decades after the Reformation. Its application to stone circles illustrates the fusion of Christian cautionary tales and the earlier pagan petrification legends.

Further west in Cornwall are the four stone circles of Penwith, known variously as the Nine Maidens, the Dancing Maidens or the Merry Maidens. The Merry Maidens at

Boleigh is explained as a group of women crossing the fields on their way to evensong at St Buryan (fig. 17). When three strange men appeared, and started playing music on their pipes and fiddle, the women forgot where they were going and started dancing. Having lured the women from the path of righteousness the musicians raised the tempo and, as the rhythm got faster and faster, the dancing women went into an ever more delicious frenzy, until suddenly a bolt of lightning struck them down and they were turned to stone. The musicians were also turned to stone. The Pipers are a couple of generously sized standing stones in the nearby fields, while nearly three miles away, on the other side of St Buryan, is another stone, the smaller Blind Fiddler. He was caught trying to escape.[5] Although the circle is now universally known as the Merry Maidens, in the eighteenth century it was called Dawns Men – Cornish for dancing stones – prompting one local folklore collector to complain that the story of the dancing women was invented by an over enthusiastic author.

This would not be the first case of a writer improving a folk tale, or even transplanting a story from one place to another. Apart from the sexual connotation the final fling of the Merry Maidens has another, equally medieval element – the Devil tempting the pious from their true faith by assuming a disguise. When William Stukeley and John Wood visited the Stanton Drew circles in the early eighteenth century they were known as the Wedding. A wedding party continued their dancing throughout Saturday night then, as they were about to finish on the stroke of midnight, a stranger appeared and started playing the fiddle. The guests just could not stop tapping their feet, and soon the party was back in full swing, but as soon as the clock struck twelve they were all turned to stone – including the fiddler who is easily recognisable at Stanton Drew because he is the tallest stone of all. The straggling group of stones do a good impression

FIGURE 17.
The Merry Maidens in west Cornwall are nineteen girls petrified for dancing when they should have been at church.

FIGURE 18.
As late as the
eighteenth cen-
tury the stone
circles at Stanton
Drew were
known as the
Wedding. The
three stones mak-
ing up the Cove
are the bride and
groom with the
priest.

of a wedding party – some dancing, some tottering on the brink, others lying on the ground completely legless. Nearby (next to the pub in fact) are three stones known as the Cove, said to be the bride and groom with the priest (fig. 18).

The stones of Tinkinswood burial chamber near Cardiff are said to be maidens dancing on a Sunday. Looking at the arrangement of uprights and capstone, I dread to think what dance they were doing. The stones of Callanish are much easier to visualise as giants turned to stone by St Kiaran for refusing to accept Christianity. The Hownam Shearers, a stone row in Roxburghshire, are a line of women turned to stone for reaping on the Sabbath, much like the Duddo Stones in Northumberland, five men digging up their turnips on a Sunday.

The Devil replaces giants in English folklore just as Arthur does in Welsh folklore. The following is typical. The Devil was walking through the Wiltshire countryside to Devizes, carrying a sack of earth with which to bury the church. He met a man coming in the other direction carrying a sack of shoes, and the Devil asked him how far he had left to walk. The man showed him the shoes and said he'd worn them all out walking from Devizes. So the Devil emptied his sack of earth and went away.

This is one of the stories of how Silbury Hill was raised. The Devil seems to have been particularly active in the area. The two stones making up the Cove at Avebury were known as the Devil's Brandirons and, until one of them was broken up in about 1720, the three large stones near Beckhampton were called the Devil's Quoits. The two remaining stones are now usually known as Adam and Eve. A little further away from Avebury village are the sparse remains of a chambered barrow called the Devil's Den. If water is poured into the cup-shaped depressions on the capstone at night, it will be drunk by a demon before morning (fig. 19).

The standing stone in the churchyard at Rudston was not, according to local belief, the reason the church was built at that particular place, but was a missile thrown by the Devil in an attempt to destroy the church. He missed, as he invariably did. Further north at Boroughbridge are three tall and impressive standing stones called the Devil's Arrows. They were thrown by the Devil from How Hill near Fountains Abbey toward Aldborough, but landed way off target. Nearly hitting the mark are the Harold Stones at Trellech in Monmouthshire. Again there are three stones, launched from Trellech Beacon about a mile away and landing only a couple of hundred yards short of the church.

Alas, the Devil of these stories is a loser, neither artful nor sinister. The stone circle near Urquhart in Moray used to be known as the Deil's Stanes, because if you walked around it three times at midnight the Devil would appear. The Rollright Stones were the reverse, as they were an effective talisman. One eighteenth-century writer complained that the King Stone was 'daily diminishing in size because people from Wales

FIGURE 19.
The Devil's Den,
near Avebury in
Wiltshire. If water
is poured into one
of the cup-shaped
depressions on the
capstone at night,
it will be drunk
by a demon be-
fore morning.

keep chipping off bits to keep the Devil off'. The Devil in the folklore of the landscape is a far less powerful demon than some of the fairies, to whom propitiatory offerings had to be made. And of course the wrath of the Devil was nothing compared to the wrath of God.

Eventually people stopped believing that God would turn you to stone if you profaned the Lord's Day. The decline of tales, superstitions and charms was remarked upon by every collector of folklore, going back as far as the sixteenth century. Protestants banished all forms of idolatry and superstition in the church, and thus frowned on it in popular culture. So did the more extreme Puritans: one of the reasons they hated the Roman church was because in proselytising the pagans it had adopted too many pagan practices. In the seventeenth century John Aubrey saw folklore's demise as a product of the social upheavals of the Civil War, while in the eighteenth century it came under attack from dissenting Christians, including the Methodists and Quakers who were strongly represented among the labouring classes. Until now popular culture had come under the broad heading of antiquities. The term folklore came along just in time – the nineteenth century, when most of the information recounted here was collected and published.

The decline of rural communities in the wake of the industrial revolution, and the provision of education for all, hastened folklore's demise. The nineteenth century saw only the culmination of an intellectual development dating back to the seventeenth century, and encompassing a change in consciousness toward Nature. Hitherto religion and superstition bore a resemblance insofar as they both believed in spiritual forces and the divinity of water, trees, animals and rocks. The advent of Newtonian science was to alter this completely until Nature had triumphed over Supernature. Folklore became the culture of the naive and ignorant, an attitude that remains prevalent today, but apart from its entertainment value it shows a different and, perhaps crucially, an older way of looking at the landscape.

4

In Medieval Literature

Nearly 1500 years separate the written word of the Romans from the printed word of Caxton. In the intervening period it is difficult to find a reference, let alone a meaningful one, to old stone monuments. There are two worthwhile exceptions from medieval literature that otherwise have nothing in common. They are not written in the same language and take us to opposite ends of Britain.

Beowulf is an Old English poem preserved in a single manuscript written about AD 1000. This is a copy by two scribes of an earlier manuscript. As a literary composition *Beowulf* is thought to have been composed in the eighth century, drawing on various folk tales and legends common throughout northern Europe. It is an Anglo-Saxon poem, but the events are set in fifth-century Scandinavia and concentrate on the exploits of Beowulf of the Geats. These were a people of southern Sweden, one of the tribes lost to history during the period of migrations at the end of the Roman Empire.

Beowulf's last exploit was a fight with a dragon over a hoard of treasure, which is hidden beneath a large barrow. The poet is clearly visualising a megalithic chambered tomb, because beneath the mound 'lay a passage unknown to men' leading to a treasure house built of 'stone arches fast on pillars'. The barrow is not the work of men but 'the ancient work of giants', and inside it the lone survivor of a warrior race had hidden the treasures of his people. It was not long before the hoard was discovered by a dragon whose nature it was 'to seek out a hoard in the earth where, wise with winters, it guards heathen gold'. And so, 'for three hundred winters the scourge of the nation held a particularly immense treasure house in the earth, until a certain man enraged its heart'.

The man, described only as 'the slave of one or another hero's son', stumbled on the treasure by accident when he sought refuge in the barrow from his enemies. Once inside he crept past the slumbering dragon and made off with 'a plated flagon' which he used as a peace offering. But when the dragon woke it saw a footprint in the ground and realised that the hoard had been tampered with. It managed to restrain its huffing and puffing until nightfall, but then 'it encircled those who dwelt in the land with flame, fire and burning', before returning to its lair by daybreak. When Beowulf heard 'that his own home, the finest of buildings, the Geat's throne, source of gifts, had been melted away in the burning surges', he knew he must meet the dragon in combat. It was his final act of heroism for, although the dragon was slain, Beowulf himself was mortally wounded.

The barrow appears in the story merely as part of the scenery, and it probably does not refer to any particular chambered tomb, either in Britain or Scandinavia. However, in the 1930s, two archaeologists, Stuart Piggott and Alexander Keiller, suggested that it might be a Scottish or Irish chambered tomb, largely on the basis that 'stone arches fast on pillars' was describing a chamber with a corbelled roof. Maes Howe in Orkney seemed the most likely candidate because, with a bit of artistic licence, it was located like the barrow in the poem, 'on open ground near the sea-waves'. It is a spurious argument because the text will not bear this kind of close scrutiny, but there are other, entirely coincidental, connections between Maes Howe and the Scandinavians, in that the 'treasures' it contained were plundered by Viking raiders.

Maes Howe is one of the wonders of prehistoric Britain. From a distance it is merely a grassy mound, but a large and conspicuous one, over a hundred feet in diameter and about twenty-five feet high. The entrance on the south-west side opens into a long passage leading to a large central chamber. This is about fifteen feet square and was once about eighteen feet high, but the most impressive features are its slabs of coursed masonry and the superb corbelled roof (fig. 20). In January 1153 Earl Harold

FIGURE 20. Maes Howe is one of the wonders of prehistoric Britain. It was robbed of its 'treasures' by Viking raiders in the mid twelfth century. (*Historic Scotland*)

and his men sheltered in the central chamber 'while a snowstorm drove over them, and there were two of their band lost their wits', but if they were looking for treasure they would have left empty-handed. The robbery of Maes Howe probably took place a couple of years earlier, carried out by Viking raiders led by Rognwald and Eindrid the Younger in the winter of 1150–51. On the walls they left twenty-four runic inscriptions, made on several occasions and including fourteen personal names. There are also carvings of a walrus, a serpent knot and, perfectly in keeping with its guardianship of buried treasure, a large dragon. Four of the inscriptions refer to the removal of treasure, but are not very specific. One reads, 'It is true what I say, that treasure was carried off in the course of three nights'; also 'Hakon single-handed bore treasure from this Howe'. Another reads, 'Away to the north west is a great treasure hidden'. Coincidentally a hoard of Viking silverware was found in 1858, about seven miles north west of Maes Howe.

The only prehistoric monument referred to specifically by medieval writers is Stonehenge, which was first mentioned in a history of England written by Henry of Huntingdon in 1130. Then came Geoffrey of Monmouth's *History of the Kings of Britain*, written in Latin and completed about 1136. It purports to trace the history of the British kings, beginning with, the great-grandson of the Trojan Aeneas, Brutus, who landed in Britain in the twelfth century BC, and ending with Cadwallader, after whose death in 689 the reign of the Britons was eclipsed by the invading Saxons. Like *Beowulf* it recounts an heroic age, but Geoffrey was a Welshman and the tone of the book is distinctly patriotic. Of the three principal characters two – Brutus, and Belinus, who is supposed to have captured Rome – are fictitious. The third is Arthur, but the Arthur of medieval romance, not the Arthur of medieval history described by earlier writers such as Nennius.

It was Geoffrey who first referred to Stonehenge as the Giants' Ring, and it was Geoffrey who first wrote about the amazing medicinal properties of the stones. Where did he get his information from? He claimed that his book was based on 'a certain very ancient book written in the British language', which is possible although not very likely. Folklore seems to have provided him with plenty of background material – for instance he describes Cornwall as having more giants than any other part of Britain – but the story of Merlin and Stonehenge is by general consensus a product of his own imagination.

The episode begins with Vortigern, who had usurped the throne of Britain and had become the reluctant ally of his father-in-law, the Saxon King Hengist. Hengist proposed a summit meeting between the feuding Britons and Saxons, which took place on Salisbury Plain at the Cloister of Ambrius (Amesbury) on May Day. The Britons (Christian and Welsh) attended the summit unarmed and in good faith, but the Saxons (pagan and English) went there intent on treachery. At a signal from Hengist the Saxons reached

FIGURE 21. In this fourteenth-century view of Stonehenge, Merlin reassembles the stones after having them brought from Ireland. (*British Library*)

for their concealed daggers and massacred the British, all except Vortigern who was captured and forced by Hengist to surrender all he possessed.

The rightful king of the British, Aurelius Ambrosius, now returned from exile in Brittany. 'When news of this reached Hengist and his Saxons, he was greatly frightened, for he dreaded the courage of Aurelius.' And so Aurelius Ambrosius assembled an army and duly defeated Hengist in battle. Then Aurelius visited Mount Ambrius to pay his respects at the grave of his massacred countrymen, and decided that it was worthy of some lasting memorial. But nobody could think of a suitable building. Tremornius, Archbishop of the City of the Legions (Caerleon in Monmouthshire, probably Geoffrey's birthplace), suggested that Merlin, a wizard and the prophet of Vortigern, would be equal to the task. When summoned, Merlin told the king: 'If you want to grace the burial-place of these men with some lasting monument send for the Giants' Ring which is on Mount Killarus in Ireland. In that place there is a stone construction which no man of this period could ever erect, unless he combined great skill and artistry. The stones are enormous and there is no one alive strong enough to move them.'

When Aurelius heard this he laughed. Why would they want to go to Ireland when there were plenty of big stones in Britain? Because 'these stones are connected with certain religious rites and they have various properties which are medicinally important. Many years ago the Giants transported them from the remotest confines of Africa and then set them up in Ireland . . .' The King liked the idea and he sent his brother, Uther, together with 15,000 men, to fetch the stones. When this uninvited army landed on Irish soil, the Irish thought they were about to be attacked. But as far as Geoffrey is concerned, 'the Irish were spoiling for a fight' and were wholly to blame for the carnage that ensued. The Britons won a bloody battle, in the course of which several thousand Irishmen, and who knows how many Britons, were killed so that 460 massacred Britons could have their memorial.

Led by Uther the victorious British now tried to move the stones, but rigging up hawsers and ropes was useless. The stones would not budge. Merlin waited till tempers were fraying and then calmly stepped in. With the same ropes he managed to dismantle the ring of stones single-handed, and the amazed troops set to work dragging them back to the ships. Once Merlin had reassembled the Giants' Ring on Salisbury Plain (fig. 21), Aurelius summoned all the Bishops and Abbots and 'men from every rank and file under the King's command' for a ceremony of rededication. He had no idea that he would soon be joining his slain brothers. Merlin, a soothsayer as well as a magician, prophesied that Aurelius would die by poisoning, and when this came to pass he too was laid to rest inside the Giants' Ring. The story then moves on: Aurelius' brother, now called Utherpendragon, is proclaimed king, and he in turn is succeeded by his son Arthur.

The History of the Kings of Britain was an immediate literary success, although Geoffrey always had his critics. William of Newburgh suggested that Geoffrey had written his book 'either from an inordinate love of lying, or for the sake of pleasing the Britons'. Almost 200 manuscript copies of the book survive, including translations into English and French. William Caxton printed a version of it in 1480.

Henry of Huntingdon had put Stonehenge on the map by declaring it one of the wonders of Britain, but for him it ranked lower than Cheddar Gorge in Somerset and the Devil's Arse in Derbyshire. The success of Geoffrey's book gave Stonehenge much better publicity, and his account was never challenged until the sixteenth century. Stonehenge was a monument to slain warriors erected on Salisbury Plain by magic. Moreover, the construction was masterminded by the son of an incubus. The Merlin story was repeated in the middle ages by three Welsh authors – Gerald of Wales, Robert Wace and Alexander Neckham – and the story of the massacre of the British found its way into Spenser's *The Fairie Queene*, where he writes of Hengist:

> three hundred Lordes he slew
> Of British bloud, all sitting at his bord;
> Whose dolefull moniments who list to rew,
> Th'eternall markes of treason may at Stoneheng vew.

And then of the triumphant Aurelius:

> peaceably did rayne,
> Till that through poyson stopped was his breath;
> So now entombed lyes at Stoneheng by the heath.

> (book 2, canto 10, stanzas 66 and 67)

Merlin, magic and menhirs took a long time to disentangle themselves. In 1591 Sir John Harington's translation of Ariosto's *Orlando Furioso* mentioned a Merlin's Castle, 'the old ruines whereof are yet seene in our highway from Bath to London. Also the great stones of unmeasurable bignesse and number, that lie scattered about the place, have given occasion to some to report, and others to beleeve wondrous stratagems wrought by his great skill in Magike'.[1] The great stones referred to here are not those of Stonehenge but of Avebury.

Geoffrey's account of Stonehenge was the theory of one individual, a theory challenged in 1534 by Polydore Vergil. Vergil was an Italian from Urbino, and patriotic enough to find Geoffrey extolling the genius of the Britons over and above the Romans and Macedonians intolerable. He modified Geoffrey's account by dropping the Irish and Merlin, but otherwise could find no other explanation for Stonehenge that would have made sense. So it remained the tomb of Aurelius Ambrosius, 'a rioll sepulcher in the fashion of a crowne of great square stones, even in that place wheare in skirmished he received his fatall stroke'. Despite an obvious debt to his predecessor, Polydore Vergil described Geoffrey's version of events as 'moste impudent lyeing'.[2] Later an apologist for Geoffrey returned the compliment by accusing Vergil of 'foul-mouthed railery'. This is the way it goes with academic rivalries: their little dispute was a omen of greater controversies to come.

5

The Wonder of Britain

In 1533 Henry VIII granted a commission to John Leland 'to peruse and diligently to serche al the libraries and collegies of this yowre noble reaulme'. For eight years Leland toured the country describing many things of antiquarian interest, mainly libraries, monasteries and assorted buildings. In 1546 he dedicated the first fruits of his studies as a 'New Yeares Gifte' to the King, and signed it 'Joannes Lelandius antiquarius scripsit'.[1] It was the first time a British scholar had referred to himself as an 'antiquary'.

The word came from Italy. The study of classical antiquities – like that of architecture, sculpture, coins and inscriptions – had an acknowledged place in Italian Renaissance humanism, and Leland, who had studied at the universities of Oxford and Cambridge, and also in Paris, considered himself equally a part of this new approach to learning. But Leland was English and personified a new spirit of national self-consciousness, of a nation about to pursue its own individual destiny – independent, assertive and patriotic. As we shall see, patriotism recurs frequently in antiquarian writings, and indeed a self-consciously patriotic note was struck by another early antiquary, William Camden, whose *Britannia* was published in Latin in 1586. Camden tells us that the geographer Abraham Ortelius 'did very earnestly sollicit me to acquaint the World with *Britain*, that ancient Island; that is, to restore Britain to its Antiquities, and its Antiquities to Britain'. He added that, despite the difficulty of the task presented to him, he 'could not decline doing what I was able for the Glory of my Country'.[2]

Antiquarian interests were to give birth to many forms of historical study, such as archaeology, numismatics, heraldry and philology. As observers and recorders of Britain, the antiquaries dabbled in everything. An amusing portrait of 'gentlemen of this musty vocation' was given in the *New Dictionary of the Terms Ancient and Modern of the Canting Crew*. Although it was published in 1690, it is as valid for the sixteenth as it is for the seventeenth century: '*Antiquary*, a curious Critick in old Coins, Stones and Inscriptions, in Worm-eaten Records, and ancient Manuscripts; also one that affects and blindly doats, on Relicks, Ruins, old Customs, Phrases and Fashions.'[3]

Given such promiscuous tastes, the earliest antiquarian books offered nothing much in the way of theory. The writers were on a voyage of discovery. When they described ruins in the landscape it was as topographers, not archaeologists, but for the first time these ruins were thought to be worth writing about for their own sake. Coming to the River Kennet near Avebury John Leland wrote: 'Kenet risithe northe northe west at Selberi Hille bottom, where by hath be [sic] camps and sepultures of men of warre,

as at Aibyri a myle of, and in dyvers placis of the playne.'[4] At Boroughbridge in north
Yorkshire he found three stones known as the Devil's Arrows (fig. 22), but his curiosity
yielded nothing: 'Inscription could I none find yn these stones: and if ther were it
might be woren owt: for they be sore woren and scalid with wether.'[5] Arriving at
Long Meg in Cumbria William Camden saw inside the ring 'two heaps of stones, under
which they say are dead bodies bury'd'. Hearsay was almost the sole source of
information, and these topographers were the first to record the folklore of the
monuments. Richard Carew, a friend of William Camden, told him about the tradition
of the Hurlers in Cornwall being men turned to stone, and in his own *Survey of
Cornwall*, written in the 1580s, he recounts a story of a man digging for treasure beneath
a menhir called the Tristan Stone. Another Cornish topographer, John Norden, writing
in 1584, had heard about the digging of a barrow in Withiel parish, at the bottom of
which were '3 whyte stones sett triangularly as pillars supportinge another stone nere
a yard square, and under it an earthen Pott verie thyck, haulfe full of black slymye
matter, seeminge to have been the congealed ashes of some worthy man'. Norden's
speculation goes no further than suggesting the occupant was killed 'in the time of the
Romish, Saxon and Danish warrs'.[6]

For the explanation of stone monuments there was still one place that monopolised
attention. Largely thanks to Geoffrey of Monmouth, Stonehenge was renowned as an
ancient wonder of Britain and attracted a trickle of curious visitors. In 1620 James I
went there and was so impressed that his host and favourite, the Duke of Buckingham,
tried to buy it off the owner. The Duke had a hole dug in the centre of the monument,
but the artefacts unearthed were not very enlightening. The King decided that Stonehenge was worthy of a more expert study, so he commanded the architect Inigo Jones,
Surveyor of the King's Works, to make a plan of the monument and to give an account
of its origins.

Unfortunately neither his plan nor his account was published before Inigo Jones died
in 1652. But in 1655 his observations, worked up for publication by John Webb,
appeared in a book called *The Most Notable Antiquity of Great Britain, Vulgarly Called
Stone-heng on Salisbury Plain, Restored*. While it is not possible to distinguish the ideas
of Jones from those of Webb, the latter was Jones's assistant, his loyal disciple and his
son-in-law, so we can presume that the two men were of like mind. Jones treated
Stonehenge as a work of architecture: he drew up a list of candidates from the work
of classical authors which he then scrutinised as to its potential builders. However, it
could not have been built by the ancient Britons: 'who cast their eies upon this Antiquity
and examine the same with judgement, must be enforced to confesse it erected by
people, grand masters of the Art of building, with liberall sciences, whereof the ancient
Britans utterly ignorant, as a Nation wholly addicted to wars, never applying themselves
to the study of Arts, or troubling their thoughts with any excellency therein'.[7] Nor

FIGURE 22. One of the three Devil's Arrows, in north Yorkshire. The Devil's Arrows was one of the earliest monuments to attract antiquarian interest. However, John Leland's curiosity yielded nothing: 'Inscription could I none find . . . for they be sore woren and scalid with wether.'

could it have been built by the priests of the Britons, the Druids: 'I find no mention, that they were at any time either studious in *Architecture* . . . or skilfull in anything else conducing thereunto.'[8] The period after the fall of the Roman Empire, as Geoffrey of Monmouth had advocated, was equally implausible: 'in the last declining of the *Roman* Empire, the *Arts* of *Design*, of which *Architecture* chief, were utterly lost even in *Rome* it self, much more in *Britain*, being then but a Tempest-beaten *Province*, and utterly abandoned by the *Romans*'.[9]

Therefore 'more propitious times, must be sought out for designing a structure, so exquisite in the composure as this', and that meant of course the Romans. He claimed, quite erroneously, that the plan of Stonehenge exhibited a perfect geometric symmetry, a shape defined by four equilateral triangles within a circle (fig. 23). More to the point, he found a classical building with just such a plan in Vitruvius' treatise on proportions in architecture. As to the elevation, its proportions were assigned, again quite erroneously, to the Tuscan order (fig. 24). Jones was able to conclude that Stonehenge had been built in the first century AD, probably while Agricola was governor of Britain, as a temple to the god Coelus, otherwise known as Uranus.

A few years later, in 1663, a counterblast was issued by Dr Walter Charleton, Physician

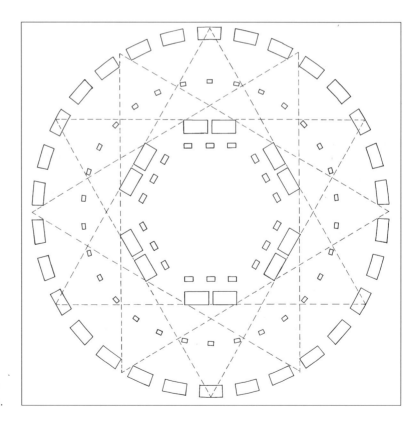

FIGURE 23.
Inigo Jones' plan
of Stonehenge
conformed to the
geometric
proportions in
architecture advo-
cated by Vitruvius.

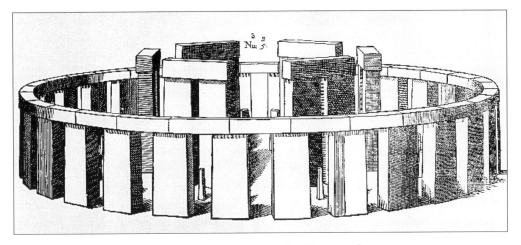

FIGURE 24. Stonehenge, restored by Inigo Jones to the Tuscan order.

to Charles II, in a book called *Chorea Gigantum: or The Most Famous Antiquity of Great-Britain, Vulgarly Called Stone-heng, Standing on Salisbury Plain, Restored to the Danes.* Dr Charleton, claiming to have 'diligently compared STONE-HENG with other Antiquities of the same kind, at this day standing in *Denmark*, and finding a perfect *Resemblance* in most, if not all particulars', concluded that Stonehenge must be Danish. It was built in the time of Alfred the Great, after the king of Wessex had been forced back into Somerset. Stonehenge was constructed for the inauguration of Danish kings, and its plan was reminiscent of the shape of a crown. This was a very tactful suggestion, given the recent restoration of the monarchy and Charleton's own employment in the court of Charles II. Even so one of Webb's friends thought it a 'capricious Conceit', and two years later Webb himself published a rejoinder, *A Vindication of Stone-Heng Restored.*

This mini controversy was a sterile one, parochial in both the geographical and the intellectual sense. There were other theories to choose from, including Edward Bolton's idea that Stonehenge was the tomb of Boadicea. Everyone, it seemed, including 'Pedlars and Tinckers, vamping on London way near it, may, and do, freely spend their mouthes on it'. These words appeared in a manuscript circulating in the 1660s, called *A Fool's Bolt Soon Shott at Stonage*, whose author wished to remain anonymous. But since everybody else had had their say, he decided to 'provoke my friends' by shooting his own bolt, in case 'by art or accident, [it] shall hit the mark'. Stonehenge is described, tongue in cheek, as 'an old British triumphall tropicall temple erected to *Anaraith*, their Godess of victory, in a bloudy field there, wone, by illustrious *Stanengs* and his *Cangick Giants*, from K. *Divitiacus* and his *Belgae*. In which temple the Captives and spoiles were sacrifised to the said Idol *Anaraith*.'[10]

But although Stonehenge was unique, it became apparent that it was not the only ancient stone monument in England. Charleton's theory was quite a serviceable one when applied to these other monuments, and in Robert Plot's *Natural History of Oxfordshire* of 1667 the Rollright Stones are similarly ascribed a Danish origin. Camden himself had been inclined to connect Rollright with Rollo the Dane. In 1723 Thomas Twining published a book which set out to prove the origin of Avebury, but we need go no further than the title, *Avebury in Wiltshire, the Remains of a Roman Work.* As for the classical temple scheme of Inigo Jones, it attracted derision from the start. A refutation of it is a convenient way of introducing John Aubrey, who read the book when it was first published: 'There is a great deale of Learning in it: but having compared his Scheme with the Monument it self, I found he had not dealt fairly: but had made a Lesbians rule, which is conformed to the stone: that is, he framed the monument to his own Hypothesis, which is much differing from the Thing it self.'[11] Aubrey had visited Stonehenge, but more importantly he had discovered a few years earlier a monument that 'did as much excell *Stoneheng*, as a Cathedral does a Parish church'. Now having read Inigo Jones it 'gave me an edge to make more researches'.

6

John Aubrey and Friends

John Aubrey was born in 1626 at Easton Piercy in Wiltshire, and went up to Oxford University in 1642. Thereafter fate was less than kind to him. His studies were curtailed by the Civil War, his father died leaving debts, a situation exacerbated by his son's own lack of business acumen, which led eventually to the lost of the family's estates. For most of his life Aubrey (fig. 25) was an impoverished scholar. He was forever owing money, but he did have an extraordinary talent for making friends, which he combined with an ear for gossip in the writing of his chief literary work, *Brief Lives*. It is for these witty, uninhibited portraits of his contemporaries, and near contemporaries, that Aubrey's name is best known, although the collection was not published during his lifetime. Sir John Birkenhead, satirist and Member of Parliament, was 'exceedingly bold, confident, witty, not very grateful to his benefactors, would Lye damnably', while Sir Henry Blount, a famous traveller, was 'pretty wild when young, especially addicted to common wenches'.

Aubrey wrote that 'I was inclin'd by my *Genius*, from early childhood to the Love of Antiquities: and my Fate dropt me in a Countrey most suitable for such Enquiries'.[1] He began a 'Naturall Historie of Wiltshire' in 1656, and it was largely his natural history and antiquarian interests that got him elected a Fellow of the newly formed Royal Society in 1663. As a scholar he was prolific, delving into science, the supernatural, architecture, folklore, place-names and archaeology, but he had one major shortcoming: his habit of starting books but not finishing them. The only one of his books published during his lifetime was the *Miscellanies* of 1696. This was an entertaining compendium of supernatural phenomena, containing everything you always wanted to know about 'Local-Fatality; Ostenta; Omens; Magick; Transportation in the Air; Visions in a Beril or Glass; Corps Candles in Wales; Extasie', and much more. His friend, the antiquary Ralph Sheldon, remarked that Aubrey's 'head is so full that it will not give his tongue leave to utter one word after another', and his estranged friend Anthony Wood described him as 'magotie-headed'. On his death in 1697 it looked as if fate would continue to conspire against him.

Aubrey's restoration as a serious man of letters has been a slow one, but his status as Britain's first field archaeologist has never been in doubt. His acquaintance with the standing stones of antiquity began by chance while out hunting on the Marlborough Downs in the New Year of 1649. He later wrote:

the Chase led us (at length) through the village of Aubury, into the Closes there: where I was wonderfully surprized at the sight of those vast stones: of which I had

FIGURE 25.
John Aubrey
(1626–97).
Despite having a
chaotic mind,
Aubrey can claim
to be the founder
of archaeology as
a discipline.
(*Ashmolean
Museum*)

never heard before: as also at the mighty Bank & Grasse about it: I observed in the Inclosures some segments of rude circles, made with those stones: whence I concluded that they had been in the old time complete. I left my Company a while, entertaining my selfe with a more delightfull indaegation: and then (steered by the cry of the Hounds) overtooke the company, and went with them to *Kynnet*, where was a good Hunting dinner provided.[2]

Aubrey had discovered Avebury. But the place as he first saw it is far removed from the Avebury we know today, although the village had already half sprawled across the stones, confusing the ancient structures to the casual eye. Avebury is by far the largest and most complex megalithic ruin in Britain, and is better described as an archaeological landscape than an archaeological site. The main concentration of stones is contained within a circular earthwork defined by a huge ditch with external bank. Around the edge of the ditch was a circle of about 100 stones, the biggest of which stand athwart the four entrances. Inside this massive enclosure were two adjacent circles. At the centre

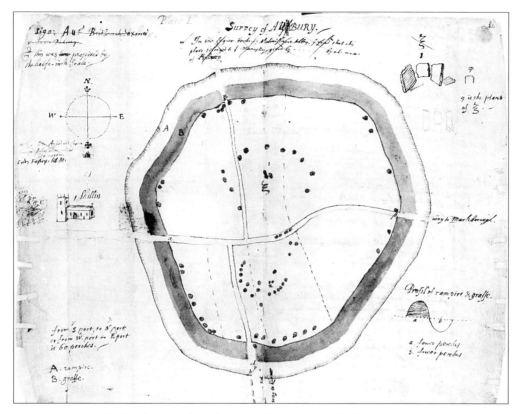

FIGURE 26. John Aubrey's plan of Avebury, made in 1663 at the behest of Charles II. (*Bodleian Library, MS Top. Gen. c.4, fos 39v–40*)

of the north circle was an arrangement of three upright stones, resembling the chamber of a dolmen, and known as the Cove. The centre of the south circle was marked by the tallest stone at Avebury, known as the Obelisk.

From the south side of the great circle a double line of stones, known as the Kennet Avenue, ran for one and a half miles to Overton Hill where it ended in a stone circle made up of two concentric rings, now known as the Sanctuary. Another double line of stones ran for some distance from the west of the great circle, known as the Beckhampton Avenue, but so little of it was left by the seventeenth century that Aubrey did not notice it. In fact its existence is still disputed by some archaeologists. Less than half a mile south of Avebury is Silbury Hill, the largest artificial mound in Britain, and the hill crests of the surrounding downland are covered with barrows, including the famous chambered long barrow at West Kennet.

It took more than ten years for Aubrey to knuckle down and make a serious study of Avebury. This came about at the behest of Charles II. Aubrey had discussed his findings with his friend Dr Charleton, who admitted that he had previously passed by the stones *en route* to Bath, but had not recognised what they were. Charleton promptly visited the stones and showed a plan of them to the Royal Society in 1663. Shortly afterwards he brought Aubrey's discovery to the attention of the King, who was surprised to hear that there was an antiquity in Britain more impressive than Stonehenge, and remarked of Avebury that 'none of our Chorographers had taken notice of it'. This was more or less true. As already quoted, Leland's description of Avebury was fleeting. Inigo Jones knew of it, but seemed to think of it as a quarry, while it was not even mentioned in the first edition of Camden's *Britannia*. The 1610 edition compensated slightly, thanks to additional material added by the translator, Philemon Holland, but its true nature remained unrecognised: 'It is environeth with a faire trench, and hath foure gappes as gates, in two of which stand huge Stones as jambes, but so rude, that they seeme rather naturall than artificiall.'[3]

Aubrey, as the acknowledged expert, was summoned before the King, and took with him a drawing 'done by memorie only'. The King was impressed and about a fortnight later, in August 1663, he, with the Duke of York and Dr Charleton, stopped off on his way to Bath so that Aubrey could show them 'that stupendious Antiquity'. The royal visit was evidently a great occasion – sixty years later the locals were still talking about it. Aubrey later wrote: 'He and his Royal Highnesse the Duke of Yorke were very well pleased. His Majesty then commanded me to write a description of it, and present it to him: and the Duke of Yorke commanded me to give an account of the Old Camps, and Barrows on the Plaines.'[4]

In September 1663 Aubrey made a plane-table survey of Avebury (fig. 26), a year later he surveyed the circles and avenues at Stanton Drew, and in 1666 he made a sketch plan of Stonehenge (fig. 27). He supplemented his account of Avebury with his thoughts on Stonehenge, and presented his discourse, in manuscript form, to the King, addressing it 'to King Charles by his Majestie's most loyale and obedient Subject John Aubrey'. The King was well pleased and asked Aubrey to have it printed, which he did not. Also 'His Majestie commanded me to digge at the bottom of the stones [of the Cove] . . . to try if I could find any humane bones: but I did not doe it'.[5]

His reluctance to undertake any form of excavation was admirable. 'I never was so sacrilegious as to disturbe or rob the urne', he wrote of a barrow near his farmland at Broad Chalke, but in any case his time could be much better spent in recording for posterity. He had first-hand knowledge of the vulnerability of ancient monuments, and at Avebury there was an urgent need to record the stones as they then stood. Aubrey made acquaintances in the village, and was told about the destruction of stones by John Brinsdon:

I have *verbum sacerdotis*, for it, that these mighty stones . . . may be broken in what part of them you please, without any great trouble: *sc.* make a fire on that line of stone, where you would have it crack: and after the stone is well heated, draw over

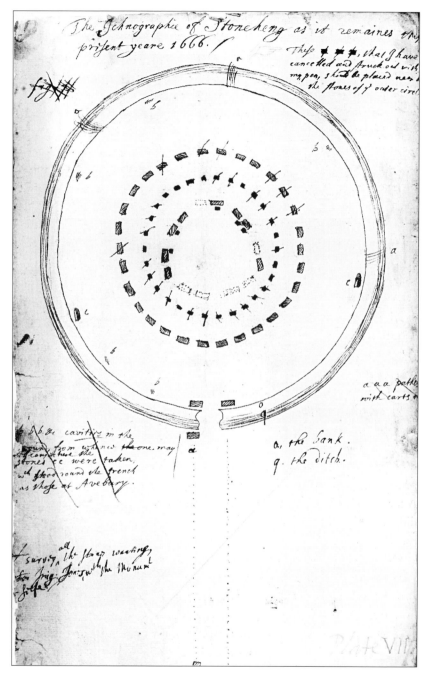

FIGURE 27. In this survey of Stonehenge, made in 1666, John Aubrey was the first to record the pits in the inner circumference of the bank. The pits have subsequently been named the Aubrey Holes. (*Bodleian Library, MS Top. Gen. c.4, fo. 4v*)

a line with cold water, & immediately give it a knock with a Smyth's sledge, and it will break like the Collets at the Glass-House.[6]

One of the reasons the discourse presented to Charles II was never printed was because it rapidly expanded into an ambitious project to describe the ancient monuments of Britain, the 'Monumenta Britannica'. The first part, called 'Templa Druidum', was devoted to stone circles, and in the next part, the 'Chorographia Antiquara', there were chapters on camps, barrows, urns and roads. This was the first time antiquities had been divided up into categories, and it was the first time stone circles were studied as a distinct species. The analogy with natural history is an appropriate one, not only because many antiquaries were also natural historians, because Aubrey and his antiquarianism were part of a new scientific movement, whose approach to learning was especially associated with the Royal Society.

The society was explicitly engaged in the 'promoting of Physico-Mathematicall-Experimental Learning', whereby natural and artificial phenomena were observed, described, then interpreted by inductive reasoning. This empirical approach had been championed by Francis Bacon at the beginning of the seventeenth century, but had its roots in the Renaissance. It ultimately replaced superstitions with mechanisms, and its ultimate protagonist was Sir Isaac Newton, with whom Aubrey was acquainted. The approach was paralleled in historiography, particularly by Sir William Dugdale's acclaimed *Antiquities of Warwickshire* of 1656, where documents and records were searched out, then collated, questioned and interpreted, thus helping to lay the foundations for modern historical scholarship. Aubrey used the same empirical approach to antiquities, and this, together with his categorisation of monuments, is why modern archaeologists see him as the father of their profession. There is a nice irony here, because despite having one of the most chaotic minds in British archaeology, it was Aubrey who stamped it with discipline.

'These Antiquities are so exceeding old that no Bookes do reach them',[7] he wrote of the stone circles, so he would have 'to make the Stones speake for themselves'. Aubrey overdid it when he talked grandly of his attempt 'to work out and restore after a kind of Algebraical method, by comparing them that I have seen, one with another; and reducing them to a kind of Aequation',[8] but it does demonstrate his alliance with the new philosophy. The huge ditch surrounding the stone circle at Avebury was inside the bank, so he figured out that it could not have been a military encampment, but was a temple of some sort. Furthermore the 'antique rudeness' of the structures was considered 'clear evidence that these monuments were Pagan-Temples: which was not made out before'.[9] This was not entirely true, but the important point was that previous authors had confined their attentions to Stonehenge, treating it as a freak. Aubrey recognised that it belonged to a class of monuments, and it was stone circles generally which he attributed to the pagan Britons. Confirmation of his argument that stone circles were British was to come later in the seventeenth century from Edward Lhwyd and others, who found circles beyond the limits of Roman, Saxon or Danish influence. But at this level it was far from being an original idea. Edward Bolton and the author of *A Fool's Bolt Soon Shot at Stonage* both cited the British as the builders of Stonehenge; and in a book called *Origines sacrae* of 1662 Edward Stillingfleet, later Bishop of Worcester, said that standing stones were places of worship used by the Ancient Britons. The 'Ancient Briton' was an idea whose time had come.

To Geoffrey of Monmouth and his fellow medieval scholars he would have meant very little, but the profile of the Ancient Briton was raised during the Renaissance when Greek and Roman texts were rescued from obscurity and put into print for the first time. The study of classical languages and literature was part of every gentleman's education, and for the convenience of antiquaries relevant quotations referring to pre-Roman Britain appeared in the 1610 edition of *Britannia*. These were largely found in the works of Tacitus, Julius Caesar, Pliny, Diodorus Siculus, Pomponius Mela and the Greek geographer Strabo. So Aubrey and his contemporaries were not, and could not be, as free of book-derived knowledge as they claimed.

Another factor that structured contemporary thought was the discovery of the New World. By the early seventeenth century the Ancient Briton was habitually visualised by reference to the natives of America. This was aided by explorers who had a nasty habit of bringing home a prize Indian to show off with: in 1532 William Hawkins presented to Henry VIII a Brazilian king, whose 'apparel, behaviour and gesture, were very strange to the beholders'. In 1584 the artist John White accompanied Raleigh on his expedition to Virginia, making a number of watercolour sketches of the natives. These and similar drawings were engraved and circulated widely (fig. 28). William Camden may even have seen the real thing: writing in the *Annals of Great Britain under Queen Elizabeth,* published between 1615 and 1628, he referred to the Indians as 'apparelled in sea-calves' skins, the women painted about the eyes and balls of the cheek with a blue colour like the ancient Britons'.[10]

This temptation to link the Indians with the Ancient Britons was irresistible. The use of body paint, mentioned by Tacitus, was the first obvious link; the second was their material technology. The Indians were living in the Stone Age, and antiquaries had in their collections numerous stone tools from Britain. There were some significant looking material links between the two continents, as in the curious case of 'elf bolts'. These were the flint arrow heads supposedly made by witches and fairies and fired at cattle and people. The argument about whether such artefacts were the relics of former epochs or whether they were celestial objects of miraculous properties had already been played out in Italy where, among others, Michele Mercati (1541–93), superintendent of the Vatican botanical gardens, established that they were genuine archaeological remains. In Britain, Sir Robert Sibbald, a Scottish antiquary, accepted the traditional explanation

FIGURE 28. John Speed's fanciful portrait of an Ancient Briton was influenced by contemporary descriptions of American Indians, right down to the body paint.

and found confirmation for it in Pliny's *Natural History*. However Edward Lhwyd, Keeper of the Ashmolean Museum in Oxford, wrote to a friend in 1699 that the so-called elf bolts 'are just the same chip'd flints the natives of New England head their arrows with at this day; and there are also several stone hatchets found in this kingdom, not unlike those of the Americans'.[11] Aubrey followed the trend when he described the inhabitants of ancient Wiltshire as 'almost as salvage as the beasts whose skins were their only rayment . . . They were 2 or 3 degrees less salvage then the Americans'. Aubrey presented an unromanticised view of the past (and of the Indians), a hard primitivism, perfectly in accord with his friend Thomas Hobbes' assessment of the lives of primitive people as 'solitary, poor, nasty, brutish and short'.

However the most influential aspect of Aubrey's interpretation of stone circles stemmed, ironically, not from his 'Algebraical method', but from his reading of classical texts. Tacitus, Julius Caesar and Pliny all clearly stated that there was an order of priests in Britain before the Roman conquest called Druids, who Aubrey described as 'the most eminent Priests (or Order of Priests) among the Britaines'. He therefore supposed 'that these ancient Monuments (sc. *Aubury, Stonehenge*, Kerrig y Druidd &c.) were Temples of the Priests of the most eminent Order, viz, *Druids*, and it is strongly to be presumed, that Aubury, Stonehenge & c: are as ancient as those times'.[12] Later he qualified this, stating 'I now think it a surer way to say, monuments erected by the Britains', but the connection was so logical and inevitable that he had already titled his study of stone circles 'Templa Druidum' and the connection stuck. However, unlike many of his contemporaries, Aubrey had no real opinion on Druids as such. His subject was stone circles, and there is no better summary of his work than his own: 'This Inquiry I must confess is a gropeing in the Dark: but although I have not brought it into a cleer light; yet I can affirm, that I have brought it from an utter darkness, to a thin Mist: and have gonne farther in this Essay than any one before me.'[13]

Aubrey's field studies dwindled after about 1670, but he continued to extend and revise the 'Monumenta Britannica', largely as new information came to light from other field working antiquaries. The Reverend James Garden was Professor of Theology at King's College in Aberdeen, and Aubrey wrote to him enquiring of stone circles in Scotland. Garden assumed that these circles had never been written about, so he was obviously unaware of the *Scotorum historiae* of Hector Boece, published in 1526. Here he would have found the earliest reference to the Aberdeenshire circles in a story about a legendary pre-Roman Scottish king:

> In the times of King Mainus . . . huge stones were erected in a ring and the biggest of them was stretched out on the south side to serve for an altar, whereon were burned the victims in sacrifice to the gods. In proof of the fact to this day there stand these mighty stones gathered together into circles . . . and whoso sees them will assuredly marvel by what mechanical craft or by what bodily strength stones of such bulk have been collected to one spot.[14]

With no knowledge of this reference Garden had to rely on fieldwork. Conversations with local people established the folklore of the stones, that it was unwise to remove any of them, that they were sometimes referred to as 'chapels' or 'law stones', and that they were heathen places of worship. His travels took him as far as Keig on the River Don, where he found the Cothiemuir Wood circle, and was told that 'ashes of some burnt matter' had been dug out from a cist in the centre. Nearer to home was the Authquhorthies circle, five miles south of Aberdeen, where he found cavities in the tops of the stone, which he assumed 'served for washing the priests, sacrifices, and other things esteemed sacred among the heathen'. This was another enquiry by empirical methods, and Aubrey himself could have written Garden's concluding remarks: 'Albeit from the general tradition, that these monuments were places of pagan worship, and the historical knowledge we have that the superstition of the Druids did take place in Britain, we rationally collect, that these monuments have been temples of the Druids.'[15]

More information on the antiquities of the Celtic countries came from Edward Lhwyd. First as assistant (to Robert Plot), then as Keeper of the Ashmolean Museum, he was at the hub of the antiquarian scene. He of course knew Aubrey, whom he described as 'an ingenious Gentleman of the Royal Society', and he worked with Robert Plot for long enough to despise him with a passion: 'a man of as bad morals as ever took a doctor's degree'. He first distinguished himself as a palaeontologist, publishing *Lithophylacii Britannici ichnographia*, in 1699. This was a catalogue illustrating nearly 2000 fossils, although crucially he did not recognise them as extinct species. In the 1690s he also started work on his *Archaeologia Britannica, Giving Some Account . . . of the Languages, Histories and Customs of the Originall Inhabitants of Great Britain*, of which his studies of archaeological monuments were to form part.

These enquiries took him to Ireland and Scotland as well as his native Wales. His principal claim to fame now is his discovery in 1699 of the chambered cairn at Newgrange in Ireland. Like Garden, Lhwyd's interpretations were partly informed by folklore. In Cornwall, for example, he found the Merry Maidens stone circle which at that time was known as Dawns Men, meaning dancing stones, 'so called of the common people on no other account, than that they are placed in a circular Order, and so make an Area for Dancing'.[16]

It was the discovery of so many stone monuments in Celtic Britain and Ireland that satisfied both himself and Aubrey that they were pre-Roman. Lhwyd came to a similar conclusion in the case of barrows and cairns. At Trelech in Carmarthenshire he had a barrow opened, in the centre of which was

> such a barbarous monument as we call a *Kist-vaen,* or *Stone-Chest,* which was about four foot and a half in length, and about three foot broad . . . And considering the rudeness of the Monument describ'd, and yet the labour and force requir'd in erecting it, I am apt to suspect it the Barrow of some British Prince, who might live probably before the Roman Conquest. For seeing it is much too barbarous to be supposed Roman, and that we do not find in History that the Saxons were ever concern'd here, or the Danes any farther than in plundering the Seacoasts, it seems necessary to conclude it British.[17]

The first volume of Lhwyd's *Archaeologia Britannica* was published in 1707. This was his *Glossography*, a study in comparative philology, analysing the relationships between the Cornish, Welsh, Breton and Irish languages. He had no time to publish any of the remaining volumes before his early death in 1709. The dispersal and subsequent loss of most of his papers has deprived us of many of his thoughts and discoveries. Aubrey was more fortunate. In 1692 he seemed to be taking positive steps towards publishing his 'Monumenta Britannica', even to the extent of advertising its imminent printing. However there were so many corrections and additions made to the original manuscript that it would have required a major editing job to see it through to publication, and he himself admitted that he lacked 'patience to go through Knotty Studies'. He naively hoped that some younger scholar would come along and finish what he had started, but in the short term Aubrey was acutely aware of the need to safeguard his works, pointing out that many a valuable manuscript had 'wrapt Herings by this time', or 'been putt under Pyes'. When Elias Ashmole offered to take them into his museum Aubrey eagerly accepted: they stayed at the Ashmolean until transferred to the Bodleian Library in Oxford, where they remain.

Some of Aubrey's work did find its way into print before he died in 1697. In 1695 a new, extended edition of Camden's *Britannia* was published, edited by the young Edmund Gibson, later Bishop of London, with the help of Thomas Tanner, later Bishop of St Asaph, and others. An indication of the greater scope of antiquarian studies since Camden's day is the fact that to revise and extend his original text it was now deemed necessary to invite a number of leading antiquaries to contribute material relating to their own special interests. Gibson persuaded Aubrey to lend him the manuscript of 'Monumenta Britannica', and also secured contributions from such luminaries as Robert Plot, Edward Lhwyd, John Evelyn, William Nicolson (the Saxon scholar) and Samuel Pepys, who chipped in with a section on naval history.

This edition of *Britannia* put antiquarian studies where they belonged, with the discovery during the seventeenth century of rural Britain. Two other topographical books published near the end of the century increased the antiquaries' knowledge even further. James Wallace's *An Account of the Islands of Orkney*, published in 1693, gave the first description of the monuments at Stenness, while even more widely read was Martin Martin's *Description of the Western Islands of Scotland* of 1703, which included one of the earliest descriptions of Callanish in the Outer Hebrides. But the definitive statement of antiquarian studies was the 1695 *Britannia*. It achieved the original aim of Camden 'to restore Britain to its Antiquities, and its Antiquities to Britain', and became a national institution. Its contributors may have hoped it would serve as a foundation for future antiquarian studies. In the event it marked not the beginning of an era, but the end of one.

7

William Stukeley

Having been discovered by John Aubrey, and endorsed by Charles II, Avebury attracted its first tourists. Samuel Pepys went there in 1668 and paid a local a shilling to show him round. But a tragic irony – predicted by Aubrey himself – was unfolding: Avebury was undergoing a cool, calculated and rapid destruction. By the 1720s many of the stones, shattered by fire and water, either had been or were still being broken up to build houses, barns, garden walls, the local alehouse and a nonconformist chapel (fig. 29). It was a sad sight for an antiquary to behold: 'the barbarous massacre of a stone here with leavers and hammers, sledges and fire, is as terrible a sight as a Spanish Atto de fe . . . the straw, the faggots, the smoak, the prongs, and squallor of the fellows looks like a knot of devils grilling the soul of a sinner'.[1]

The arch 'stone-killers' are known by name: Farmer Green and Farmer Griffin, John Fowler, Walter Stretch and, worst of all, Tom Robinson, a housing speculator. Not only did they break up the stones within the earthwork, they also exploited the easy quarry of the Avenues and the Sanctuary as well (fig. 30). Lord Stawell, owner of Avebury Manor, even levelled part of the bank to make room for a barn. We know all this because Avebury's destruction was chronicled in detail by one powerless onlooker, William Stukeley. Of the Sanctuary he wrote: '13 May, 1724. This day I saw several of the few stones left on Overton Hill carryed downwards towards W. Kennet & two

FIGURE 29.
William Stukeley's drawing of the destruction of stones at Avebury in the 1720s: 'the barbarous massacre of a stone here . . . is as terrible a sight as a Spanish Atto de fe'.
(*Bodleian Library, Gough Maps 231, 5*)

FIGURE 30. William Stukeley's drawing of the Sanctuary at Avebury was made only a year before the stones were broken up for building material in 1724.

thirds of the temple plowed up this winter and the sods thrown in to the cavitys so that next year it will be impossible ever more to take any measure of it.'[2]

William Stukeley was born in 1687 and came from Holbeach in Lincolnshire. His interest in antiquities and the English countryside began as the perfect antidote to London life, where he was studying to become a physician. He later blamed an over indulgence in lavish dinners 'where we drank nothing but French wine' for leaving him laid up every winter with gout. As a remedy 'I was oblig'd to ride for my health, and that brought me in the humour and love of travelling; whereby I indulg'd myself in the study of the antiquities of my country'.[3] In 1710 he made the first of many tours throughout Britain, journals from which were published in 1724 under the title *Itinerarium curiosum*. On that first tour he discovered the Rollright Stones in the Cotswolds, and mused 'I cannot but suppose 'em to have been an heathen temple of our Ancestors, perhaps in the Druids' time'.[4]

After qualifying as a physician Stukeley practised in Lincolnshire, but by 1717 he was back in London, where he found intellectual life more stimulating. In 1718 he was elected a Fellow of the Royal Society and became the first Secretary of the newly-formed Society of Antiquaries of London. Through his friends Roger and Samuel Gale he discovered and copied notes, made by their father, from Aubrey's 'Monumenta Britannica', which impressed on him the importance of Avebury, a place he had already read

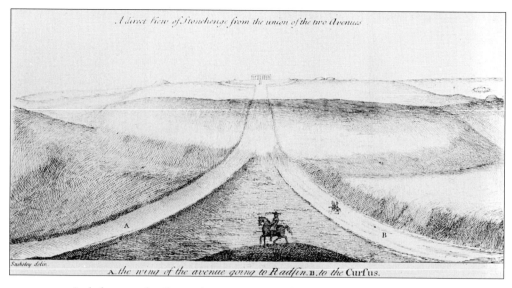

A direct View of Stonehenge from the union of the two Avenues

A. *the wing of the avenue going to* Radfin. B. *to the* Curfus.

FIGURE 31. Stukeley was the first antiquary to notice the Stonehenge Avenue and its orientation to the midsummer sunrise.

about in *Britannia*. He first went there, and to Stonehenge, in 1719, and for six years first-hand investigation at the two places was his consuming passion.

Stukeley's fieldwork at Avebury and Stonehenge has had a lasting impact on archaeology. He discovered the Beckhampton Avenue, the Stonehenge Avenue (fig. 31) and the long linear earthwork near Stonehenge called the Cursus. The names for the features at Avebury – Cove, Obelisk, Sanctuary, Kennet Avenue – all come from Stukeley, as do the words 'trilithon', describing two uprights supporting a lintel at Stonehenge, and 'cursus', so-called because its shape suggested a track for races. He made copious notes; he took measurements in his efforts to establish what unit of length had been used by the builders; and he took compass bearings to establish the orientation of the temples. Stukeley also believed that 'the position of the stones, their number & site' would help elucidate its meaning (fig. 32). Occasionally he dug into barrows in the vicinity, which satisfied him that they were not the graves of warriors slain in battle, but 'the single sepulchres of kings, and great personages'.[5] He and his friend Lord Pembroke, of Wilton House, supervised these diggings, although they employed Richard Hayns, 'an old man of Amesbury', to do the heavy spade work (fig. 33). Around Stonehenge most of the barrows contained cremations, with a variety of grave goods. In one of them he found an urn containing burned bones 'crouded all together in a little heap, not so much as a hat croune would contain'. These remains appeared to him 'to have been a girl of about fourteen years old, by their bulk and the great quantity of female ornaments mix'd with the bones, all of which we gathered'.[6] In another barrow 'I found bits of red and

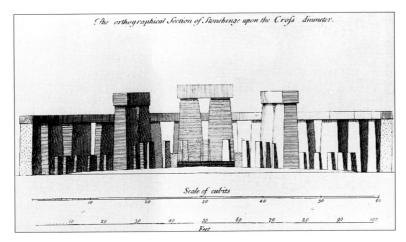

The orthographical Section of Stonehenge upon the Cross diameter.

Scale of cubits

Feet

FIGURE 32.
Stukeley looked
for the unit of
measurement used
by the builders of
Stonehenge, and
he claimed to
have found it –
the Druid Cubit.

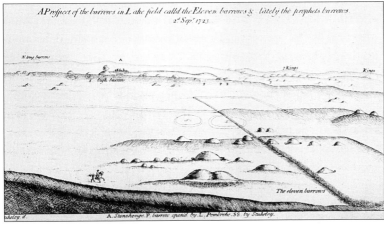

A Prospect of the barrows in Lake field calld the Eleven barrows & lately the prophets barrows.
2ᵈ Sep.ʳ 1723.

The eleven barrows

A. Stonehenge. P. barrow opend by L. Pembroke. SS. by Stukeley.

FIGURE 33.
Stukeley's excava-
tions in the
barrows near
Stonehenge
satisfied him that
they were the
'sepulchres of
kings, and great
personages'.

blue marble, chippings of the stones of the temple. So that probably the interr'd was
one of the builders.'[7]

These were halcyon days. He worked sometimes alone, at other times with friends
such as Roger Gale, Lord Pembroke or the antiquary Lord Winchelsea: 'Lord Winchilsea
has workt very hard, and was ravisht with Stonehenge, it was a great strife between
us, which should talk of leaving it first.'[8] On another occasion, he and Lord Winchelsea
brought a ladder and climbed on top of one of the lintels and had dinner. He remarked
that the stone was large enough 'for a steady hand and nimble heels to dance a minuet
on'. In six years he gained an unrivalled knowledge of Avebury and Stonehenge, but
this alone was not enough to find their meaning, particularly of Avebury, which he
thought the more important of the two, and which he later described as 'the most
extraordinary work in the world'.

Like Aubrey, Stukeley attributed Avebury to the Druids, but he also assumed that
the configuration of circles and avenues in the landscape was a symbolic picture of the

Druid theology. On a 1721 plan of Avebury the two inner circles are labelled as Solar and Lunar Temples. The Sanctuary was drawn in 1723 and labelled the 'Temple of Ertha', meaning Mother Earth. He could not trace the end of the Beckhampton Avenue but presumed it must have ended in a stone circle to balance the Sanctuary, and on a 1723 plan he provisionally dotted it in and named it the 'Temple of the Infernal Regions', representing the souls of the dead. These were not gods in the plural, however, because Stukeley believed that monotheism was the archetypal religion, and that in early religions there was a subordinate pantheon of divine agents.

In 1722 he started writing a four-volume history of the Celts of which three manuscript volumes survive: on 'Celtic Religion', 'Stonehenge', and 'The History of the Temples of the Ancient Celts'. For any eighteenth-century scholar studying religious history the foremost text was the Bible, especially the Pentateuch, the first five books of the Old Testament, which were traditionally ascribed to Moses. The chronology of events given in the Old Testament allowed scholars to count backwards and arrive at a date of 4004 BC for the creation of the world described in Genesis. This date appeared in the margin of the Authorised Version or King James Bible, first published in 1611. However for the antiquaries the key date in history was not the Creation but the Flood, which happened in 2448 BC, after which Noah's sons – Shem, Ham and Japheth – dispersed and peopled the world, taking the first, true religion with them. Because the origin of the dispersal was the Near East, the western nations were thought to have derived from the eastern nations, giving them common roots which were discernible in the Pentateuch.

Stukeley had also read the writings of the oracular Egyptian sage, Hermes Trismegistus, who was thought to have been a contemporary of Moses. These mystical writings, known collectively as the *Corpus Hermeticum*, foresaw the coming of Christianity, which led scholars to suppose that Hermes had a knowledge of the true God. Although in fact the texts were written between AD 100 and 300, as Isaac Casaubon had demonstrated in the early seventeenth century, the Hermetic tradition was still believed in by Stukeley, who saw Hermes as the patriarch of Egyptian religion, and by many of his contemporaries. Egyptian esotericism had a strong influence on Stukeley, not only because of Hermes, but also because he had read *Oedipus Aegypticus* by the Jesuit natural philosopher Athanasius Kircher, published between 1652 and 1654. This tried to interpret Egyptian esotericism as an exposition of divine truths of timeless universality. As soon as he started to look for them, Stukeley inevitably saw links between the Druid and Egyptian theologies. By 1724 he had also decided that there had never been a stone circle at the end of the Beckhampton Avenue, and so had to rethink his initial interpretation. Then he came up with the theory that the plan of Avebury represented a serpent through a circle. In 1724 he wrote in his field notes: 'this is the representation of God or the great soul of the world among the Persian magi & the Egyptian priests & we find it here among the western Druids doubtless tis of vastest antiquity & borrowed by them all from the post diluvian times.'[9]

His projected four-volume work was never published, for reasons which have never been clear. However in 1724 he published *Itinerarium curiosum*, based on journals of his tours, but it seems not to have been a great success. The book was 'universally condemn'd as strange, weak, ridiculous stuff', according to the venomous tongue of Thomas Hearne, the Oxford historian. In 1726 Stukeley left London for his native Lincolnshire. Four years later he had married and had become ordained as the Reverend William Stukeley, Vicar of All Saints, Stamford. So the London physician, who in his mid thirties had investigated Avebury and Stonehenge in the 1720s, was a provincial clergyman in his mid fifties when he came to publishing two great classics of antiquarian literature: *Stonehenge: A Temple Restored to the British Druids* was published in 1740, followed by *Abury: A Temple of the British Druids* in 1743.

These books were the high point of the so-called Druid Revival, a product of the awakening of interest in the past which had begun during the Renaissance. Aubrey had made only cursory reference to them, but among other antiquaries Druids were an important part of what the English thought about their own history. In 1534 the Italian Polydore Vergil had called them 'preestes . . . of hethen religion, sainge their accursed prayers', a sentiment perfectly in accord with the grim picture painted of them by most classical authors. But to Hector Boece, in his *Scotorum historiae* (1526), they were experts in natural and moral philosophy, and their role was to make sacrifices in honour of their gods, and to instruct the sons of noblemen in virtue and the sciences. In Michael Drayton's *Poly Olbion: Great Britaine* of 1613 the Druids are described in a similar vein as 'sacred bards', 'very proportionat in many things to Cabalistique and Pythagorean doctrine', and ultimately as philosophers 'like whom great Nature's depths no man yet ever know'. John Leland felt a certain kinship with the Druids because Julius Caesar had said they practised astronomy, mathematics and jurisprudence. In doing so they gave Britain and the British a respectable ancestry.

By the seventeenth century the average appreciation of the Druids was becoming less charitable. The title page of *De dis Germanis* by Elias Schedius, published in Amsterdam in 1648, depicts a grove littered with sacrificial corpses. A Druid is holding a chalice and a sacrificial knife, and at his feet is a decapitated victim. Beside him stands a priestess banging a drum with someone else's thigh bones. Hardly sage and philosophical. Aylett Sammes, in his *Britannia antiqua illustrata* of 1676, was again less interested in the supposed philosophical achievements of the Druids than with their idolatry and human sacrifice. Sammes included an illustration showing several men being ritually sacrificed inside a huge wickerwork idol (fig. 34). This practice was described by Julius Caesar, who said that captured Roman soldiers were burned to death inside these images. More usually thieves and robbers were the victims, but in their absence even

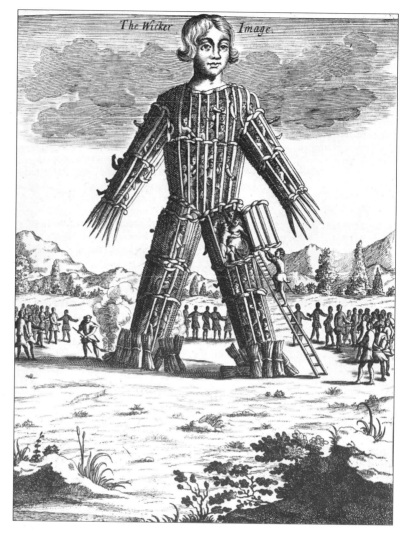

FIGURE 34.
Aylett Sammes'
'Wicker Image'
dramatised the bar-
baric practices of
the Druids rather
than their philo-
sophical
achievements.
Ritual human
sacrifice inside a
wicker image had
been described in
the first century
BC by Julius
Caesar.
(*British Library*)

poor luckless innocents were sacrificed to the flames. Human sacrifice was mentioned
consistently by classical authors, another gory account appearing in Tacitus' *Annals*
(book xiv, c. 31): 'It was their religion to drench their altars in the blood of prisoners
and consult their gods by means of human entrails.'

Tacitus was writing about a Druid stronghold on Anglesey, an island whose antiquities
were described in the Reverend Henry Rowlands' *Mona antiqua restaurata*, first published
in 1723. Rowlands outlined the orthodox view of Europe peopled by the sons of
Japheth, and even speculated that some of the first settlers of Anglesey may have had 'one
of Noah's sons for grandsire or great-grandsire'. Although these first settlers 'conveyed
here some of the rites and usages of that true religion, pure and untainted . . . though
I must confess they soon after became . . . abominably corrupted, and perverted into

the grossest heathenish fictions and barbarities'.[10] You can sense Rowlands' pulse quicken whenever the Druids are mentioned: 'They were not only vile and abominable' but their human sacrifice was 'the foulest and most unassociable crime' which bore 'the most odious marks of both divine and human indignation'.[11] John Toland, in an essay called 'Specimen of the Critical History of the Celtic Religion and Learning', published posthumously in 1726, also took the cynical option. The Druids were a heathen priesthood who 'calculated to beget ignorance', and who were well versed in 'the art of managing the mob, which is vulgarly called *leading people by the nose*'.[12]

Both Rowlands and Toland linked Druids with stone monuments. Tacitus tells us that, after conquering the Druids' stronghold on Anglesey, 'Suetonius garrisoned the conquered island' and 'the groves devoted to Mona's barbarous superstition he demolished'. Rowlands also argued that stones were used as altars and idols, which according to the Bible was a common heathen practice. The cromlechs on Anglesey were built over the graves of the earliest settlers, but only when these ancestors had become subject to a cult of veneration. It was the capstones of these cromlechs 'on which, when the true religion became depraved and corrupted, they might make oblations and other sacrifices to their departed ghosts. From this practice, it is likely, grew the apotheosis of the first heroes, and from thence the gross idolatries of the Gentiles.'[13]

To Rowlands and Toland the Druids represented a corruption of the true religion, but to Stukeley they *were* the true religion. As he says in his *Abury*, 'the true religion has chiefly since the repeopling mankind after the flood, subsisted in our island'.[14] It was brought here by a Phoenician colony led by Hercules of Tyre; and from Hercules, who had been a scholar of Abraham, 'the Druids learn'd the groundwork of learning, religion and philosophy, which they were so famous for ever after' (fig. 35). Moreover, these Druids left 'works, still visible with us, which for grandeur, simplicity and antiquity, exceed any of the European wonders'.

This is the first hint that Stukeley saw Britain's monuments, and Avebury especially, as a source of national pride. In fact his Druids side with the patriotism of Drayton and Leland rather than the cynicism of Toland and Rowlands. But in the 1720s Stukeley developed something more than a scholarly interest in Druidism. In 1722 he and a group of friends established the Society of the Roman Knights, dedicated to the preservation of Roman remains. Its members took pseudonyms from the Celtic princes associated with the Roman conquest of Britain, except for Stukeley, who chose to be named after a Druid called Chyndonax. The name came from the celebrated, and highly dubious, discovery in France of a cinerary urn with Chyndonax inscribed on its base. The use of assumed names in contemporary intellectual clubs was not meant to be taken seriously. However, the frontispiece of *Stonehenge* shows a portrait of the author in profile, with an oak twig in his hair and the legend CHYNDONAX – the clearest indication that Stukeley fancied himself as an Arch-Druid (fig. 36). This was partly vanity

A British Druid

FIGURE 35. To William Stukeley, the Druids were patriarchal Christians in the time of Abraham.

no doubt but it had a serious side, too, in the fusion of Druidism and Christianity that pervades his work.

Stukeley's investigations at Avebury and Stonehenge were far more profound than Aubrey's, and they allowed him to put forward some authoritative and original theories. In one year he and Lord Winchelsea made 2000 measurements at Stonehenge, from which Stukeley claimed to have detected the unit of measurement used by the builders. This was the Druid Cubit of 20.8 inches, and he expressed the dimensions of everything in these terms. The sarsen circle was sixty cubits in diameter, the diameter of the court (to the outsides of the ditches) was 240 cubits, and the Cursus was 6000 cubits long. At Avebury the Kennet and Beckhampton Avenues were both 4000 cubits long; Silbury was 100 cubits high.

Traditionally temples were laid out according to the cardinal points of the compass, and generally faced east. Using a compass, which he believed the Druids also possessed, he noticed that Stonehenge, with its Avenue oriented north east, was in fact 6–7° away from the cardinal points, but could account for this apparent discrepancy by the rate of the Earth's magnetic change. Over a cycle of about 700 years the position of magnetic north was thought to vary steadily.[15] Through his friend Dr Edmond Halley, Stukeley had access to data on magnetic variation, and figured that if he had taken his compass readings in 1620 then Stonehenge would have conformed to the cardinal points. Therefore he could leap back through time in steps of 700 years to pick the most likely date for its foundation. Three cycles equalled 2100 years, which subtracted from 1620 gave 460 BC (Stukeley's arithmetic, not mine), a date which Dr Halley would have agreed with. The two men were at Stonehenge in 1720 when 'The Doctor observ'd from the general wear of the weather upon the stones, that the work must be of an extraordinary antiquity, and for ought he knew, 2 or 3000 years old'.[16]

Once he had decided that Avebury represented a serpent through a circle, he assumed that the symbolic figure would be facing east. In fact the serpent's head – the Sanctuary – does face east, but the whole work stood roughly 10° to the east of north, a similar discrepancy to that at Stonehenge. Stukeley argued that Avebury was the older of the two, and so '*Abury* must be above 700 years prior in time to *Stonehenge*', and so went back two cycles, or 1400 years, to 1860 BC. According to Archbishop Ussher's biblical chronology this was 'the year of the death of *Sarah*, *Abraham's* wife, which happened in the summer time of the 1859th year before Christ'. At the same time 'our *Tyrian Hercules* made his expedition into the ocean . . . and most likely 'tis that *Abury* was the first great temple of *Britain*, and made by the first *Phoenician* colony that came hither'.[17]

FIGURE 36. In this self-portrait, William Stukeley styled himself as an Arch-Druid, with an oak twig in his hair and the legend 'Chyndonax' – a mythical Druid from Gaul.

The Stonehenge Avenue was 'oriented full north east, being the point where the sun rises, or nearly, at the summer solstice'.[18] Stukeley therefore assumed that midsummer was a Druid festival celebrated with religious ceremonies and sports. The latter were staged in the Cursus which was laid out over a gentle valley, 'conveniently under the eye of the most numerous quantity of spectators', and overlooking Stonehenge to the south (fig. 37). It gave 'a delightful prospect from the temple, when this vast plain was crouded with chariots, horsemen and foot, attending these solemnities, with innumerable multitudes'.[19] As for the religious ceremonies, 'I suppose only the priests and chief personages came within [Stonehenge], who made the procession with sacrifices along the avenue. The multitude kept without, on foot or in their chariots.'[20] Stukeley visualised a procession of priests and sacrificial victims, which he specifies as animals, proceeding around the temple, stopping at certain stones to bow to the deity; then the animals were washed and anointed with holy water before being sacrificed. In one of the barrows nearby he found 'one of those brass [bronze was always called brass] instruments call'd *celts*, which I hold to belong to the Druids, wherewith they cut off the mistletoe' in the ceremony described by Pliny.[21]

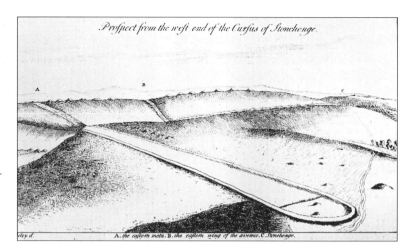

Prospect from the west end of the Cursus of Stonehenge.

A. the eastern meta. B. the eastern wing of the avenue. C. Stonehenge.

FIGURE 37.
William Stukeley
was the first to
discover the Stone-
henge Cursus, so
named because its
shape suggested a
track for races.

Another bronze axe-head had been dug up at Avebury, 'near the smith's shop by the church', and when Lord Stawell's workmen were levelling part of the earthwork they found lots of 'buck's horns, bones, oyster shells, and wood coals'. For Stukeley these were 'remains of the sacrifices that had been performed here'. Avebury was an even bigger arena for religious ceremonies than Stonehenge – 'when the *vallum* all around was cover'd with spectators, it formed a most notable amphitheater'. The inner sancta were the two central circles, at the centre of which were the Cove and Obelisk. These Stukeley termed the 'Kibla', an Arabic word, 'whereunto they turn'd their faces, in the religious offerings there performed',[22] and which were found in a number of other stone circles such as Stonehenge, Callanish and Boscawen-un in Cornwall.

His journeys around the country had quickly established that not all stone circles were alike, so Stukeley divided them into two categories. The first was the simple ring of stones which he called a 'temple'. The second was 'those with the form of a snake annext' which he called '*Dracontia*, by which they were denominated of old'. Avebury was the supreme expression of this second type, but he also enlisted Callanish into this category by giving its straight avenues a little twist. A third kind of temple was a serpent 'with the form of wings annext', which he dubbed 'alate or winged temples'. But these do not concern us – they do not seem to have concerned anyone – and as examples he cited and illustrated the thoroughly unconvincing looking earthworks at Barrow in Humberside and Navestock Common in Essex. As so often, Stonehenge defied categorisation and remained a freak.

An example of the first kind of temple he cited Rollright, whose stones he described as 'corroded like worm-eaten wood by the harsh Jaws of Time'. Beside the stone circle is a long barrow, which like all long barrows Stukeley assumed to be the burial place of an Arch-Druid. The stone circle was erected beside the barrow as a sepulchral monument. This 'proceeded from a strong notion in antiquity of a future state, and that in respect of their bodies as well as their souls; for these temples are thought prophylactic, and have a power in protecting and preserving the remains of the dead'.[23]

Avebury was an even bigger mausoleum, centred on Silbury Hill (fig. 38): 'As this immense body of earth was rais'd for the sake of the interment of this great prince, whoever he was: so the temple of *Abury* was made for the sake of this *tumulus*.' The great Prince he calls Cunedha, whose remains were apparently found in the top of the mound in 1723 when some trees were being planted on it. According to his compass work Silbury stands exactly south of Avebury, and stands exactly midway between the ends of the Kennet and Beckhampton Avenues. Therefore 'the work of *Abury*, which is the circle, and the two avenues which represent the snake transmitted thro' it, are the great *hierogrammaton*, or sacred prophylactic character of the divine mind, which is to protect the *depositum* of the prince here interr'd' (fig. 39).[24]

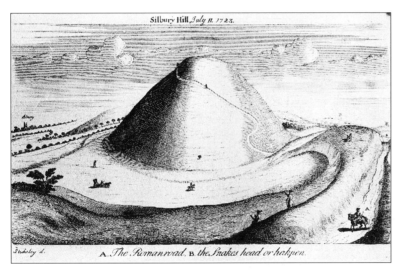

A. The Roman road. B. the Snakes head or halcyon.

FIGURE 38. According to Stukeley, Silbury Hill was the burial place of a Phoenician prince called Cunedha.

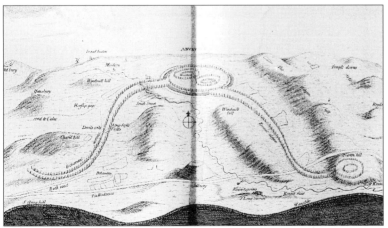

FIGURE 39. William Stukeley's reconstruction of Avebury, with Silbury Hill due south of the stone circle. Stukeley called Avebury 'the most magnificent mausoleum in the world'.

So far so good. Stukeley presented death and regeneration as the themes of Avebury, themes which have been investigated ever since. He came to these conclusions largely via his fieldwork, plus some imaginative and ingenious interpretation. True, some of his evidence is suspect, for example he could not show where the Beckhampton Avenue really ended, only where it should end. He also doctored some of the evidence: the Sanctuary was circular when he surveyed it in 1723 but now that it had become the serpent's head he drew it oval. But it should be obvious by now that Stukeley did not trumpet inductive reasoning in the way that Aubrey did. In the preface to *Abury* he outlined his own position. The antiquary must proceed 'without a childish pointing out every particular, without a syllogistical proving, or mathematical demonstration'. Instead, 'the subject of antiquities must be drawn out with such strong lines of verisimilitude, and represented in so lively colours, that the reader in effect sees them'.[25]

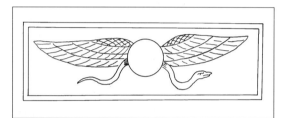

FIGURE 40. The Egyptian hierogram, as drawn by Stukeley, was based on the work of the seventeenth-century philosopher Athanasius Kircher. The serpent through a circle was to influence Stukeley's interpretation of Avebury.

In order to do this the antiquary had to have some prior conception, and this is where Stukeley brought his knowledge of religious history, the Egyptian tradition and, ultimately, his personal beliefs to bear.

The plan on which Avebury is built is explained as 'that sacred hierogram of the Egyptians', the circle, the serpent and wings (fig. 40). This derived from Egyptian hieroglyphics, and demonstrates Stukeley's debt to *Oedipus Aegypticus*, where Kircher describes the symbol as 'ophio-cyclo-pterygo-morphus'. According to Stukeley the symbol represents the nature of the divinity: 'The circle meant the supreme fountain of all being, the father; the serpent, that divine emanation from him which was called the son; the wings imported that other divine emanation from them which was call'd the spirit, the *anima mundi*.'[26] Here he has described the Trinity – Father, Son, and Holy Ghost. The Druids were therefore patriarchal Christians in the time of Abraham.

This is the underlying message in *Stonehenge* and *Abury*. They were the first, and in the event the only two books published, of a projected seven-volume study of 'Patriarchal Christianity: or A Chronological History of the Origin and Progress of True Religion, and of Idolatry'. It was to include books on 'a mosaic Chronology from the Creation to Exodus', the 'mysteries of the ancients and of idolatry', the patriarchal history of Abraham, the Phoenician colonisation of Britain, and the origin of the alphabet. At the beginning of *Stonehenge* he made his intentions clear:

My intent is . . . to promote, as much as I am able, the knowledge and practice of ancient and true religion; to revive in the minds of the learned the spirit of Christianity; . . . to restore the first and great Idea of the Deity, who has carry'd on the same regular and golden chain of Religion from the beginning to this day; to warm our hearts into that true sense of Religion, which keeps the medium between ignorant superstition and learned free-thinking, between slovenly fanaticism and popish pageantry, between enthusiasm and the rational worship of God, which is no where upon earth done, in my judgment, better than in the Church of England.[27]

What on earth have Stonehenge and Avebury got to do with the Church of England? In his manuscript on Celtic temples, probably written in 1724, he described Avebury as 'the greatest drought [draught] of the trinity that ever was', and this discovery certainly influenced his desire to enter the priesthood. In 1729, before his ordination, he wrote to William Wake, Archbishop of Canterbury, saying that he had discovered 'some notions about the doctrine of the Trinity which I think are not common'.[28] Stukeley later used this theory of Avebury in a contemporary religious dispute, and in doing so he manipulated the past in order to claim authority in the present. The dispute was between Anglican orthodoxy and natural religion, caused by an inevitable clash between science and theology.

Francis Bacon had called science the study of the works of God, and argued that God had provided two channels of revelation, Scripture and Nature. Sir Isaac Newton, a devout if unorthodox Christian, found in Nature a universe obeying design, order, law and certainty, but this did not negate the existence of God; it proved it, because the world was shown to be a great machine, and the great machine needed a divine mechanic. By the eighteenth century the Church of England could accept this order and harmony of the universe − Nature's law − as the work of a divine and beneficent Creator, work that could be understood by reason. But its divine nature was also validated by the fulfilment in the New Testament of the prophecies of the Old, and in miracles, especially the Resurrection. This tolerant, or Latitudinarian as it was known, position was challenged by, among others, the Deists, followers of Natural Religion.

Deists maintained that it was impossible to believe in both Nature and Supernature (or miracles) because one cancelled out the other. They based their faith on that 'beautiful and harmonious Order of Things' demonstrated by Newton, and believed that every human being possessed a natural morality. God gave this morality to all mankind and it was 'therefore not to be destroyed or altered by every whiffling Proclamation of an Enthusiast', to quote one of its adherents, Charles Blount. So if God could be discovered through Nature, why look for him in the annals of an obscure semitic tribe? Natural Religion thus rejected Revelation and the supernatural doctrines of Christianity. It stripped away the mythology of the church, and took away its jealous and vengeful God.

Immediate confirmation of natural morality came from across the Atlantic, from where the Noble Savage entered the modern European consciousness. Pigafetta, who sailed around the world with Magellan, described the native Brazilians as if they were still living in the Garden of Eden: they wore no clothes, lived to 140 years of age and were free of civilised vices. Arthur Barlowe, who travelled to Virginia in 1584 with Sir Walter Raleigh, found the native Americans 'most gentle, loving and faithfull, void of all guile, and treason, and such as lived after the manner of the golden age'.[29] It was therefore reasonable to assume that the Ancient Britons shared this natural morality until their descent into idolatry.

This was John Toland's view, and Toland, who made his name as a religious polemicist, was an arch exponent of Deism. Born in Ireland in 1670, he studied at Edinburgh University, where he caused a sensation by declaring himself a Rosicrucian; later he publicly burned a prayer-book in a coffee house. His pamphlet *Christianity Not Mysterious* of 1696, one of the earliest and most influential of Deist tracts, had him denounced from the pulpits of Britain and Ireland. Another Deist, Lord Shaftesbury, maintained Natural Religion as the most reasonable of Christian doctrines because it occupied the middle ground between the 'Chaos and Atoms of the Atheists' and the 'Magick and Daemons of the Polytheists'. For most Latitudinarians in the Church of England, however, Deism stood on the slippery slope towards a godless world.

Stukeley considered himself an orthodox churchman, and his work on Patriarchal Christianity was intended 'to combat the deists from an unexpected quarter'.[30] He tried to show that the religion of the ancient Britons was far from natural or idolatrous because they had a knowledge of the Trinity, which ultimately could only have been revealed by God. The Druids, like the Chaldeans, the Gymnosophists of India and the Egyptians, were disciples of the Persian Magi, the first patriarchal priests after the Flood. They came to Britain

> as a *Phoenician* colony . . . during the life of the patriarch *Abraham*, or very soon after. Therefore they brought with them the patriarchal religion, which was so extremely like Christianity, that in effect it differed from it only in this; they believed in a Messiah who was to come into the world, as we believe in him that is come.[31]

By the time *Stonehenge* and *Abury* were published the Deist controversy was already petering out, but Stukeley's Druids, patriarchal Christians and Phoenicians were well-established myths by the time of his death in 1765. For the next hundred years the average antiquarian offering leaned heavily on Stukeley's example. In another respect Stukeley was to be an influential figure. He was lucky enough to see Avebury in nearly all its glory and it stirred his patriotic heart. Avebury was a 'noble monument of our ancestors' piety, I may add, orthodoxy'. It was 'the most magnificent *mausoleum* in the world' and a 'stupendous production of labour and art' that ranked with the work of

FIGURE 41.
The 'Serpent Temples thro' the Earth' from William Blake's *Jerusalem* owes an obvious debt to Stukeley, combining the lintels of Stonehenge with the Avenues of Avebury.
(*British Museum*)

the Egyptians, and equalled the wisdom of Pythagoras and Plato. This strain of romantic nationalism found its way into the writings of, among others, William Blake. In Blake's *Jerusalem: The Emanation of the Giant Albion*, begun in 1804, there are two Stukeley-inspired engravings, a Stonehenge trilithon and 'The Serpent Temples thro' the Earth', obviously derived from Avebury (fig. 41). Meanwhile in the preface to the second chapter, addressed 'To the Jews', we find ourselves on familiar territory when we read:

> Jerusalem the Emanation of the Giant Albion! Can it be? Is it a Truth that the Learned have explored? Was Britain the Primitive Seat of Patriarchal Religion? . . . All things Begin & End in Albion's Ancient Druid rocky shore.
>
> Your ancestors derived their origin from Abraham, Heber, Shem and Noah, Who were Druids, as the Druid Temples (which are the Patriarchal Pillars & Oak Groves) over the whole Earth witness to this day.

The style may be all Blake, but the content is decidedly Stukeley.

8

William Borlase

Depending in which direction you are travelling, Boscawen-un is either the first or the last stone circle in Britain. It lies tucked away at the end of a farm track near the main Penzance to Land's End road. Without the aid of a map you would not know it was there. As stone circles go it is small, a ring of nineteen stones with a tall, leaning pillar in the middle. At one time William Stukeley thought it was the first circle in Britain, erected by the Phoenician colonisers immediately after they had come ashore. To Daniel Defoe in the 1720s it was the last thing he noted on his journey to the end of 'this utmost angle of the nation'. Boscawen-un was a relic that time forgot; the stones had 'no inscription, neither does tradition offer to leave any part of their history upon record; as whether it was a trophy, or a monument of burial, or an altar for worship, or what else; so all that can be learn'd of them, is, That here they are'.[1]

Defoe's comments are a reminder that not everybody was impressed by antiquarian speculation, but ironically Boscawen-un is one of the most written about stone circles in Britain. Defoe also seemed unaware that Cornish stone circles had been an object of enquiry for well over a century. The topographers William Camden, Richard Carew and John Norden had all made records of Cornish monuments during the Elizabethan era. A century later John Anstis, Garter King of Arms and a Cornishman, was active in the field. Encouraged by him, Edward Lhwyd came here, although neither of them published any of their work.

In 1722, just before Defoe passed through, the young William Borlase was installed as Rector of the nearby parish of Ludgvan. For Borlase it was a homecoming. He had been born in 1696 at Pendeen and after coming down from Oxford spent the remainder of his life back where he was born: in the district west of Penzance known as Penwith. Borlase (fig. 42) would have agreed with Defoe about one thing. In this part of Cornwall he felt a keen sense of isolation: he once remarked that were he not so cut off from the intellectual life of London and Oxford he would never have put so much effort into his study of geology and antiquities.

It was as a geologist that Borlase first made his name. He was elected a Fellow of the Royal Society in 1750 after submitting a treatise on 'Spar and Sparry Productions, Called Cornish Diamonds'. He was also a friend of Alexander Pope, to whom he sent several mineral samples for a private grotto. Pope wrote back to thank him, saying 'in some part of [my grotto] I must fix your name, if I can contrive it agreeably to your modesty and merit, in a shade but shining'.

The study of antiquities in Penwith was an obvious pursuit for any man with an education and time on his hands. In 1749 he wrote to William Stukeley: 'I found in a short time, that though we had few remains about us of any striking beauty or magnificence, yet that we had a great variety of monuments here which were of the most remote antiquity.'[2] The quoits and circles are the best known of these, and the proliferation of standing stones and barrows complete a rich prehistoric landscape. The average Penwith quoit is now denuded of its barrow or cairn, and some are in a ruinous condition, but they are undeniably striking in appearance and blend well with the region's granite scenery. Mixed with a variety of Iron Age domestic sites and field systems, numerous Christian

FIGURE 42. The Reverend Dr William Borlase (1695–1772). (*Royal Institution of Cornwall*)

crosses, holy wells and saints' shrines, not to mention the more recent mining industry, Penwith strikes the visitor as a place with more than its fair share of ghosts. In addition, it is the richest repository of ancient folklore in Britain, a culture assimilated by Borlase as he made his rides through the countryside.

Borlase began studying these antiquities in the 1720s, but it was a good ten or fifteen years before he started recording them in earnest. In 1748 two friends, Charles Lyttelton and Jeremiah Milles, respectively the Dean and Precentor of Exeter Cathedral, and both future Presidents of the Society of Antiquaries, persuaded this unambitious and unassuming antiquary to publish his work. Borlase now stepped up the pace of his research: through Milles and Lyttleton he obtained manuscripts by Edward Lhwyd and John Anstis, and in 1752 he sent a questionnaire to all the Cornish clergy and gentry soliciting information, although the response was poor. He also had other issues to deal with, especially a demon in the shape of John Wesley. Borlase was vehemently anti-Methodist, but unfortunately for his peace of mind Cornwall was 'one of the quack's constant stages'. In 1756 he made it plain in a letter to the Bishop of Exeter that the vacant curacy at St Just should be filled by a man with 'a due sense of the irregularity and ill tendency of Mr Wesley's principles and practice'.[3] Ironically, John Wesley was an admirer of the scholarship, both antiquarian and geological, of Borlase.

The *Antiquities, Historical and Monumental, of the County of Cornwall* was finally published in 1754. To call it a comprehensive study of Cornwall's prehistoric remains would be misleading. The reason he sent out a questionnaire was because even as late as 1750 Cornwall's internal communications were poor, and many of the county's ancient monuments are in remote places. So the book is heavily biased towards Penwith, and even here he misread some of the evidence. Many of his stone circles were in fact the foundations of Iron Age round dwellings which survive as circles of closely packed stones (fig. 43). The only genuine stone circles he mentions are the four in Penwith (the Merry Maidens, Boscawen-un, Tregeseal and Boskednan), plus a ruined pair of circles further east at Wendron, and the Hurlers. The remainder of the Bodmin Moor circles were as yet undiscovered, and even the impressive Trethevy Quoit, which Stukeley illustrated in his *Abury* volume, went unnoticed.

Borlase began his disquisition with a familiar historical overview. Mankind spread across Europe from the sons of Japheth, and the first settlers reached Britain from Gaul, Spain and Germany. But these early settlers were not Phoenicians, who did not come to Britain until late, about 450 BC, and then only to Cornwall to buy tin. Free of any Deist or Patriarchal Christian connotations, Borlase saw the Druids as having the same 'customs, tenets, rites, and superstitions of other gentile nations': their religion was intended 'to promote the delusions of the people, and gain of the Priests'.[4] As a Christian, Borlase was obviously no lover of pagan Druids: 'the frequency of their human sacrifices shocks us, their magick exceeds belief; their oak worship looks singular and absurd'.[5]

Founded on biblical historiography, his antiquarianism became a vision of the Cornish landscape informed by the scriptures and the folklore of the stones. On Mount Sinai God told Moses: 'If thou wilt make me an altar of stone, thou shalt not build it of hewn stone: for if thou lift up thy tool upon it, thou hast polluted it.' Cornwall has (or had) many weird rock formations which Borlase believed were just as wonderful to the early inhabitants of Cornwall as they were in his own day. Geologists have shown that they are purely the result of weathering, but Borlase thought flint tools had had a hand in their appearance. Apparently this was a common Gentile practice: 'after Rocks became Symbols, they were occasionally varied and shaped for a variety of superstitious reasons'. In particular the natural hollows he found on the stones were dubbed 'Rock-Basins', and were deliberately cut 'for an holy oil . . . and the sacred instruments; for wine to sprinkle the sacrifice; for Oak leaves dipped in their holy water to purify their Altars afresh'.[6] These 'polluted' rocks were not temples but idols. Borlase wrote:

> Consecrated rocks were called anciently by the name of some God, that is, named, ritually dedicated, and advanced into Divinities. After these Rocks had been con-
> secrated, the Ancients paid them all manner of reverence imagined, that henceforth
> some spiritual intelligences resided within them, and that whatever touched them
> was sacred, and derived great virtue and power from them. Hence arose a Custom,

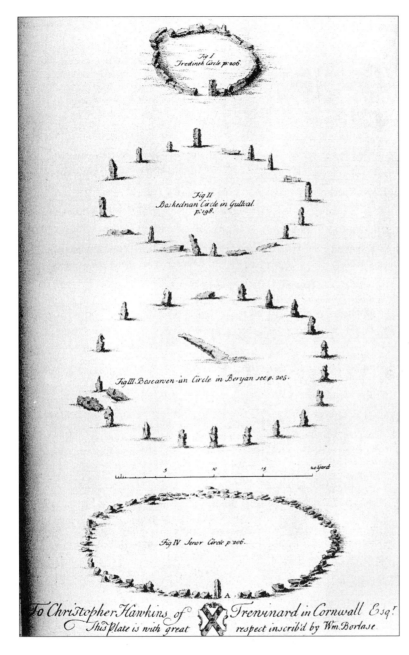

Fig I
Tredineh Circle p. 206.

Fig II
Boskednan Circle in Gulval.
p. 198.

Fig III. Boscawen-un Circle in Beryan see p. 205.

Fig IV Jenor Circle p. 206.

To Christopher Hawkins of   Trevinard in Cornwall Esq!
This Plate is with great   respect inscrib'd by Wm. Borlase.

FIGURE 43.
Stone circles in
west Cornwall by
Borlase. In fact
only the middle
two, Boskednan
and Boscawen-un,
are genuine circles.

which continues to this day, of lying down, and sleeping upon Rocks, in order to be cured of lameness.[7]

One of the strangest of the natural rock formations is the Cheesewring, near the Hurlers on Bodmin Moor (fig. 44). It is a tall, thin rock pile standing in an exposed position overlooking a vast tract of the moor, conspicuous and strange enough for Borlase to assume it was a rock idol. On top of the stones are various hollows in which water was collected, water that 'was accounted holy, of great use to purification, to cure distempers, and forestall future events'. Having climbed on top of the rock pile, the Druids would 'harangue the audience, pronounce decisions, and foretell future Events'.[8]

Many of the rock formations referred to by Borlase have since been destroyed, especially logan stones to which a variety of superstitions were attached. The only surviving example is at Treryn Dinas in Penwith. It was well known to Borlase, who wrote that 'any hand may move it to and fro; but . . . it is morally impossible that any lever, or indeed any force . . . can remove it from its present situation'.[9] By the early nineteenth century it had become a tourist attraction. 'Logan' is a west country pronunciation of 'logging', to log meaning to rock. These stones were supposed to rock only at certain times of the day (usually midnight) and could cure all manner of diseases or turn you into a witch. Although logan stones are perfectly natural, 'it is not

FIGURE 44.
Although it is a
natural rockpile,
Borlase believed
that the Cheese-
wring on Bodmin
Moor was a rock
idol from which
the Druids
addressed the mul-
titudes.

at all improbable, that the Druids, so well versed in the Arts of Magick (the sole business of which is to deceive), observing this uncommon property . . . soon learned to make use of it, as an occasional miracle'.[10]

At Constantine was the Cornish Pebble, another natural formation – a large rock perched precariously on two smaller rocks, creating a natural aperture. The Druids refined this natural wonder to produce the artificial, and genuinely prehistoric, holed stones. The Men-an-tol in Penwith is flanked by two short stones, beside one of which is a prostrate stone 'like a cushion or pillow, as if to kneel upon' (fig. 45). The purpose of the holed stone was 'to initiate, and dedicate Children to the Offices of Rock Worship, by drawing them through this hole, and also to purify the Victim before it was sacrificed'. To account for the celebrated curative properties of the stone he suggested:

> considering the many lucrative juggles of the Druids . . . it is not wholly improbable, that some miraculous Restoration of health might be promised to the people . . . upon proper pecuniary gratifications, provided that, at a certain season of the Moon, and whilst a priest officiated at one of the Stones adjoining, with prayers adapted to the occasion, they would draw their infirm children through this whole hole.[11]

A similar baptismal function is suggested for the trilithons at Stonehenge. They were symbolic doorways 'used for Proselytes, or Novices, people under Vows, or about to sacrifice', to initiate them 'into their more sublime mysteries'.[12]

Rocks and standing stones were the altars and idols of the Druids, stone circles were their temples. The circle was a symbolic figure necessary for the Druids to conduct

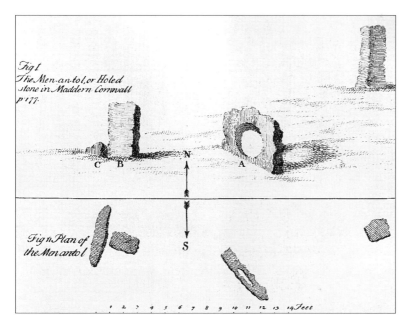

FIGURE 45.
William Borlase
believed that the
Men-an-tol had
initiated children
'to the Offices of
Rock Worship'.

'their nefarious Rites of Witchcraft, and Necromancy'. The prototype of all stone circles were those supposedly erected by Moses and Joshua beneath Mount Sinai and at Gilgal. 'This Gilgal was first a place of worship, then of national Council, and Inauguration.' Borlase believed that many 'Eastern Superstitions' were enacted in open air temples, and that the Druids followed their example, maintaining that 'the Gods were not to be confined within walls'.

Religious ceremonies, generally with the air of satanic rituals, are vividly brought to life by Borlase. The special times of devotion were midday and midnight, while assemblies were held at new or full moon. Near the Merry Maidens stone circle Borlase found a number of small standing stones with small apertures. To these the intended victims were 'tied while the Priests were going through their preparatory Ceremonies, and making Supplications to the Gods to accept the ensuing Sacrifice'.[13] The Druids – clean-shaven novices and bearded elders – were dressed in white and wore wreaths of oak leaves around their temples; meanwhile their wives and daughters-in-law were admitted into the sanctuary of the stone circle, but stripped naked, their bodies painted with herb juice. All this was necessary before they could 'appease the Gods with human victims'.

Borlase maintained that, in pagan society, religion and civil administration were not only conducted in the same place but usually at the same time: 'the Ancients took care that all civil Treaties, Laws, and Elections should be attended by Sacrifices'. He went on to say that 'whilst any election or decree was depending, or any solemn compact to be confirmed; the principal persons concerned stood each by his pillar; and where a Middle Stone was erected in the Circle, there stood the Prince, or General elect',[14] which explained the central stone at Boscawen-un. But the number of 'pillars' in a circle could have another meaning. The four Penwith circles each have nineteen stones, which he suggested might be a division of the year into the seven days of the week and the twelve months of the year. 'The priests were the only Chronologers and Registers of Time' and so the stones were used in their 'endeavour to perpetuate the memory of their Learning, and Astronomical Computations'.[15] Then again he suggested some of the circles might also be sepulchral, based on reports that burials were discovered within them, or were trophies erected after battles, for which he could turn to folklore for evidence. In this way he found room for just about every conceivable use for these enclosures.

Barrows were much less complicated, especially as he found scriptural authority for their purely sepulchral function. Cornish sepulchral monuments come in all shapes and sizes, 'but generally large in proportion to the Quality of the deceased, or the Vanity, Affection, and Power of the Survivors'. While cromlechs were also considered by Borlase to be sepulchral, he was not impressed with Rowlands' sacrificial altar theory because of its impracticalities. In any case the importance of the cromlechs was not the

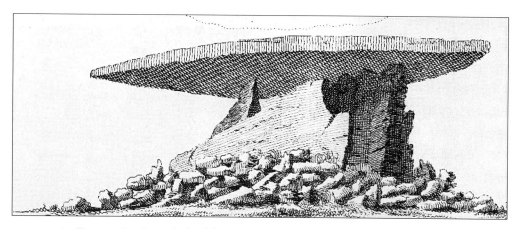

FIGURE 46. Zennor Quoit, typical of the graves of 'Princes and Great Commanders'.

surface of the capstone, and its possible uses, but the chamber it enclosed (fig. 46). These chambers were just glorified versions of the small stone cists found in barrows, and were probably the last resting places of 'Princes and Great Commanders'. Borlase dabbled a little in excavation, and his book contains drawings of urns, bronze daggers and coins. He also dug at some of the quoits, but without success. Mulfra Quoit yielded nothing, while at Lanyon Quoit someone had beaten him to it. In essence he was a topographer, whose antiquarian imagination was informed by the Cornish landscape rather than artefacts.

Predictably William Stukeley did not like the book. The two men had corresponded briefly, Stukeley being delighted to find a contact in remote Cornwall, but their ideas about Druids were poles apart and Stukeley was not a man to tolerate views he disagreed with. What he said about the book we do not know, but Jeremiah Milles wrote to Borlase in 1754 saying: 'You need not be in any pain on account of your differing from Dr Stukeley about any point of Druid history. What you assert is founded on authority, but he makes a system out of his own head.'[16] Now in the most creative period of his life, Borlase soon enhanced his reputation with two further publications. In 1756 he published *Observations on the Ancient and Present State of the Isles of Scilly*; and in 1758 came his other labour of love, *The Natural History of Cornwall*, over half of which was devoted to geology. A second edition of *Antiquities* was to appear in 1769, but by now Borlase was an old man. To free himself from the wearisome tasks of overseeing book production, he sold this edition to a London bookseller for 100 guineas.

Borlase received an honorary doctorate from Oxford University in 1766, and as Dr Borlase he has long been hailed as the 'Father of Cornish Archaeology'. But he was not an archaeologist, he was an antiquary, although one who stood apart from his contemporaries. His influence was to be limited, although the reason for this was topographical rather than intellectual. Until the mid nineteenth century Borlase provided the definitive model for interpreting Dartmoor's monuments, while in 1796 Hayman Rooke wrote an account of monuments in the Peak District, which quotes liberally from Borlase and includes many Borlaseian rock idols.

The *Antiquities* differs from eighteenth-century antiquarian literature because Cornwall is different from Wessex. Borlase had to contend with a folklore heritage unlike anything Aubrey or Stukeley encountered in Wiltshire. In these popular beliefs he recognised supernatural forces which were older than Christianity, and they were applied equally to natural rock formations and genuine archaeological remains. Borlase combined this evidence into a symbolic whole, further enhanced by a belief that he was writing about an age of darkness before the light of Christianity. Then there was the intangible quality of the place. Penwith has attracted and inspired a long list of artists and writers: D. H. Lawrence, Katherine Mansfield, Virginia Woolf, Patrick Heron, Barbara Hepworth. To these the name of William Borlase should be added. The uniqueness of his book is really the uniqueness of the Cornish landscape.

9

Romantic Druids and the Picturesque

Stanton Drew, nine miles west of Bath, is the third of the great Wessex stone circles, and the one that tourism forgot. To be precise, Stanton Drew is actually three stone circles, but they have none of the visual compactness of Avebury, spread out as they are in the green fields behind the village. There is a cove, similar to the one at Avebury, which looks absurdly out of place in the beer garden of the Druids Arms, but the nucleus of the village has its back turned away from the circles, which stand neglected like old rusting farm machinery put out to grass (fig. 47).

Aubrey and Stukeley had both come here and recognised Stanton Drew's obvious significance, but the first antiquary to make a proper survey of it was the Bath architect John Wood the Elder. According to the local people previous attempts to count or make a plan of the Wedding, as it was known, had all failed because the surveyors were either struck dead on the spot, or were taken so ill they could no longer continue. 'This was seriously told me', wrote Wood,

> when I began to take a Plan of them, on the 12th of August 1740, to deter me from proceeding: And as a Storm accidentally arose just after, and blew down Part of a Tree near the Body of the Work, the people were then thoroughly satisfied that I had disturbed the Guardian Spirits of the metamorphosed Stones, and from thence great Pains were taken to convince me of the Impiety of what I was about.[1]

Wood tells us that 'Stantondrue' means 'Oak Men's Town', and 'Achmanchester' means 'Oak Men's City'. The oak men were of course Druids, and Achmanchester was the Saxon name for Bath. Where Stukeley saw Avebury as the supreme achievement of ancient Druidism, Wood staked a rival claim for Stanton Drew and Bath in his book, *An Essay towards a Description of Bath*, first published in 1742. Wood's Druids have nothing to do with the religious patriarchs of Stukeley – they are Pythagorean philosophers – but Wood is just as patriotic in seeing the British Druids as the fount of the most sacred wisdom of the Ancients. Wood, as a native of Bath, also allowed his patriotism to take on a more regional bias. In Michael Drayton's *Poly Olbion* King Bladud, grandson six times removed from the Trojan Brutus (the founder of Britain according to Geoffrey of Monmouth), is credited with discovering Bath's hot springs. Moreover he was learned in 'the Liberall Arts' of Greece. Wood latched on to this and hailed Bladud, who began his twenty year reign in 483 BC, as the founder of Bath

FIGURE 47.
According to John
Wood, the circles
at Stanton Drew
were a university
of the Druids, and
were built with
stone quarried
from Wookey
Hole in the
Mendips.

as the 'Metropolitan Seat of the *British Druids*'. He also identified Bladud as the person
known to the Greeks as Abaris the Hyperborean, and so Bladud 'appears to have been
a great Prophet, and the most Eminent Philosopher of all Antiquity: He was the
Renowned *Hypoborean* High Priest of *Apollo* that shined in *Greece* at the very time
Pythagoras flourished; He was a Disciple and a Colleague to that Celebrated Philosopher'.[2]

Stanton Drew was the university of the Druids, founded by Bladud for a colony of
philosophers who came here from Greece. The stones were quarried from the Mendip
Hills near Wells, gouged out from the bowels of the Earth, leaving behind the cave
known as Wookey Hole. This became 'the place where the *Druids* practised Part of
their Magick, and initiated their Disciples into the Mysteries of that Art'. The stones,
meanwhile, were used to 'cure the Diseases of the People, to honour the Gods, and
to instruct Mankind in the Liberal Sciences'.[3]

The liberal sciences, as Pomponius Mela and Caesar had written, included astronomy.
The three circles and outlying stones 'form a perfect Model of the *Pythagorean* System
of the Planetary World', its three circles representing sun, moon and Earth, with the
outlying stones representing the other planets. The stones could also be used calend-
rically – the large central circle was 365 Jewish Yards in circumference, giving the days
of the solar year – and incorporated the 'grand mystical Numbers of the ancient *Britons*',
about which more in due course.

Here we need to digress for a moment because, although Wood's antiquarianism
was uncritical and its bias transparent, it informed the symbolism in his architecture, in
particular the King's Circus in Bath (fig. 48). The idea of the Circus as an arena for
sports – a highly impractical idea – was first projected in 1725, when Wood was only
twenty-one, but building work did not start until 1754, the year of his death. In 1740,
after his survey of Stanton Drew, he speculated in a letter to Lord Harley that the two
smaller circles were temples of the sun and moon, while the central, larger circle was

FIGURE 48. The King's Circus in Bath is John Wood's masterpiece, symbolically recreating a circle of houses Wood thought he had found at Stanton Drew. The acorns on the parapet are the only overt Druid symbol.

the remains of a circle of houses in which the priests lived. This is probably what the Circus, with its thirty middle-class houses, symbolically recreates. Wood also projected the building of the Royal Crescent, which his son later superintended to a different design. In the Circus and Crescent were the symbolic recreations of the temples of the sun and moon. The Circus is widely regarded as a masterpiece of Palladian architecture, but Wood never explained its arcane symbolism. A hint can be seen in the Circus itself with its giant acorns, representing the Druids, on top of the parapet.

A year before his work at Stanton Drew Wood was at Stonehenge, where he aimed to rectify his complaint that nobody had made an accurate survey of it. In the course of his work he nearly got mugged by 'a Couple of lusty Fellows who bore the marks of a late Fray', and who were a bit too interested in the colour of his watch. Here also he gave his son, John Wood the Younger, his first lesson in surveying. In 1747 he ventured into print with a book called *Choir Gaure, Vulgarly Called Stonehenge*, which offered an interpretation to rival Stukeley's. Stonehenge was now a lunar temple dedicated to the goddess Diana, and Wood claimed to have discovered how the Druids used it as a solar and lunar calendar.

The key to unlock this mystery was to count and then to interpret the number of stones. These are the grand mystical numbers which Wood had already interpreted at Stanton Drew, drawing on the idea that everything is assimilated to number which

originates from Pythagoras. At Stonehenge the thirty upright stones of the sarsen circle
represented the thirty days of the month, while the thirty lintels stood for a Druid 'age'
of thirty years. These and other schemes combined every nineteenth revolution of the
sun to represent the perfect harmony of the celestial spheres. The nineteen-year period,
covering all the changes of the moon's position relative to the sun, is known as a
Metonic Cycle, after the Athenian philosopher who discovered it in the fifth century
BC. Wood calls nineteen the 'Golden Number', but far from being of Greek origin,
he gives us 'a sufficient Demonstration that this GOLDEN NUMBER was of *British*, instead
of *Grecian* original'.[4]

There was nothing especially clever about all this and, with typical self-importance,
Stukeley described *Choir Gaure* as 'an account of Stonehenge, written to contradict me'.
A entry in his diary during 1763 shows that sixteen years after the book was published,
and nine years after its author had died, Stukeley was still fuming:

> 'Tis such a heap, a ruin of trifling, nonsensical, impertinent and needless measuring
> of the stones . . . The whole performance he stuffs with fabulous whimsys of his
> own crackt imaginations, wild extravagancys concerning the Druids, without the
> least true foundation and knowledge concerning them . . . the whole of this *wooden*
> performance is no more than the fermented dregs and settlement of the dullest, and
> most inveterate mixture of ignorance, malice, and malevolence. His entrance into
> this sacred enclosure, seems to me like Satan breaking over the hallowed mound of
> Paradise with no other than a murderous intent.[5]

Stukeley could rant and rave all he liked, but Wood's brand of astronomical symbolism
was the shape of things to come.

In Julius Caesar's *Gallic War* there is a passage lauding the Druids' knowledge of
astronomy: 'They . . . discuss and impart to the youth many things respecting the stars
and their motion, respecting the extent of the world and of our earth . . .' Once the
idea of sage and philosophical Druids became fashionable, their apparent astronomical
wisdom captured the popular imagination. In 1793 Wordsworth spent three days walking
over Salisbury Plain. Later, in *The Prelude*, he described the 'Lines, circles, mounts, a
mystery of shapes' as:

> the work, as some divine
> Of infant science, imitative forms
> By which the Druids covertly express'd
> Their knowledge of the heavens, and imaged forth
> The constellations.
>
> (book 13, lines 338–44)

Ancient astronomy was seen as one of Britain's most impenetrable mysteries and, thanks to the turgid schemes of those who tried to unravel it, it remained one. Dr John Smith's theory of Stonehenge had much in common with Wood's, not least in the arbitrary nature of his numbers game. Smith's *Choir Gawr: The Grand Orrery of the Ancient Druids, Called Stonehenge, Astronomically Explained, and Proved to be a Temple for Observing the Motions of the Heavenly Bodies* was published in 1771. Stonehenge was a temple from which the heavens were observed, and at its centre was the Arch-Druid's stall, from where he watched the summer sun rise over the Heel Stone. The thirty uprights of the sarsen circle, representing the days of the month, multiplied by the twelve stones of the bluestone horseshoe, symbolising the twelve signs of the zodiac, equalled the 360 days of the solar year. Meanwhile the inner circle of thirty bluestones signified the twenty-nine days and twelve hours of the lunar month. So Stonehenge was used as a solar and lunar calendar.

The Reverend Thomas Maurice calculated a slightly different scheme. The sixty stones in the sarsen circle, which included the lintels, corresponded to the sexagenary cycle of Asiatic astronomy. The circle of thirty bluestones represented a generation of Druids, while the nineteen stones of the sarsen horseshoe represented the length of the Indian lunar cycle. Nineteen stones could also have been the well-known Metonic Cycle, but Maurice was not the only author to make comparisons with India. The gradual acquisition of Indian territory in the latter half of the eighteenth century was the beginning of Britain's complicated love affair with Indian culture. In India there were not only megaliths but an ancient astronomical tradition. In his *Oriental Collections* of 1798 General Charles Vallancey compared Druid and Indian astronomy, and in his *Indian Antiquities* of 1796 Maurice speculated that the Druids were descended from a tribe of Brahmins. In fact there was nothing odd about seeing the Brahmin as the counterpart to the British Druid: Henry Wansey, writing in 1796, seriously believed that 'was a learned Brahmin to contemplate the ruins of Stonehenge, he might, possibly, comprehend more of its design than we do, and trace some vestiges of an art wholly unknown to us'.

Godfrey Higgins preferred a connection with Babylon. After all, the Babylonians were the most famous of ancient astronomers, according to classical literature and the Bible. His book *Celtic Druids*, published in 1829, suggested that there was a numerical correlation between the astronomical cycles and the number of stones in every 'Druidical circle'. As per usual, Stonehenge, which he calculated was built in 4000 BC, was used to illustrated the point:

> The outer circle of Stonehenge consists of 60 stones, the base number of the most famous [i.e. Babylonian] of all the cycles of antiquity. The next circle consists of 40 [sic], but one on each side of the entrance is advanced out of the line, so as to leave 19 stones, a Metonic cycle on each side, and the inner of one Metonic cycle or 19 stones.

John Wood had visualised a symbolic representation of the planets at Stonehenge and Stanton Drew, and in the title of his book Dr Smith had described Stonehenge as a 'Grand Orrery'. An orrery is a clockwork model of the planetary system, named after Charles Boyle, fourth Earl of Cork and Orrery, for whom one of the earliest models was made in 1712. The theory of a planetarium, or 'stationary orrery', has never been entirely in fashion, but then again never entirely out of it. In 1777 a Mr Waltire gave a series of lectures in Salisbury, claiming that the barrows around Stonehenge accurately represented not only the position but the magnitude of the fixed stars, forming a complete planisphere. Other barrows were placed so as to register eclipses which had taken place, and the Stonehenge trilithons were 'the registers of the transits of Mercury and Venus'. Stonehenge itself he considered to be at least 17,000 years old.

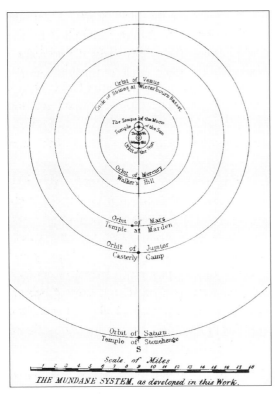

The Reverend Edward Duke, in his *The Druidical Temples of the County of Wilts*, published in 1846, was just as overblown. His planetarium was postulated on a north–south line with a radius of thirty-two miles (fig. 49). The Earth was represented by Silbury Hill and the orbits of the sun and moon were the south and north circles at Avebury respectively. Three ancient earthworks – Walker's Hill, Marden and Casterly Camp – represented Mercury, Mars and Jupiter, and resembled the 'hill altars of holy scripture'. A circle of stones at Winterbourne Bassett represented Venus and Stonehenge was Saturn. These two, plus the two circles at Avebury, made up the four planetary temples in stone, and 'by an analysis of the details are resolvable into every known astronomical cycle of antiquity'. Moreover, 'these planetary temples, taken synthetically, and as a whole, were intended to represent the *magnus annus*, the great year of Plato': the precession of the equinoxes, an astronomical cycle which at the time was measured at 25,920 years.[6] Today the best-known planetarium has nothing to do with megaliths: it is the Glastonbury

FIGURE 49. Edward Duke's planetarium, whereby the ancient temples of Wiltshire were postulated, incorrectly, as standing on a true north–south line.

Zodiac either discovered or imagined (take your pick) by an artist, Katherine Maltwood, in 1929.

Avebury never attracted the same kind of astronomical speculation as Stonehenge. Nevertheless, and despite its ruination, it still inspired its visitors with awe, wonder, and Stukeleyite tendencies. The Reverend William Cooke published in 1755 *An Enquiry into the Patriarchal and Druidical Religion, Temples, &c, Wherein the Primaeval Institution and Universality of the Christian Scheme is Manifested*. The title tells us all we need to know. Later on there was William Lisle Bowles' *Hermes Britannicus* of 1828: 'The vast pile I consider as sacred to the great instructor, symbolised and worshipped in Egypt, who unfolded the heavens, and brought intelligence of one infinite God, and of eternal life to Man; which knowledge, in remote ages, was communicated to the Celtic Druids by the Phoenicians.'[7] He continues by fusing God, the stars and the serpent, allowing him to speak of Avebury 'representing the God over the Heavens, stretching on each side in the form of the *serpent*, the well known emblem, both of the course of the stars and of restoration and immortality'.[8]

And so on. In the absence of a new Big Idea this kind of writing lasted well into the nineteenth century, by which time it had become stale, second-hand and stultifyingly boring. Lacking the freshness and originality of Stukeley and Borlase, or even Wood, writers lapsed into a smug self-glorification: 'I must now take the key in my hand', wrote Edward Duke, 'and endeavour to unlock the sacred chest, in which the grand arcanum of our heathen ancestors has been for ages reposited.'[9] However, Duke's 'strong and continuous series of well established facts' precluded any form of debate. When he thinks that 'Abiri' is a corruption of 'Cabiri', which in Hebrew meant 'the mighty ones', there is no way of arguing with him. In the pages of the *Archaeological Journal* in 1857 J. M. Kemble tried another method, humour:

> The avenue you see [again at Avebury], which my friends the Ophites consider so mysterious, was only a common stone row, and the 'temple' itself of the snake, the sun, the Helio-Arkite cult, the mystic zodiac, and a number of other very fine things – so fine that one cannot understand them – is very probably, in the eyes of this dull dog of a surveyor, only a burial place.[10]

Kemble was writing as an archaeologist whose knowledge was based on digging artefacts out of the earth. Until there were improvements in excavation methods, and until astronomical theories were based on scientific know-how rather than esoteric numerology, there was no alternative to fashionable pseudo-mysticism. In *Cyclops Christianus* of 1849 Algernon Herbert argued quite plausibly that Stonehenge, Avebury, Carnac and the like could not have been built before the Roman conquest, otherwise Caesar, Tacitus and the other Roman authors would have mentioned them. According to Herbert, the Druids had worshipped in oak groves which were imitated in stone by the later

Britons. It was a reasonable theory, but hopelessly wide of the mark. William Borlase had declared optimistically that 'conjecture may sometimes strike a new light, and the truths of Antiquity be more effectually pursued than where people will not venture to guess at all'.[11] A century later Herbert was left to sum up his own efforts, and the doomed efforts of all his fellow antiquaries, when he wrote: 'Few things have interested antiquarians more than the remarkable systems of unhewn stone erected with prodigious labour in these islands. Many conjectures have been expended [on them] . . . with singular ill success.'[12]

Ironically, just as British antiquarianism reached its low point British antiquities had never been more popular. The topographers of the seventeenth and early eighteenth century were being superseded by writers and artists who were formulating a new aesthetic response to the landscape and its monuments. Sir Walter Scott's popular novels, written in the early decades of the nineteenth century when the countryside was noticeably changing, recalled an earlier world of rural simplicity, and offered the comforts of nostalgia as an antidote to the insecurities of the present. *The Pirate* of 1821 is set in Shetland and Orkney in about 1700, and in one of the closing scenes the pirate, Captain Cleveland, meets his lover Minna Troil, in secret at the Stones of Stenness (fig. 50). Scott found in the stones a dramatic backdrop for melodramatic events: 'The immense blocks of stone . . . stood around the pirate in the grey light of the dawning,

FIGURE 50. The Stones of Stenness in 1772, later used by Sir Walter Scott as a backdrop for one of the closing scenes in his novel *The Pirate*. To the right is the Stone of Odin, destroyed in 1814, and in the distance is the Ring of Brodgar. (*British Library*)

like the phantom forms of antediluvian giants.' As for his lover: 'If we hold the circles of Gothic or Scandinavian origin, she might have seemed a descended Vision of Freya, the spouse of the Thundering Deity, before whom some bold Sea-King or champion bent with an awe, which no mere mortal terror could have inflicted upon him.' The Dwarfie Stane in Hoy and the Stone of Odin at Stenness were also requisitioned for the story, again as romantic stage scenery, and yet Scott was unable to leave Orkney without indulging his own theories about them. These are found, appropriately enough, not in the novel but in the footnotes. The Dwarfie Stane was 'a temple of some kind to the Northern *Dii Manes*', while the 'promise of Odin', as he termed it, was traced back to the Eyrbrigga Saga, where oaths are pledged by joining hands in a silver ring. As for the origin of the stones, he was adamant that the Druids could have had nothing to do with them in this land of Norse people.

Scotland had already been romanticised as a land of myth by James Macpherson. In 1762 he published *Fingal*, and a year later *Temora*, which he claimed were the work of the ancient Gaelic bard Ossian. Irish scholars dismissed them as fakes, as did Samuel

FIGURE 51. William Geller's fanciful recreation of Stonehenge, of 1832, replete with rocky outcrops and oak groves, represents Druidomania in all its baroque excess.
(*Salisbury and South Wiltshire Museum*)

Johnson (who was about to be fooled by Chatterton), but the public did not care who
had written them. They loved the high romance in a misty Celtic past, and possibly
the influence of Macpherson led to landmarks in the west of Scotland acquiring Ossianic
associations. A 'four poster' stone circle in Perthshire is known as the Grave of Diarmid,
while the Trotternish standing stones on Skye are three stones on which Fin MacCoul's
cauldron was placed, as was the self-explanatory Fingal's Cauldron Seat, a stone circle
on Machrie Moor in Arran.

Even Wordsworth was not averse to conjuring up a dramatic past. 'Guilt and Sorrow'
is a poem written in his early twenties, based on his walk across Salisbury Plain in 1793.
In an earlier draft he had a rush of blood, and evoked Stonehenge in all its Druid
glory:

> For oft, at dead of night, when dreadful fire
> Unfolds that powerful circle's reddening stones
> Mid priests and spectres grim and idols dire
> Far heard the great flame utters human moans
> Then all is hushed . . .

Later he had second thoughts, and chose instead to savour the mystery of a ruin:

> Pile of Stone-henge! so proud to hint yet keep
> Thy secrets, thou that lov'st to stand and hear
> The Plain resounding to the whirlwind's sweep,
> Inmate of lonesome Nature's endless year.[13]

Nearly thirty years later, in 1821, he again preferred to contemplate Long Meg and
her Daughters as a ruin which will refuse to yield its secrets:

> A weight of awe, not easy to be borne,
> Fell suddenly upon my Spirit – cast
> From the dread bosom of the unknown past,
> When first I saw that family forlorn.
> Speak Thou, whose massy strength and stature scorn
> The power of years – pre-eminent, and placed
> Apart, to overlook the circle vast –
> Speak, Giant Mother! [14]

But she told him nothing.

The pleasure of ruins is intimately bound up with the aesthetic movement known
as the Picturesque. It was artistically and intellectually undemanding, and became
very popular. In the eighteenth century Stonehenge, the greatest ruin of all, became a
tourist attraction. A Mrs Powys from Oxford recorded in her diary in 1759 that it 'gave

FIGURE 52.
Ystumcegid
cromlech, in
north Wales, in
the restrained
pages of *Archaeo-
logia* in 1852.

one sensations pleasingly awful'. Awe became a byword for all that the eighteenth century loved about ruins in the landscape; you will find it written in the journals of tours through Britain, and expressed in countless paintings and engravings of the period. Artists found a large, if not always lucrative, market for picturesque scenery and the weird and wonderful things in it. Of these, standing stones and dolmens may have been less popular than castles or monastic ruins, but they were just the kind of Gothick curiosity that inspired follies in the artificial landscape of gardens and parks.

In the park at Alton Towers in Staffordshire, begun in 1814, is a megalithic construction of piled stones and slabs, improbably titled the Druids' Sideboard. George Henry Law, the Bishop of Bath and Wells from 1824 to 1854, replanted woodland at his country residence at Banwell, where he executed a variety of Druid fantasies. One of them is an avenue marked with pairs of tufa standing stones, leading to a belvedere. William Beckford had a vast Gothic pile built in Wiltshire, called Fonthill Abbey, and had an imitation dolmen set up in the grounds. This whole Gothic fantasy, completed in 1807, must have been the last word in vulgarity until the badly-built towers unceremoniously tumbled to the ground within twenty years of being raised. The dolmen did not survive either.

'Druid Circles' also occasionally caught the imagination. The unassuming circles at Ipsden and Stonor Park in Oxfordshire could be mistaken for the real thing, unlike the folly built by Major Frederick West in Shropshire in the 1830s. It stands in a field visible from his home, Quinta House near Weston Rhyn, and its tall thin stones with equally slender lintels look like a matchstick Stonehenge (fig. 53).

This all seems harmless enough, but there was an unfortunate tendency to dismantle and remove dolmens, which had stood quite happily for 4000 or more years, out of the fields and into private gardens. One such was taken for a 'rock work' at Wardour

Castle in Wiltshire, and was described by one commentator as the 'most Gothic of Grottoes'. In the early nineteenth century the Earl of Darnley had a dolmen removed and reerected at Cobham Park in Kent, where it was born again as Merlin's Grotto. But the most bizarre 'rescue mission' was the removal of a Jersey chambered tomb to Park Place near Henley-on-Thames. In August 1785 the Colonel of the St Helier Militia was having some ground levelled for a parade square, when the workmen found some fallen stones that once formed a chambered cairn. The interests of military parades being paramount the stones had to go. They were offered to Marshall Conway, the Governor of Jersey, by the Vingtaine de la Ville, as a gift from the people of Jersey on the occasion of his retirement. The only snag was that Conway was expected to pay his own transportation costs. He reacted coolly to this idea, but his cousin, Horace Walpole, implored him: 'Pray do not disappoint me but transport the Cathedral of your island to your domain on our continent'. Presently the stones came floating up the Thames on a barge and were rebuilt at Conway's Park Place overlooking the river. Walpole, who fancied himself as an expert in these matters, declared that the monument had been accurately reassembled. A simple inscription commemorating 'Cet ancien Temple des Druides' provided the finishing touch.

So cromlechs and standing stones became, for some, a luxury item of garden furniture. William Danby, of Swinton Hall near Ilton on the Yorkshire Moors, had bigger ideas. His own Druid's Temple, dating from the 1820s, was an attempt to outdo Stonehenge

FIGURE 53. A Stonehenge folly, at Quinta in Shropshire, erected in the 1830s.

FIGURE 54. The Druid's Temple, near Ilton in north Yorkshire, is the last word in megalithic overstatement. William Danby had it built in the 1820s by the local unemployed.

as a megalithic spectacle (fig. 54). He had it built on the cheap by the local unemployed in exchange for their dole of a shilling a day. The Temple has trilithons, a Slaughter Stone and an Altar Stone, plus several outlying dolmens and a Cornish Cheesewring. Today it resides in the middle of a forestry plantation, surrounded by evergreens, but in its prime it must have been the height of overstatement.

Equally kitsch was the popular image of the wise old Druid. This has survived to the present day virtually intact, still wearing his white robes, and up until the early twentieth century still wearing his Father Christmas beard. Stone circles remained the focus of his ancient rites, partly due to the influence of a Welshman, Edward Williams. Williams was a mason from Glamorgan and is better known by his bardic nom de plume, Iolo Morgannwg. He claimed that druidical lore had been passed down unbroken from the Druids of prehistory, but only amongst the Glamorganshire poets. In fact the only two ordained Bards of the old tradition surviving were Edward Evans of Aberdare and himself. His talent for fabricating evidence was nothing if not audacious. In 1792 he presided over the first of the 'revived' Gorsedd ceremonies on Primrose Hill in London, together with a group of other expatriate Bards. The *Gentleman's Magazine* reported that 'the wonted ceremonies were observed. A circle of stones formed, in the middle of which was the *Maen Gorsedd*, or Altar, on which a naked sword being placed, all the Bards assisted to sheath it.'[15]

Later Iolo succeeded in getting his ceremonies tacked on to the genuinely ancient Welsh cultural festival, the Eisteddfod. At the Carmarthen Eisteddfod of 1819 he took a series of pebbles from his pockets and laid them out in a ring in the garden of the

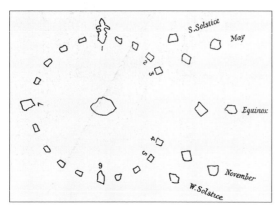

FIGURE 55. Iolo Morgannwg's supposed Gorsedd circle, found among his papers after his death, confirms the bard's reputation for fabrication.

Ivy Bush hotel, and the first bardic ceremony at an Eisteddfod took place. The idea caught on. A new ancient ceremony was invented where the Ovates, the Bards and the Druids paraded with their costumes and regalia. It took place inside a circle of nineteen stones especially constructed for the occasion (fig. 55). Ever since the National Eisteddfod of Wales was constituted in 1861 a similar ceremony has taken place, and this is why in Wales you can find stone circles in the most unlikely places, such as the heart of Cardiff's civic centre and the leafy suburbs of Merthyr Tydfil (fig. 56).

Cornwall too adopted a similar Gorsedd ceremony in the twentieth century, but there they prefer to stage them in the many prehistoric circles of the county. The first of them was held in 1928, when Boscawen-un was the chosen venue for a special reason. A Welsh triad written down in the sixteenth century by Llewelyn Sion reads:

> The three principal Gorsedds of the Isle of Britain:
> The Gorsedd of Meriw hill;
> The Gorsedd of Beiscawen;
> And the Gorsedd of Bryn Gwyddon.[16]

Boscawen-un is therefore a special place to the Cornish Bards.

The Druids associated with the midsummer sunrise at Stonehenge have nothing to do with the Welsh Gorsedd, apart from their origin in the romantic inclinations of the eighteenth century. The Ancient Order of Druids was founded in 1781 by Henry Hurle, a carpenter and builder, who gave it many of the mystical trappings of Freemasonry. It was constituted partly as a benefit society but on this contentious point a majority of hardliners split to form the Albion Lodge of the Ancient Order of Druids, who initiated Winston Churchill in 1908. There is a photograph of the ceremony showing the future Prime Minister surrounded by wizened old sages in long, white stick-on beards.

The history of these new Druid orders is marked by continual splits and splinter groups, but one enduring feature is the solstice ceremony conducted at Stonehenge,

FIGURE 56. A late nineteenth-century Gorsedd circle at Thomastown in Merthyr Tydfil.

which started in the late nineteenth century and soon attracted a flurry of rowdy spectators. In the 1940s jazz bands livened up the occasion, but by the 1960s the ridicule they regularly attracted was turning to disdain – the astronomer Gerald Hawkins referred to their crepuscular performances as a 'sad little made-up ritual'.[15] Celebrating the solstice seems a harmless enough thing to do, but there has occasionally been an ill-wind in the summer night air. At the 1914 solstice the Chief Druid, Dr MacGregor Reid, was ejected from Stonehenge by the owner, Edmund Antrobus, who had decided to prohibit all religious ceremonies at the place. Dr Reid, so the Druids say, put a curse on the owner which was particularly potent: both Antrobus and his nephew were dead within a year. So much for peace, love and understanding. The right of the Druids to hold their ceremonies at Stonehenge was not questioned again until the 1980s when the monument became a focus of wider social conflicts and the Druids were forced to conduct their ceremonies elsewhere.

In 1975 the Secular Order of Druids was initiated. They claim lineal descent from the eighteenth century, declaring that former Arch Druids have included William Blake, Lord Winchelsea and William Stukeley, and that they began with their secret foundation in 1716 by, of all people, John Toland. This is a curious claim given that Toland, who hated all priestly institutions, saw the Druids as charlatans who 'calculated to beget ignorance' among the people. But the authenticity of their claims has no bearing on their right to worship in a Neolithic temple, and the Druids are adamant that Stonehenge is their rightful place of worship. In 1918 when the then owner Cecil Chubb gave Stonehenge to the nation, he invited the Arch-Druid formally to hand over the title-deed. According to Tim Sebastian, the current secular Arch-Druid, this 'alone secures and legitimises the Druidic claim to Stonehenge as a Temple of the Druids'.[17]

10

Richard Colt Hoare
and William Cunnington

Bring the *Urn* – the relicks in;
Now the Mystic rites begin.

Richard Fenton, 1806

In 1807 the travel writer Richard Fenton visited William Cunnington at his home in Heytesbury, on the west side of Salisbury Plain. Inside the 'moss house' in his back garden Cunnington had stored all the artefacts he had dug up from Wiltshire barrows. 'Nothing could be more curious', wrote Fenton, 'than the arrangement of the museum: the contents of every tumulus was separate, and the articles so disposed as in the case of ornaments, such as beads, in such elegant knots and festoons, as to please the eye.' Cunnington's shelves were piled high with urns and pottery of various styles, flint arrowheads, buttons and beads in bone, glass and amber, bronze axes and daggers, iron spearheads, whetstones, bone tokens, 'grape cups' and the skeleton of a goose. 'The story of several' of these barrows 'was so perfectly told by the relics they contained, that an epitaph could not have let us more into the light of the rank and character of the dead.'[1] If only that were true.

William Cunnington (fig. 57) was the first of a venerable family dynasty of Wiltshire archaeologists, but it was left to the last of them, Robert, to write a biography of their illustrious ancestor, published in 1975. Its title, *From Antiquary to Archaeologist*, sums up William Cunnington's career precisely. Elected to the Society of Antiquaries in 1801, he was as 'naturally curious and inquisitive' as any other Fellow, but he stood apart from them in one important respect. The society was peopled with men of education and private means but, as a wool merchant, Cunnington came from a lower social class. Perhaps it was his lack of classical learning and biblical scholarship that led him to an alternative method of seeking the past, but whatever the reason he was perhaps the first person in Britain who could properly call himself an archaeologist. Rather as a result of his work than the intention of it, subsequent archaeologists realised that if they wanted to write with any authority on ancient Britain they would have to forego the civilised comforts of the library and step out into the field and get their hands dirty.

Barrow digging had always been part of the antiquarian repertory. Borlase and Stukeley, and before them Edward Lhwyd, had all dabbled a little. In the mid seventeenth century Dr Thomas Browne of Norwich suggested that 'subterraneous enquiry by cutting through one of them either directly or cross-wise' would establish whether barrows were raised by the Romans, Saxons or Danes. But the excavation of barrows as a consciously intellectual pursuit seems to have begun in the early 1600s with Sir John Oglander, who went to live in the Isle of Wight in 1607. Here he noted 'divors buries on ye topp of oure Island hills' and, 'I have digged for my experience in soome of ye moore auntientest, and have found manie bones of men formerlye consumed by fyor, according to ye Romane custome'.[2] In 1658 Browne wrote:

FIGURE 57. William Cunnington (1754–1810). His portrait appeared at the beginning of the first volume of *Ancient Wiltshire*.

surely many noble bones and ashes have been contented with such hilly tombs; which neither admitting ornament, epitaph or inscription, may, if earthquakes spare them, out-last all other monuments . . . Obelisks have their term, and pyramids will tumble, but these mountainous monuments may stand, and are like to have the same period with the earth.[3]

Well, maybe, but few of their ashes were allowed to rest in peace.

Cunnington had become interested in Wiltshire antiquities during long rides in the country, and he soon came into contact with the Wiltshire antiquarian fraternity. John Britton, a topographer, H. P. Wyndham, the Member of Parliament for Wiltshire, the Reverend W. Coxe of Bemerton and the Reverend Thomas Leman of Bath, all encouraged Cunnington in his barrow-digging activities which began in 1800. Coxe and Wyndham both sponsored excavations by Cunnington, but their motives were not entirely altruistic. Both wanted to write a definitive history of Wiltshire antiquities, and Coxe even went to the extent of preventing Cunnington from divulging information about the excavations carried out at his expense. Cunnington benefited from this arrangement insofar as without a sponsor he would not have been able to afford to take time away from his drapery business. When Wyndham and Coxe lost interest in

FIGURE 58. Sir Richard Colt Hoare, Cunnington's patron, without whose financial resources *Ancient Wiltshire* would never have been

his field work Cunnington was lucky
enough to find a new patron with
whom he enjoyed a much more fruit-
ful relationship.

Sir Richard Colt Hoare was the son
of a banker, was hugely wealthy and
was a connoisseur of the arts and literature (fig. 58). Every year thousands
of people visit his home at Stourhead
with the magnificent landscaped park
laid out by his grandfather in the 1740s.
After his marriage was tragically cut
short by the death of his wife and
second child in 1785 he took himself
off around Britain, making several
tours through Wales. In 1803 he
agreed to take on the expense of Cunnington's excavations, and to write the
much mooted history of Wiltshire.
Cunnington was by this time well into
his stride, and had found two reliable
diggers in the father and son team of

Stephen and John Parker. Hoare also employed Philip Crocker as a surveyor and
draughtsman, seconded from the newly-formed Ordnance Survey.

By 1801 Cunnington had opened twenty-four barrows and was gaining in confidence.
'I now begin to flatter myself that with a little more experience I shall be able to say
on first sight of the Tumulus what interment it contains – I think I can already point
out the barrow under which Cremation has been practised.'[4] Throughout the ensuing
decade barrows were opened at a rapid pace: if everything went well Cunnington could
do three a day. In all Cunnington and Hoare opened more than 450 barrows. In each
of them they left a lead or brass token inscribed WC or RCH, together with the date,
to show future investigators who had opened them. They employed two methods of
digging – one was to drive a trench through the centre of the mound, the other was
to sink a shaft from the top. In only a few cases did they fail to find a burial. However,
with rudimentary techniques, there were many unfortunate accidents, and at times the
record of these barrow openings is a catalogue of blunders. In a barrow near Marlborough
was a 'black cup curiously ornamented, but an unlucky stroke of the labourers spade
cut it in two'. On finding a beaker in another barrow Cunnington reported: 'it is much
to be regretted that this little vessel of such superior taste . . . should have been beaten

to pieces by the pick-axe, and what occasioned me to greater vexation, I saw the pick-axe go into it before I could cry out to the man to stop'.[5] Anyone can make mistakes, and it should be pointed out that disasters still sometimes happen in excavations, the only difference being that today's archaeologists are far more reluctant to admit their misfortunes in print.

In the vicinity of Stonehenge Cunnington literally struck gold, especially at the barrow cemetery on Normanton Down, a mile south of Stonehenge. Bush barrow, to the south west of Stonehenge, had already been investigated by Stukeley, but without success. Cunnington hit the jackpot. He found a single skeleton accompanied by two bronze daggers, a bronze axe, two decorated lozenges of sheet gold and a gold belt hook. An array of bronze rivets mixed with wood fragments was probably the remains of a shield. The handle of one of the daggers had a chevron pattern made up of thousands of tiny gold pins, 'but unfortunately John [Parker] with his trowel had scattered them in every direction before I had examined them with a glass'.[6]

Round barrows, which contained both inhumations and cremations, concealed the richest grave goods. Long barrows were soon found to be a different species, being more difficult to excavate because it was not obvious where to dig. Cunnington noticed that 'they differ very materially from the circular barrows in their contents; for we have never found any brass weapons or trinkets deposited with the dead . . . with very few exceptions, we have always found skeletons on the floor . . . lying in a confused and irregular manner'.[7] When it came to tackling the barrow cemetery on Winterbourne Stoke Down (fig. 59), west of Stonehenge, the long barrow was left alone, the diggers 'being so well satisfied about this species of *tumuli*'.[8]

When an excavation was completed the bones remained in the barrows when the hole or trench was back-filled, much to the chagrin of later

FIGURE 59. The barrow cemetery at Winterbourne Stoke Down. The long barrow was not considered to be worth excavating.

archaeologists to whom skeletal remains were of vital importance. Sometimes artefacts were discarded if they were considered insignificant, including 'many small rings of bone' unearthed from the Bush barrow. Broken pottery was also cast aside. The more presentable artefacts found their way on to the shelves of Cunnington's moss house. An account of each excavation was posted in a letter to Hoare, who used these as the basis for describing the barrows in *The Ancient History of South Wiltshire*, which was published in two parts, in 1810 and 1812.

Hoare did not attend as many of the excavations as he led his readers to believe – 'circumstances prevented my being present' often meant he was away on his travels. At other times he brought along a party of friends. Cunnington claimed to have been 'gratified with the presence of several learned and well-informed people on the scene of action'. They included the budding barrow diggers Dean Merewether and the

Reverend John Skinner, whose exploits will be described in due course. Possibly Cunnington found these people irksome, but he would have been obliged to take advice from them simply because they were higher up the social ladder. Cunnington was quite capable of writing his own book – he had a firmer grasp of his subject than Hoare and company – but did not have the financial resources to get it published. Instead a portrait and a dedication appeared at the beginning of the first volume of *Ancient Wiltshire*, which is appropriate given that it was largely Cunnington's book. Hoare's great contribution was financial. The book was a lavish production – he spent £1271 merely on the surveys, drawings and engravings for the first volume – and consequently very expensive. For a title of only local interest this was commercial suicide. *Ancient Wiltshire* sold poorly and Hoare was heavily out of pocket.

The half-title page of the book has a decidedly romantic air: it is bordered

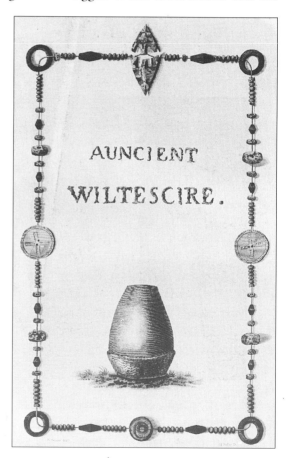

FIGURE 60. The frontispiece of *Ancient Wiltshire* was the only romantic indulgence that Richard Colt Hoare allowed himself.

with prehistoric beads and flints, in the centre of which is the drawing of an urn, plus the title, in archaic lettering, spelled *Auncient Wiltescire* (fig. 60). Thereafter the book is entirely a sober affair. The introduction is sub-headed with the proud boast 'We speak from facts, not theory', which was clearly a swipe at the Stukeleyites, as well as being a declaration of intent. But did this new approach to the study of the past, based on the facts of excavation rather than the theories of literary scholarship, furnish us with a new and revitalised vision of ancient Britain?

No. Hoare had impressed upon Cunnington the 'need to be perfectly unbiased, and to judge only from certain proof', but they had no clear idea of what is was they were trying to prove. This was their undoing. The facts did not explain themselves and so, instead of a historical synthesis based on the finds from the barrows, Hoare embarked on a topographical journey through Wiltshire, stopping at every barrow to itemise its contents. He defended the need to describe the barrows in detail by pointing out that 'they throw a strong light on the customs of our rude ancestors at a period when they lived in savage and pastoral wildness'.[9] He was unable to elucidate the customs, but a grim picture emerged of the ancient Britons progressing gradually 'from the bleak hill to the fertile valley, and from barbarism to civilisation'.[10] It was an unromanticised view of the past, containing passages that John Aubrey could have written: 'our Britons resided upon the hills, sheltered by huts from the inclemency of the weather, and subsisting on the produce of their cattle, and the venison which the woods supplied in abundance'.[11]

Cunnington was an archaeologist in a pre-scientific age, and the finds from his barrows are presented as the curiosities of an antiquary rather than the data for archaeological research (fig. 61). But Cunnington's biggest problem was that he dug too many barrows. The more finds he discovered, the more burials he unearthed, the more confusing the picture became. Some skeletons were extended full length, others lay in a crouched position, while in the long barrows the bones were all mixed up. As for the cremations, some were deposited on the original ground surface, some were contained in urns. Which came first, inhumation or cremation? After all their joint investigations Hoare simply did not know, and concluded that 'burying the body entire, and . . . consuming it by fire, were adopted at one and the same period'. The fact that he was more or less right was due solely to luck.

As for the finds stacked up on Cunnington's shelves they were no easier to differentiate. The Reverend Thomas Leman offered Cunnington the best advice when he wrote to him: 'I think we distinguish three great eras in the arms of offence found in our barrows'. The first was the era of bone and stone 'which may be safely attributed to the Celts'; the second was the era of bronze objects 'probably imported . . . from the more polished nations of Africa'; and the third was the era of iron 'introduced but a little before the invasions of the Romans'.[12] Hoare could write that barrows were the 'sepulchral memorials of the Celts and first Colonists of Britain; and some may be appropriated to the subsequent colony of Belgae who invaded our island'. However, neither of them appreciated that the long barrows, 'so very unproductive in articles of curiosity', were earlier than the round barrows.

Instead of suspecting a chronological sequence, they assumed that different types of barrow reflected the hierarchy of early British society. Hoare divided the barrows into several types, along the lines of Stukeley's system, with Long, Bowl, Bell, Druid, Pond, Twin, Cone and Broad, but when they were considered in relation to the artefacts they contained a pattern refused to emerge (fig. 62). Neither did Cunnington make much progress on this score: the Ancient Britons 'had no regular system in regard to

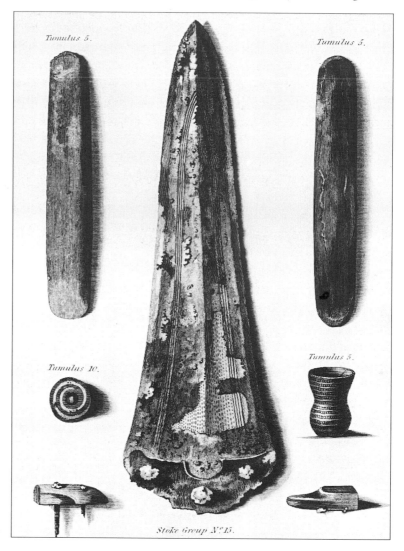

FIGURE 61.
William Cun-
nington amassed a
vast array of arte-
facts from his
barrow openings,
but could not see
that stone was ear-
lier than bronze.

the form of the tumulus, nor many other things practised at the interment of their dead; but appear to have been influenced by caprice than by established rules'.[13] In the end, Hoare had to admit that 'after the result of ten years' experience and constant research, we are obliged to confess our total ignorance as to the authors of these sepulchral memorials'.[14]

Nor did Cunnington's dig at Stonehenge offer any enlightenment (fig. 63). He did, however, establish a chronological sequence, believing that the sarsens were earlier than the smaller bluestones: 'the smaller circle and oval, of inferior stones, were raised at a later period; for they add nothing to the general grandeur of the temple, but rather give a littleness to the whole'.[15] Hoare could do no better than describe the stones through the eye of the traveller. The architecture of Stonehenge meant nothing to him, it was just a picturesque ruin (fig. 64).

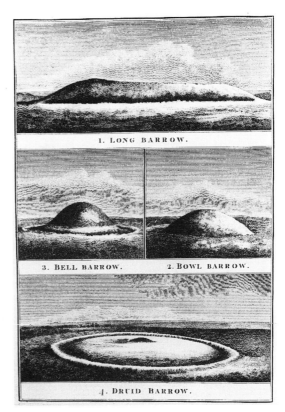

FIGURE 62. Barrow types in Wiltshire, as deduced by Hoare and Cunnington.

For a man who had seen many antique curiosities on his travels, and whose landscaped park was dotted with ornamental temples, Hoare was conditioned to fall back on his aesthetic sensibilities: 'even the most indifferent passenger over the plain must be attracted by the solitary and magnificent appearance of these ruins; and all with one accord will exclaim, "HOW GRAND! HOW WONDERFUL! HOW INCOMPREHENSIBLE!"'.[16] Of all the sentences contained in *Ancient Wiltshire* this was the one he enjoyed writing most. But it does not mean anything.

William Cunnington died in 1810, but Hoare continued work on *Ancient Wiltshire*, completed with *The Ancient History of North Wiltshire* in 1819, and the final part, on the Roman era, published in 1821. He did undertake a few excavations of his own but lacked Cunnington's vigour and, by this time, his optimism. In a barrow on Whitesheet Hill he found a skeleton whose 'mouth was wide open, and it grinn'd horribly a ghastly smile'. Later, General Pitt Rivers quipped that the skull was only laughing at Hoare's primitive excavation technique. In 1812 Hoare and Philip Crocker

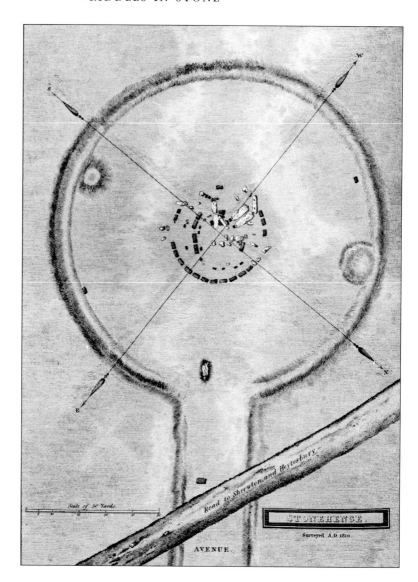

FIGURE 63.
Philip Crocker's
1810 plan of
Stonehenge,
published in
Ancient Wiltshire.

made, to that date, the most accurate survey of Avebury, correcting Stukeley's circular and symmetrical plan (fig. 65). 'I have no doubt but the original British constructors of this work had the circular form in view, though they did not possess the mathematical means of drawing it to a nicety.'[17] A comparison between the plans of Crocker and Stukeley also shows that a number of stones had been destroyed in the intervening period.

Stukeley was still the authority on Avebury and, given that he had nothing original to offer, Hoare deferred to the serpent theory of his predecessor. That Avebury was much older than Stonehenge, and was built by a more primitive people, seemed to be

FIGURE 64.
As an inveterate traveller in Britain and the Continent, Richard Colt Hoare was conditioned to see Stonehenge as a Picturesque ruin.

FIGURE 65.
In 1812 Philip Crocker made a fresh plan of Avebury. This reconstruction of its original appearance was the most accurate to date, even though he neglected to show the causeways across the ditch.

confirmed after digging some of the barrows on Overton Hill near the Sanctuary. 'The result of these underground researches will prove to us the very high antiquity of the tumuli . . . and at the same time the poverty of those Britons over whose ashes these sepulchral mounds were elevated. We find no costly ornaments of jet, amber or gold, but very simple articles of brass, and vessels of the coarsest pottery.'[18] Avebury was erected 'for the joint purposes of religion and legislature'. Stone circles in general were 'national edifices, constructed according to the rude fashion of the times, and at period when the Deity was worshipped in the most simple and primitive manner, under the open canopy of heaven, not in stately covered temples'.[19]

Nothing in this passage, or in *Ancient Wiltshire* generally, advances beyond the researches of Stukeley and Borlase. Cunnington and Hoare's greatest contribution was in methodology: how to obtain facts rather than how to advance theory. On his death Cunnington's collection of artefacts was passed on to Hoare; after gathering dust in the cellars at Stourhead it was passed to the Wiltshire Archaeological and Natural History Society. In 1883 the trustees of the society paid £250 to purchase them outright for their museum in Devizes. The contents of the display cabinets, and their description in Hoare's books, are why these unlikely partners have been called the 'Fathers of Archaeological Excavation in England'.[20] Their precedent was widely followed during the nineteenth century. For a while enquiries into stone circles were of secondary interest. The barrow was the thing.

11

The Barrow Diggers

'The way to open a barrow', said the Reverend Charles Woolls, 'is either to remove the mound of earth entirely, or to make a section through it at least six or eight feet wide from north to south, or from east to west, or sink a shaft down the centre from top to bottom.'[1] Woolls' talent for stating the obvious was matched only by an unfortunate tendency to versify his exploits. In his book *The Barrow Diggers*, published anonymously in 1839, he writes:

> Clasps, Celts and Arrow-heads, I'll try
> To claw within my Clutch,
> And if a Shield I should espy,
> I'll vow there ne'er was such.
>
> With Popist Tricks, and Relics rare,
> The Priests their Flocks do gull,
> In casting out the earth take care,
> Huzza! I've found a skull.

Woolls was not the only barrow-digging clergyman with a penchant for verse. In his *Barrow Digging by a Barrow-Knight* of 1845, written to celebrate the opening of a barrow in Derbyshire by Thomas Bateman, the Reverend Stephen Isaacson describes the delicate unearthing of its contents:

> hither bring my trusty scratcher
> 'Mongst barrow-tools there's none to match her,
> And tread not heavily, because it
> May seriously affect deposit,
> For Briton's skull so long in ground
> Is very seldom perfect found;
> And what we scarcely deem a less ill
> You may destroy a potter's vessel,
> Which formed of potter's clay, though thick,
> Can scarce withstand the blow of pick!

Pity it doesn't scan. In another poem Isaacson also reminds us that a barrow digging in the mid nineteenth century could easily turn into a social occasion, an agreeable alternative to hunting or shooting:

Such dragging of skirts! such giggling of flirts,
As you see in a storm on Hyde Park;
With no end of umbrellas to shelter the Fellows,
Who seemed bent on digging till dark.

The poet continues with the gentlemen 'down on their knuckles' exchanging 'chuckles o'er buckles', our cue to move quickly on. In Orkney, Captain F. W. L. Thomas was referring to the opening of barrows near the Ring of Brodgar when he wrote: 'not infrequently in summer a group of hungry antiquaries may be seen gazing with fixed attention not into the musty recesses of a kistvaen, but the still more interesting interior of a provision-basket'.[2] What more civilised pursuit could there be for a warm summer's day than sunshine, fresh air and a picnic, and the pretence of being on a scientific quest. But things did not always go to plan. During excavation of the Beedon barrow in Berkshire in 1815, 'the work was much impeded . . . by a violent thunder storm, which the country people regarded as in some manner caused by the sacrilegious undertaking to disturb the dead. One of the labourers employed left the work in consequence, and much alarm prevailed.'[3] There were red faces all round when, in digging the tall barrow on Veryan Beacon in Cornwall in 1855, 'a mass of earth . . . unfortunately fell in, completely overwhelming two of the workmen, and partially interring one or two amateur excavators'.[4]

As often as not the amateur excavators went home with a trophy for the mantelpiece. Very rarely was anything unearthed of any intrinsic value, one reason why so many landowners were indifferent to their barrows being plundered, but just occasionally the results surpassed all expectations. Rillaton barrow near the Hurlers on Bodmin Moor looks like any other barrow in the district. When it was opened in 1837 the diggers

FIGURE 66.
A romanticised
reconstruction
of a Beaker burial
from a barrow on
Roundway Down
in Wiltshire.

found more or less what they expected, an inhumation inside a stone cist. Not until they examined the contents of a large earthen pot did they realise they had found something special. Inside the pot was a handled beaker of corrugated sheet gold, the like of which had only been seen, and then very rarely, on Salisbury Plain. Rumour of this stupendous find spread rapidly and, a few years later, when William Copeland Borlase, great-great-grandson of the antiquary the Reverend Dr Borlase, came here hoping to excavate the remaining barrows he found, not

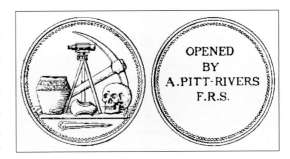

FIGURE 67.
Most of the nineteenth-century barrow diggers left personalised tokens in barrows when they backfilled them, a practice started by William Cunnington. This one belonged to General Pitt Rivers.

surprisingly, that every barrow for miles around had been turned out.

In the second half of the nineteenth century there was a backlash against the wholesale ransacking of barrows. In his *Celtic Tumuli of Dorset* of 1866, Charles Warne accused past diggers of 'desecrating these time-hallowed monuments for no better purpose than the indulgence of craving acquisitiveness and the adornment of glass cases with ill-understood relics, to be paraded with empty admiration of those who may descend to flatter the equally vain and ignorant collector'.[5] That was well said, but in a few year's time the trenching and shafting techniques, as well as the manner of recording, of Warne's own generation would seem equally primitive and irresponsible. During the second half of the nineteenth century the standard of recording excavations greatly improved (fig. 68), but by the 1950s Stuart Piggott was decrying methods that 'fail lamentably to satisfy even the most moderate demands of the modern archaeologist'.[6]

Few people have criticised the barrow diggers' lack of respect for the dead. Hoare and Cunnington reburied the human remains when they restored a barrow, but later diggers had, and still have, no such qualms. The dead have had to suffer a variety of indignities – thrown away as rubbish, paraded in museums, donating carbon for dating, and one day perhaps being DNA tested. The great chambered tombs of prehistory are tombs no longer because the dead have been cleared out of them. Excavation of any sacred ground is by its very nature a desecration, and yet it is difficult to find an archaeologist prepared to admit this. We respect the past on our own terms, exploiting it as we have exploited everything else.

Irrespective of the ethics, excavations undoubtedly yield results, although to call the barrow diggings of the nineteenth century excavations would on the whole be to flatter them. The sad truth is that never in the history of British archaeology was so much

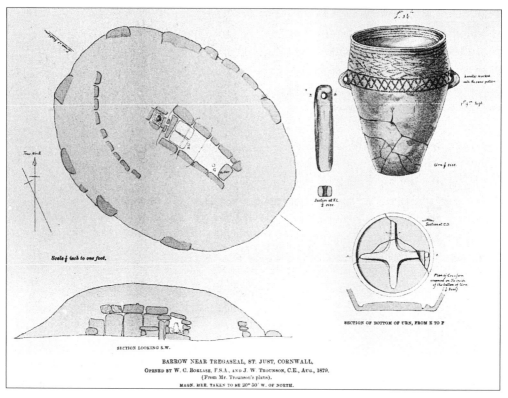

BARROW NEAR TREGESEAL, ST. JUST, CORNWALL,
OPENED BY W. C. BORLASE, F.S.A., AND J. W. TROUNSON, C.E., AUG., 1879.
(From Mr. Trounson's plans).
MAGN. MER. TAKEN TO BE 20° 50' W. OF NORTH.

FIGURE 68. During the second half of the nineteenth century the standard of recording barrow openings improved. William Copeland Borlase opened Tregeseal barrow in 1879.

damage done by so few in so short a space of time. Only a fraction of the material dug up in this period has survived. The casual treatment of even so unique and priceless an artefact as the Rillaton cup shows how relics survived often by pure luck. The contents of the Rillaton barrow were declared treasure trove and were given, as the law required, to the Crown. This fact was quickly forgotten and soon it was widely supposed that the cup had simply been lost. In 1936 one of the other artefacts from the barrow – a bronze dagger – appeared in a list of curios in the royal collection at Osborne. Discreet enquiries about the gold cup were now made, and Queen Mary was approached by the librarian of Windsor Castle. She recalled seeing a similar cup in her husband's dressing-room. As it transpired, there it was: George V was using it to keep his shaving kit in. The cup is now in the British Museum (fig. 69).

Amid the damage and despoilation lies a great contradiction. With Hoare and Cunnington having led the way, antiquaries turned away from book learning and were trying to reconstruct the past using material remains. They were no longer antiquaries but archaeologists. For John Mortimer and company 'the pursuit of archaeology, and the diversion it affords' may have remained 'a delightful relaxation', but these amateur excavators were the direct antecedents of the modern archaeologist.

Thomas Bateman was born in 1821, and at the age of twenty-six inherited his family's vast country estates in Derbyshire. It set him up for a life of leisure, much of which he gave over to his archaeological pursuits, including the accumulation of a considerable library and personal museum. His father had been a sometime excavator of barrows, and Bateman junior developed his interest as a young man – his first book *Vestiges of the Antiquities of Derbyshire* was published in 1848. In all he was responsible for nearly 400 barrow openings in Derbyshire, Staffordshire and the East and North Ridings of Yorkshire. The work in Staffordshire was largely supervised by his lieutenant, Samuel Carrington, and in Yorkshire by James Ruddock. These works were summarised in his later book, *Ten Years Digging in Celtic and Saxon Grave Hills in the Counties of Derbyshire, Staffordshire and Yorkshire from 1848 to 1858*, published in 1861, the year of his death.

FIGURE 69. The gold cup from Rillaton barrow in Cornwall is now in the British Museum. It was originally seized by the Crown as treasure trove. George V at one time used it to keep his shaving equipment in. (*British Museum*)

Wessex remained prime hunting ground for the barrow digger. The Reverend John Skinner of Camerton, a good friend of Hoare, opened barrows in north-east Somerset between 1815 and 1821, including the chambered long barrow at Stoney Littleton. Woolls was busy in Dorset during the 1830s, and was succeeded by Edward Cunnington and Charles Warne. Wiltshire had Dean Merewether of Hereford, who had a go at the West Kennet long barrow, fortunately without doing too much damage, and then in 1849, at the expense of the Royal Archaeological Institute, had a tunnel driven into the centre of Silbury Hill. The results of his investigations, or lack of them in the case of Silbury, were published in 1851 under the misleading title *Diary of a Dean*. Merewether's contribution was followed by the work of John Akerman and the Reverend W. C. Lukis, who was vociferous in criticising Hoare's 'unscientific opening of innumerable barrows'.

Dr John Thurnam is known less for his barrow digging than for his interpretation of their contents. He was born in 1810 into a Quaker family in York, and was for a time medical superintendent of the city's Friends' Retreat. He was educated in London and Aberdeen, and went to Wiltshire in 1849 as medical superintendent at the new county asylum in Devizes. In the *Archaeological Journal* of 1850 he announced that he was studying skull types from British barrows, and he hoped that readers would be able to show him examples that he could measure. A year later the Royal Society awarded him £50 to continue his 'craniometric' researches. In the course of his work he had to excavate barrows already dug by Hoare and Cunnington, who had left the bones behind. He dug some more barrows in Wiltshire and Gloucestershire, publishing the results of his work in the 1869 and 1871 editions of *Archaeologia*. He died from a stroke in 1873.

Cornwall remained stimulating territory for early archaeologists, principal among whom was William Copeland Borlase. Coming from a family with an illustrious antiquarian pedigree, he carried out his first excavation, of a fogou (a subterranean stone-lined chamber), at the age of fifteen, and published his major work on Cornish barrows, *Naenia Cornubiae*, in 1872 at the age of twenty-four. In 1880 he was elected Liberal MP for East Cornwall, but seven years later revelations by his Portuguese ex-mistress left him jobless, bankrupt and shunned by both his family and polite society. Thereafter he led an unsettled life – he worked for a time as the manager of tin mines in Spain and Portugal – but continued with his archaeological pursuits, publishing an account of Irish dolmens in 1897 just two years before his death at the age of fifty-one.

Yorkshire, England's biggest county, suffered more than any other from the depredations of pick and shovel. Bateman, Lukis, the Reverend J. C. Atkinson and others were active in the county, but their efforts were overshadowed by the two giants of Yorkshire barrow digging, Canon William Greenwell and J. R. Mortimer.

William Greenwell was born in 1820 and lived to the grand old age of ninety-eight. He was made a Canon of Durham Cathedral in 1854, becoming Librarian to the Dean and Chapter eight years later, a post he held until he was eighty-seven. His barrow digging ranged over the north of England from Northumberland down to Yorkshire, with the occasional foray into Wiltshire and Gloucestershire. His magnum opus, *British Barrows*, was published in 1877. In all he dug nearly 300 barrows, about the same number as his contemporary and 'rival', John Mortimer. Mortimer was born in Fimber in 1825 and was a corn chandler by trade. His area of interest was the Yorkshire Wolds, and he clashed briefly with Greenwell. The two exchanged words of the 'that scoundrel Mortimer' variety, but were careful to mind their manners in print. Mortimer published his life's work in 1905 under the authoritative title of *Forty Years' Researches in British and Saxon Burial Mounds of East Yorkshire*.

Scotland's cairns came through the nineteenth century relatively unscathed, if only because archaeologically speaking much of Scotland remained *terra incognita*. In 1909 a Mr A. O. Curle, all alone with only a bicycle or a pony for transport, embarked on a trek through Caithness and Sutherland to complete an inventory of known sites,

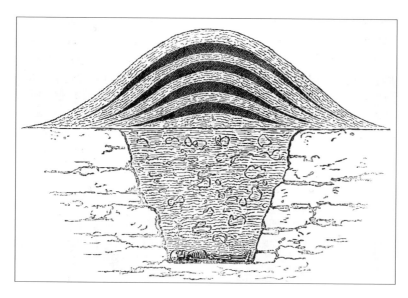

FIGURE 70. John Thurnam's graphical reconstruction of a Bronze Age burial under a round barrow.

a challenge for the dedicated, not the dilettanti. In the 1860s Joseph Anderson, later to be Director of the National Museum of Antiquities in Edinburgh, and R. I. Shearer had dug seven tombs in Caithness, thanks to funds provided by the Anthropological Institute, but early barrow-digging activity in Scotland was concentrated on the more accessible terrain of Orkney. As late as the 1850s the chambered cairns here were still known as Picts' Houses, but twenty years of digging put the record straight. Captain Thomas of the Royal Navy, who was stationed in Orkney while Admiralty charts were being drawn up, soon became intrigued by the islands' impressive monuments. He dug a large tomb on Holm of Papa Westray in 1849, aided by the crew of his ship, the *Woodlark*, and two years later published a résumé of Orcadian monuments, *The Celtic Antiquities of Orkney*. James Farrer, who was MP for Durham, was a prolific digger and was asked by the owner of the land to dig into Maes Howe in 1861. George Petrie, however, is probably the best known of the early Orkney archaeologists. He led a busy life, having to find time for his excavations amid a hectic schedule – he was Sheriff Substitute, Elder of the Free Presbyterian Church, and Factor of a large estate.

The barrow diggers very quickly acquired an enormous amount of data to work on. It had been established in the eighteenth century that barrows belonged to pre-Roman Britain; now it was a case of organising artefacts into a more refined chronological sequence. Hoare and Cunnington had singularly failed to do this, despite some sound advice from the Reverend Thomas Leman of Bath. Bateman meanwhile had detected a Stone Age before the Age of Metal. However, the definitive statement on the chronology of prehistory was made not in Britain but in Denmark. In 1836 Christian Jurgensen Thomsen, Curator of the National Museum of Denmark in Copenhagen, produced a guide book to the museum which was published in Britain in 1848 as *Guide to Northern Antiquities*. It divided artefacts according to three ages: Stone, Bronze and Iron. This is the Three Age System on which prehistoric archaeology has since been based, although as a classification of artefacts it was prefigured in the work of French antiquaries of the eighteenth century such as Montfaucon and Mahudel, in the unpublished 'Metallotheca' by the sixteenth-century Italian antiquary Michele Mercati, who in turn found the same chronology in *De natura rerum*, written in the first century BC by Lucretius. The Three Age System was first applied to Britain in 1851 in Daniel Wilson's *The Archaeology and Prehistoric Annals of Scotland*, where it is 'justly esteemed the foundation of Archaeology as a Science'. A further refinement to it came in 1865 when Sir John Lubbock (later Lord Avebury) published his *Pre-Historic Times*. Here he adopted a division of the Stone Age into two eras, along lines put forward by a number of French archaeologists, and coined the words Palaeolithic and Neolithic.

In 1843 Thomsen's assistant at the National Museum, Jens Jacob Worsaae, published *Danmarks Oldtid*, translated into English in 1849 as *The Primeval Antiquities of Denmark*. This was an application of Thomsen's model to the antiquities in the field, and it showed that Denmark's megalithic remains belonged to both the Stone Age and the Bronze Age. Back in Wessex archaeologists could apply this system to barrows and immediately solve the enigma of the long barrows – they belonged to the Neolithic, or New Stone Age, and were therefore earlier than the Bronze Age round barrows. Because of the prevalence of Neolithic round barrows in Yorkshire, Mortimer was understandably less than impressed with this idea, and there was initially some confusion about the date of the Orkney and Caithness cairns. In the *Archaeological Journal* of 1863 Petrie argued that the 'Picts' Houses' were in fact tombs, although five years later Farrer was claiming that Quoy Ness in Sanday was a broch subsequently converted into a burial place (fig. 71). Joseph Anderson initially thought that the tombs he dug in Caithness were likewise the burial places of the broch builders. By the time he published his *Scotland in Pagan Times* in 1886, however, it was established that the cairns were not from the historic period, but were Neolithic.

After a close examination of the burials from the Peak District Bateman found that the skulls belonging to these two ages showed marked differences, a subject studied in more depth by Dr John Thurnam. Thurnam's examination of skulls from Wiltshire barrows showed again two distinct types. He found that the people buried in the long barrows were short in stature and had long heads, or 'dolicocephalic' skulls, while a small sample of those in the round barrows were of a taller stature and had broad heads, or 'bracycephalic' skulls. This suggested to him that a long-headed race had inhabited Britain during the Neolithic period; and that then a round-headed race had invaded Britain and become the dominant culture, introducing the rite of cremation. Taking Thurnam's lead, Greenwell found much the same thing in his own investigations, and

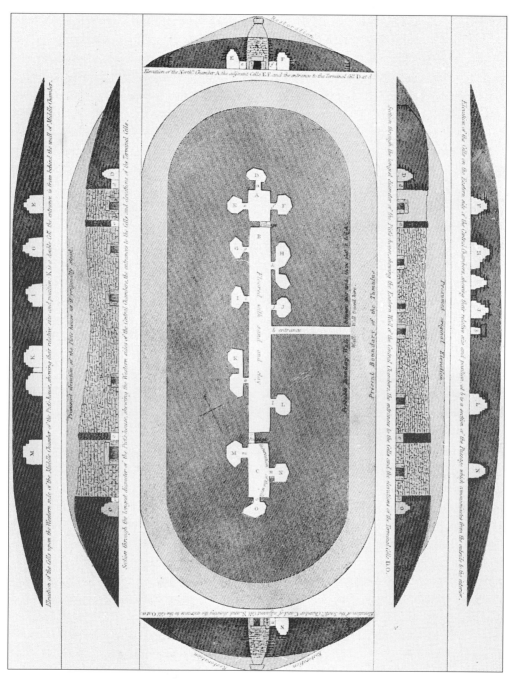

FIGURE 71. Until the latter half of the nineteenth century Orkney's chambered tombs were known as Picts' Houses, and were generally assumed to contain burials from the historic era.

concluded that the two races existed in the Bronze Age in about equal numbers, to judge from the number of each type of skull found in the round barrows.

William Copeland Borlase stood apart from the Three Age consensus because it did not tally with his own findings. As far as he was concerned, Cornwall was not populated 'until the early centuries of the Christian era'. None of the 200 plus barrows he dug contained Roman deposits but, relying on suspect and second-hand accounts of Roman coins being dug out of Cornish barrows, he concluded that the accompanying urns must be of the same date. As if to strengthen this argument, he pointed out that many Cornish barrows contained cremations, and that cremation was a Roman practice.

The dates Borlase gives are, like *Naenia Cornubiae* generally, wild and illogical. Other archaeologists got it right and put the barrows before the Roman invasion, but beyond that their dating was guesswork. Bateman was thinking of 'perhaps tens of centuries before the lust of conquest tempted the Roman legions across the Channel'; Greenwell thought his long barrows Neolithic, while the round barrows belonged to the Bronze Age, which he guessed started about 1000 BC. Thurnam was not so interested in this matter, being much more concerned with the funeral practices of his barrow people, and what level of civilisation they had reached.

A reconstruction of ancient Britain based on the artefacts yielded by excavation inevitably led archaeologists to consider their subject afresh. Druids by now had been relegated to 'the quaint speculations of a few individuals, fresh from the classics of the eighteenth century'. This kind of 'absurd fancy', wrote William Copeland Borlase, would no longer survive 'the withering glance of a nineteenth-century critic'.[7] Where the antiquaries of the eighteenth century had been romantics, the archaeologists of the nineteenth century considered themselves scientists.

Stone and bronze artefacts persuaded them that the people of ancient Britain lived in a primitive society. This view was current as far back as the seventeenth century when the discovery of Stone Age people in America gave it added credibility, and even throughout the Romantic period the idea was never far away. Man was born savage and progressed slowly towards civilisation: that is the theme implicit in Aubrey's 'Monumenta Britannica', and in Hoare's *Ancient Wiltshire*. In 1881 the anthropologist Sir Edward Tylor proposed three stages in the progression of mankind: Savagery, Barbarism and Civilisation, a classification that remained in use until the second half of the twentieth century. Savagery was the primeval state, Barbarism began with the progression to agriculture. Civilisation required the written word, it implied urbanisation, and its ultimate achievement was empire. Given that Britain was the most technologically advanced nation in the world, had the largest cities and ruled over the largest empire the world had ever known, British archaeologists were generally quite comfortable with this idea. In fact it was a general attitude that went beyond the relatively innocuous pursuit of archaeology. A clear parallel was seen between the Roman colonisation of Britain, and consequent civilising of the ancient British, and the European colonisation of Africa, with its mission to civilise the 'savages', the so-called White Man's Burden.

Of other studies of the origins of mankind, Darwin's theory of biological evolution, expressed in *The Origin of Species* in 1859 and *The Descent of Man* in 1871, had only a limited direct influence on archaeology, where cultural evolution was already strongly presumed. A more significant text for archaeologists was Charles Lyell's *The Principles of Geology*, published between 1830 and 1833. With this the biblical chronologists, who still believed the world was created in 4004 BC, were undone. So were the Catastrophists, who believed the human remains buried beneath stalagmites in caves were sinners who perished in the Flood. Lyell declared what many of his fellow geologists had themselves deduced – that the world was many millions of years older than anyone had ever believed.

The earliest inhabitants of Britain were found to be cave-dwelling hunters. The barrow builders lived in a much later and more advanced society, implied partly because a degree of social organisation was necessary to undertake barrow building, but also because the barrows revealed evidence that the builders farmed the land. Canon Greenwell collected up the animal bones found under barrows and used them to postulate the activities of Bronze Age man. On the Yorkshire Wolds he found ox, pig, goat or sheep, the occasional horse, and the domesticated dog. This led him to suppose that animal husbandry was established here by the Bronze Age, but the profusion of arrow heads (which he conceded could also have been fired at people), with remains of red deer, suggested that hunting was still a part of the local economy. Furthermore, they 'cultivated grain, manufactured cloth, and pottery', leading him to conclude that the 'semi-savage state had been well-nigh passed, and that the dawn of an advanced civilisation was approaching'. This was in about 250 BC, according to Greenwell's chronological reckoning.

Animal bones were found in barrows for two possible reasons: they were offerings made to the dead; or they were the remains of funeral feasts. At Wideford Hill in Orkney Petrie discovered animal bones 'in the mouths of the passages leading to the cells, as if the animals had been intended to be offerings made to the *manes* of the departed'.[8] From his study of long barrows Thurnam speculated that oxen had been slaughtered for the funeral feast, and that the unused parts of the body – the head and hooves – had been thrown into barrows as offerings. But scatters of animal bones were less controversial than the jumbles of human bones found in Neolithic barrows and cairns. Thurnam, Greenwell and Mortimer all believed that the long barrow builders must have practised cannibalism. The skeletons in long barrows were invariably found to be 'lying in a promiscuous state', for which several theories were put forward. When the Reverend John Skinner and Sir Richard Colt Hoare opened Stoney Littleton long barrow in 1821 they thought it must have previously been ransacked (fig. 72). The diggers of West Lanyon Quoit in Cornwall came to the same conclusion. After excavating East Tilshead long barrow in Wiltshire, Thurnam saw that the bones had been so closely packed they could not have been placed in the barrow until they had been defleshed. He therefore deferred to Greenwell, who claimed that the disarticulated bones were evidence of 'feasts, at the interment, where slaves, captives, and others were slain and eaten'.[9] Mortimer took the issue further: 'All races of men, in their march towards civilisation, appear to have passed through the stages of cannibalism.' To illustrate the point he added a footnote: 'The Agheri Fakirs of India eat human flesh, and they believe some of this sect have the power to eat human flesh and make it alive again. They make drinking cups of human skulls.'[10] The barrow diggers expected to find evidence of uncivilised practises, and so they duly did. It is also significant to note that in the eighteenth century Henry Wansey and the Reverend Thomas Maurice had found ancient wisdom in India. A hundred years later, with the Indian Mutiny still fresh in mind, there was only Indian savagery.

Cleft skulls had been noted by Cunnington as early as 1801. The act of trepanning, cutting a disc out of the skull, was correctly assumed by Thurnam to have been deliberate, but then he confused it with evidence of ritual killing – 'the skeletons with cleft skulls are those of human victims immolated on the occasion of the burial of a chief'.[11] At the West Kennet long barrow, which he partially excavated in 1860, he found two badly-damaged skulls. One, belonging to a 'youth of about seventeen years of age', was 'extensively fractured at the summit by what appeared to have been the death blow'. The other, belonging to a man 'of about fifty years of age', had a fracture extending 'from one temple to the other, through the forehead into the right cheek'.

This seemed to be evidence of the ritual killing of a chief's subjects and was likened to the contemporary Hindu practice of suttee. Greenwell was in no doubt that 'it was

FIGURE 72. Stoney Littleton chambered tomb, near Bath, was restored by the Somerset Arch-aeological and Natural History Society in the 1850s. It had been opened in 1821 by John Skinner, who thought it must previously have been ransacked, since none of the bones formed a complete skeleton.

the habit to slay at the funeral and to bury with the dead man, wives, children, and others, probably slaves'.[12] He referred his readers to a passage in Herodotus which describes the death of a Scythian king: 'The corpse is laid out in the tomb . . . with spears fixed in the ground on either side to support a roof of withies laid on wooden poles, while in other parts of the great square pit various members of the king's household are buried beside him: one of his concubines, his butler, his cook, his groom, his steward, and his chamberlain — all of them strangled.' Greenwell also described the burial of a Fijian chief, where the dead man's mother, wife and servant were all ritually killed. Here he was using literary sources in a different way to Stukeley and the Romantics. The British barrow builders were presumed to be at the same stage of civilisation as the Scythians and Fijians, so it was argued that their funeral practices would be similar. He therefore quoted Herodotus not to prove the ethnic origins of the British but to show an ethnic parallel.

Virgil's *Aeneid* was also useful in this respect. When Aeneas visited the barrow under which his father was buried he performed the following rite: 'In formal libation he poured on the earth two bowls of unwatered wine, two of fresh milk, and two of hallowed blood. Then he scattered some bright flowers.' (book v, lines 77–78) This helped Thurnam in his effort to imagine the funeral rites performed by the British, but a more difficult question to answer was whether they believed in an afterlife. Julius Caesar was adamant that the later Celts did. Thurnam described the chambered long barrow at Belas Knap in Gloucestershire as a place where 'the *manes* of the dead may have been worshipped . . . and necromancy practised', but it was the round barrows that contained grave goods, although for what reason was debatable. Perhaps a 'super-stitious dread' of retaining the belongings of a dead man caused them to be buried with the body. Native Greenlanders were supposed to practise this. In the opinion of Borlase they were 'merely votive offerings of affection', but the most popular theory was a belief in some future state — 'almost every modern savage grave gives the like evidence of the custom'.[13] A large proportion of the round barrows contained inhumations in a crouched position. This was thought by Greenwell to represent a sleeping posture, because 'most savages sleep after that fashion' in the open air. In 1860 a Monsieur Troyon likened the crouched posture to the foetal position and wondered whether after death the body reentered the bosom of the Universal Mother.

If the bodies were being laid to rest in preparation for the next world, why were there apparently contradictory practices? For one thing, cremation looked pretty final, and a high proportion of the inhumed dead were being sent to the next world with no belongings at all. Less than half of the burials were accompanied by grave goods, and even then the quality and quantity varied greatly. William Copeland Borlase found Cornish grave goods uninteresting and thought they had little significance, but this could hardly be said of many Salisbury Plain barrows. Apart from containers like cinerary urns, beakers and incense cups (it was supposed that incense was burned during cremation to alleviate the stench of burning flesh), Thurnam listed an impressive range of grave goods found in Wiltshire: stone and bronze axes, daggers, hammers, knives and scrapers, whetstones and amulets; ornaments made of bone, ivory, glass, amber, jet, gold and bronze, used to craft beads, buttons, pins, armlets, hooks and belt buckles. Thurnam thought that some of the more impressive had been specially made for the occasion, and that while most of the interments accompanied by ornaments were of women, the richest graves were obviously of men: 'Such is everywhere common in the lower stages of civilisation',[14] wrote Thurnam, subject of an Empire whose figurehead was a Queen.

The barrow-digging era was brought to a close by a military man, General Pitt Rivers. He was born Augustus Lane-Fox in 1827 and, after Sandhurst, was in the Army for over thirty years, which included service in the Crimea (fig. 73). His lifelong passion for collecting began with old firearms, which he learned to arrange in typological sequences in order to demonstrate their technological development. By the late 1870s

he was also collecting prehistoric flints. When his vast private collections outgrew the confines of his own home they were exhibited in Bethnal Green and South Kensington before, in 1885, being given to the University Museum in Oxford, which had to build a special annexe to house them, now known as the Pitt Rivers Museum.

In accordance with the will of his great uncle George Pitt, the second Baron Rivers, General Lane-Fox inherited the family's Rushmore Estate in 1880, assuming the name Pitt Rivers by royal licence. Two years later he retired from the Army and became the first Inspector of Ancient Monuments in Great Britain, with the job of persuading landowners to allow ancient monuments on their land to be given statutory protection. Pitt Rivers was a wealthy, energetic and resourceful man with an appetite for new challenges, and he had soon embarked

FIGURE 73. General A. L. F. Pitt Rivers (1827–1900) took archaeology into the twentieth century with his disciplined methods of excavation. (*Pitt Rivers Museum*)

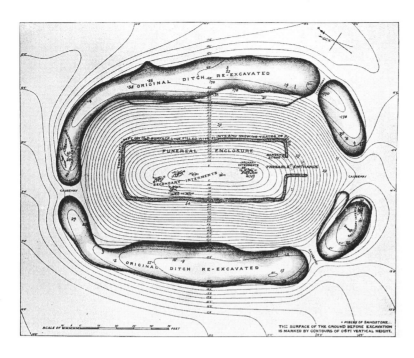

FIGURE 74.
Pitt Rivers'
exemplary plan of
Wor Barrow on
Cranborne Chase,
excavated in 1893.

on a series of excavations on own his land at Cranborne Chase, on the Wiltshire–Dorset border.

A Pitt Rivers excavation was undertaken with strict military discipline and thoroughness, applying all the experience he had gained from organising his private collections. A comprehensive written account was accompanied by photographs and detailed scale drawings (fig. 74). The exact location of every artefact was recorded, and he argued the case for preserving all the artefacts uncovered, not just the ones that would look good in a display cabinet. He once described Thurnam's discovery of two different skull types in prehistoric Britain as 'one of the most important discoveries of our time', and the dimensions of all the skulls he discovered in his excavations were measured for this purpose. The results were published in tabulated form which allowed his readers to evaluate and interpret the evidence for themselves, an opportunity not granted by the earlier barrow diggers. The results of his excavations appeared in the four volumes of *Excavations in Cranborne Chase*, privately published between 1887 and 1898. The books were way ahead of their time and prefigure twentieth-century methods and standards.

However, we still have some ground to cover in the nineteenth. The middle of the century saw the study of stone circles in the doldrums but, with the slow accumulation of knowledge by the barrow diggers, there were suddenly possibilities for a whole new range of interpretations.

12

Stone Circles and Stone Age Man

In the *Proceedings of the Society of Antiquaries of Scotland* for 1857 there is an article by Henry Callender entitled 'Notice of the Stone Circle at Callernish, in the Island of Lewis'. Despite being one of Scotland's best known stone circles (fig. 75), the author told his readers that 'owing to its remote, and comparatively inaccessible situation, it has not been particularly examined, or very accurately described'.[1] Callender could have been speaking for the whole of Scotland when he said this. Of over 650 stone circles in Britain nearly 400 are north of the Border, but by the 1850s only a handful of them had been discovered and described.

In the latter half of the nineteenth century there was a sustained effort to map, catalogue and classify the stone circles of Scotland, just when they were in most danger of disappearing. Until the end of the eighteenth century much of Scotland had an essentially peasant economy. Arable land remained open and was divided into strips or 'rigs', with the soil still being turned over by wooden ploughs. Cattle and sheep grazed on lands which were largely held in common. The first Improvers to adopt English methods of agriculture were dilettanti following a fashion rather than financial gain — one did the Grand Tour, one improved one's land. Fields were enclosed, wastes were reclaimed, the old hamlets, or 'farmtouns', were broken up, and new steadings were built. Then a new breed of landowner emerged, parvenus who had made fortunes in trade at home or abroad, or from lucrative government contracts during the wars with France. To recoup some of his capital investment he raised the rents, forcing the tenants into improving their land or giving up farming altogether.

The Agrarian Revolution prefigured the Industrial Revolution, which provided a market for the increased yields, and by the 1830s Scotland had transformed itself from the most backward agricultural country in Europe to the most advanced. The new capitalist farmers were businessmen with a businesslike approach to the landscape. In 1885 James Peter reflected ruefully on the consequences for prehistoric monuments of this new commercial attitude:

> So long as agriculture was in its infancy, and where there was little disposition to cultivate any land but that which was of fair quality or free from obstacles . . . they had an impunity from the hand of the destroyer; but when land increased in value, through improved methods of agriculture, and the introduction of extraneous manures, old boundaries and the most sacred enclosures were ruthlessly swept away.[2]

Perhaps the most infamous of Scotland's 'Improvers' was Captain Mackay, who broke up the Stone of Odin and some of the Stones of Stenness in 1814, to the universal outrage of native Orcadians. One of the reasons no court proceedings were issued against him was that, in the words of the Sheriff Substitute, 'it may lead the vulgar to confound every improving farmer with the idea of a desolator'.[3]

Superstition had been part of the old way of life but, as the evidence of wholly or partially destroyed stone circles demonstrated, there was nothing to be feared from breaking up stones. In 1779 James Anderson had given an account of the Hill of Fiddes stone circle in Aberdeenshire to the Society of Antiquaries of London, but a hundred years later the field archaeologist Fred Coles could only report that it was now 'a poor remnant' of 'a once noble specimen' (fig. 76). James Peter cited the final indignity of the Gaval circle in Old Deer, where the large recumbent stone was 'shattered by

FIGURE 75. Callanish, on the island of Lewis, has attracted antiquarian interest since the early eighteenth century. The true scale of the monument was only revealed in the 1850s when a thick layer of peat was removed from the site, exposing the full height of the stones and a cist in the centre. (*Historic Scotland*)

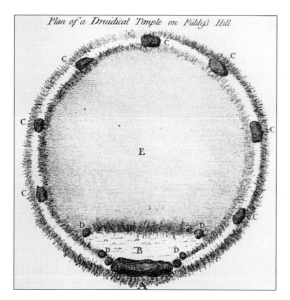

Plan of a Druidical Temple on Fiddes Hill

FIGURE 76. The Hill of Fiddes stone circle, as published by James Anderson in 1779. A hundred years later it was 'a poor remnant' of 'a once noble specimen'.

thoughtless young apprentice masons working in the neighbourhood'.[4] The last remaining upright stone was subsequently used as a rubbing post for cattle.

A survey of Scottish stone circles was organised by the Society of Antiquaries of Scotland, who appointed Fred Coles, assistant keeper of the society's museum in Edinburgh, to take charge. He began his excursions into the Scottish countryside in the early 1890s and continued working on the project for twenty years, although even by this time he had covered none of the islands. He was aided in his search by the 6 inch and 25 inch maps produced by the Ordnance Survey which were the first to record the existence of many of these sites. They were marked as 'Druidical Circle', or 'Circle of Stones', or just 'Stones', and Coles and his team had to cover many miles of countryside to find and verify them. Others were not marked on the maps and were only discovered after questioning the locals.

This programme of surveying and recording was repeated across the rest of Britain on a more informal basis by a few indefatigable investigators. The results appeared in the national archaeological journals, the county archaeological journals, most of which were first published in the latter half of the nineteenth century, and in the early volumes of the *Victoria County History*, the first of which were published in the first decade of the twentieth century. The Reverend W. C. Lukis headed off into the wilds of Cornwall and Wales, but success was patchy. With William Copeland Borlase he found a number of circles on Bodmin Moor, which was surprising given that Cornish antiquities were supposed to have been thoroughly examined already. His travels in Wales were less productive and he returned home disappointed: 'It is a deplorable fact that since the Ordnance Survey was issued in 1843, many of these ancient buildings have disappeared', resulting in 'several long, fatiguing and fruitless journeys along very rugged and mountainous roads'.[5]

The terrain of Dartmoor was hardly any less strenuous, but it offered rich pickings to anyone prepared to do the legwork. Richard Nicholls Worth, a journalist by trade, and his son Richard Hansford Worth, a civil engineer by profession but now best known for his writings on Dartmoor, were joined by Robert Burnard in making a comprehensive survey of Dartmoor monuments, particularly the stone rows, over a long period from the end of the 1880s. In 1894 they formed the nucleus of the Dartmoor Exploration Committee of the Devon Association for the Advancement of Science. Burnard, with the assistance of the Reverend Sabine Baring-Gould, was active in reerecting fallen stones. Worth senior published his first article on stone rows in 1892, while Worth junior published his last in 1947, by which time sixty-two rows had been discovered.

Along with the survey and description of these newly-discovered sites, the resurvey of well-known ones corrected many of the inaccuracies of earlier writers. C. W. Dymond complained that 'it is remarkable how often incorrect drawings have stirred the embers of strife, and bewildered the patient student by their fabulous data'.[6] As an example, he cited John Aubrey's account of Long Meg and her Daughters. Aubrey was given the description by a friend at Oxford who told him that Long Meg was accompanied by 'a Circle of Stones about two hundred in number', and 'the Diameter of this Circle is about the diameter of the Thames from the Herald's Office'.[7] You can see what Dymond was complaining about.

The discovery of so many new circles and rows stimulated new ideas about their purpose. Ideas about cultural evolution had shifted the emphasis away from Romantic notions of the Druids to the more prosaic Stone and Bronze Age man. It was generally agreed that the stones and barrows were of a much earlier date than the Druids described by Caesar, but in any case theories about the Druids were becoming too restrictive. As early as 1821 Samuel Seyer, after describing Stanton Drew in his *Memoirs Historical and Topographical of Bristol*, was musing that stone circles 'were not raised without a prodigious expence of labor, perhaps the personal exertions of the whole tribe; and, therefore, it must have been for some purpose interesting to the whole nation' rather than the preserve of an hermetic priesthood.[8]

Far from shedding light on the mystery of the circles, the vast accumulation of new data only complicated the issue. In Scotland, for example, not only are there circles large and small, many of them with cairns in the centre, some with central stones, avenues, or encircled by a bank and ditch (the circle henges), there are also some special types. On the south side of the Moray Firth near Inverness and Nairn are the Clava cairns which are chambered cairns surrounded by a ring of stones. About eighty miles east of there, in the foothills of the Grampians in Aberdeenshire, are circles with a large recumbent stone on the south side. Moving south to Perthshire there is a concentration of sites with four stones arranged in rectangles, known as Four Posters. On islands such as Arran or Lewis the visitor might see another type, the concentric circles (familiar from Avebury), circles with a double ring of stones. In addition a sizeable minority, about a fifth, of the circles of north-east Scotland have at least one stone decorated with cup marks.

The problems of interpreting this bewildering array of variations and inconsistencies was summed up in Daniel Wilson's *The Archaeology and Prehistoric Annals of Scotland* (1851), where he admits that the 'uniformity of the Scottish monolithic groups is not sufficiently marked to prove a common origin for all; the differences are so striking, that we look in vain for evidence of uniformity of faith or object in their builders'. The best that could be said was that 'instead of being the temples of a common faith, they are more probably the ruins of a variety of edifices designed for diverse purposes – perhaps for the rites of rival creeds'. He concluded by suggesting that the circles were erected as 'courts of law and battle rings, wherein the duel or judicial combat was fought, though this, doubtless, had its origin in the invariable union of the priestly and judicial offices in a primitive state of society'.[9]

Some sites could only be interpreted by a fresh analysis of the surface remains. Writing in the *Transactions of the Plymouth Institute* in 1830, the Reverend Samuel Rowe thought that the stone rows of Dartmoor were 'constructed for gymnastic performances in connection with the celebration of religious worship', because the rows he had discovered, like the two at Merrivale, were double lines of stones. The Worths rejected this because they had found single, double or, occasionally, treble lines of stones. The longest, on Stall Moor, is just over two miles long, crosses the River Erme, and has a barrow at each end. At Drizzlecombe the Worths found three stone rows, between 100 and 200 yards long, each with a barrow at one end and a standing stone at the other. Of the two rows at Merrivale, one has a barrow midway along its length. This clear association with barrows led Worth senior to suppose that the rows were sepulchral: 'the length of the rows and the number of stones indicate with more or less precision the number of what I may call active mourners'.[10]

FIGURE 77. A large proportion of Scottish megalithic sites are adorned with cup marks, but the early archaeologists failed to make any headway with these numinous decorations.

If stone rows were an enigma, then cup marks, found primarily on Scottish stone circles and cairns, were a riddle within an enigma (fig. 77). Dr Stuart's *Sculptured Stones of Scotland* had described some of them, while there were comprehensive surveys made in the Inverness district by William Jolly, a schools inspector, and in Aberdeenshire and Banffshire by James Ritchie, a schoolmaster and keen photographer. These studies, published in 1882 and 1918 respectively, provided detailed catalogues, but could not advance beyond Professor James Simpson's *On Ancient Sculpturings of Cups and Concentric Rings,* published by the Society of Antiquaries of Scotland in 1867. Simpson recounted previous theories, that the cup marks were crude representations of the sun and the stars, symbolic enumerations of families or tribes, archaic writing, or even 'objects for the practice of magic and necromancy', but his own position was a negative one. He pointed out that, whatever their meaning, cup marks are too impenetrable for any theory to be either proved or disproved. The best that his 140 page monograph can offer is that 'whatever else was their object . . . they were emblems or symbols connected in some way with the religious thoughts and doctrines of those who carved them'.[11]

The use of folklore in interpreting standing remains became unfashionable once progress steamrollered its way through the countryside, labelling the old tales and traditions the culture of credulous country bumpkins. Therefore the old theories about places like Men-an-tol in Cornwall needed updating. When the British Archaeological Association held their conference in Cornwall in 1877, C. W. Dymond wrote a short note on Men-an-tol as a guide to visitors. You can sense his blushes as he goes trespassing on forbidden territory: 'Is it possible that some of the ceremonies may have been phallic?'[12]

In the first volume of the *Victoria County History of Cornwall,* published in 1906, G. F. Tregelles took up the theme again. 'The Phallic cult is an obscure subject', he wrote, but 'in other parts of the world menhirs, single or grouped, are often associated with Phallism'. Even so, Tregelles was not quite prepared to admit that they did it in Cornwall: 'it is not unreasonable to suggest that the Cornish stone circles may in part have owed their origin to some far away echo of this ancient worship'.[13] This is a rather vague use of the ethnic parallel, but in 1891 A. J. Evans, Keeper of the Ashmolean Museum in Oxford, chose a much more precise example to explain the Rollright Stones. In India 'some of the barbarous hill tribes' were still erecting stone circles 'in memory of departed spirits'. They were specifically connected with the cycle of fertility and death: 'there was one interesting case in which the stones were said to be erected to an old woman who had recently died, and whose spirit was supposed to be the cause of a large harvest which came after her death'.[14]

Dymond's surveys of the Cumbrian stone circles led him to the conclusion that, despite superficial differences, all circles were the product of the same religious thoughts and doctrines. Furthermore, where Swinside, Long Meg and Castlerigg, all in Cumbria, had distinct entrances, and Stanton Drew and Callanish had avenues, 'the inference is irresistible . . . that processional services were a common feature of their use. Whether these were connected with religious, political, judicial, or sepulchral objects, or with

all of them, we know far too little of the customs of our remote ancestors to decide.'
In the end Dymond opted for 'temples, primarily; courts of judicature, secondarily;
sometimes memorial buildings, thirdly'.[15] This conclusion was a product of his own
method of study – the field survey. If he had used different techniques he would have
reached different conclusions.

When Henry Callender described Callanish in 1857 he was in no doubt that it was
an astronomical temple, with its radiating lines of stones marking the four cardinal
points of the compass. But in 1860 another article in the *Proceedings of the Society of
Antiquaries of Scotland*, this time by Cosmo Innes, described the removal of a thick layer
of peat moss from the site which exposed a cairn at the centre of the circle. Further
investigation revealed that the cairn contained human bones, giving the impression that
Callanish was a giant sepulchre. Theories of astronomical temples and evidence of
sepulchral rites came to dominate ideas about stone circles at the end of the nineteenth
century. Although the two seemed to be mutually exclusive, they managed to thrive
side by side until the more elaborate theories of Sir Norman Lockyer in the early 1900s
stretched the credulity of archaeologists too far.

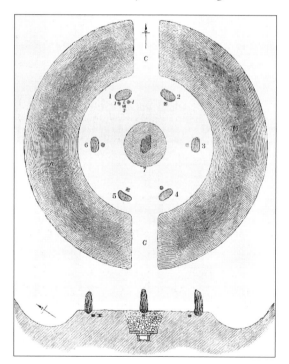

FIGURE 78. Broomend o' Crichie was excavated
in 1855. In typical barrow-digging style, the
excavators went straight to the centre of the
circle in a successful attempt to find a burial.

The archaeologist's principal tools
were the trowel and the shovel, and
excavation (at least in Scotland) revealed plenty of evidence that stone circles
had been used for burial. Broomend o'
Crichie is a much despoiled circle in
Aberdeenshire enclosed within a
henge. It was excavated in 1855, when
the work focused on the centre of the
circle beneath a missing central stone
(fig. 78). Charles Dalrymple reported
some thirty years later that well below
the surface they found 'a cist containing
the remains of a human skeleton; of
which the skull and leg bones were
tolerably entire, and along with which,
about the centre of the cist, lay a quantity of incinerated human bones'.[16]
Similar finds were made by James
Bryce when he excavated several sites
on Machrie Moor, on the west side of
Arran, including five stone circles, in
1861. He conceded that circles may

have been used as courts and temples, 'but they seem evidently to have been designed in the first instance . . . as sepulchral monuments, marking off the sacred precincts where lay the ashes or the bones of the dead. Any other supposition seems unwarranted by the facts'.[17]

In his *Scotland in Pagan Times* of 1886 Joseph Anderson treated the sepulchral interpretation as self-evident, but it was difficult to write with the same level of certainty about the English and Welsh circles. If an excavation yielded a burial, it indicated that the stone circle was a sepulchral monument. If no burial was found, the insignificant artefacts recovered seemed beyond meaningful interpretation, so the archaeologists had to look elsewhere for a sepulchral connection. In 1877 W. C. Lukis argued that because stone circles 'frequently occur in localities which abound in graves, and are often intimately associated with graves, the presumption is that they were sacred enclosures, in some way connected with the burial of the dead'.[18] Not everybody agreed, especially astronomers like A. L. Lewis, who habitually pointed out that churches are surrounded by graveyards but are not sepulchral monuments.

Some of the early archaeologists would have talked more sense if they *had* indulged in excavation. James Fergusson, described by one modern archaeologist as 'that unamiable eccentric',[19] wrote a book called *Rude Stone Monuments in All Countries*, published in 1872, which was much discussed but not highly regarded. He claimed that stone circles were not even prehistoric: they were built by the pagan Britons in between the departure of the Romans and the arrival of the Saxons. As proof he cited Silbury Hill, which according to his reckoning was built on a Roman road. Meanwhile at Avebury, 'if I am not much mistaken, two of Arthur's generals of division lie buried, one in each of the stone circles inside the inclosure'.[20] Another latter-day advocate of the post-Roman theory was A. H. Allcroft, whose *The Circle and the Cross* of 1927 tried to show that stone circles were moot places of the Celts and Saxons.

Before he made his name as an Egyptologist, Sir Flinders Petrie made a thorough and accurate survey of Stonehenge in the summer of 1877. He assumed that the builders had used a standard unit of length and, as usual in such cases, he discovered what is was: the Roman foot of 11.68 inches. This posed a contradiction. On the one hand, the archaeology said Stonehenge was prehistoric; on the other, the metrology said it was post-Roman. In the end Petrie plumped for the latter and believed, with Geoffrey of Monmouth, that Stonehenge was the burial ground of British kings. Nevertheless, his escape clause was that the only way 'to settle this much-disputed subject, is careful digging'.[21]

The real issue, as far as dating was concerned, was to place the stone circles in the Three Age System, or more specifically within the Neolithic or Bronze Age, and this was one question that excavation could answer. In 1899 the British Association for the Advancement of Science formed a committee to study 'The Age of Stone Circles', and

in 1901 appointed Harold St George Gray to direct their excavations. Gray was one
of Britain's first professional field archaeologists. He was born in Lichfield in 1872, and
in 1888 became assistant to General Pitt Rivers, with whom he stayed for over ten
years. In 1901 he was also appointed Secretary of the Somerset Archaeological and
Natural History Society, remaining curator of their museum (now the County Museum)
in Taunton until 1949.

The first stone circle he dug was Arbor Low in Derbyshire (fig. 79). The site is an
unusual one because it is contained within a steeply banked henge, and all but one of
the stones are lying prostrate. A Bronze Age round barrow was added to the bank
which attracted the attention of the barrow diggers and made the stone circle an object
of considerable speculation. Early writers disagreed about whether the stones were
originally upright. In *A View of the Present State of Derbyshire* (1803), Mr J. Pilkington
thought the stones were laid flat because they were 'seats or supports for those who

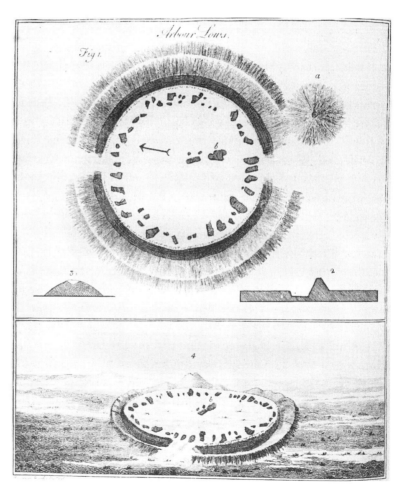

FIGURE 79.
Hayman Rooke's
survey of Arbor
Low in Derby-
shire, published in
1798, was one of
the earliest records
of the monument.

attended the celebration of the rites of worship'. The barrow was a repository for the bones of the victims sacrificed in the ceremonies. Writing in 1900, just before Gray's excavation, T. N. Brushfield suggested that the stones were originally upright, which Gray's evidence would discount. He also suggested that Arbor Low was Neolithic and was the burial place of a 'leader of men': the burial took place in the centre of the ring, above which the cove was constructed, then came the outer ring of stones and the bank and ditch. Two entrances allowed ceremonial access to the sacred enclosure where religious rites took place.

Gray was able to confirm or deny only some of this. The dig, organised by the Anthropological Section of the British Association, produced few finds, and even these were not very interesting. The highlight was a human skeleton found near the centre of the enclosure; the skull (Gray had become well versed in skull types during his association with Pitt Rivers) was midway between the long- and round-headed types. If this suggested a date at the end of the Neolithic and the beginning of the Bronze Age, it was only confirmed by the other artefacts recovered.

In 1905 Gray was in Cornwall making a survey of the Bodmin Moor circles. He dug at the Stripple Stones, Cornwall's only circle henge, but the results were disappointing. There was no burial, and the paucity of finds was not enough to date the site to the late Neolithic with any confidence. Meanwhile, at the Fernacre and Stannon circles, he noted the absence of barrows in the vicinity, but instead found 'dozens of hut circles' which he assumed, correctly, to be contemporary.

Gray's biggest project was excavation at Avebury, which had already attracted interest from eager archaeologists, notably the Reverend A. C. Smith and Edward Cunnington in 1865. The objective of their dig was to locate the former position of missing stones and to test the theory of James Fergusson that Avebury was a vast burial ground. In the *Athenaeum* in 1865, Fergusson absurdly suggested that the bank at Avebury was 'nothing but a long barrow of circular shape', and that the graves of Arthurian warriors would be found 'wherever they are looked for'. In the event Smith and Cunnington found 'a good deal of British pottery, and many animal bones . . . but *no human bones whatever*'.[22] Fergusson was unperturbed by the news, and continued to defend his theory regardless.

Gray worked at Avebury in 1908, 1909, 1911 and 1914, and then after the war returned for another short season in 1922. Avebury could therefore claim to have been the most scientifically investigated stone circle to date. What did these excavations achieve? Gray's sections through the bank and ditch showed how much silting there had been, and revealed the original profile of the ditch (fig. 80). In later years this kind of information was invaluable for calculating how many man hours were needed to raise the earthwork, which in turn had implications for deducing the kind of society that produced it. Also, by the time the excavations were summarised in *Archaeologia* in

FIGURE 80.
Harold St George
Gray's excavation
through the ditch
at Avebury.
(*Alexander Keiller
Museum, Avebury*)

1935, Gray was able to call upon the assistance of two rising stars of prehistoric studies, Stuart Piggott and Grahame Clark, to aid him in dating Avebury to the end of the Neolithic. As to the meaning of Avebury, Gray wrote that the bank and ditch 'were apparently designed to enclose a sacred area. The ditch being on the inner side could not have been intended for defensive purposes . . . Presumably the vallum served as elevated ground from which spectators could watch ceremonies in progress within the circles, without being allowed to go closer.'[23] This is more or less what William Stukeley had said, without the benefit of five years of excavation.

Gray's excavations answered the question of date but had not been particularly

FIGURE 81.
Professor William
Gowland, in the
centre of the
picture, supervises
excavations at
Stonehenge in
1901.

successful in explaining the purpose of stone circles. The same could be said of the excavations at Stonehenge in 1901, directed by Professor William Gowland of the Royal School of Mines in London (fig. 81). On the last day of the nineteenth century two stones fell in a storm, and a committee drawn from interested parties – the Society of Antiquaries, the Society for the Protection of Ancient Buildings and the Wiltshire Archaeological and Natural History Society – was formed to advise on conservation at what was now universally regarded as a national monument. One of their recommendations, immediately adopted, was the erection of a wire fence around Stonehenge. In the event the fallen stones were not reerected, but a leaning stone was pulled upright and set in concrete, which allowed a limited amount of excavation to take place before the workmen moved in.

Gowland unearthed a variety of artefacts, but 'no object of bronze, iron, or other metal occurred in the excavations except in the superficial layers'. Much of this material seemed to be the refuse of the builders: the 'employment of deer's horn picks for the extensive excavations made in the chalk around the base of the monoliths . . . tends to support the view that bronze implements cannot have been in common use'.[24] Gowland did not realise that the bluestones belonged to an earlier phase of Stonehenge, and that they had been removed before the sarsen circle and horseshoe were erected, then placed in a new setting when it was complete. He therefore decided that 'the monument as a whole is of one date. Its parts do not belong to different ages'.[25] This date seemed to be the overlap between the end of the Neolithic and the beginning of the Bronze Age, which he guessed must have been about 1800 BC.

In 1901 Sir Norman Lockyer had tried to date Stonehenge by astronomical means, his final date of 1680 BC being close enough to Gowland's for both men to feel satisfied.

Gowland was himself interested in astronomical theories and the orientation to the summer solstice was the basis of his ideas about Stonehenge. He seemed confident that Stonehenge 'was not a sepulchre', although had he dug at the centre of the monument the evidence might have been more forthcoming. Similarly, he overlooked the presence of Stonehenge amid Britain's biggest barrow cemetery because his attention was fixed on the Avenue. For Stonehenge 'was a place of sanctity dedicated to the observation or adoration of the sun'.[26] The evidence of his excavation had not told him any of this. Instead he chose to illustrate an ethnic parallel with Shinto sun worship in Japan, where he found the same combination of solstice ceremonies in a temple with trilithons. Again, when he came to consider how such vast stones were transported across Salisbury Plain he went back to Japan, describing the building of Osaka Castle in the seventeenth century, where two huge blocks of stone, apparently weighing 160 tons each, were transported on a wooden frame with 'rude solid wheels of wood'.

Sun worship in both Japan and Britain did not to Gowland signify a common racial origin: 'it by no means follows that the practice or the forms were copied by one race from another, but rather that they were the outcome of a similar development of the human mind and had an independent origin in many and remotely separated regions'.[27] Daniel Wilson came to much the same conclusion about the Scottish circles, seeing them as comparable to Asian megaliths in the sense that they represented 'a remarkable phase of the human mind' long since passed.

Lewis Morgan, an American anthropologist, developed this concept and argued that mankind had evolved 'from savagery to civilisation through the slow accumulation of experimental knowledge'. This was the theory of the 'psychic unity of man', meaning that all savages will eventually attain civilisation by their own efforts. Daniel Wilson, after emigrating to Canada, argued the same thing in 1862 in his *Prehistoric Man: Researches into the Origins of Civilisation in the Old and New Worlds*. But there was a rival theory. The revered Swedish archaeologist Oscar Montelius wrote in *Der Orient und Europa* in 1899 that 'our continent was for a long time only a pale reflection of Near Eastern Culture'. European history is full of invasions, and the written word did not come to Britain by independent development – it was introduced by the invading Romans. The possibility that in prehistory technological developments had an external source was also suggested by the archaeology: long-headed Iberians of the Stone Age and the arrival of broad-headed Celts at the beginning of the Bronze Age. This dichotomy between separate development and external influence was to be the single most important issue for the next generation of archaeologists.

13

Diffusionism

From the beginning, British antiquaries knew that megaliths were not a uniquely British phenomenon. As early as 1663 Dr Walter Charleton was claiming that Stonehenge was a Danish monument, an idea gleaned from his correspondence with the Danish antiquary Olaus Worm, whose *Danicum monumentorum* of 1643 illustrated a number of Danish megaliths. At the end of the seventeenth century Edward Lhwyd was in Ireland where he found the great chambered cairn of Newgrange in the Boyne Valley; and in the 1720s, just after Stukeley had finished his field studies at Avebury and Stonehenge, de Robien was describing the megaliths at Carnac and Locmariaquer in Brittany. By the early twentieth century the map of megalithic Europe had expanded considerably, taking in Scandinavia and the North Sea coasts of Germany and Holland, most of France, Portugal and southern Spain, and the Mediterranean coast as far as the Greek Islands. In all these places chambered tombs, as they were now called, had been built for collective burials: their engineering and architecture were clearly comparable to the chambered tombs of Britain.

The occurrence of these tombs throughout a sizeable portion of Europe posed questions that the nineteenth-century archaeologists were not equipped to answer. Did they constitute the remains of a single race of people, or just a single religion? Where exactly did the practice originate, and how did it spread over such a vast area? To answer these questions someone had to write a prehistory of Europe, describing not just a sequence of artefacts but a sequence of events.

James Fergusson had already attempted this in his *Rude Stone Monuments in All Countries* of 1872. For him the origin of megalith building was India, whence it had spread to North Africa and Europe. However, as he placed the events in Europe immediately before the Christian era, his theory was fatally flawed from the outset. In 1911 Grafton Elliot Smith published a book, *The Ancient Egyptians*, which was the first of a long series of publications advancing a new theory, that all human progress in antiquity was due to travelling Egyptians known as Children of the Sun. Smith was an anatomist who had taught in Cairo before taking up a post at Manchester University. Here he joined forces with W. J. Perry and others to form what was referred to informally as the Manchester School. They maintained that the first megaliths were the Egyptian tombs known as *mastabas*, and that the Children of the Sun who introduced them to Britain and elsewhere were travelling in search of mineral wealth. Therefore you will find megaliths in Cornwall where they looked for tin, in Derbyshire where they mined lead, and in Wales where they found copper and gold.

A variation on this theme was Lord Raglan's *How Came Civilisation?* of 1939, in which he replaced the Egyptians with Sumerians. He wrote: 'The natural state of man is a state of low savagery', and 'savages never invent or discover anything',[1] implying that they owed their rise to some more advanced race. This was Fascism, a strain of thinking that was to find its fullest expression in Germany. When Himmler declared that 'prehistory is the doctrine of the eminence of the Germans at the dawn of civilisation', he was merely repeating a racist message which had matured in Germany earlier in the century. The leading advocate of what became Nazi prehistory was Gustav Kossina, Professor of German Prehistory in the University of Berlin from 1902 until his death in 1931. In his *Die deutsche Vorgeschichte: eine hervoragend nationale Wissenschaft* (German Prehistory: A Supremely National Science) of 1912, he began by claiming that 'only a thoroughly manly and efficient people could have conquered the world at the end of the Roman Empire'. If the Germans had triumphed in the fifth century AD, Kossina wondered what was happening two thousand years earlier. Again, it was the Germans who spread out across Europe and the Near East, imposing their burial rites and megalith building on all other races. Kossina also redefined the Indo-European languages as Indo-German, a linguistic root which became 'an eternal symbol of the world-historical vocation of our race'.

FIGURE 82. Professor Vere Gordon Childe was the leading Diffusionist thinker. In 1927 he became the first Professor of Prehistoric Archaeology at a British university. (*Institute of Archaeology, University College, London*)

Like Kossina, Vere Gordon Childe (fig. 82) began his academic career as a philologist, but politically and intellectually the two men had nothing else in common. Childe was an Australian who won a scholarship to Oxford University in 1914. He took up archaeology while still an undergraduate, but did not prosper with it until he had made a tour through Europe, where he studied the objects in the major museums, before finally settling in London in 1922. Even though as a scholar of artefacts Childe was a direct descendant of the nineteenth century, he nevertheless criticised his predecessors for being first and foremost collectors. Although they had arranged their objects into chronological sequences, presenting the prehistoric past as a series of epochs, their artefacts remained only objects, not expressions of human society.

To Childe, who made no secret of his interest in Marxism, 'the "materialist concept of history" asserts that the economy determines the ideology'.[2] He argued that

> any tool is a social product; its manufacture and use, and therefore its form too, are conditioned by the traditions of social groups which make and use it. American table-knives and forks are quite different from those current in Great Britain. The difference in these everyday utensils, serving the same simple purpose, reflects one divergence in traditions, in habits of eating, between two kindred peoples.[3]

He therefore urged prehistorians to 'interpret in the same way slight differences in the forms of axes, knives or pots, and more marked variations in house-plans or burial rites as reflecting the divergent traditions of distinct social groups'. These distinct social (not ethnic) groups were known as 'cultures', a concept which ironically he had picked up in Germany.

Cultures could be placed in a relative chronology, and they could also be plotted on a map. Childe had read *Man and his Past*, published in 1921 by O. G. S. Crawford, the Archaeology Officer with the Ordnance Survey, which advocated that prehistoric communities could be studied in a geographical context. Since cultures were not static either in time or place, Childe proposed that changes and developments in technology and society were due either to the actual movement of people, or at least to interactions between different cultures. Ideas and innovations were thus transmitted by a process of diffusion.

Childe had studied classics at Oxford, and people used to say that an education in the classics was the ideal preparation for anything in life. This was to be particularly true of archaeology, where the preeminence of Greece and then Rome dominated concepts of Europe's rise to civilisation. It is perfectly true that agriculture, urbanisation and the written word were advanced in the Near East and the eastern Mediterranean long before they were in northern Europe. Nevertheless, a classical education impressed certain mental habits which caused archaeologists to underestimate the independent capabilities of north Europeans.

The Swedish archaeologist Oscar Montelius had argued that 'one does not have to probe deeply . . . to see that the original homeland of the dolmens cannot be sought in northern Europe. They could not have spread from here to the southern shores of the Mediterranean'. Naturally Childe agreed, as his encyclopaedic knowledge of sites and artefacts throughout Europe encouraged him to look south to the Continent for the sources of the interactions and migrations that affected Britain. The result was a pan-European view of prehistory, whereby whatever happened in Britain was conditioned by what had happened in the Near East, the Iberian peninsula or the Danube. The movement of people and ideas was from south to north, east to west, or what Childe described as the 'irradiation of European barbarism by Oriental civilisation'. However, barbarian Europe was not a pale reflection of the Near Eastern world, partly because these barbarians had to adapt to the particular environmental conditions in which they lived. In doing so they created something distinctly and recognisably European. These are the essential ingredients of Childe's Diffusionism. His definitive statement of these views was *The Dawn of European Civilization*, which was first published in 1925 and eventually ran to six editions. It remained the standard text book for students of European prehistory for nearly forty years.

In 1927 Childe was appointed Abercromby Professor of Prehistoric Archaeology in the University of Edinburgh, the first chair for prehistoric studies to be founded at a British university. At this time the number of archaeological posts in the universities had yet to reach double figures, and most of Childe's colleagues were therefore museum curators. After 1945 archaeology expanded exponentially as an intellectual discipline, as public funds became available and many universities opened departments of archaeology offering degree courses and research facilities. A new generation of archaeologists, led by Stuart Piggott (fig. 83), Childe's successor as Abercromby Professor at Edinburgh, continued to elaborate and refine prehistoric Britain within the Diffusionist framework, until the mid 1960s when the Invasion Hypothesis, as it became known, was seriously challenged.

It was an exciting time for archaeology, and a period when it enjoyed a broad popular appeal. The BBC responded with two popular television programmes in the 1950s, *Buried Treasure* and the quiz show *Animal, Vegetable, Mineral?* whose chairman, Glyn

FIGURE 83.
Professors Stuart
Piggott (*left*) and
Richard Atkinson
(*right*) explain
their work at
Wayland's Smithy
in 1962 to Sir
Mortimer
Wheeler.
(*Reading Museum*)

Daniel (fig. 84), was elected Television Personality of the Year in 1955. However, it was generally a barren time for the study of circles and standing stones. Archaeology was now about people and their material lives: a fragment of all-over-corded beaker, or a barbed and tanged arrowhead, spoke the kind of language that stone circles did not. In any case, ceremonial monuments could no longer be studied for their own sake in a spirit of outmoded antiquarianism. They were seen in the context of the progression of mankind from the savage state of hunting, through barbarism, to Rome and civilisation.

The principal technique by which the past was reconstructed was excavation. The methods pioneered by Pitt Rivers were refined by Sir Mortimer Wheeler, R. G. Collingwood and others, and supplemented by specialist

FIGURE 84. Professor Glyn Daniel shortly before his death in 1986. Daniel was the doyen of television archaeology in the 1950s. (*Gwil Owen*)

contributions from scientists, for example in the analysis of human, animal and plant remains. A theory of interpretation was also established. In an influential paper, published in 1954, Professor Christopher Hawkes argued that four levels of inference could be drawn from archaeological evidence, and that they have a descending level of reliability.[4] They are, put simply, technology, economy, society and religion. As far as the first level is concerned, the artefacts are often the technology; they also speak directly about the economy, or methods of livelihood, of the people being studied. Indications of social structure are less certain. Take, for example, a chambered long barrow like West Kennet. It was obviously beyond the capacity of a traditional family unit to construct, so it implies some wider social organisation. But who was chosen for burial in the tomb? Was the society ranked, with a ruling chieftain, or was it more egalitarian? There is no incontrovertible evidence to answer these questions, nor does the evidence tell you other things you might wish to know, such as how many wives the men had, or how many husbands the women had. Moving on to a higher forms of culture, such as what sort of religious or spiritual beliefs caused such tombs to be built, the evidence was deemed to be slim, and so was the interpretation.

FIGURE 85.
During the 1930s
Avebury was sub-
stantially restored
by Alexander
Keiller, one of a
number of restora-
tions that helped
to stimulate popu-
lar awareness of
Britain's pre-
historic heritage.

With these general rules in mind, Stuart Piggott was able to write 'what rites were celebrated in such structures as the stone or timber circles of the British Isles, at Avebury or Stonehenge, must remain unknown, thanks to the very nature of archaeological evidence'.[5] For an archaeologist writing in 1959 this was a very proper, even admirable, thing to say. A later generation would deem this approach too negative, yet it reveals a caution-neurosis in archaeologists which even today has not been eradicated. In the preface to his *Stonehenge* of 1956, aimed at a popular readership, Richard Atkinson informed his readers that 'I have not scrupled to indulge in certain speculations, of a kind which my more austere colleagues may well reprehend'. He points out that an application of Hawkes's theory of inference was very often a disingenuous ploy to avoid delving into the tricky areas of society and religion: 'Silence upon such questions is too frequently justified by an appeal to the strict canons of archaeological evidence, when in fact it merely serves to conceal a lack of imagination.'[6]

Three definitive surveys of prehistoric Britain were published during the time in question. Childe's *Prehistoric Communities of the British Isles* (1940) and Stuart Piggott's *Neolithic Cultures of the British Isles* (1954) were both text books, or at least that is their style. *Prehistoric Britain*, written by Jacquetta and Christopher Hawkes, was published as a Pelican paperback in 1944 and presented the same information to a popular audience. In outline the story they narrate is as follows.

The long barrows of southern England were erected by the first farmers to reach Britain. They came as immigrants from the chalk lands of Gaul, and they settled on the downs and uplands between Sussex and Devon. They also built earthworks known as causewayed enclosures. These consist of rings of concentric ditches with a series of gaps, or causeways, allowing access to the interior. The first of these causewayed enclosures to be recognised was near Avebury, at Windmill Hill, and so these first farmers became known as the Windmill Hill Culture. The long barrows found in Lincolnshire and Yorkshire reflected the northward expansion of this culture once it had become established.

Slightly later than the arrival of the Windmill Hill Folk, several bands of immigrants arrived by sea to colonise west and north Britain. Unfortunately no settlement sites were found, so these people were known primarily through their tombs, which is why they were called the Megalith Builders. A detailed analysis of tomb architecture, encompassing the shape of the covering mound, the layout of the burial chambers, the use of upright slabs (orthostats) and lintels, as opposed to drystone walling and corbelled roofs, ordered these tombs into geographical groups and were indicative of separate cultures. Antecedents were sought and traced to France and Iberia, whence the colonisers came.

Chambered tombs belong to the Neolithic, the duration of which in Britain was estimated by Piggott to have lasted no more than 500 years. He argued that the Windmill Hill Folk had settled in Britain just after 2000 BC, while Childe had put the figure at 2700 BC, Jacquetta Hawkes at 2500 BC. These dates, always intended to be approximate, were derived by cross-reference to dates from the calendars of ancient Egypt, allowing for a time-lag as innovations spread slowly out from the eastern Mediterranean. The arrival of a new race of people in Britain was dated to between 1900 and 1700 BC. They colonised Britain not after a single invasion but in a series of migrations over a period of about 200 years. These were the round-headed people identified from round barrows by John Thurnam, and they came from the area of modern Germany, although their ultimate origin seemed to have been southern Europe. Their material culture, reconstructed primarily from grave goods, was characterised by the ubiquitous drinking cups, or beakers, from which they were christened the Beaker Folk.

We are now in the Bronze Age. The Beaker Folk, as Childe saw them, were 'generally able to impose their material culture and burial rites to the virtual extinction' of collective burial in chambered tombs. Childe thought the Beaker Folk had introduced stone circles to Britain, but later work suggested they had merely adapted a native tradition to their own purposes. They did, however, appear to have introduced individual burial under round barrows, often with elaborate grave goods. These barrows suggested the emergence of a more stratified society, since only a select few were honoured with barrow burial. Furthermore, the appearance of rich grave goods in some Wessex barrows, together with the outstanding structure of Stonehenge, suggested that this area, located favourably among the trade routes of southern England, was the home of Britain's first affluent society, showing attestable links with the more advanced civilisation of Mycenae.

As the Wessex Culture established itself in one small part of England, the Beaker Folk elsewhere were transforming themselves into a new archaeological culture, the Food-Vessel People, who in turn metamorphosed into the Urn Folk. These latter, as their name implies, cremated their dead and collected up the ashes into urns. Like their predecessors they built barrows, but gradually this practice declined. Instead they chose to bury urns in existing barrows and stone circles until, slowly but surely, the great monumental works of the Early Bronze Age were discarded. More than a thousand years before the Romans reached our shores, the barrows and stones had become monuments of times past.

14

Megalith Builders

Chambered tombs are rich repositories of archaeological data. In the absence of known settlement sites in large parts of Britain, the houses of the dead were asked to explain the world of the living. One of the ways this was attempted was by architectural classification, considering both the shape of the covering mounds and the internal arrangements of passage and chambers. A detailed elucidation of this would be (and always was) a tiresome business, but these were the main regional groups: the Severn-Cotswold tombs, the Clyde tombs covering south-west Scotland and the Isle of Man, the Outer Hebridean tombs, the Orkney-Cromarty type covering north-east Scotland, and the Clava cairns of Inverness. Finally, there was the Maes Howe type, comprising only a limited number of tombs in Orkney, and thought to have derived from the Boyne Valley chambered tombs in Ireland.

Each of these regional distributions had a maritime bearing, so they were interpreted as representing colonisation by sea, from the south, by the Megalith Builders. If the tombs were plotted on a map, together with the sites of the Windmill Hill Culture, they showed the areas of primary Neolithic settlement in Britain. Moreover, enough of them survived the depredations of nineteenth-century diggers for a widespread programme of excavations to take place. An examination of the finds recovered from the tombs revealed a Stone Age people who bred cattle, kept sheep, goats and pigs, hunted deer, ate shellfish and cultivated crops. Wheat was grown in southern England, while barley was grown in Orkney. Glyn Daniel's summing up of early rural England has come to sound rather quaint: 'We may then picture the builders of chambered tombs in southern Britain living in small villages, cultivating wheat and barley in their small fields, tending herds of oxen and flocks of sheep, with some pigs and goats – and perhaps horses – about their little farmsteads.'[1] The existence of chambered tombs, which demanded considerable time and effort to build, was seen as symbolising the success of the colonisers in establishing a farming economy in Britain.

The more localised distribution of chambered tombs and long barrows raised questions about their social context, a subject Childe speculated upon in his *Prehistoric Communities*: 'Each block of downland in Sussex boasts its own tiny cluster of long barrows. In a word, a family vault corresponds to an area of arable land and pasture . . . and to the social unit exploiting it.'[2] Elsewhere in Britain the idea of family vaults looked similarly promising: 'On Rousay there would seem to be almost as many family vaults of the Stone Age as there are farms today. Each vault might correspond to a social and economic unit of similar size. In that case the Neolithic population would correspond to the present, less landlords, shopkeepers and artisans!'[3] This implied that everyone had been entitled to chambered tomb burial in an egalitarian society, but on the Orkney mainland was Maes Howe, an outstanding monument that seemed to demand an outstanding individual – surely 'the tomb of a chieftain of the Boyne'.

There was another question to be answered by way of the labour involved in quarrying, transporting and erecting heavy blocks of stone, then covering them with large mounds of earth or stone. As Childe again wrote: 'It was not necessarily beyond the bounds of a single household who could rely on the co-operation of neighbours' to build such tombs, but 'it is intrinsically more likely that the unit engaged was larger, and that the single family whose members enjoyed the privilege of burial in the vault was that of the clan chief'.[4]

The whole issue of transporting and erecting huge blocks of stone was considered by Professor Richard Atkinson in the late 1950s when he was working at Stonehenge. He discounted the idea that draught animals could have been used. Therefore the only effective way of moving a large stone was to place it on a timber sledge, then pull it along on a track of rollers. If this method were adopted, two men per ton could shift the stone, with another two manoeuvring the rollers. Raising the capstones of the tombs would prevent few difficulties 'if it is assumed that the mound surrounding the chamber was first built up to the level of the tops of the walls, to provide a sloping ramp'.[5]

One of the heaviest capstones used in a chambered tomb in Britain is at Tinkinswood, a Severn-Cotswold tomb near Cardiff (fig. 86). The stone weighs about fifty tons, so Atkinson figured that 'not less than 200 able-bodied persons, representing a total population of not less than 300, would be needed to get it into its present position

FIGURE 86. Tinkinswood chambered tomb, near Cardiff, was estimated to have contained about forty-eight individuals, but Richard Atkinson estimated that not less than 200 able-bodied persons would have been required to raise the capstone in place.

with the means currently available'. The chamber was excavated in 1912, when the remains of about forty-eight individuals were recovered, a number well above the average for chambered tombs.

If we assume, as we safely can, a crude death rate of 40 per thousand per annum, a population of 300 souls would incur that number of deaths in just over *four years*, an impossibly short period of use for a structure of this character. We may thus assume that this tomb, and by inference many others, are not the mausolea of a whole local population, but only of one small fraction of it.[6]

The evidence from the excavation of chambered tombs was by itself too ambiguous to draw such a firm conclusion. Grave goods were few, giving no indication of elite social or economic status, and the bones recovered from them showed that they had been used as collective tombs for people of both sexes and all ages. Fortunately for the archaeologists, inhumation was practised everywhere in Britain by the Megalith Builders, although some cremations were discovered in tombs of the Clyde group and those of northern Scotland, and in the long barrows of Yorkshire. Bones, however poorly preserved, provide a lot more information than ashes.

The Pant-y-Saer chambered tomb on Anglesey was excavated in the early 1930s by Sir Lindsay Scott and contained the remains of fifty-four inhumations. Thirty-six of these were adults, three were adolescents, six were children and nine were foetuses. Unfortunately, it was not possible to ascertain the division of the sexes. If they had been represented in about equal proportions this would have agreed with the burials in the Severn-Cotswold tombs, a number of which were excavated in the first half of the twentieth century. Of these West Kennet yielded upwards of forty-six burials, Ty Isaf thirty-three, while in Gloucestershire Nympsfield yielded twenty-four, Lanhill nineteen and Notgrove only nine burials. Anatomical reports on the remains from these tombs established that the people were the long-headed people common throughout Neolithic Britain, but among these people dirt pyorrhoea and osteoarthritis were common, while two cases of spina bifida were found at West Kennet. Keiller and Piggott's excavation of Lanhill in the 1930s recovered nine individuals they thought were members of one family group – there was a striking family likeness in their features, and seven of the nine had rare 'Wormian ossicles' in their skulls. There was nothing, however, to indicate conclusively whether they were ordinary peasant farmers or the family of a clan chief.

All this enriched our knowledge of the way of life of Neolithic cultures, but it did not explain the tombs themselves. The material culture of the Megalith Builders in Britain and Europe showed no obvious uniformity, except in the nature of the tombs. As Jacquetta Hawkes wrote, 'it is unlikely that the megalith building communities living in different regions would have been found to speak the same language, and they certainly did not have any common tradition for the manufacture of their tools, weapons and pottery'.[7] The only common tradition they had was seemingly their predisposition to build monuments to the dead. Childe saw the Megalith Builders as 'missionaries', implanting their religious beliefs, as well as their knowledge of agriculture, on indigenous populations, which allowed him to speak of a 'megalithic religion' disseminated across Europe like Christianity. A slightly different interpretation was offered by Glyn Daniel who, while not disputing this spread of religious belief, thought that 'the primary driving force of the megalith builders was a colonial and trading one and a prospecting one'.[8] Therefore the diffusion of chambered tomb building was a secondary process.

But what was the nature of this religion? Perhaps there was a clue in the underlying concept of the tomb, about which opinions differed. Some thought they were substitutes for natural caves, others that they were houses of the dead adapted from the homes of the living, others again that they represented the womb from which the spirits of the dead were reborn, which implied the cult of a mother goddess. Childe speculated that perhaps the Megalith Builders 'formed a spiritual aristocracy of "divine" chiefs whose magic powers ensured the fertility of crops and herds, of game and fish'.[9]

There was in fact evidence that fertility cults were practised by these Neolithic farmers. Crudely worked chalk figurines and phalli had been discovered during excavation of the causewayed enclosures of the Windmill Hill Culture. 'Both are fertility charms used in magic rites to ensure the germination of the grain and the multiplication of the herds and flocks', thought Childe.[10] In 1939 excavation at the Neolithic flint mines of Grimes Graves in Norfolk revealed an underground gallery with a shrine. A crude chalk image, less than five inches high, of a fat and pregnant woman was placed on a pedestal. She had a chalk phallus alongside her and antler picks at her feet. To Piggott 'this obvious shrine of an Earth Goddess may represent an appeal to the chthonic powers for more abundant flint'.[11]

Cult objects were also found deposited at chambered tombs. At Pant-y-Saer Scott found a white quartzite pebble which he decided served 'a magical purpose', and at Cairnholy Piggott found in the forecourt 'ritual deposits' of shellfish, broken pottery and a jet bead. At Bryn Celli Ddu a stone was unearthed which was called the Pattern Stone because of its Boyne-style carvings. W. F. J. Knight interpreted these carvings as 'maze symbolism', which was 'expected to create a field of magical force of the right kind' during ritual performances. The stone may have been intended as 'a chart to direct ritual dancing at the foundation; and it may afterwards have been dug into the monument, in the hope that its sympathetic presence might help to maintain the conditions originally intended by the dance'. This imaginative interpretation was extremely radical, written as it was in 1932, 'but it is better not to go too far', Knight concluded, suddenly suffering the archaeologist's brand of vertigo.[12]

Inside the chamber at Bryn Celli Ddu is a single pillar which has no structural significance. The excavator of the site, W.J.Hemp, thought it might have been a symbolic offering to the 'dolmen goddess' because it was clearly a 'phallic emblem'. A similar pillar was found at Clettraval in North Uist, while a single standing stone stood in the forecourt at Cairnholy in Kirkcudbright. Another example of sexual symbolism was spotted at Wayland's Smithy. Of the huge sarsen stones that form the façade of the tomb the two stones flanking the entrance to the chambers have shapes suggestive of penis and vulva.

Once it was looked for, all chambered tombs excavated using modern scientific methods showed traces of ritual activity. Lindsay Scott argued that 'ritual is the only key likely to open the door to a coherent understanding of the chambered tombs'. Where the barrow diggers of the nineteenth century made straight for the burials in a tomb, archaeologists now cut trenches through the mounds, exposing the original ground surfaces in the process, where they found evidence that rituals had been performed at these sites before the tombs were erected. Small rings of stones, or pits, were found beneath both chambered tombs and long barrows, often showing evidence that fires had been lit in them. The purpose of the ceremonies was a mystery but, at Notgrove in Gloucestershire, Elsie Clifford found a ring of stone slabs, at the centre of which was a polygonal cist containing the remains of a man in his late fifties. Perhaps his burial consecrated the site.

The tombs themselves were used for collective burials over a considerable period of time. At Cairnholy, in Kirkcudbright (fig. 87), Piggott found six hearths in the forecourt, leading him to conclude that 'there had been six burials made in the tomb, which on a twenty-year generation would give it a life of a century or so'.[13] Given that the Neolithic period was thought to have lasted about 700 years this comment, written in

FIGURE 87.
At Cairnholy
chambered tomb
Stuart Piggott
found evidence
of ritual deposits
in the tomb's
forecourt.
(*Audrey Henshall*)

1951, seemed quite plausible. However, as radiocarbon dates became available in the 1950s, such thinking had to be revised. West Kennet, which Piggott and Atkinson excavated in the mid 1950s, was calculated to have been in use for somewhere around a thousand years.

Glyn Daniel, in his *Prehistoric Chamber Tombs of England and Wales* of 1950, wrote: 'The general practice was probably to store a few bodies in some convenient place and to open the chamber tomb ceremonially perhaps once or twice a year to accommodate the three or four bodies that had accumulated.'[14] When a new burial was introduced the bones of the earlier skeletons were either carefully stacked against the chamber walls, or unceremoniously pushed aside to make room for the latest occupant, who was usually placed in a crouched position. This accounted for the disarticulated state of some remains and the more complete state of others.

At the Unival passage grave on North Uist, excavated in the late 1940s, Lindsay Scott found something slightly different. Unival has a single burial chamber, inside which a cist was built of thin slabs. It contained 'the extremely decayed remains of the upper half of the skeleton of a mature woman' and the condition of the bones 'must be due to the piling of burning charcoal on them'. The sequence of burial rites here began with placing the body into the cist, accompanied by pots containing food offerings. After an interval during which most of the flesh decomposed, the remains were scorched by throwing charcoal on them. When a new corpse was introduced the previous body had to be cleared out of the cist to make way for the new incumbent. The larger bones were piled against the chamber wall while the smaller bones and broken pottery were shovelled out on to the chamber floor.

Scott thought that fire had been introduced 'to drive the ghost away from its decomposed body'. Similarly burnt bones were found in the tombs of southern Britain. Fires were also lit during the elaborate ceremonies that took place in the forecourt of the tomb. Jacquetta Hawkes thought 'it is not too fanciful to see it filled by a circle of dancers moving in some revolving figure, while offerings might be made at the portal to propitiate the ancestral spirits'.[15] Daniel envisaged 'fires, funeral feasts, and the sacrificing of animals – and just possibly in rare cases, human beings'. Evidence of human sacrifice was difficult to pinpoint, but at Maiden Castle in Dorset one hapless individual, uncovered during Sir Mortimer Wheeler's excavation there in the 1930s, certainly came to a sensationally gruesome end.

Long before the famous Iron Age hillfort came into existence a causewayed enclosure was built at Maiden Castle, over which a barrow was subsequently raised. It was not an ordinary long barrow because the mound is nearly a third of a mile long, so it was classified as a bank barrow. At its eastern end Wheeler found the remains of two children and a man of about thirty. The man 'had been systematically dismembered immediately after death. The bones bore axe-marks, and the whole body had been cut up as by a butcher for the stewpot. The skull had been hacked to pieces as though for the extraction of the brain.' The immediate impression was that 'the body had been cooked and eaten'.

Recent analysis of these remains show them to be of Anglo-Saxon date, but even so it was always quoted as a freak incident. Of more general significance was evidence for the extraction of bones from the tombs. One of the problems in ascertaining the number of burials in a tomb was that skeletons were rarely found complete. In particular, excavators commonly found many more jaw bones than skulls. At West Kennet Piggott thought that the only possible reason for the absence of skulls and thigh bones was that they had been deliberately removed from the tomb. The skull in particular was an obvious object of veneration. He also pointed to the belief in classical antiquity that linked the head and the thighs as the seats of generation and fertility. The skull and thigh became 'an emblem of the whole human body after death', and the chambered tomb builders were seen practising an ancestor cult.

Until the late 1950s there had only been two complete excavations of long barrows: General Pitt Rivers' work at Wor barrow in 1893; and C. W. Phillips' excavation of Giants' Hills long barrow near Skendleby in Lincolnshire in the 1930s. Excavation of three long barrows at the end of the 1950s, however, at Nutbane in Hampshire by Faith de Mallet Morgan, Fussell's Lodge near Salisbury by Paul Ashbee, and Wayland's Smithy by Professors Piggott and Atkinson, showed that long barrows were clearly related to chambered tombs (figs 88, 89). Each had a wooden mortuary enclosure, although at Nutbane it was smaller than the adjacent roofed forecourt building where rituals had taken place. Fussell's Lodge contained fifty-seven disarticulated skeletons, which Ashbee thought had been previously buried elsewhere. At Wayland's Smithy fourteen variously articulated skeletons were thought to have been defleshed in the open air, a ritual known as excarnation: 'the evidence seems to require the provision of some kind of platform, elevated above the ground and thus out of reach of mammals, but open to the sky and to birds of prey'.[16] The defleshed corpses were then placed inside a small wooden chamber, 'resembling a low ridge tent, with massive posts at either end' supporting a ridge pole. The posts were so large that Atkinson supposed they were projected far above the mound and were possibly carved and painted, making the long barrow a conspicuous landmark for miles around. Fussell's Lodge had an equally striking appearance. Ashbee found a bedding trench which held vertically set wooden posts, the purpose of which was to contain the earth dug from the flanking ditches. So when it was newly built the barrow looked, because of its timber 'retaining walls', like the 'trapezoidal long houses current upon the mainland of Europe during the 3rd millennium BC'. In his *The Earthen Long Barrow in Britain* of 1970, Ashbee argued that other long barrows were originally timber retained, and that the decay of the wood is responsible for their present earthen appearance (fig. 90).

FIGURE 88. Excavations at Wayland's Smithy in 1962. In the background are the façade stones awaiting restoration. (*Reading Museum*)

FIGURE 89. Wayland's Smithy after its restoration.

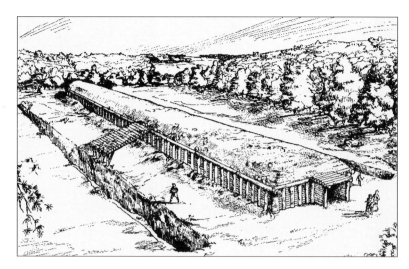

FIGURE 90.
Paul Ashbee's
excavation of
Fussell's Lodge
long barrow near
Salisbury in 1957,
by showing that it
originally had a
timber revetment,
radically changed
our perception of
earthen long
barrows.
(*Society of Anti-
quaries of London*)

A class of structure associated with long barrows was the cursus, named by William Stukeley after finding the one near Stonehenge. The Greater Stonehenge Cursus had a long barrow at one end. The more extensive Dorset Cursus, six miles long, has a barrow at each end and two along its course. Dr J. F. S. Stone excavated a trench through the Greater Stonehenge Cursus in 1947 and found it to be of Neolithic date, but probably later than the barrow it was aligned to. However, as his excavation had yielded fragments of bluestone, he wondered whether a stone circle had stood at the western end of the cursus. If so the Cursus may have been some form of processional way linking a stone circle with a long barrow. 'We seem to have here – if stone and timber circles can be construed as meeting-places or assembly-grounds for the living – the material embodiment of an attempted connecting link between the living and the dead.'[17]

There is also a hint here of cultural continuity from the long barrows to the stone circles, but Diffusionist thought discouraged it. The Invasion Hypothesis demanded a separation of one phase of prehistory from the next. The Neolithic people believed one thing, but Bronze Age people believed something else. As Jacquetta Hawkes wrote:

the earth goddess and phallic fertility rites which preoccupied the mind of Neolithic man seem to have lost their hold. There was a shift of interest from the earth and the womb upwards to the sun and the heavens – well symbolised by the change from the dark, closed tomb to the open sun-orientated temple.[18]

15

Beaker Folk

In 1927 Graham Callander, Director of the National Museum of Antiquities of Scotland, was invited to London to speak to the Society of Antiquaries about recent research north of the Border. One of the topics he chose to dwell on was the origin of the Scottish stone circles. Just as Diffusionist ideas were entering their ascendancy, Callander confounded his peers by proposing that these circles owed nothing to outside influence but were an independent invention. He tried to show that they evolved in stages out of the building of chambered tombs. In studying the round cairns of the Hebrides he noticed that many of them have a pronounced kerb of large stones. Gradually the significance of the kerb increased while that of the cairn decreased, until after a succession of intermediate stages the stone circle emerged inside which there was either no cairn at all, or a cairn with minimal architectural significance. In his *Megalithic Monuments of North-East Scotland* of 1934, Alexander Keiller argued much the same thing, suggesting that the Recumbent Stone circles of Aberdeenshire were a degeneration of the neighbouring Clava cairns. Although most of Britain's stone circles are in Scotland, and with a couple of rare exceptions are unique to the British Isles, this theory did not generate much enthusiasm. When archaeologists were studying the origin of anything prehistoric, they invariably looked across the English Channel for inspiration.

During the 1914–18 war O. G. S. Crawford had been an observer with the Royal Flying Corps, in the course of which he became involved with aerial photography. In a series of books published in the 1920s he advocated its use in identifying sites invisible from the ground. Right on cue, another Royal Flying Corps veteran, Squadron Leader G. S. M. Insall VC, discovered two important sites in southern England, one near Stonehenge in 1925 and the other at Arminghall in Norfolk in 1929.

In the former case the aerial photograph revealed a ploughed-down circular earthwork with concentric rings of spots visible in the interior. Their configuration reminded archaeologists of Stonehenge. An excavation led by Maud Cunnington was soon underway which showed that the spots were wooden post holes. This led immediately to the site being nicknamed 'Woodhenge'. The rings of posts formed an oval shape which had a definite axis pointing toward the midsummer sunrise. In the centre was a single burial. The skeleton of a young girl, apparently killed by a blow to the head that split her skull in two, was carefully exhumed and labelled 'dedicatory sacrifice'.

The meaning of Woodhenge seemed obvious: it was a place of ritual, a wooden precursor of the stone circle. Confirmation of this seemed to come in 1930 from another of Maud Cunnington's excavations, the Sanctuary at Avebury. Using Stukeley's notes, she managed to pinpoint where the long-vanished Sanctuary on Overton Hill had once stood, and then confirmed its exact location by excavation. She duly unearthed the pits into which the stones had been sunk, but she also found concentric rings of post holes. Meanwhile the skeleton of the adolescent 'may have been of a dedicatory nature'.

Stuart Piggott later argued convincingly that the Sanctuary post holes represented three successive wooden buildings, all of which were earlier than the stone circles. He also saw the Woodhenge post holes as the remnant of a building – a circular ridge-roofed structure with an open atrium in the centre. It was a discovery that opened up exciting new possibilities: 'the reconstruction I have suggested brings to mind nothing so much as the Globe at Southwark: a "wooden O" wherein perhaps were enacted those crude ritual dramas of harvest and springtime in which the whole great tradition of the European theatre finds its birth'.[1]

Arminghall, meanwhile, was excavated in the 1930s by Grahame Clark of the University of Cambridge. The site was defined by two concentric ditches, in the centre of which a horseshoe configuration of wooden posts had once stood. These posts were nearly three feet in diameter, sunk seven feet into virgin soil, and may have risen to a height of twenty feet above ground. Despite the fact that there was no grave in the centre, and the site had no obvious orientation like Stonehenge or Woodhenge, Clark was certain that the posts 'were not the uprights of a house, but the pillars, as it were, of an open-air temple'.[2]

The origin of Clark's 'open-air temples' and Piggott's 'great dim raftered halls of magic and ritual' was sought across the Channel, coming to rest initially with the 'palisade barrows' studied by a Dutch archaeologist, Dr A. E. van Giffen. Beneath these Dutch barrows similar rings of post holes had been found, which were interpreted either as the remains of wooden buildings or as rings of free-standing posts. Clark ultimately decided that henges and palisade barrows are essentially different things, but a precedent for wooden ceremonial structures had been found on the Continent. Childe followed this up by arguing that wooden structures 'are more appropriate to the inhabitants of forested plains, like the Beaker Folk in East Anglia and their Battle-axe ancestors in Northern Europe, than to the megalith builders of the rock-bound Atlantic coasts'.[3] However the crux of the Arminghall/Woodhenge problem rested not with the post holes but with the earthworks enclosing them.

Arminghall and Woodhenge are both henges, a type of circular earthwork found throughout southern Britain, and with less regularity in the north. Most of them have the bank outside the ditch (Stonehenge is an exception), so could not have been used for defensive purposes. Some contained wooden structures, some stone circles, some contained both, some nothing at all. Two henges excavated in the late 1940s by Richard Atkinson, then of the Ashmolean Museum, at Dorchester-on-Thames had an internal ring of pits. So did the henge at Cairnpapple in West Lothian, excavated by Piggott in the early fifties. At all three sites the pits were found to contain cremations.

A study of the pottery recovered from these sites indicated that they were not built by the invading Beaker Folk, but had an indigenous origin. In the later Neolithic a new culture appeared in the archaeological record, but not as the result of an invasion. When the Windmill Hill Folk established themselves in southern England they had to live side by side with the native hunter-gatherers of Mesolithic Britain. Eventually the two cultures merged and formed a secondary Neolithic culture which, for want of inspiration, was named Secondary Neolithic. These people were deemed responsible for the earliest henges.

The Beaker Folk, when they invaded or colonised Britain, were thought to have appropriated these henges for their own purposes. They also built new henges with rings of stones instead of wooden posts, and so the origins of Stonehenge and Avebury, the greatest of stone circle henges, seemed to be established. Although there are other stone circles in henges – Arbor Low in Derbyshire, Stenness in Orkney and the Stripple Stones in Cornwall – this version of their origin was constructed primarily with Wessex in mind.

In Wales Sir Mortimer Wheeler noted in 1925 that the stone circles stand in areas apart from the chambered tombs, implying that they were built by a different people. But could they be ascribed to the spread of Beaker ideas from southern England? Not on archaeological evidence. And what about the circles of south-west and north-west England? With less conviction it was argued that these and the Welsh circles were inspired by invaders from Brittany, whose stone rows and occasional circles, such as the half drowned Er Lannic in the Gulf of Morbihan, suggested an affinity between Britain and Brittany in the Early Bronze Age. Moving north to Scotland, where there was supposedly a Beaker invasion along the east coast, the preponderance of cairns inside the circles only served to complicate the issue further. There was no real evidence to dispute Callander and Keiller's claims for independent invention, so archaeologists found themselves unable to write about the spread of a stone circle religion as they had about the 'megalithic religion' of the chambered tombs.

It soon became apparent that stone circles would not be a fertile area of study for archaeologists of the Diffusionist school. W. F. Grimes' 1936 survey of megalithic monuments in Wales for the *Proceedings of the Prehistoric Society* devotes only two of its thirty-four pages to stone circles. He comments that 'any suggestion as to [their] meaning would seem to be little more than unprofitable guesswork'.[4] Excavation of these sites was rarely attempted because in the past they had yielded disappointing results, except where the circle contained a cairn. In the 1930s H. E. Kilbride-Jones excavated Loanhead of Daviot and the Standing Stones of Cullerlie, while Childe excavated Old Keig, all three of them in Aberdeenshire. At Cullerlie the stone ring was erected before eight

FIGURE 91. Loanhead of Daviot stone circle, in Aberdeenshire, was excavated in the 1930s, revealing evidence that a funeral pyre had been lit before a cairn was raised over the burial. (*Historic Scotland*)

small cairns, containing cremations, were built inside it. At Loanhead (fig. 91) the centre of the circle revealed so much evidence of burning that Kilbride-Jones thought a funeral pyre had been lit there before a cairn was raised over the burial. But, alas, 'beyond drawing attention to these facts, one is not prepared to say anything'.[5] Childe was more forthcoming. Old Keig also has a cairn in the centre, containing a cremation, which 'must be regarded as primary and revealing its purpose'. The original ground surface beneath the cairn showed evidence of being pounded by countless feet:

> in other words, the circle of uprights, the erection of which would involve a great deal of trampling about, must presumably have been set up before the cairn. This is quite in order. Just as a Pharaoh would build his pyramid before his death, so the barbaric Aberdeenshire chief would have the enclosure which was to guard his ashes completed during his lifetime.[6]

Turning his attention to southern England, Childe had to find a different explanation. The scale and self-importance of Avebury and Stonehenge implied that 'each might be fairly compared to a cathedral and contrasted with smaller local sanctuaries, presumably filling the role of parish churches'.[7] In her *Prehistoric Britain* Jacquetta Hawkes envisaged worshippers assembling to watch the priests perform magic rituals inside Avebury and Stonehenge. 'What these mysteries were we shall never know', she wrote, but the midsummer orientation of Stonehenge was a clue. 'The sun certainly played some part', and this change in emphasis from the Earth to the sky 'is exactly what known religious history would lead one to suspect. It is typical of Indo-European religion that Zeus, a sky god, should rule the Greek pantheon.' With the triumph of the Beaker Folk in Britain 'we are witnessing the triumph of some more barbaric Zeus over the ancient Earth Mother dear to the Neolithic peasantry'.[8]

Stonehenge and Avebury had by now been hailed as among the greatest monuments of the 'Old World', yet as late as the 1930s they were enjoying vastly different fortunes.

Stonehenge had been given to the nation in 1918 but by this time Avebury was in a sorry state. The earthwork and the Kennet Avenue remained the property of a number of private owners and were still not safe from occasional vandalism. The village was anything but a picture postcard, with piles of domestic and agricultural rubbish cluttering up the stones, and with part of the bank obscured by a dense cover of trees and undergrowth. In 1934 Alexander Keiller purchased as much of the land as he could, then started tidying up the place. However in 1937, when Keiller tried to raise £11,000 to purchase the monument for the nation, the Government refused to contribute a penny. Eventually ownership passed to the National Trust, but not before it had been rescued from squalor by Keiller and his assistant, the young Stuart Piggott.

Alexander Keiller was one of the last of the great amateur archaeologists, perhaps the last who could afford to be. Born in 1889, his wealth came from the family's Dundee marmalade firm. He inherited the family's Morven estates in Aberdeenshire when he was nine years old. After a brief spell working in the family business he set up his own car business, then served as a pilot in the Royal Naval Auxiliary Service in the 1914–18 war. His archaeological pursuits began with a survey of stone circles in north-east Scotland, after which his attention was diverted to Avebury. Keiller was active in scuppering plans to build a Marconi wireless station at Windmill Hill near Avebury in 1923. He used the same tactic here as he would later use at Avebury – he bought the site. Meanwhile in 1924 he and Crawford hired an aircraft and took 300 photographs in two months, which formed the basis of their amazing book *Wessex from the Air*, published in 1928. The importance of Windmill Hill was not merely its proximity to Avebury. On its summit is an early Neolithic causewayed enclosure, the first to be recognised and properly studied. Keiller started excavating it in 1925. Because Keiller himself had little previous experience, Harold St George Gray agreed to direct operations for the first two seasons.

After this Keiller took over full responsibility, turning his attention to Avebury itself. Apart from purchasing land there he also bought Avebury Manor, in which he lived until his death in 1955. There he founded the Morven Institute of Archaeological Research, named after his Scottish estate. During the late 1930s fallen stones were hauled upright, stones buried during the middle ages were unearthed and reerected, while the positions of missing stones were marked with concrete posts (fig. 92). Stuart Piggott later described this work as 'more like megalithic landscape gardening than research archaeology', and posterity has criticised Keiller for giving Avebury its present sanitised appearance. This is unfair. When Keiller went to Avebury it was, as he says, 'the outstanding archaeological disgrace of Britain'. His purpose was corrective and to that extent his work was a great success.

It was Keiller and Piggott who found the unfortunate barber-surgeon crushed by a buried stone (fig. 93). In the Kennet Avenue burials were found in association with

FIGURE 92. The restoration of stones in the Kennet Avenue at Avebury in the 1930s. The method of erecting these stones in prehistory cannot have been much different.

FIGURE 93. The remains of this barber-surgeon were found at Avebury in the 1930s during the restoration of fallen stones. He died in the 1320s when stones were being felled at the behest of the church. (*Alexander Keiller Museum, Avebury*)

four of the stones. Two of them had accompanying beakers, making Avebury the only stone circle which could be associated with the Beaker Folk with absolute confidence. Moreover, they noticed that the shape of the stones conformed to two distinct shapes, in which they saw a sexual connotation. Tall thin stones alternated with broader, diamond-shaped stones, which were classed as Type A (male) and Type B (female) (fig. 94). Even restoration work could be turned into experimentation: one of the smaller stones, weighing about eight tons, was raised upright using prehistoric equipment in about five days.

Keiller's excavations at Avebury were curtailed by the outbreak of war in 1939. After 1945 ill health prevented him from pursuing his work with his former vigour, and he died in 1955 before a full report of his excavations could be published. This task was then taken on by Isobel Smith, who published *Windmill Hill and Avebury* in 1965, a work that looked back to the excavations of the 1920s, but whose conclusions

FIGURE 94.
Stones in the
Kennet Avenue at
Avebury, showing
the alternate male
and female shapes.

foreshadowed the concerns of archaeologists up to the present day. Using pottery styles to construct a chronology, she proposed a sequence of construction: first came the outer circle and the bank and ditch; later the inner circles, with their central Cove and Obelisk, were built, more or less contemporary with the Kennet Avenue; and finally the concentric stone circles of the Sanctuary replaced the earlier timber structure.

Her explanation of Avebury was based on finds from Keiller's and Gray's excavations, plus an interpretation of its architecture. Architecturally the Cove is suggestive of a megalithic burial chamber, like those of West Kennet, while the other inner circle has the Obelisk, a possible phallic symbol. This led her to argue that the builders' system of beliefs 'embraced the concept of a close relationship between death and fertility'. Moreover, with the Type A and Type B stones of the circles and Avenue, 'the implication must be that the monuments were dedicated to a fertility cult'.[9] But there were also human remains recovered by Gray from the ditch. These were 'fragments of human skeletons, all from skulls, mandibles, and long bones', and there was 'no reason why the bones from the Avebury ditch may not have been taken from skeletons in a chambered long barrow, at West Kennet or elsewhere'.[10] This possibility was strengthened by showing that the outer circle and ditch, unlike the Kennet Avenue, were pre-Beaker, while Piggott's excavation at West Kennet had shown it to have been in use for about a thousand years, overlapping with the use of Avebury itself.

Smith's conclusions raised some other problems. Human remains in the ditch at Avebury were found in circumstances 'strongly reminiscent of those in which human bones occurred in the ditches at Windmill Hill, and the question arises whether the same interpretation applies'. Certainly the evidence from Avebury suggested 'a continuity of ritual and ceremony extending over a long period and through successive changes of material culture'.[11] But the probable use of bones from Neolithic chambered tombs for rituals at Beaker stone circles was not what archaeologists had come to expect.

The people who had used Britain's stone circles were hitherto identified as the people buried in the round barrows. Thanks to the earlier diggers their display of worldly goods could be studied at leisure in museums: earrings and necklaces with gold sun disks were their show of vanity, daggers their aggression, while the contents of their beakers remained a mystery. Was the spiritual or magical power of alcohol a factor in the Beaker Folk's domination of Britain? Or was it just the way they let their hair down?

On a social level, the artefacts spoke of a hierarchical society in Bronze Age Britain, one in which the individual rather than the clan or family took precedence. Even though there was no incontrovertible evidence from the barrows that any priests existed to preside over ceremonies at Stonehenge, Avebury or anywhere else, a priesthood still figured in the imagination of Sir Cyril Fox when he visualised a Bronze Age funeral: 'priests or shamans, on behalf of an important local family . . . who had suffered bereavement, performed ritual acts by virtue of which contact was obtained with an underworld Power, and a place provided for the ashes of the dead in the shadow of Its Presence'.[12]

Rings of posts, like those discovered in Holland, had been found under barrows as early as 1850 by Charles and Henry Long at Beedon in Berkshire, and also by John Mortimer in the East Riding. He interpreted them as the remains of dwellings, an idea that did not find much favour. By the late 1950s several more examples had been revealed. Reviewing the evidence in *The Bronze Age Round Barrow in Britain* (1960), Paul Ashbee noted that single or concentric circles of posts were in nearly all cases only temporary, being removed before the barrows were raised. He thought they were temporary mortuary houses, or enclosures, and performed the same function as the rings of stones marking the perimeter of cairns in western Britain. As Thurnam and Greenwell before him, Ashbee turned to early literature to visualise a barrow funeral. In the *Aeneid* Misenus was cremated in a huge pyre and 'the Trojans were weeping as bitterly as ever for Misenus as they paid their last dues to his ashes' (book vi, line 212), over which a barrow was raised. This seemed to strike the right note. No longer were tombs revisited by later generations for ritual performances; and no longer were bones to be venerated in a cult of the dead. When the barrow was raised over the body, the spirit was allowed to rest in peace – at least until the barrow diggers got to work.

16

Stonehenge and the Wessex Culture

For an ostentatious display of material wealth no barrows in Britain can compare with those of Wessex. In 1938 Stuart Piggott took a fresh look at the treasures from ninety-nine of these barrows, mostly dug up in the nineteenth century, and in an article in the *Proceedings of the Prehistoric Society* proposed that they formed 'the material equipment of an aristocratic minority' – the Wessex Culture.

The Wessex chieftains were thought to have come from Brittany, men who muscled their way past the Beaker aristocracy and exploited the lucrative trade routes across southern England. Able to levy a toll on consignments of copper and gold from Ireland, and tin from Cornwall, destined for the far reaches of the Baltic, central Europe and the Aegean, they amassed a fortune which they spent on the most luxurious items Europe could offer: faience beads from the eastern Mediterranean, amber from Scandinavia and north Germany, bronze work from Brittany and south Germany, and gold from Ireland. They also imported amber and gold as raw materials and enlisted craftsmen to produce original products. The ribbed gold cup from Rillaton barrow in Cornwall – a Wessex outlier – was deemed a Wessex copy of a type fashionable in Mycenae. Meanwhile the gold-mounted amber disks from the Late Minoan 'Tomb of the Double Axes' at Knossos were so similar to those in Wessex that they should have been stamped 'made in England'.

Illustrators visualised these chieftains as hirsute brutes posing with bronze axes and daggers, spears and shields. The man Cunnington found in Bush barrow had two bronze daggers, one with gold inlay, and a sceptre which was surely the regalia of pomp and circumstance. These chieftains visualised themselves as warrior heroes. To archaeologists they were the nearest thing Britain had to an heroic age, and they were the inspiration behind Stuart Piggott's poem 'Wessex Harvest':

> Now the ancient Wessex hills
> seize their lost splendour
> once, Stonehenge-building, their princes
> proud with their Wicklow gold
> strode into sunshine;
> now earth inherits
> their dust, who are chalk-graved,
> dry frail and brittle
> pale bones under barrows –
> poor fragments, the great ones.

The full flowering of the Wessex Culture, about 1500 BC, coincided with the apogee of Mycenaean civilisation. As any informed archaeologist was aware, Mycenae was the city of Agamemnon: it represented the heroic age of classical antiquity. It was even possible that the poems of Homer described a world that the northern barbarians in Wessex would have found familiar. And just maybe those most famous of all merchant-venturers, the Argonauts, had come to Britain in their search for the Golden Fleece. This was romantic stuff, and scholars could find themselves dizzied by the thought that the light of Mediterranean civilisation had briefly illumined the dark centuries of barbarian Britain. Too far fetched, their more austere colleagues might have claimed, until in the one and only monument built by the Wessex Culture the influence of Mycenae was suddenly there for all to see.

If there was one site archaeologists dreamed of getting their trowels into, Stonehenge was it. And who can blame them? Wessex was the region where most of the great discoveries of early twentieth-century archaeology had been made. The names Windmill Hill and Woodhenge, unfamiliar to the general public, were permanently etched in the minds of every archaeology student. What with the presence of Avebury and Stonehenge as well, Wessex became the epicentre of Neolithic and Bronze Age Britain. Wessex also took on its primary importance because it was more intensively studied than any other region, so the term Wessex Culture can be taken as having two meanings. It describes both a culture of Bronze Age Britain and the work of archaeologists in the mid twentieth century.

The leading lights in this latter-day Wessex Culture were ironically two prehistorians from the other end of Britain – the University of Edinburgh. Of the five prime prehistoric monuments in Wessex, Stuart Piggott had worked with Keiller at Avebury; Richard Atkinson was later to dig Silbury Hill; while Piggott and Atkinson in partnership dug West Kennet, Wayland's Smithy and, first of all, Stonehenge.

A comprehensive programme of excavations at Stonehenge had been in progress as recently as the 1920s. They were directed for the Society of Antiquaries by Colonel William Hawley, who had assisted Gowland in his 1901 dig. However, the project was so badly resourced that Hawley often worked alone on the site, a problem compounded by his lack of ambition. Archaeological excavation has been described as testing a hypothesis by destructive analysis; an archaeologist with no hypothesis will have no analysis to compensate for the destruction. Where Gowland dug with the express purpose of dating the monument, Hawley was determined to keep an open mind, which recalls the saying that if your mind stays open your brains will fall out. The inevitable happened: 'the more we dig, the more the mystery appears to deepen', he once confessed to a group of journalists, but unfortunately he kept on digging.[1] A series of reports published in the *Antiquaries Journal* during the 1920s only confirmed the obvious – that Hawley had been out of his depth.

After the war the Society of Antiquaries agreed to a fresh series of excavations whose aim was to do what Hawley had not – provide a definitive written account of the monument. Atkinson and Piggott were to join with the Wiltshire archaeologist Dr J. F. S. Stone, in directing the work. The first season's digging took place in 1950, continuing periodically until 1964. Because Hawley had stripped nearly half the area of the site, digging was now confined to small, strategically important areas, plus a limited reexploration of Hawley's trenches. A definitive excavation report did not appear in print until 1995, but a popular and stimulating summary was published by Atkinson in his now classic *Stonehenge*, first published in 1956.

Stonehenge was shown to be not the product of a single undertaking, but of three main phases of construction over a 500 year period, or so they thought then. The first phase, Stonehenge I, began about 1900 BC and consisted of the bank and ditch and the digging of fifty-six pits – called the Aubrey Holes after the man who first noticed them – around the edge. The henge had an entrance to the north east, outside which stood the Heel Stone. During the next phase of activity, Stonehenge II, the axis of the earthwork was altered and the Avenue was constructed in the direction of the mid-summer sunrise. The bluestones of Pembrokeshire origin were brought to the site and holes were dug to contain them. The plan was evidently to construct a double ring of stones at the centre of the enclosure, but it was never completed. Stonehenge III was started soon after the abandonment of the bluestone circles, and is the one we are familiar with. Sarsen stones were brought from near Marlborough, were tooled and dressed, then erected in a great lintelled circle with a horseshoe arrangement of trilithons in the centre. The whereabouts of the bluestones at this time remained a mystery, but after the sarsen structures were completed an attempt to rearrange the bluestones was abandoned before they were finally set up in harmony with the sarsens: a bluestone circle within the sarsen circle, a bluestone horseshoe within the sarsen horseshoe (fig. 95). This was the end of the building of Stonehenge, except for an extension of the Avenue one and a half miles to the River Avon. At last an excavation had made Stonehenge intelligible.

These three main phases could be slotted neatly into the Invasion Hypothesis as the work of three consecutive cultures: the Secondary Neolithic, the Beaker Folk and, finally, the Wessex Culture. Although the site had been continually reused, its meaning had changed over time. Excavation had avoided the very centre of the site but Atkinson believed that a wooden building had been constructed at the centre of Stonehenge I 'in which resided the numinous principle of the place, either as a disembodied presence or represented by some tangible object of worship and veneration'. The only evidence of ritual practices during this period came from the Aubrey Holes which were interpreted as ritual pits, used in a ritual designed 'to open the way to the chthonic deities, the Gods of the Nether World'.[2]

FIGURE 95.
Alan Sorrel's
reconstruction of
the final phase of
Stonehenge,
placed at around
1300 BC.
(*English Heritage
Photographic Library*)

The Beaker Folk changed the axis of Stonehenge. It appeared that they had changed the emphasis from the underworld of spirits to the sky because the Avenue was aligned to the midsummer sunrise. This presented the classic dichotomy between Neolithic and Bronze Age beliefs. Stonehenge III was more of a problem. Although the axis remained the same, implying the same skyward orientation, the unique lintelled circle and trilithons were interpreted as a fusion of the two previous cultures. The lintels were held in place by mortise and tenon joints, clearly a technique borrowed from carpentry. Moreover, the circle and trilithon horseshoe were suggestive of a wooden building. Did they therefore combine 'the stone circle of the Beaker cultures and the framed wooden shrine of the Secondary Neolithic, now no longer roofed but open to the sky?'[3]

Stonehenge is unique among stone circles because, among other things, it stands in a place where there is no natural supply of stone. So how were the stones brought there? There was no wheeled transport and there were no pack animals in prehistory. The only possible modes of transport seemed to be sledges over land and rafts on water. In the case of the bluestones the question of water transport was particularly important. If the stones really were taken from the Prescelly Mountains the only practical route was by sea. The idea of transporting bluestones up the Bristol Channel immediately called to mind Geoffrey of Monmouth's story of Utherpendragon bringing the stones across from Ireland, and raised the suggestion that Geoffrey had latched on to some distant folk memory of the actual building of Stonehenge.

The largest of the Welsh stones at Stonehenge is the Altar Stone, weighing over six tons. Before it was dressed it weighed nearer seven tons. With dug-out canoes well attested in Neolithic Britain, Atkinson calculated that three canoes lashed together side by side would have been able to take the weight of most of the foreign stones. The theory was tested in a BBC television programme broadcast in 1954, where three dug-out canoes made of elm were floated on the River Avon near Salisbury, then a replica bluestone made of reinforced concrete was lowered on to it. Some local schoolboys acted as the crew and floated up and down the river as easily as students punting on the Cherwell in Oxford.

In contrast, the stones could not be moved over land without breaking sweat. In the same broadcast, an experiment with a sledge pulling the replica bluestone was also tried. Where one schoolboy could punt the raft along the river fourteen boys were needed to drag the sledge on rollers. But the bluestones are the small fry, whereas the heaviest of the sarsens weigh in the region of fifty tons. Atkinson reckoned they would have needed 1100 men to move them effectively, and that the twenty-four mile journey could not have been completed in much under nine weeks.

The thought of so many people engaged in the work brought the question of social organisation into play. Surely no one but the rich Wessex chieftains could 'command the immense resources of labour and craftsmanship necessary for the building of Stonehenge III', and yet 'for all their evident power and wealth . . . these men were essentially barbarians'.[4] To explain its incomparable refinement Atkinson looked further afield for its influences, and this inevitably led him to Mycenae. For example, the Lion Gate at Mycenae is very similar to the trilithons at Stonehenge in appearance, and the lintel is held in place by mortise and tenon joints. Trade contacts between the two areas seemed well attested. The link was further cemented, however, by a sensational discovery made by Atkinson in 1953 as he was preparing to photograph the graffiti on one of the stones. Having waited for the angle of the sun to show the engraving in relief, he noticed beneath it the carving of a dagger and four axe-heads. More axe-head carvings were soon found on two other stones, and the best preserved of them seemed to be representations of a type made in Ireland in the Bronze Age. But the significant find was the dagger: it looked like a type known only from Mycenae and had been in use until about 1500 BC.

This led Atkinson into the belief that the architect of Stonehenge was quite possibly Mycenaean. He was either 'the skilled servant of a far-voyaging Mycenaean prince' or was working 'at the behest of a barbarian British king, whose voice and gifts spoke loudly enough to be heard even in the cities of the Mediterranean'.[5] And so Stonehenge, in the imagination of an archaeologist who had studied classics at Oxford, stood as a symbol 'of the first incorporation of Britain, however transitory, within the orbit of the Mediterranean world, the cradle of European civilisation'.[6]

Stonehenge was the only monument that could be assigned to the Wessex Culture, which therefore was not the expression of the common will but imposed from above.

FIGURE 96. How the Stonehenge lintels were raised. A reconstruction based on the work of Richard Atkinson. In 1996 the BBC filmed a method of raising the uprights by means of an A-frame. (*English Heritage Photographic Library*)

Atkinson believed that Stonehenge is 'evidence for the concentration of political power . . . in the hands of a single man, who alone could create and maintain the conditions necessary for this great undertaking'. But who he was, and where he came from, would remain unknown – 'yet who but he should sleep, like Arthur or Barbarossa, in the quiet darkness of a sarsen vault beneath the mountainous pile of Silbury Hill? And is not Stonehenge itself his memorial?'[7]

As luck would have it, Atkinson was given the opportunity to answer one of these questions in the last of the great Wessex excavations. In 1967 the BBC announced that it was to sponsor a three-year dig at Silbury Hill. After his much acclaimed work at Stonehenge Richard Atkinson, now of University College, Cardiff, was the obvious person to take charge. However, the warning signs were there from the beginning. Silbury Hill remained one of the enigmas of prehistoric Britain. If it was classed as a barrow it was certainly no ordinary barrow; and if it contained a grave it was certainly the grave of an extraordinary person. The sponsors evidently hoped for something special, otherwise there would be no point broadcasting the events live on television. In a press release a spokesman for the BBC positively gushed with anticipation: 'We shall be deploying every latest scientific skill and modern resources to solve the mystery: the unfolding of the story on BBC 2 should be one of the major events in television over the next three years.'[8] Although it was not mentioned specifically, the possibility of finding the grave of some Wessex supremo was the hope and expectation of the project.

The prognosis was not good. In 1776 a shaft had been dug by Cornish tin miners from the top of the mound to the bottom, but nothing had been found. In 1849 the Archaeological Institute sponsored a tunnelling to the centre, but again found nothing. In 1867 a couple of trenches were dug into the mound to prove that it was prehistoric, an absurd and vain attempt to shut James Fergusson up. Finally, a resistivity survey in 1959 failed to locate a stone chamber. Atkinson was careful to point these facts out, but nevertheless got carried away in the excitement. He talked of driving a new tunnel to link up with the old, after which the interior of the mound would be 'supplied with a light railway, mains lighting, forced-air supply and telephones'. It sounded more like a Journey to the Centre of the Earth.

Viewers tuned in expecting to see the discovery of Britain's own Tutankhamun. But it was not to be. In the centre of this great mound, the largest prehistoric mound in Europe, was another mound. In its construction a low mound of turf covered with soil had first been built inside a fence, but immediately this was enlarged by the raising of the great mound. It had been built up in terraces, strengthened by chalk retaining walls. Lastly, the terraces were concealed by an outer skin of chalk to give it a smooth profile. For Atkinson and his colleagues this discovery was more success than failure, but it was not prime time television. As the viewing public sighed and put the kettle on, archaeology had unwittingly become a victim of its own publicity.

The timing of the Silbury anti-climax was not without its significance. By 1970 the new technique of radiocarbon dating had undone the Diffusionist framework of pre-historic Europe. A radiocarbon date of 2600 BC for Silbury was far earlier than Childe's generation thought possible, and it also showed that Silbury Hill belonged to the Neolithic, not the Bronze Age. Stonehenge III was also found to be much earlier than expected, so the brief flirtation between Wessex and Mycenae was at an end. The major task facing archaeologists at the beginning of the 1970s was to replace Diffusionist thinking with a fresh approach which would allow a new archaeology to be written. On a popular level, they also had to compete with alternative ideas that had come to fruition in the 1960s. Theories about advanced astronomy at stone circles, and the linking of prehistoric sites by invisible lines of terrestrial energy – leys, now became better known than the orthodox views they so bluntly contradicted.

17

The Sun and the Stars

The standing stones of Callanish are the most impressive of a group of stone circles clustering around the sheltered waters of Loch Roag on the island of Lewis (fig. 97). Although the site is visible from a considerable distance, the circle itself is surprisingly small, only forty feet across, but built with tall stone slabs, with a taller stone in the centre. Radiating from the circle are three rows of stones, and to the north is a double row of stones (or avenue if you prefer), giving the whole configuration a rough, upturned cruciform shape.

In 1808 Thomas Headrick claimed that the circle was laid out to the cardinal points of north, south, east and west, which is not in fact true. However, as Henry Callender pointed out in 1857, the fact that 'its position was chosen and laid down by astronomical observation can easily be demonstrated by visiting the spot on a clear night, when it will be found that, by bringing the upper part of the single line of stones extending to the south to bear upon the top of the large stone in the centre of the circle, the apex of that stone coincides exactly with the pole star'.[1] It is probably the most convincing orientation of stones in prehistoric Britain. Meanwhile Headrick went on to claim that the stones marked 'the rising of the sun, moon and stars, the seasons of the year, and even the hours or divisions of the day'. He was therefore suggesting that specific astronomical observations were made at Callanish and that they could be used to construct a calendar.

Neither of these ideas was new. The antiquaries of the eighteenth and nineteenth centuries were fond of penetrating the obscure numerical symbolism embodied in stone circles to prove that they were used as calendars, and Stukeley had earlier shown that Stonehenge was oriented to the summer solstice. But whereas the astronomical symbolism beloved of the Romantics faded away, the concept of astronomical orientation was to become a subject in its own right. In the wake of Sir Norman Lockyer, who gave the subject its scientific focus, the study of ancient astronomy was termed astro-archaeology, although today it is defined more accurately as archaeo-astronomy. It is a branch of archaeological research that requires specialist knowledge and, partly as a result of this, has been noticeably influenced by the contributions of individual researchers – principally Norman Lockyer, Gerald Hawkins and Alexander Thom – working independently of each other and of mainstream theories.

Before we delve deeper into astronomical theories, there is the little problem of technical details. One of the criticisms repeatedly levelled at Sir Norman Lockyer by archaeologists was that he did not know anything about archaeology. In turn Lockyer bemoaned the ignorance of archaeologists regarding all things astronomical. In a history of ideas we need not go into the more theoretical aspects of astronomical cycles, but we do need to understand something of the movements of the sun, the stars and later the moon, as seen by an observer on the ground.

Most of us know that the Earth's axis is tilted in relation to the sun. Even if we cannot explain the mechanics of the Earth's orbit we know the effect that this tilt produces – warm summers, cold winters, and long summer days with long winter nights. The further north or south you travel from the Equator, the more extreme the difference between summer and winter becomes.

FIGURE 97. Callanish in the Outer Hebrides has attracted astronomical speculation since the early nineteenth century. The avenue to the south is oriented on a true north–south axis. (*Crown Copyright: RCAHM Scotland*)

On two days of the year the sun rises in the east and sets in the west. These are the equinoxes, which in our modern calendar are 21 March and 23 September. During the spring and summer months the sun rises and sets north of a line due east–west, and the days are longer than the nights. During the autumn and winter months the reverse is true – the sun rises and sets south of line due east–west, and the nights are longer than the days. The longest day is the summer solstice, when the sun rises and sets in its most northerly position, when daylight hours are longest and when the midday sun reaches its highest point in the sky. The shortest day is therefore the winter solstice, when the reverse is true. The solstices are six months apart, the sun moving gradually from one extreme to the other. Midway between the solstices are the equinoxes, so the solar year is naturally divided into four quarters, although they are not quite equal because the Earth's orbit is not a circle.

There are two possible ways of observing the changes in the sun's position throughout the year, observations which would enable a calendar to be constructed. The first method is to use a sundial, by erecting a tall pole, or gnomon, and reading the shadows it casts. At midday the sun is at due south, so its shadow runs on a true north–south line; the time during the rest of the day is measured according to the amount of deviation from this north–south axis. The time of year can also be calculated by measuring the length of the shadow at midday. The winter solstice is the shortest day: the sun is at its lowest point in the midday sky and will therefore cast the longest shadow. However, in practice, it is very difficult to measure this. To allow for the minuscule changes in the length of the shadow approaching the solstices a tall gnomon is needed but, unfortunately, the taller the pole the more blurred the edges of its shadow become.

During the nineteenth century the idea of gnomons in ancient Britain enjoyed a measure of popularity, suggested partly by their use in India. The Reverend Edward Duke thought one had been erected at Avebury, while in 1899 Dr Alfred Eddowes claimed that a grooved bluestone near the centre of Stonehenge was used to support a pole which served as the gnomon for a giant sundial. In *The Rational Almanac*, published in 1902, Moses Cotsworth, from York, calculated that the Egyptian pyramids could, by means of the shadows they cast, accurately record the time of day, the progress of the seasons and the true length of the year. Back in England he calculated that Silbury Hill was surmounted by a gnomon 95 feet tall which cast a shadow on to the artificially levelled ground to the north. Midwinter was determined by the midday sun casting the tip of its shadow on to a marker stone. Cotsworth determined the exact spot where this marker lay then, with one of the cries of 'Eureka' exclaimed regularly in the history of archaeo-astronomy, he found it – a small boulder carved with many symbols, including a fish.

There is another, potentially more accurate, method of charting the course of the solar year, one which by common consent would have been used in prehistory, always assuming astronomical observations were made. That is to observe the place on the horizon where the sun rises or sets, and to set up a foresight on the horizon behind which the sun will rise or set on important days such as the solstices. The Heel Stone at Stonehenge is the most famous of these foresights, but unfortunately is not a good example. In theory the further the foresight is away from the observing position, or backsight, the more accurate the alignment will be. Near the equinoxes the sun's rising and setting positions change noticeably from day to day, but near the solstices the changes are minuscule and much more difficult to detect by eye.

Unfortunately for the astronomers, their task was not simply a case of observing the sunrises and sunsets at the solstices to see if they corresponded with the alignments suggested by the stones. Standing at a fixed position the sun would appear to rise from a slightly different place on the horizon from one millennium to the next, due to changes in the Earth's axial tilt in relation to the sun. This is known as the Obliquity of the Ecliptic. In 1500 BC, on the basis of the present rate of change in the obliquity, the summer solstice sunrise in the latitudes of southern England was about half a degree further away from its present equinoctial position. This may not seem very much in theory but, in practice, means that precise alignments made 4000 years ago can now only be verified by calculation.

The early astronomers were also looking for alignments made to the stars – Lockyer knew, for example, that the Egyptian New Year was associated with the rising of Sirius and wondered if a similar practice existed in Britain. The Precession of the Equinoxes is the astronomical cycle which accounts for the alteration in the positions of the stars. It takes about 26,000 years to complete a full cycle, but the shifts of a star along the horizon during this period become quite marked as the centuries progress. Lockyer, and later Alexander Thom, hoped that once they had identified which star they were looking for they would be able to date individual sites to within a range of 100 years or so. This had already been attempted at Stonehenge by J. H. Broome in 1869. He dated the monument to 977 BC, when Sirius rose over the Heel Stone.

As early as 1796 Henry Wansey had written: 'Stonehenge stands in the best situation possible for observing the heavenly bodies, as there is an horizon nearly three miles distant on all sides; and on either distant hill trees might have been planted as to have measured any number of degrees of a circle, so as to calculate the right ascension or declination of a star or planet.' The isolation of Stonehenge on Salisbury Plain is something every visitor will notice, but few people also notice as they walk up to look at the sarsen circle that there are two stones, not four feet tall, standing on the inner perimeter of the bank. They certainly do not look very important, but originally there were four of them, known as the Station Stones, and they formed very nearly a perfect rectangle. It was the Edward Duke, in his 1846 *Druidical Temples*, who first noted that the shorter sides of the rectangle pointed one to midsummer sunrise, the other to midwinter sunset. Although this was reiterated in Lewis Gidley's *Stonehenge* of 1873, the tide of opinion was by this time against astronomical theories. Given the fantastical claims made by John Wood, Dr Smith and their friends, few archaeologists had an open mind on astronomy. Furthermore, now that excavation had become the principal means of reconstructing the past, the occasional burials found at stone circles were thought to be good evidence that they were sepulchral monuments.

When, in the 1880s, A. L. Lewis began arguing the case for an astronomical interpretation, he had repeatedly to emphasise that stone circles were temples for the living; and that because graves are found in churches it does not mean that churches are constructed for the dead. Lewis made a systematic, but by no means scientific, study of British stone circles, and all subsequent studies have followed to some extent his ideas. He noticed that stone circles tended to be oriented to the north or north east. For example Stonehenge and the Rollright Stones have an outlying stone to the north east – the Heel Stone and the King Stone respectively – while the Swinside circle in Cumbria is oriented toward three small hills. Due north of the Fernacre circle on Bodmin Moor in Cornwall is the prominent rock outcrop of Rough Tor. The northerly orientations signified alignments to the rising stars, while the north-easterly orientations were alignments to the summer solstice. He concluded that they were the work of two distinct immigrant cultures: star-worshippers and sun-worshippers.[2] Like many of his contemporaries, his researches took him first to Cornwall. He then visited the less accessible stone circles of Scotland, where he found two distinct variations in circle types, which apparently confirmed his theory that there were two skywatching races in ancient Britain. The Recumbent Stone circles of Aberdeenshire, with their recumbent stone placed on or near due south, were star temples, while the nearby Clava cairns, with their entrance passages running roughly north east to south west, were solar temples.[3]

Lewis was the first archaeo-astronomer to give the azimuths, or compass bearings, for his orientations, but they were always rounded to the nearest degree. If later researchers have found his method insufficiently accurate, Lewis was not suggesting pinpoint accuracy for any of his alignments. The stone circles were oriented in the general direction of the rising sun or stars, or perhaps merely to the direction of the dawn light, and the purpose was symbolic, not scientific. His moderate views would be deemed acceptable by many archaeologists today but, come the turn of the century, his work was to be overshadowed by the more extravagant theories of Sir Norman Lockyer.

18

Sir Norman Lockyer and his Followers

The year 1894 saw the publication of two literary landmarks in archaeo-astronomy. *Standing Stones and Maeshowe of Stenness* was a pamphlet written by Magnus Spence about an impressive but none the less little known group of prehistoric structures on the fringes of the ancient world. The second was Sir Norman Lockyer's *The Dawn of Astronomy*, a study of the orientation of Egyptian temples. Apart from their interest in astronomy, the authors appear to have had little in common. Magnus Spence was a schoolmaster in the Orkney Islands; Lockyer was a Professor at the Royal College of Science, Director of the Solar Physics Observatory and the founding editor of the scientific current affairs journal *Nature*. In 1870 he had detected lines of an unknown element in the sun which we now call helium, a discovery which gained him international recognition as a scientist.

The coincidence of their publication marks a turning-point in the history of our study. Spence belonged to the tradition of astronomical enquiry started by Stukeley. He was an informed amateur, as confident researching history and folklore in a library as he was working in the field measuring angles with a sextant. Of course Lockyer shared these qualities: but he was also a polymath, the epitome of the learned gentleman, author of such diverse books as *Chemistry of the Sun*, *Surveying for Archaeologists*, *Tennyson as a Student and a Poet of Nature* and *The Rules of Golf*. However, his talk of azimuths and declinations, obliquity and precession, all quite incomprehensible to the casual reader, signalled a changing world of intellectual enquiry. Suddenly, we are listening to the voice of the expert.

He had long been interested in ancient astronomy – he had made a survey of the Rollright Stones in 1868 – but his most active phase began after a trip to Greece in 1890, where he was struck by the difference in orientation between the old and new Parthenon. He was already aware of work by German and French archaeologists on the orientation of temples and pyramids in Egypt, and he knew the tradition that churches were oriented toward sunrise on the feast day of their patron saint. The orthodox view of Egyptian temples was that they were oriented either to the River Nile or some other topographical feature. Lockyer wondered whether they had astronomical orientations – after all Egyptian religion was largely preoccupied by the sun god Ra – and during the early 1890s he spent several seasons in Egypt testing his hypothesis.

Although he surveyed a large number of sites, he found seven temples oriented toward the star Sirius but only a disappointing six temples oriented to the sun. Lockyer had enough self-belief to consider this a triumph and, although many Egyptologists found him unconvincing, he did have his followers. His astronomical alignments were not strictly speaking based on observing distant foresights, but on orientations whereby, on the day of the solstice, the first gleam of light shone down the axis of the temple. He had some supporting evidence in the form of inscriptions, found on the walls of Karnak, Denderah, Edfu and other temples, to show how these axes were laid out. This was by a foundation ceremony which he translated as the 'stretching of the cord'. An outstretched rope was used to make an alignment to the rising sun on a particular day of the year, then stakes were driven into the ground at either end, thereby fixing the axis of the temple.

Lockyer assumed that the axis of Stonehenge was laid out in a similar way. In 1901 he went to Stonehenge with a friend and colleague, F. C. Penrose, to attempt to calculate the date of its construction. If he could find the axis of Stonehenge he could then calculate its azimuth and work out when the midsummer sun rose exactly over that point. Flinders Petrie had already tried to date Stonehenge in the same way but, by faulty reasoning about changes in the Obliquity of the Ecliptic, he had come up with the impossible date of AD 730. Lockyer, in contrast, could not be faulted on his astronomy. He chose the axis of Stonehenge as the mid line of the Avenue and when he extended this line on a map he found it very nearly passed through an Ordnance Survey bench-mark on Sidbury Hill, eight miles away. Inexplicably, he chose a line to the bench-mark – set up in the nineteenth century and not even visible from Stonehenge – as the axis, and deduced the date from that.

It was an obvious error, as has been pointed out on many occasions; the kind of mistake he made when his approach became too sloppy. Even so, he came up with the plausible date of 1680 BC ± 200 years.[1] This happened to agree very nicely with the date of 1800 BC which was given, in the same year 1901, by William Gowland, who had been examining artefacts revealed by excavation. Gowland deduced that the monument was Neolithic but his date of 1800 BC was, educated or not, guesswork. Nevertheless, Lockyer congratulated himself on this apparent endorsement of his methods.

The date of Stonehenge was a minor issue. The greater challenge was in proving that British stone monuments, primarily stone circles, were systematically aligned to the rising of the sun and the stars. One of his collaborators once wrote to Lockyer that, 'I seem never to see anything until you point out what to look for'.[2] Lockyer could have said this himself, for he was not entirely an original thinker; his achievement was to synthesise and expand on the disconnected theories of previous writers.

He was fully aware of the work already done by Lewis, but where Lewis gave approximate azimuths for his orientations Lockyer was arguing for precise alignments. He had also read *L'astronomie préhistorique,* a study by Félix Gaillard on the orientation and alignments of the chambered tombs and avenues at Carnac in Brittany. Another Frenchman, Lieutenant de Vasseau Devoir of the French Navy, stationed at Brest, had studied the Breton sites and found that they were not only oriented to the solstices but also to sunrises on the quarter days of the Celtic calendar, what Lockyer was to call the May Year. These are the first days of May, August, November and February, the Celtic festivals of Beltane, Lugnasad, Samhain and Imbolc; known in the Christian era as May Day, Lammas, All Hallows and Candlemas. Lockyer was able to 'prove' Devoir's hypothesis at the first site where he tested it, Stonehenge. An analysis of the Station Stones gave him alignments to the May sunset and the November sunrise, as well as a repeat of the midsummer sunrise of the Avenue. He was later to argue that the earliest stone circle builders used a solar calendar for worship, as well as to construct a farmer's almanac, and that the calendar was based on the May Year. Much later this was replaced by solstice worship with Stonehenge the perfect illustration of this change – the Station Stones belonged to an earlier temple which was later reconstructed with a new axis to the midsummer sunrise. The reuse of temple sites, with a rededication and a new orientation, was a well-authenticated practice in ancient Egypt.

Arguably the most important influence on Lockyer's thinking was Magnus Spence's Stenness pamphlet. Orkney was too remote for Lockyer to travel to in person, so his study of it was based on Spence's survey drawings and a large-scale Ordnance Survey map. Lockyer radically revised Spence's astronomy (one line that Spence claimed marked midwinter sunrise Lockyer reinterpreted as November sunrise), but more importantly Spence showed Lockyer a way of looking at the interrelationship of sites in the landscape (fig. 98). The most important of the astronomical alignments at Stenness was deemed to be a straight line which links three sites – the Ring of Brodgar and two standing stones called the Watchstone and the Barnhouse. It was claimed that a famous holed stone, the Stone of Odin, also stood on this alignment before it was destroyed. A line from the Watchstone to the Maes Howe chambered cairn signalled the equinox sunset; and a line from Maes Howe south west to the Barnhouse stone, which according to Spence signalled the winter solstice, was according to Lockyer 'for the exchange of signals', whatever that means.

In discovering and describing an interrelationship of sites Lockyer was years ahead of his time, although maybe Spence should take the credit for seeing it first. Here was a ritual landscape, a place where stones and cairns were carefully sited in relation to one another. While it was a concept he did not make the most of, and he would never have approved the phrase 'ritual landscape' anyway, Lockyer had evolved a way of looking at the landscape for astronomical alignments which during his visit to Cornwall began to pay dividends. Standing inside a stone circle he looked to the foresights on the horizon, usually a standing stone, but sometimes a barrow.

Stonehenge and Stenness had failed to yield any alignments to the stars but in Cornwall Lockyer found plenty. Sightlines to the stars were to be, by general consensus, the least convincing element in Lockyer's theories. As the Reverend G. H. Engleheart put it in 1923: 'It was a suspicious circumstance in Sir Norman Lockyer's system that when the Sun did not explain the orientation of a stone circle, one star or another was adopted in its place.'[3] But the stars were necessary for Lockyer to make his cultural connections with ancient Egypt. In Egypt he had learned that the rise of certain stars was observed near dawn as 'warning stars', signalling to the priest to prepare the sunrise sacrifice. Similarly, there were stars rising near enough due north which were used as clock stars during the night.

Lockyer's main interest was in warning stars indicating the coming festival days. In Cornwall the stars were observed from the centre of stone circles like Tregeseal, the Merry Maidens and Boscawen-un. The Hurlers on Bodmin Moor were constructed to watch for the star Arcturus, which warned of the coming August festival. Lockyer soon believed he knew the reason why the site consists of three adjacent stone circles. Alignments to the stars have a limited lifespan because of the precession cycle, so he claimed that three successive circles had to be built to compensate for this. These he

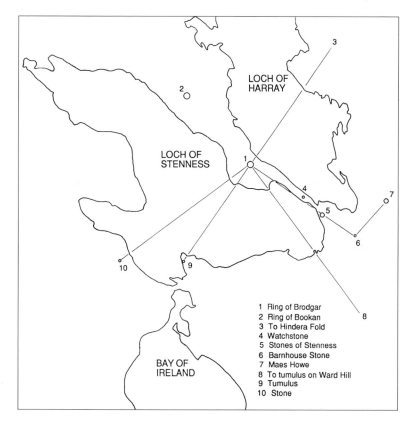

1 Ring of Brodgar
2 Ring of Bookan
3 To Hindera Fold
4 Watchstone
5 Stones of Stenness
6 Barnhouse Stone
7 Maes Howe
8 To tumulus on Ward Hill
9 Tumulus
10 Stone

FIGURE 98. Lockyer's study of astronomical alignments in Orkney, centred on the Ring of Brodgar stone circle, leant heavily on the earlier work of Magnus Spence. (*After Lockyer, 1909*)

FIGURE 99. Lockyer at work in Aberdeenshire, photographed by his wife.

gave dates of 2170, 2090 and 1900 BC. More evidence of stellar orientation came from the stone rows of Dartmoor. In particular, the two rows at Merrivale were aligned to the rising of the Pleiades (also known as the Seven Sisters) in 1580 and 1420 BC. Because it was roughly parallel on an Ordnance Survey map, Lockyer now thought there was enough evidence to declare that the Stonehenge Cursus was constructed as a processional way to watch the rising of the Pleiades in about 1950 BC.

At stone circles the observer would search out the sun on the horizon; in Egypt the solstitial sun penetrated the interior of the temples, the dawn light slowly creeping its way along the axis to the centre. This concept he applied to Britain to account for the orientations of chambered barrows and dolmens. Lockyer had some strange ideas about these sites. He argued that they were dwellings from where observations were made, presumably because it was too inclement for the astronomer-priests to venture outside. He also claimed that Neolithic man was ignorant of carpentry, so the huge blocking stones that sealed off the chambers were to Lockyer only the doors that kept out the elements. Perhaps the astronomer-priests made their observations lying flat out on the floor, having done their backs in trying to get the doors open. Furthermore, the bones found in these chambers were, to Lockyer, not human remains at all but the bones of animals cast aside after meals. Had Lockyer seen any of the skulls that had been excavated from these chambers he would have had to join with Dr Thurnam and Canon Greenwell in claiming that the ancient Britons were cannibalistic.

Lockyer studied several dolmens in Cornwall, plus some others in Wales, and gave precise astronomical orientations to many of these denuded, sometimes even incorrectly restored, monuments: places like Lanyon Quoit in Cornwall (fig. 100) and the Devil's Den near Avebury where only the bare bones of the original structure survives. This lapse into uncritical speculation earned him plenty of derision at the time but, typical of Lockyer, he managed to stumble on something interesting in the process. After surveying the chambered cairn of Bryn Celli Ddu in Anglesey he decided it was oriented

FIGURE 100.
Lanyon Quoit in
Cornwall, one of
many restored
chambered tombs
for which
Lockyer offered
unconvincing
astronomical
orientations.

to the midsummer sunrise. He then described the discovery inside the chamber of a single pillar, which he claimed was placed there so that the midsummer sun would shine down the passage and illuminate it for a few hours after sunrise. Unfortunately the stone stood outside the line of the passage so the sunlight could never have fallen on it, but Lockyer was speculating seventy years before archaeologists made a similar claim for Newgrange in Ireland, where a stone in the chamber *was* briefly illuminated at midwinter.[4] The idea that the sun was supposed to shine into the central chamber at a certain time of the year was inspired thinking, but was no more than half an answer. He wrote of Bryn Celli Ddu that 'the common people still suppose this to be the habitation of spirits' but could not develop the spiritual connection himself.

Lockyer was a scientist, not an ethnographer. When it came to examining the origins and meaning of ancient astronomy in Britain he relied heavily on the work of J. G. Frazer, whose *The Golden Bough*, an encyclopaedic synthesis of world ethnography, was published in twelve volumes between 1890 and 1915. In folklore Lockyer found plenty of confirmation of his theories. He laid particular emphasis on the fire festivals that took place at the summer solstice, or St John's Eve as it is known in the Christian era, and the Celtic festivals of Beltane and Samhain. According to Lockyer the myriad rites and superstitions connected with trees, wells and stones 'were not separate but part of one whole'. Via a long-winded and convoluted argument, he concluded that all folklore comes from a single source – the Sumerian and Semitic Babylonians, the source of all civilisation. Lockyer was therefore arguing his own brand of Diffusionism before the Manchester School and before Childe. The birth of civilisation and the birth of astronomy were naturally coeval, although astronomy did not come to Britain direct from Babylon, but rather via Egypt.

These expert Egyptians he called 'astronomer-priests', men who travelled from place to place orienting new temples on the correct alignment, in effect performing the 'stretching of the cord' ceremony he had picked up in Egypt. Because of his special knowledge the astronomer-priest became a holy figure. He functioned as the 'chief sacrificer, and guardian of the sacrificial altars and fires'. Everything connected with him was also deemed sacrosanct; holed stones now gained their curative properties, as did the streams and wells where he took water and where offerings were subsequently made. The astronomer was the holiest of holies, and people worshipped the ground he walked on, a very attractive idea to Lockyer. The astronomer-priest had a sub-class, 'priest-druids', who performed the wonted ceremonies once the astronomer-priests had laid out the correct alignment and moved on. The later Druids of classical literature were, according to Lockyer, the lineal descendants of the original astronomer- priests.

Lockyer had published a number of articles on his researches before, in his seventieth year, he published his results as *Stonehenge and other British Stone Monuments Astronomically Considered* in 1906. After its publication he persuaded the Royal Society to set up the Society for the Astronomical Study of Ancient Monuments. It soon had an active Cornish branch, and a season of observations from the Tregeseal stone circle followed.

There was also interest in his work in Wales. The Reverend J. Griffith was Vicar of Llangwm, a historian of the Welsh Gorsedd tradition and a student of ancient astronomy. He believed that the Welsh Gorsedd circles, which the bard Myvyr Morgannwg had identified over half a century earlier with the Neolithic stone circles, were oriented to mark the rising sun of the May Year. Griffith found little difficulty in gaining Lockyer's attention, and an article by Griffith duly appeared in *Nature* in 1907. In the same year Lockyer was invited to attend the National Eisteddfod of Wales which was to be held in Swansea. Every year a Gorsedd circle of nineteen stones was set up for the Eisteddfod. Lockyer, on whom the title of Gwyddon Pyrdain (meaning Britain's Man of Science) was conferred, was asked to speak from the central stone. Obviously flattered, Lockyer returned the compliment, saying that only recently he had been studying other circles of nineteen stones, that Tregeseal and Boscawen-un in Cornwall were places where similar assemblies had taken place for forty centuries, and that the Gorsedd was therefore probably the oldest continuing tradition on the planet. Griffith went further, saying that 'we are able to see at the Welsh National Eisteddfod in this twentieth century the actual use to which the temple observatory was put'.[5]

In Wales Lockyer advocated the formation of a society for the astronomical study of stone monuments, similar to the one in Cornwall, and subsequent to his Swansea visit he studied a number of Welsh monuments in the field. All this and more was included in a revised and extended edition of his *Stonehenge* which came out in 1909.

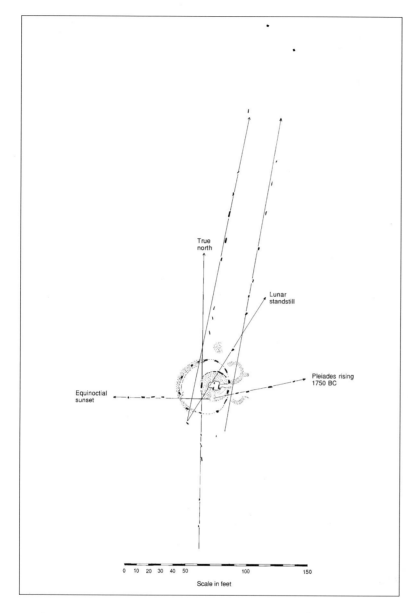

True
north

Lunar
standstill

Pleiades rising
1750 BC

Equinoctial
sunset

0 10 20 30 40 50   100   150
Scale in feet

FIGURE 101.
Boyle Somerville's
survey of
Callanish was the
first astronomical
study to suggest
alignment to the
moon.
(*After Somerville,
1912*)

In this volume he gave more of the same information, and none of his new research required his earlier conclusions to be revised. Only at Avebury did he encounter difficulties. Stukeley was a great admirer of the serpentine avenues at Avebury; Lockyer disliked them for the opposite reason – they were not straight and so messed up his theory. Just as Stukeley introduced a curve to the avenues at Callanish, so Lockyer put the Avebury avenues into the straitjacket of his preconceptions, joining them up with the two inner circles, claiming the bank and ditch were a later, non-astronomical addition. You can always make the evidence fit your theory if you are determined enough.

For nearly sixty years Lockyer's work remained the most comprehensive study of prehistoric astronomy in Britain. He had a number of collaborators but, although he generously acknowledged their contributions, none could assume the mantle of Gwyddon Pyrdain when, at seventy-three, the master opted for less demanding pursuits. One of the few who had the specialist knowledge to do so was Captain (later Rear-Admiral) Boyle Somerville, who, after reading Lockyer's *Stonehenge*, began surveying sites in Ireland. He then turned his attention to Scotland, beginning with a survey of Callanish in 1909 (fig. 101). He worked from the same premise as Lewis, that if Stonehenge had an orientation then so did other stone circles; and like Lockyer he looked for distant sightlines as the only way to record precise alignments.

According to Somerville, the initial purpose of these orientations was to create an agricultural calendar. But then, as society developed, so astronomy became more associated with religion. Although he believed the origins of ancient astronomy in Britain lay in the eastern Mediterranean, in most other respects his ideas diverged from those of Lockyer. In particular, Somerville noticed that barrows face roughly east. If the builders believed in death and resurrection then the dead would rise out of their tombs and be facing the rising sun or star. Chambered cairns and barrows became 'temples of the dead' whereby the cult of the dead and the cult of the heavens were reconciled. Later Somerville became a follower of the ley theory of Alfred Watkins and was an active member of the ley hunters' Straight Track Club. Meanwhile he had studied the construction of stone circles and deduced that most of them were not, and deliberately not, circles. Having surveyed twenty-seven (mostly Irish) circles with a theodolite, Somerville concluded that 'in not one case are the stones composing the ring placed in a true circle . . . the best that can be done is to draw two consecutive circles . . . within which the stones forming the ring may fall'.[6] He was not the first person to notice this but, significantly, it was from Somerville that Alexander Thom picked up the idea. Somerville also continued his interest in astronomical alignments. Given his track record on the fringes of archaeological thought, it is surprising to find him respectably delivering a lecture on orientation to the Society of Antiquaries in 1923 and writing an article on the subject for *Antiquity* four years later.

Sir Norman Lockyer died in 1920. To say that by this time archaeo-astronomy was out of fashion would be misleading, since it had never enjoyed more than a cult following. Although the subject was seriously debated, there was a general resistance to Lockyer's theories for two reasons. First, and only the British could have dreamt this one up, it was thought that astronomical observations were impossible in a country where it rains all the time. Secondly, and more seriously, was that a mastery of astronomy suggested, as Somerville put it, an 'unexpected degree of culture'. This is what became a thorn in the flesh of some professional archaeologists. *Stonehenge Today and Yesterday*, published in 1916 by Frank Stevens, Curator of Salisbury Museum, complained that 'the astronomer . . . will convert barrows into observation mounds, without reference to their uses and contents, and *without allowing for the ignorance of the period*' (my italics).[7] Sir Mortimer Wheeler, in his *Prehistoric and Roman Wales* of 1925, was not exactly dismissive, but was certainly very sceptical. The idea of astronomer-priests 'has led a generation of antiquaries to waste much time and ink upon the supposed astronomical properties of these circles'. He conceded that 'ritualistic observance of the great seasonal changes' might be 'sometimes indicated in the plan of the monument', but pointed out that 'not one of the Welsh circles has yet been found to conform with any nicety to a convincing astronomical formula'.[8]

Gordon Childe wavered on the subject. 'It is fantastic to imagine', he wrote in 1930, 'that the ill-clad inhabitants of these boreal isles should shiver night long in rain and gale, peering through the driving mists to note eclipses and planetary movements in our oft veiled skies.'[9] However, ten years later, writing about the Recumbent Stone circles of Aberdeenshire, he mused, 'the Recumbent Stone with its straight upper edge would form an admirable artificial horizon for observing heliacal risings of stars for calendrical regulation'.[10]

Other archaeologists were quite equitable in their approach. Orientation to events in the solar year seemed reasonable on religious or ceremonial grounds, but no archaeologist was going to flatter Neolithic and Bronze Age barbarians by calling them 'astronomers'. Nor were archaeologists prepared to accept that observations with the naked eye could be made with precision. In the first issue of the mainstream journal *Antiquity*, published in 1927, A. P. Trotter offered a critical appraisal of Lockyer's Stonehenge work. Trotter accepted the case for astronomical orientation, and accepted Lockyer's theory that it provided an agricultural calendar, but dismissed his argument that the alignments were precise enough to allow the date of Stonehenge to be calculated. The latter point was reiterated by R. J. C. Atkinson in his *Stonehenge* of 1956.

Atkinson remained interested in astronomy, although in the end it contributed little to his ideas about Stonehenge. Another Stonehenge archaeologist, R. S. Newall, who had worked on the excavations of the 1920s, suggested that it was not oriented to the midsummer sunrise but in the opposite direction, to midwinter sunset. The reasoning behind this was that the Avenue was evidently a processional way, and if a procession made its way down the Avenue it would have done so facing the sun – the deity being worshipped – rather than with the sun to its back. Thus Newall saw ancient astronomy as symbolic and connected with religious rites. When the astronomical debate flourished again in the 1960s Stonehenge was again at the centre of the controversy, but by this time the magic and religion had been replaced by eclipse predictors and Pythagorean triangles.

19

Stonehenge Decoded

The 1950s had been a good decade for Stonehenge studies. The excavations by Atkinson, Piggott and Stone had compensated for Colonel Hawley's poor showing in the 1920s, and the division of Stonehenge into three main periods of construction was a significant advance in knowledge, as well as being a triumph of archaeological technique. As to its purpose, Atkinson made several tentative suggestions concerning its use as a temple for fertility rites, dancing, propitiation of the gods; and secular uses like markets. In contrast to this steady advance, over the next decade the archaeologists and the astronomers were to clash in what became a very public showdown.

The first challenge to orthodox opinion came from two astronomers working independently of each other, a David and Goliath combination of C. A. Newham, a retired gas industry engineer from Yorkshire, and Dr Gerald Hawkins, Professor of Astronomy at Boston University. Both had begun their studies after visiting Stonehenge and reading Lockyer's work which, though flawed, they considered was at least methodologically correct. Newham and Hawkins came to remarkably similar conclusions, even though their working methods were markedly different. If Stonehenge had been oriented to the summer solstice, Hawkins wondered if it could also mark other celestial events. There were many alignments of stones which were potential sightlines, while the centre of the monument presented many controlled vistas through the sarsen horseshoe and circle. Hawkins decided to test whether they had any astronomical significance. Assuming that the third phase of Stonehenge was built in 1500 BC, he turned to his trusty assistant, an IBM 7090 computer, for the answer. The computer determined the azimuths and declinations of all the potential alignments but, although there were good correlations with sunrises and sunsets, many of the sightlines were outside the arc of the sun's rising and setting positions. Hawkins then tested to see whether these were possibly oriented to the rising of the stars or the planets, but the results were negative. Only when he calculated the declinations of the moon's risings and settings did it seem that he had hit the jackpot (fig. 102).

Newham had come to a similar conclusion. This was a new avenue for archaeo-astronomy, as Lockyer had confined his attentions to the sun and the stars. The first possible lunar alignment had been given by Somerville in his study of Callanish, but mixed in with the solar and stellar orientations it looked unimportant. Mindful of the criticisms levelled against Lockyer regarding his lack of archaeological knowledge, Newham made sure he was up to date on Stonehenge archaeology, even sending copies of his researches to R. S. Newall, and through him to Richard Atkinson. From these two he had an encouraging response. Newham, in turn, also had to make the archaeologists understand something of the moon's movements across the sky.

The moon is the brightest object in the night sky but, to untrained eyes, its path across the heavens seems haphazard and unpredictable. Repeated observations show that its movements are ordered and regular but, whereas it takes only a year to understand the motions of the sun, it takes nearly nineteen years to observe all the permutations of the moon's movements; and of course many more years to understand the pattern of those movements. Whereas the sun takes a year to travel from its most northerly and southerly positions and back again, it takes the moon only 27.32 days to move from its extreme northerly to extreme southerly position and back again. This 'lunar year' we call a month.

Although it is possible to observe the maximum northerly and southerly positions for each lunar month, these maxima are not constant. If, for example, a foresight were set up to mark the most northerly rising of the moon, in a few months the foresight would be useless because the most northerly moonrise would have shifted its position on the horizon. These extreme positions vary over a period of 18.61 years. Therefore every 18.61 years the moon reaches its most northerly and southerly positions on the horizon, which is known as a major standstill. At this time the angle between the northerly and

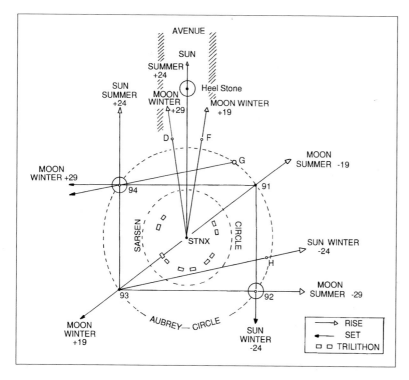

FIGURE 102.
Gerald Hawkins'
diagram of Stone-
henge sightlines,
first published in
Nature in 1963.
Baffling to the
uninitiated, such
diagrams were
part of the
Hawkins mystique.
(*After Hawkins,*
1963)

southerly risings is greatest, while 9.3 years later the angle between northerly and southerly positions is at its smallest. This is known as a minor standstill (fig. 103).

Hawkins argued that no society which practised astronomical observation would have worked in terms of 18.61 years. If their observations, and indeed their way of life, were based on a solar calendar, they would have had to round the figure up to nineteen. They could thus predict the year in which the moon would reach its most northerly and southerly positions, but after two lunar cycles they would have had to count only eighteen years. Thus to predict the lunar cycle the ancient astronomers counted nineteen, nineteen, eighteen, so three lunar cycles added up to fifty-six, a number which seemed to Hawkins to be of the utmost significance.

Nineteen is also an important lunar number. In the fifth century BC the Athenian astronomer Meton discovered that after a lapse of nineteen years the phases of the moon recurred on the same days of the same month (to within about two hours). Also there are very nearly 235 lunar months in nineteen Julian years (364.25 mean solar days). The nineteen-year cycle is quite an accurate one – only after 310 years do the new moons fall one day earlier than they should. The Metonic Cycle formed the basis

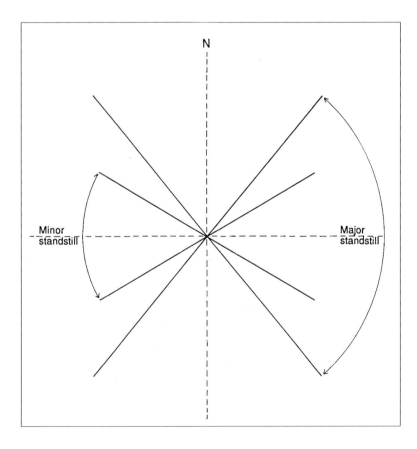

FIGURE 103.
The standstill positions of the moon over its 18.61 year cycle.

of the calendar used by the Seleucid Babylonian empire in antiquity, and also the Jewish and Christian calendars of the middle ages, particularly with regard to computing Easter. It is also mentioned in the *Histories* of Diodorus Siculus, in a passage about a race of northern people called the Hyperboreans.

While Diodorus wrote his work in about 8 BC, the passage concerning the Hyperboreans was based on an account written by Hecateus of Abdera in the fourth century BC. The Hyperboreans were described by many Greek authors, beginning with Aristeas in the seventh century BC. These classical writers were not, however, quite consistent on who the Hyperboreans were and where they lived. Herodotus thought they were a mythical race because they were described in terms of the Golden Age, but after Hecateus they were generally considered to live in the Celtic west. Quite apart from the who, what and where of the Hyperboreans, Hecateus and Diodorus certainly thought they were talking about the British Isles, because the land of Hyperboreans is described as an island across the sea from the land of the Celts:

> This island . . . is situated in the north and is inhabited by the Hyperboreans, who are called by that name because their home is beyond the point whence the north wind blows; and the island is both fertile and productive of every crop, and since it has an unusually temperate climate it produces two harvests each year. Moreover, the following legend is told concerning it: Leto [mother of Apollo and Artemis by Zeus] was born on this island, and for that reason Apollo is honoured among them above all other gods; and the inhabitants are looked upon as priests of Apollo, after a manner, since daily they praise this god continuously in song and honour him exceedingly. And there is also on this island both a magnificent sacred precinct of Apollo and a notable temple which is adorned with many votive offerings and is spherical in shape . . .
>
> They say also that the moon, as viewed from this island, appears to be but a little distance from the earth and to have upon it prominences, like those of the earth, which are visible to the eye. The account is also given that the god visits the island every nineteen years, the period in which the return of the stars to the same place in the heavens is accomplished; and for this reason the nineteen-year period is called by the Greeks the 'Year of Meton'.

How many people have been able to read this account of Britain and its spherical temple without thinking instantly of Stonehenge? And might not the sacred precinct of Apollo be Avebury? Perhaps, but to many the evidence is too good to be true. Whatever the accuracy of the account, it has certainly been generously embellished. Written by a Greek for a Greek audience, its gods conform to the Greek pantheon, and its infusion of fanciful travellers' tales with Golden Age myths is typical of classical history writing from Herodotus to Pliny. Stukeley thought this passage referred to

Stonehenge; John Wood insisted it was Bath and Stanton Drew. In the *Gentleman's Magazine* in 1849, the Reverend J. Bathurst-Deane suggested that the temple referred to was Avebury. The first astronomer to quote it was Somerville, who thought it was referring to Callanish, and perhaps he had the strongest case. In the Shetland Isles the lunar equivalent of the midnight sun can occur when, roughly every nineteen years, the moon never sets but merely brushes the northern skyline. Irish farmers also knew a period called Duibhre when, once every eighteen or nineteen years, the moon is so low in the sky that it fails to rise above the surrounding mountains. Newham and Hawkins both found in Diodorus a vindication of their own theories. After all, although layers of fabrication could be peeled away from it, it only needed 'spherical temple' and 'every nineteen years' to be genuine for the astronomers to have a case.

When it came to publication of their findings Newham, as an expert but none the less amateur astronomer, had nowhere to go. Atkinson suggested he try *Antiquity* but an outline of the proposed paper was rejected by the editor, Glyn Daniel, because it was too technical. An article eventually appeared in March 1963 in the *Yorkshire Post*, written in the form of an interview with a journalist. In 1964 Newham privately published his work in a pamphlet, *The Enigma of Stonehenge*. It raised not a flicker of interest. Hawkins meanwhile was able to get a paper printed, appropriately enough in Lockyer's old journal *Nature*, under the presumptuous title of 'Stonehenge Decoded'. It was published in October 1963 and the media response was instant. Hawkins had estimated that the probability of his correlations occurring by chance was about one in a million, and that the 4000-year-old secret of the stones had been unlocked in approximately one minute by an IBM 7090. This was good copy for newspapers and magazines, which quickly made Gerald Hawkins a household name throughout the western world. The idea was perfect for the 1960s: an ancient preoccupation with the moon and the stars made the ongoing space programmes of the sixties seem the logical conclusion to the first steps towards knowledge of outer space made by the builders of Stonehenge. The implication that only a computer could understand the stones was lapped up by a public in love with a world where technology promised exciting, limitless possibilities. Three decades later the only thing that Stonehenge and an IBM 7090 have in common is that they are both ancient monuments.

After these publications Newham and Hawkins discovered each other, but apart from a brief exchange of data they continued working independently. Hawkins was developing his theories of eclipse prediction, destined to become the most controversial and technical aspect of his work on Stonehenge. Eclipses occur when the sun, moon and Earth are aligned on the same plane, and can only happen at full or new moon. A new moon will cause a solar eclipse, while a full moon will result in a lunar eclipse. The latter is the easiest to observe, as a lunar eclipse is visible anywhere on the Earth where the moon is above the horizon. A solar eclipse is only visible across a very narrow track of land at one time.

At Stonehenge the midwinter sun sets almost exactly opposite the point where the midsummer sun rises (the angle is actually 178°). Hawkins pointed out that whenever the midwinter moon (i.e. the full moon nearest the winter solstice) rose over the Heel Stone there would be a lunar eclipse. By this reckoning the winter moon rose over the Heel Stone twice in the lunar cycle of 18.61 years, or once every 9.305 years. In practical terms Hawkins argued that eclipses were expected every 9, 9, 10, 9, 9, 10 years and so on. Doubling these up gave eighteen, nineteen and nineteen years, which added together make fifty-six. Now, fifty-six is the number of Aubrey Holes at Stonehenge, those evenly spaced pits which had been dug just inside the bank and which never held stones. Hawkins argued that six marker stones could be placed in or by the Aubrey Holes, spaced at the intervals given above, then each moved anticlockwise one space per year (fig. 104). A specific Aubrey Hole would be used to signify an eclipse, which would occur every time a marker stone was by that particular hole. However, only about half of these lunar eclipses would have been visible from Stonehenge, so the moonrise over the Heel Stone acted merely as a warning. In practice there would be a lunar eclipse at midwinter about once every nineteen years. His counting method could also predict eclipses at harvest time every 18.61 years, or in practice every nineteen, nineteen, then eighteen years by using a different Aubrey Hole as signifier. This, according to Hawkins and his IBM, was the function of the Aubrey Holes to which nobody had yet provided a valid explanation: they were a Neolithic computer. It had taken a machine to understand a machine. Hawkins pointed out, on more than one

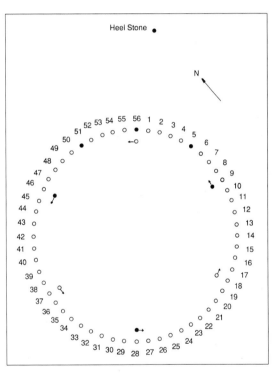

FIGURE 104. Stonehenge as a Neolithic computer. Using the fifty-six Aubrey Holes, six marker stones, each moved anti-clockwise one hole per year, would accurately predict all the major lunar events. When a stone is at Hole 56 there will be a lunar eclipse during the month of the winter solstice. A white stone at Hole 51 or 5 computes the lunar standstill years.
(*After Hawkins, 1966*)

occasion, that the only way to *prove* his theory was to use another machine, a time machine.

The use of Stonehenge as an eclipse predictor was an ingenious suggestion. The science of eclipse prediction was known in the ancient world, and priests who could calculate when they would take place were hallowed men. There is a story (whether true or not) of two Chinese court astronomers, Hsi and Ho, who failed to predict the solar eclipse of 2137 BC and were promptly executed. While the Babylonians had succeeded in predicting lunar eclipses by about 500 BC, Hawkins was claiming that Stonehenge had been used for eclipse prediction a thousand years earlier.

Hawkins aired his new hypothesis in *Nature* in 1964, at the same time as he was making a documentary for CBS Television called *The Mystery of Stonehenge*. In 1965 he published his book *Stonehenge Decoded* (in collaboration with J. B. White). The book comprised his two articles padded out with background material and the story of his own adventures with the computer. Archaeologists found his arguments glib and objected to his tabloid style of writing. The first section of the book deals with the archaeological and historical background to Stonehenge. Not only was it a poor and inaccurate paraphrase of previous publications, mainly Atkinson's, it reproduced copyright illustrations without permission. In the chapter dealing with eclipses Hawkins then made such arrogant claims as 'I think I have put forward the best theory to account for the . . . 56 Aubreys, the 59 bluestones' etc, and 'I think there is little else in these areas that can be discovered at Stonehenge'.[1] This tone of scarcely concealed smugness was guaranteed to irritate archaeologists, but they could not deny that, especially with the media attention he received, Hawkins had presented a strong challenge to the orthodox view of so-called 'primitive' society. In this he had somehow succeeded where Lockyer had failed, and his ideas had developed immeasurably from the agricultural calendars of Lockyer and Somerville. According to Hawkins, Stonehenge owed nothing to the Mediterranean world; it was built by a people possessing hitherto undreamed of intellectual powers. This was in direct contradiction to the Diffusionist theory that had dominated archaeological thinking for nearly half a century.

The archaeologists fought back, but far from defending a lost cause they found Hawkins genuinely unconvincing. In a review wittily titled 'Moonshine on Stonehenge', published in *Antiquity* in 1966, Atkinson severely criticised not only the conclusions but also the method and manner of the book. Instead of making his own survey Hawkins had used two small-scale Ministry of Works plans, one of which he got from the back of the official guide book to the monument. Also the margin of error he allowed of 2° meant that the Heel Stone could be moved twelve feet to the north east without affecting Hawkins' claim that it marked the midsummer sunrise. Finally Atkinson turned on the computer: 'The use of a computer . . . has no bearing on the validity, or otherwise, of the results obtained. What matters is the reliability of the data on which the computer operates.'[2] All in all Hawkins' scholarship was dismissed as tendentious and sloppy.

On the subject of Stonehenge as a Neolithic computer, Newham called it an 'ingenuous flight of imagination'. He also pointed out that there was no such thing as a fifty-six-year eclipse cycle, so by implication Hawkins' theory of the Aubrey Holes was flawed. But Hawkins found an ally in Professor Sir Fred Hoyle, the Cambridge cosmologist and a science fiction writer. Hoyle accepted Hawkins' theories in general terms. He also, in *Antiquity*, which had rapidly become the forum for discussion of astronomical issues, mused on the subject of eclipse prediction. After a bewildering jungle of algebraic formulae, Hoyle decided that Stonehenge was built by an isolated community, or gene pool, who lived near Stonehenge in 2000 BC and who possessed extraordinary mental gifts, a biological Golden Age soiled by gradual inter-marriage with inferior immigrants such as the Beaker People. He also showed a different way in which the Aubrey Holes could be used as an eclipse pre-dictor (fig. 105). The trouble with his theory, though, was that for the builders of Stonehenge it required a greater level of conceptual abstraction than even Hawkins had suggested. They had to know that the moon orbited the Earth, rather than merely crossed the sky; that night and day was caused by the Earth spinning on its axis; and that eclipses only occur when the moon is at one of its two nodes – the points where the planes of the terrestrial and lunar orbits intersect. If all this seemed fantastical, Hoyle summed it up by saying 'a veritable Newton or Einstein must have been at work'. Well, why not? Even so, some people thought Hoyle was getting just a bit carried away.

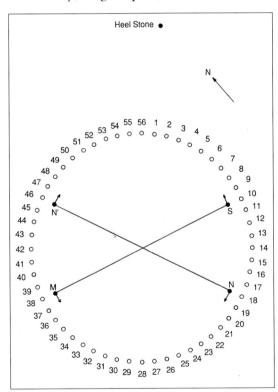

FIGURE 105. Hoyle's diagram of Stonehenge eclipse prediction. M is moved anti-clockwise one hole every half day; S is moved anti-clockwise one hole every thirteen half-days; N and N' (the nodes of the moon's orbit) are moved clockwise three holes each year. A lunar eclipse will occur when M and S coincide with the nodal positions. (*After Hoyle, 1977*)

Jacquetta Hawkes began her refuta-tion of Hoyle, in *Antiquity*, 'Every age has the Stonehenge it deserves – or desires.'[3] The article was the main response of the archaeologists to the astronomers. The gist of her argument was that Stonehenge was built for ritual, not intellectual purposes, and that the astronomical theories flatly contradicted the archaeological evidence. The major weakness in the Hawkins/Hoyle thesis, however, was that they had only considered one of 900 or so stone circles in the British Isles. Hoyle's vision of Wessex of 2000 BC as a community of gifted scientists, a kind of Neolithic Oxbridge, could perhaps only have been imagined by someone living amid the ivory towers of Cambridge. Hawkins meanwhile was more sensitive to this criticism, but his attempts to answer it were half-hearted. He made a study of Callanish based on Somerville's survey, producing the same kind of solar and lunar alignments that he found at Stonehenge, but these had to be seriously modified after he got round to visiting the site. He also referred to the work of Alexander Thom, whose methods and theories were almost the antithesis of those of Hawkins.

Amid the considerable wave of public and academic interest in the Hawkins/Hoyle debate the work of C. A. Newham was completely overshadowed. When he belatedly contributed an article on Stonehenge to *Nature*, in 1966, it followed directly after an article by the more illustrious Hoyle. Yet Newham made the greatest effort to bridge the gap between archaeologists and astronomers by a collaboration between the two disciplines. Glyn Daniel, editor of *Antiquity*, wrote of Hawkins: 'We all feel disinclined to listen to a man who has not bothered to listen carefully to archaeologists and learn what they have to say.'[4] Ironically, Daniel had been equally guilty when he had rejected Newham's work for *Antiquity*. In contrast, archaeologists continued to refer to Newham with more respect than they showed for Hawkins and Hoyle. In the guide book to Stonehenge written by R. S. Newall the work of Newham was respectfully discussed, while Hawkins' contribution was politely brushed aside. Not that Hawkins necessarily minded – infamy brings a certain kudos. In any case his *Stonehenge Decoded* was that rare thing in archaeological literature, a bestseller.

New theories claiming to have solved once and for all the mystery of the stones are regularly launched on a usually indifferent world. Hawkins was one of the lucky ones, enjoying his fifteen minutes of fame. He was a university professor with a startling and exciting new theory that started one of the greatest academic controversies of twentieth-century archaeology. After all the hyperbole for and against, no one reads his book today, but the timing of its publication was significant. The old view of Man's ascent from grunting, club-wielding savagery was being challenged by a new image of Neolithic and Bronze Age Britain as a golden age of civilisation – a civilisation crowned by scientific endeavour. Of the various elements that changed our view of prehistoric Britain astronomy was only one, and the main thrust of the argument was made not by Hawkins but by a Scottish engineering scientist, Professor Alexander Thom.

20

Pi and Pythagorean Triangles

'A dismal cirque of Druid stones, upon a forlorn moor' is how Keats described the Castlerigg circle near Keswick. Had he gone there on a good day he might instead have praised it for its dramatic lakeland setting, the reason why so many people find it an inspiring place. It was A. L. Lewis who first suggested that it was oriented to the peaks of Skiddaw and Blaencartha, and every year thousands of photographers echo the sentiment by photographing the circle against its grandiose backdrop (fig. 106).

Alexander Thom (1894–1985) was hardly renowned for his artistic sensibilities, yet his study of Castlerigg presented us with something arguably more beautiful than anything the purple prose merchants have ever mustered up. If you stand in the centre of the ring the arrangement of stones seems circular enough but, after making a precise survey, Thom found that the circle was flattened on one side. He claimed this was deliberate. In the grassy interior he attempted to discover how the ring was constructed, and found five adjoining arcs of varying radii, but all of precise lengths. This complex geometrical construction has its axes, which Thom discovered were aligned to the surrounding peaks and correspond to alignments indicating the rising and setting of the sun and moon at its extreme positions. So the external astronomical alignments at

FIGURE 106. Castlerigg stone circle near Keswick. In the early 1890s A. L. Lewis suggested the circle was oriented to the surrounding peaks.

Castlerigg are integrated with its internal geometry. This is its beauty. The site had been carefully chosen as a place to observe the sun and moon rise and fall behind the distant peaks, and the stone ring was the means by which the harmony of the Earth, the heavens and the human mind was reduced to mathematics (fig. 107).

Alexander Thom was an engineering scientist, a Professor at Oxford University from 1945 to 1961. He first encountered ancient astronomy when, as a student, he had read the paper on Callanish by Somerville in the *Journal of the British Astronomical Association*. Somerville's ideas impressed him, but it was not until some years later, in 1934, that he was reminded of it again while on a sailing holiday in the Outer Hebrides. He later described his moment of revelation in a letter to the author John Michell:

> I first saw Callanish from the deck of a small sailing vessel I had taken through the Sound of Harris and up that very exposed coast outside Lewis. As we stowed sail, the moon rose behind the stones. I went ashore in the moonlight and got to the rock at the south end of the N–S alignment and saw how perfectly the thing oriented on the pole. But there was no pole star in megalithic times. How was it

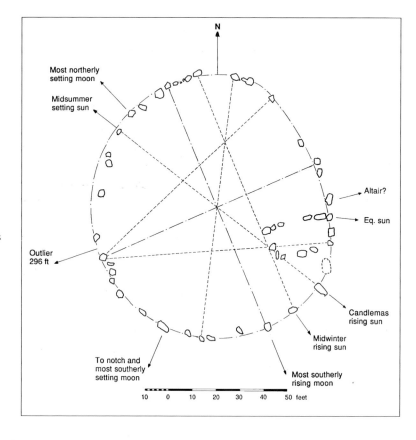

FIGURE 107. Alexander Thom's survey of Castlerigg. The astronomical orientations respect the internal geometry of the flattened circle in a way that Thom described as 'symbolic, mystical'. (*After Thom, 1967*)

done? From that moment I knew I had to deal with a highly developed culture and everything I have uncovered since lends support.[1]

Thom's studies progressed very slowly. He read and became much influenced by Sir Norman Lockyer's work, but he was also aware that Lockyer had been in too much of a hurry to find an answer. Even so there is much of Lewis, Lockyer and Somerville in Thom's theories – lines to distant foresights, the geometry of stone rings and, in his earlier work, alignments to the stars. The results of his early studies were published in scientific journals, the kind that archaeologists never read, like the *Journal of the Royal Statistical Society* and the *Journal of the British Astronomical Association*. Few archaeologists had ever heard of Professor Thom when *Megalithic Sites in Britain* was finally published in 1967. After the sensationalism of Hawkins and his computer, Thom delivered a slow, detailed and patient analysis of over 150 megalithic sites; to use Professor Atkinson's phrase, it impacted on the archaeological world like a 'well constructed parcel bomb'. A second edition was published in 1971, by which time he had surveyed 320 megalithic sites, of which nearly 250 were in his native Scotland. In the same year he expanded his theories in *Megalithic Lunar Observatories*, which was followed in 1978 by his final book, *Megalithic Remains in Britain and Brittany*, written with his son, Dr A. S. Thom.

All Thom's books make dry and difficult reading but the bare bones of his thesis are straightforward enough. British (and Breton) megalithic monuments were the product of an organised, centralised construction programme that reached its zenith in the early Bronze Age, roughly 2000 to 1500 BC. Stone circles and related structures were laid out using a standard unit of length, the Megalithic Yard (MY), and designed using integral numbers according to a Pythagorean school of geometry. The position and orientation of the megaliths was determined by astronomical considerations, and these astronomical observations were mainly to the sun or the moon. Solar observatories had a calendrical purpose, while lunar observatories were engaged in the prediction of eclipses, but encompassing all these activities was intellectual curiosity.

Thom claimed quite astonishing accuracy for many of his astronomical alignments, made from what he confidently described as astronomical observatories. One of them is Ballochroy, which overlooks the coast of the Kintyre peninsula in Argyll (fig. 108). Most people would consider the word 'observatory' a little ambitious if they saw that Ballochroy is just three standing stones. They are tall stones with broad faces, and stand together in a line. If this line is extended to the south west it passes over a stone cist which once had a large cairn over it; and if the sightline is extended yet further, across the Sound of Jura to the tiny Cara Island seven miles away, it pinpoints the place where the sun would have set at the winter solstice in about 1800 BC. Thom claimed the stones were also used to observe the sunset at the summer solstice. It is an accident of latitude that in the British Isles the sightlines to the summer and winter solstices have an angle of difference which is nearly 90°. The flat faces of two of the stones at

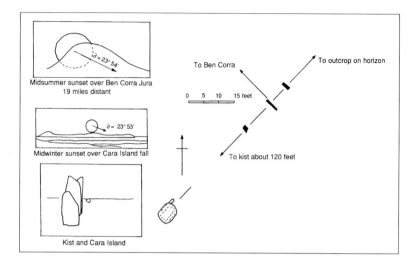

FIGURE 108.
Ballochroy in
Argyll was a solar
observatory with
sightlines to
midsummer and
midwinter sunsets.
Thom thought
Ballochroy was
erected about
1850 BC.
(*After Thom, 1967*)

Ballochroy were turned at right angles to the main alignment. According to Thom, the central stone points directly to Ben Corra, the most northerly of the Paps of Jura, and situated nearly twenty miles away, behind which the sun set at the summer solstice.

Thirty-five miles further up the coast of Argyll Thom found a similar solar observatory at Kintraw. The site stands above Loch Craignish looking south west toward the Paps of Jura, and consists of a twelve feet high standing stone and two cairns. However, from the level piece of ground on which they stand, the Paps of Jura are obscured from view. Thom puzzled over this matter for some time until he found, 100 yards away, a level platform higher up the hillside. From this elevated position it was possible, using the stone and cairns as a guideline, to survey the sun at the winter solstice setting between two of the Paps – Ben Shiantaidh and Ben a Chaolais – twenty-seven miles away.

Kintraw was always a controversial site because the solstice was observed from a hillside 'platform' to far distant hills; the cairns and standing stone being nothing more than a direction finder. In 1970, when Dr Euan Mackie of the Hunterian Museum in Glasgow excavated the platform to see if there was any evidence of the ground being artificially levelled, the results were inconclusive and, for Thom and his followers, disappointing. However, Ballochroy and Kintraw showed unequivocal alignments to the winter solstice, whether intentional or purely accidental. Thom maintained that these and other solar observations were made for the purpose of constructing a calendar. After an analysis of other alignments at sites across Britain, he concluded that the year was divided into sixteen months of twenty-two or twenty-three days: a more precise and subdivided version of Lockyer's eight-month year divided up according to the Celtic feast days, the equinoxes and the solstices.

Thom was also interested in using solar alignments to date the megaliths, calculated by reference to the rate of change in the Obliquity of the Ecliptic. Ballochroy and

Kintraw, for example, were estimated to date from about 1800 BC. This agreed well with the dates given by archaeologists at the time, but by the late 1960s, when the radiocarbon revolution threw dating of prehistoric sites into some confusion, he had to rethink his approach. By 1971 he had concluded that, because the rate of change of obliquity was a mere thirty-eight seconds per century, it would be very difficult to use it as a dating method because the alignments simply were not accurate enough.

He also found some stellar alignments which he used to date sites, for example Callanish aligned to Capella in 1800 BC, Rollright to Capella in 1750 BC. However, lines to the stars had no logic in Thom's thesis. They were not used for calendrical purposes, nor were they observed as clock stars to tell the time. Indeed, although he acknowledged that the Egyptians controlled their calendar by observing heliacal risings of certain bright stars, the method would not have been suitable for northern countries like Scotland because of their protracted twilight hours. Furthermore, stellar alignments tended to come from stone circles which in general were not designed as observatories – most of his important alignments were made from standing stones or cairns. The only purpose of these alignments seemed to be an opportunity for Thom to date sites. In 1971 he had to admit that 'astronomical dating by making use of the precession of the equinoxes looked promising 30 or 40 years ago, but it has turned out to be disappointing'.

The cycles of the moon were observed with just the same interest as those of the sun, as Thom was thinking in terms of lunar observatories long before he read Newham and Hawkins, but Hawkins' theory of eclipse prediction set him on a new path. Thom claimed to have detected interest in the slight perturbation, or continuous 'wobble', in the moon's orbit in the months approaching the standstills. It is caused by gravitational forces relative to its position with the sun, and it goes through a cycle of 173.3 days. The effect is visible as a slight variation on the horizon of the moon's position every month. There would be no reason to observe this phenomenon were it not for the fact that eclipses occur when the effects of the wobble are at their greatest. If they could discover when the lunar wobble reached its maximum, the megalith builders would know that an eclipse was due at the next new or full moon. They could then count the 173 day interval to the next maximum of the lunar wobble and the next eclipse period.

Britain's four chief lunar observatories were at Callanish, the Ring of Brodgar on the mainland of Orkney, Stonehenge (which he did not survey until 1974) and Temple Wood in Argyll. Three of these are acknowledged as among the most impressive megalithic remains in Britain, which certainly strengthened the appeal of Thom's theory. The fourth is in Argyll, close to the two solar observatories of Ballochroy and Kintraw. There are a number of impressive megalithic sites at Temple Wood in the Kilmartin Valley. The centrepiece is a stone circle (fig. 109). About 300 yards to the south east on fairly flat ground is a configuration of five standing stones running north east to

FIGURE 109. Temple Wood in Argyll, which Thom claimed was one of Britain's four chief lunar observatories. (*Historic Scotland*)

south west. About eighty yards long, the ends are marked with a pair of stones, and there is a single stone in the centre, forming a very elongated X shape. The individual members of the pairs are about ten feet apart and point approximately north west–south east, back toward the stone circle. Sightlines from the stones to the hilly horizon allowed the critical times of the lunar standstills to be observed, as well as the peak of the wobble, the most important sightline of all. This latter observation was made from the central stone, which was decorated with cup marks.[2]

According to Thom, Temple Wood was equipped to act as a self-contained lunar observatory, and the strange layout of the site was accounted for by its specific function. However, as Thom showed and as the Temple Wood observatory had allowed for, observing the peak of the wobble would have been more complicated than described above. In practical terms it was rarely possible to observe the peak, so its value had to be calculated. By mathematical argument Thom deduced that a fundamental length, which he called G, would enable the observer to discover how far left or right of the previous observation the monthly extreme had actually occurred. This length G would vary depending how far the observed foresight was from the observing position, the backsight. Thom claimed that its value was known at Temple Wood. He also developed this argument to account for the mysterious stone fans of Caithness, including the alignments of over 200 stones at Mid Clyth. By superimposing a grid pattern on a plan of Mid Clyth, Thom showed how observers could find the correction needed for the length G if the distance between successive observations was at all marked.[3]

The stone fans were therefore a kind of calculator, and a good deal more complicated one than anything suggested by Hawkins and Hoyle at Stonehenge. Even so, Thom was careful to avoid using the emotive word 'computer'. In the event it would not have mattered what he called them – few archaeologists, let alone general readers, could afford the luxury of disagreeing with him. My description is necessarily an oversimplification. Readers wanting a fuller understanding of it should turn to *Megalithic Lunar Observatories* where they will be able to follow the arguments in full.

Although precious little attention had been paid before to these stone fans in a remote corner of Scotland, Thom's idea that they were carefully laid out using mathematical principles, and involving abstract conceptualisation, accorded with his theories for the construction of stone circles. Somerville had already noticed that many stone circles are not actually circles, a fact reaffirmed by Thom. But this only became apparent after he had taken his surveys – the subtleties of shape went unnoticed to the naked eye. Even allowing for the occasional displacement or incorrect restoration of some stones, Thom decided that the shapes he found were deliberate attempts to create a variety of geometrical patterns.

It is in fact fairly easy to mark out a circle on a flat piece of ground. A stake is driven into the ground and a piece of rope is tied to it. When the rope is pulled round in a circle smaller wooden stakes can be driven into the ground to mark out the circumference, which will then determine the position of the stones. Of course if the ground surface is not level the circle will be distorted; and the longer the rope, i.e. the larger the radius, the more difficult it is to hold the rope horizontal, so more distortions will occur. However, large circles could be surveyed with impressive accuracy. The Ring of Brodgar is 340 feet in diameter and yet none of the thirty-three undisturbed stones stands more than three feet outside the arc of a true circle. Therefore the kind of misshapes Thom was finding demanded their own explanation.

Sometimes one side of the ring is flattened inwards, as at Long Meg and Castlerigg, already mentioned, where the perimeter is made up of the arcs of four circles (fig. 110). At others the circles have been elongated into an egg shape and the perimeter is drawn from the arcs of two circles. There are even some true ellipses, like the small Nine Stones in Dorset. Others have, for various reasons, even more complex designs: the so-called compound rings such as the great circle at Avebury which Thom claimed was formed from the arcs of seven circles.

An ellipse can be drawn out fairly simply on the ground using a loop of rope tied to and rotating around two stakes at a fixed distance apart. But how did Thom manage to discover the layout of the flattened circles, the egg-shaped and compound rings? And why did the builders want such obscure shapes? The key to the answer is that a

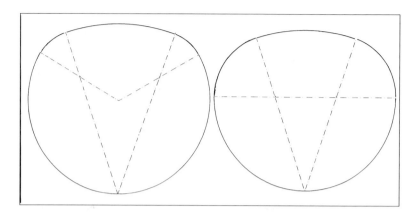

FIGURE 110.
These flattened
circle shapes were,
according to
Thom, adopted in
order that the cir-
cumference could
be measured in
whole units.
(*After Thom, 1967*)

universal unit of length was in use, the Megalithic Yard (MY) of 0.829 metres, or 2.72 feet. This standard unit of length was in use from Scotland to Brittany, and must have been verified by yardsticks issued from some central source, while its use was checked by Britain's first bureaucrats – the yard inspectors. In addition it appeared that multiples of two and a half MY, the Megalithic Rod, and two MY, the Megalithic Fathom, were also used. Thom determined the value of the Megalithic Yard, about the length of a human pace, by statistical analysis, but it compares well with other ancient units of measurement. For example the Indian *gaz* was roughly thirty-three inches long (2.75 feet) while nearer to home the Spanish *vara*, used throughout Iberia and South America, varied slightly between 2.74 feet and 2.78 feet. These historical 'short yards' seemed to have been linked to the metrologies of two of the earliest civilisations of the Old World, in the valleys of the Indus and the Tigris–Euphrates.

The specific designs Thom proposed are only valid if the Megalithic Yard is correct, and vice-versa. Of Avebury he wrote, 'without a knowledge of the Megalithic Yard . . . it is doubtful if the construction could have been discovered'. Thom claimed that the radii of the arcs were measured out in integral units. He also claimed high accuracy for his calculations, pointing out that if a value of 2.73 feet was chosen as the unit length his proposed design of Avebury would fall five feet outside the line of the stones.

The designer of a stone circle would soon have noticed that however many Megalithic Yards were used for the diameter of the circle the circumference would be a little over three times that figure, but could never be expressed as a whole number. Calculating the circumference of a circle is easy – multiply the diameter by π. But π, roughly 3.1418, is not a whole number, so the circumference can never be a whole number either. Thom suggested that the only way to correct this irregularity was to flatten or elongate the circles.

Thom also claimed that the builders of stone circles knew and regularly employed Pythagorean triangles. Pythagoras' theorem states that the square of the hypotenuse of a right-angled triangle is equal to the sum of the squares of the other two sides. The

Pythagorean triangle, which was the basic figure of megalithic geometry, is one where the length of each side is expressed in whole numbers. There are only a limited number of right-angled triangles which fulfil this condition. According to Thom, the two most widely used were the 3, 4, 5 (6, 8, 10 is the same thing) and the 12, 35, 37. There were also close approximations, for example the 8, 9, 12; but 12 squared is 144 whereas the sum of the other two squares is 145. Although there was a small error in the hypoteneuse here, the triangle was sufficiently accurate for the practical purposes of the circle builders. These triangles were never marked out in stone. They were not necessarily marked out using rope either for, although they are central to the geometry of the egg-shaped rings and the ellipses, their existence is essentially *theoretical*.

Of those archaeologists who bothered to read Alexander Thom's work when it was first published the response varied between the genuinely interested, the decidedly sceptical and the utterly bewildered. Thom had given to the builders of circles and standing stones the same kind of intellectual capabilities and achievements that Hawkins and Hoyle had, but Thom's challenge to orthodoxy was the more formidable. His discovery of the perfect ellipse, confirmed shortly afterwards by a survey of a stone ring on Arran by Dr A. E. Roy of Glasgow University, showed interest from northern Europe in a geometrical configuration not investigated by Greek mathematicians until over a thousand years later. The same was true of Pythagorean triangles, although here there was potentially more grounds for disagreement. Although the perturbation in the lunar orbit had been suspected in the tenth century AD by Arabian astronomers, it was not discovered and measured until the sixteenth century, by the Danish astronomer Tycho Brahe. Furthermore, to accomplish so many impressive feats of mathematics, Thom acknowledged that some form of writing would have been necessary. This need, however, only have been pictographic and need not have had any connection with the spoken language.

These are the kind of extravagant claims that archaeologists usually ignore. Nevertheless, Thom had surveyed over 300 sites to a degree of accuracy never before attained and his conclusions were based on thirty years of research. Even so, the shock of these new ideas provoked a hostile reaction from archaeologists more at home with pottery and pollen diagrams. Professor Glyn Daniel, editor of *Antiquity*, called the work of Thom and his ilk 'a kind of refined academic version of astronaut archaeology'. Richard Atkinson admitted that his initial reaction was to resist the implications of Thom's work 'because it is more comfortable to do so', but he later collaborated with Thom on his survey of Stonehenge.

When Thom said of the megalith builders 'they were intensely interested in measurements and attained a proficiency . . . only equalled today by a trained surveyor', he was exposing himself to a criticism levelled at all archaeo-astronomers.[4] The people who had discovered astronomical alignments were not archaeologists but engineers, astronomers, surveyors and mathematicians, who were accused of portraying the past in the image of themselves. A preoccupation with πi and Pythagorean triangles certainly seems very twentieth century, but if precise alignments were made to the sun and moon in prehistoric Britain then engineers, astronomers, surveyors and mathematicians are the only people equipped to discover it. However, for the archaeologists, there was still the bottom line – the astronomical and mathematical culture propose by Thom contradicted all the archaeological evidence. Unless the two could be reconciled, somebody had got it seriously wrong.

In his *Science and Society in Prehistoric Britain*, published in 1977, an attempt to resolve this contradiction was made by Dr Euan Mackie. He pointed out that, strictly speaking, archaeology could never prove astronomical alignments because intellectual aspirations in a non-literate society do not leave the kind of material remains that archaeologists have the wherewithal to study. One corollary of Thom's thesis was that intellectual achievements are only credible in a stratified society, one which allowed specialist groups to pursue their activities supplied with their material needs from another sector of society. By drawing a parallel with Mayan astronomy, Mackie questioned whether a theocratic elite of wise men could have lived apart from the mainstream of society in special ceremonial centres or 'monasteries'.

Mackie reinterpreted the evidence from henges in Wessex, like Durrington Walls, Marden and Mount Pleasant, all of which were excavated in the late 1960s. They were all 'superhenges', much larger than the norm, and contained wooden buildings. Although they had been interpreted as ritual centres, Mackie claimed the evidence would support an alternative theory that they were settlements for a privileged minority. Then he turned his attention to Skara Brae, a Neolithic village in Orkney, whose houses and archaeology also suggested that it was occupied by an elite group. The implication seemed to be that these special settlements were the headquarters, the training schools and the dwellings of a class of wise men who undertook, over many decades, the work at the standing stone observatories – the exact counterparts of the Mayan ceremonial centres of Central America.

Predictably enough, archaeologists were sceptical, not only of Mackie's methods but of his original premise. The prevailing view that stone circles were connected with ritual activity made Thom's theories about astronomer-mathematicians seem too narrow. For example, sites like the Ring of Brodgar, which Thom suggested was an accurate lunar observatory, have pronounced associations with burials, so if the moon was observed at all archaeologists preferred a ritualistic, not scientific, explanation. Once this religious function and the symbolic nature of the astronomy had been established, it was pointless looking for the homes of elite astronomer-mathematicians who did not exist.

By now the archaeologists were being joined in the debate by an increasing number of scientists. Dr Douglas Heggie, a mathematician from Edinburgh University, found it a popular topic for extra-mural discussion. As he wrote in 1981, 'among scientists, the new theories of megalithic astronomy became a novel and exciting issue for informal debate, as they have remained. One of the reasons for this is that the concepts involved are relatively easy to understand, especially for astronomers, and it is not hard for almost anyone to contribute a useful idea to the debate.'[5] Of those who decided to publish their contributions it is hard to find anyone, with the exception of Dr John Wood, advancing or developing the Thom hypothesis. Wood's *Sun, Moon and Standing Stones* of 1978 was a review of the story so far and an attempt to establish a consensus of astronomical studies. Professor R. Müller found three of Thom's egg-shaped rings near Boitin in Mecklenburg, Germany, but others found it more of a challenge to propose alternatives. Professor T. M. Cowan, an American psychologist, presented a simpler method of defining the egg shapes and flattened circles, but the most ingenious alternatives were proposed by Ian Angell, a mathematician from the University of London. His constructions resembled the familiar method of constructing an ellipse with two stakes and a loop of rope, except that three stakes, sometimes four, were used to create more complex shapes which seemed to fit the layout of the rings as well as Thom's designs.

In 1981 Douglas Heggie published his book *Megalithic Science*, which proved to be a turning-point in astronomical studies. Heggie was not concerned to advance new theories but to test existing hypotheses by statistical analysis. He concluded that there was no statistical proof of an accurate and standardised unit of length and that individual sites were probably laid out using an approximate unit such as a human pace. It therefore followed that there was no evidence that complex geometrical shapes were achieved by advanced mathematics. The case for astronomical alignments was far stronger, although there was no statistical proof that these were all intentional: his analysis showed that they were not accurate enough to warrant using the loaded word 'observatory'.

Where astronomical alignments did pass statistical tests, Heggie maintained they were approximate and could only have been for ritualistic purposes. When they read this, many archaeologists breathed a sigh of relief and put their *Astronomy for Beginners* back on the bookshelf. But how was Thom able to propose an honest but flawed theory so convincingly? The answer lies in his methods, to which archaeologists themselves subscribe. Thom's surveys are renowned for their accuracy, and he himself assumed that the precision of his theodolite was revealing something, which could only be that the circles were planned with an equal degree of precision. His method was to draw up plans, then to scrutinise the configurations of stones far more closely than the builders ever did. The regularities he found in the data were the product of these 'architectural' drawings. They proceeded on the false assumption that because patterns can be found after the event they must have been planned before the event. Scale drawings and measurements present stone circles in an abstract way never experienced by their builders. A comment by John Barnatt and Gordon Moir, that 'the majority of stone circles were laid out by eye to appear circular', reestablished the importance of the stone circles as they are seen on the ground. They did not need to be circular in our strict definition of the term, as long as they *appeared* so. This is what Thom's surveys have inadvertently shown us.

Nevertheless, the impact of Thom's studies put astronomy on the agenda of mainstream archaeology. Scope for fresh studies has been narrowed by the comprehensive nature of Thom's work, although in theory it still offers an opportunity for 'outsiders' to contribute to the archaeological debate. One of the few surviving lone astronomers is Christian O'Brien, a geologist by profession, who published *The Megalithic Odyssey* in 1983. This was a study of the stone circles of Bodmin Moor, which O'Brien claimed were built as calendars by itinerant Sumerians for the purpose of telling the local farmers when they should plant and harvest their crops. The book's dust-jacket (all you need to read) confidently declares that it 'persuasively argues for the appearance in prehistory of an advanced elite, a race of master builders, who travelled the world guiding and directing indigenous populations with godlike assurance'. In this fascist view of prehistory the elite Sumerians are just a repackaged version of the Children of the Sun, reminiscent also of John Ivimy's astronomical excursions in *The Sphinx and the Megaliths* of 1974. O'Brien provides a classic case of projecting oneself back into the past, to which astronomers have been particularly prone. O'Brien's narrow archaeological perspective encompasses Iraq and Britain, on which rests his entire theory. Lockyer did the same by linking Egypt and Britain; Hawkins by linking Stonehenge and computation; Hoyle Stonehenge and a Cambridge-like community of gifted minds. Even Thom does not escape this tendency. He argued that stone circles and standing stones were built by engineers bent on mathematical precision and driven by intellectual curiosity. He had an impressive range of evidence to back this up, even though his ancient astronomers seem suspiciously like professors of engineering, as one of whom Thom himself made his living.

Back at Castlerigg, a Mr Otley pointed out as long ago as 1849 that the entrance to the circle was placed at true north. According to Aubrey Burl 'the alignment was symbolic, perhaps obtained by taking a point midway between the risings and settings of the sun'.[6] Between Mr Otley and Dr Burl prehistoric science may have come and gone, but Thom's work was a short sharp shock to the bland and unimaginative interpretations archaeologists had given to the stone circles. The precedent set by Lockyer, Thom and to a certain extent Hawkins was not lost on a new generation of independent researchers, none of whom were astronomers. When he had finished his survey of Castlerigg, Thom described the circle as 'symbolic, mystical',[7] words that have encouraged dowsers, psychologists, geomancers and artists to look for their own interpretations of the monuments, against the grain of received opinion.

21

Alfred Watkins
and the Old Straight Track

'I am told there are people who do not care for maps, and find it hard to believe', wrote Robert Louis Stevenson, in a note concerning *Treasure Island*.

> The names, the shapes of the woodlands, the courses of the roads and rivers, the prehistoric footsteps of man still distinctly traceable up hill and down dale, the mills and the ruins, the ponds and the ferries, perhaps the *Standing Stone* or the *Druidic Circle* on the heath; here is an inexhaustible fund of interest for any man with eyes to see, or tuppence worth of imagination to understand with.[1]

Maps are the ultimate in armchair travel. They gave the study of prehistoric sites in the landscape a whole new dimension. Even the process of surveying relatively small areas yielded hitherto unsuspected relationships between different monuments. In most cases these were straight alignments. In 1778 William Chapple claimed that the Spinsters' Rock dolmen on Dartmoor was aligned to a stone-lined avenue leading from a stone circle. Unfortunately, the accuracy of his measurements cannot now be tested because the stone circle and its avenues have entirely disappeared. When C. W. Dymond made his survey of Stanton Drew in the 1870s he noticed that the cove, the church, the great circle and the north-east circle stood in a line; as did the south circle, the great circle and the outlying Hauteville's Quoit. Magnus Spence found similar alignments at Stenness to which he attributed an astronomical significance, as did A. L. Lewis when he noticed alignment of stone circles on Bodmin Moor to granite peaks such as Rough Tor and Brown Willy.

An Ordnance Survey map, however, allowed antiquaries to look at a much larger area of landscape at a glance. When they did so, much grander patterns emerged. As early as 1819 Richard Colt Hoare was convinced that a line between Stonehenge and Avebury, which passed through Marden Camp *en route*, was an ancient British trackway, an idea that Edward Duke developed in his grand planetarium scheme, published in 1846. In 1915 Ludovic MacLellan Mann wrote in his book *Archaic Sculpturings* that: 'certain sacred areas, covering great stretches of ground both in Scotland and Ireland . . . demonstrate that locations marked by the erections of cairns and standing stones and by prominent topographical features . . . are arranged in an exact geometrical relationship. The enquirer may, for instance, conveniently obtain evidence of this by drawing lines between such locations and salient points on the map.'[2] In the 1890s Colonel Johnson, Director of the Ordnance Survey, noted that Stonehenge, Old Sarum, Salisbury Cathedral and Clearbury Ring stood in a line. Lockyer described this twelve-mile alignment in the second edition of his *Stonehenge* which came out in 1909, where it became part of a remarkable astronomical and geometric configuration. If his solstice line to Sidbury Hill earthwork was extended in the opposite direction it passed through two other earthworks, Groveley Castle six miles away and Castle Ditches over thirteen miles away. The alignment to Old Sarum ran south east from Stonehenge. Lockyer claimed that Stonehenge, Groveley Castle and Old Sarum stood six miles equidistant, thus forming an equilateral triangle with Stonehenge at the northern apex.

Roman roads are straight, and Roman towns were planned in a grid of straight lines, so there is a natural tendency to attribute English landscape alignments to the Romans. When Sir Montagu Sharpe detected a grid pattern of north-south and east-west lines in Middlesex, marked by stones, trees, churches and mounds, he attributed them, as the title of his 1908 book says, to the *Roman Centuriation of the Middlesex District*.

An earlier researcher, William Henry Black, who devoted some fifty years to finding geometrical patterns in the landscape, suggested that ancient sites had been positioned by Roman 'geometers' as a kind of grid pattern for map-makers. Speaking to the British Archaeological Association at Hereford in 1870, he contradicted himself by claiming that 'monuments exist covering grand geometrical lines which cover the whole of Western Europe, extending beyond Britain to the Hebrides, the Shetlands, the Orkneys, right up to the Arctic Circle'. The only conclusion to be drawn from this was that 'this system is more ancient than the Roman Empire, and goes far wider'.[3]

It was also in Hereford, at the Woolhope Club, that a controversial explanation of prehistoric alignments was first aired. The talk was given in September 1921 by Alfred Watkins, a long-time member of the society and a well-known local businessman. Watkins led a busy life away from his business interests. He was a pioneer photographer and invented his own exposure metre, which he manufactured through his company in Hereford. As an amateur archaeologist he completed a range of fieldwork, including a photographic survey of Herefordshire dovecotes. He also wrote a book, *The Standing Crosses of Herefordshire*, published in 1929. None of this was particularly remarkable. Indeed the name of Alfred Watkins would hardly have been known outside Hereford had he not, in 1921, when he was sixty-six years old, made the discovery that was to lift him out of obscurity.

'The actual discovery was made on 30 June 1921', according to his son, Allen Watkins. On a chance visit to Blackwardine, Watkins senior looked at his map for features of archaeological interest. 'He noticed on the map a straight line that passed over hill tops through various points of interest and these points of interest were all ancient.' It suddenly occurred to him, or so we are told, that all ancient sites had been laid out in straight lines, although for what purpose he then did not know. Proving his theory, and explaining the purpose of the alignments, quickly became an all-consuming passion.

Later disciples of Watkins liked to claim that he had experienced a revelation, as if such a flash of divine inspiration gave his theories some kind of superior validity. In reality alignment theories already had a long history, stimulated by the publication of Ordnance Survey maps; and far from being a man for all time, as such revelatory experiences imply, his ideas and outlooks were firmly rooted in the intellectual climate of the county archaeological society. He also owed a debt to many like-minded contemporary authors. For example, by the time he spoke to the Woolhope Club, Watkins had already decided that the alignments were prehistoric trackways, an idea which leaned heavily on a book on ancient trackways by R. Hippisley Cox, called *The Green Roads of England*, published in 1914.

Watkins first ventured into print with this theory in 1922, in a book called *Early British Trackways*. He must have worked feverishly hard to develop his ideas because three years later he published a much more comprehensive book, *The Old Straight Track*. Despite writing two further books on the subject, *The Ley Hunter's Manual* in 1927 and *Archaic Tracks around Cambridge* in 1932, *The Old Straight Track* stands as the definitive statement of his theory.

Watkins called his alignments 'leys', although the name was not particularly important. A ley (or lea, lee or leigh) is traditionally a meadow, but Watkins thought that in prehistoric times it may have been a clearing in a forest for a track. Place-names that incorporate ley, such as hills, seemed to be important points in alignments, while he thought that villages with 'ley' in them were places where actual old straight tracks survived. Also people climb to the top of a hill to take in 'the lay of the land'. There is nothing especially convincing about all this. In fact Watkins is said to have dropped the word in favour of 'straight track' in his later years. But it does not matter. Ley is nicely monosyllabic and conveys a simple meaning: an alignment of ancient sites stretching for anything between one mile and many miles.

Very few of Watkins' leys were alignments of purely prehistoric sites. Many, indeed most, of his leys were marked by features much later than the Neolithic period when the system was supposedly brought to perfection. They include Iron Age hillforts, medieval mottes, pre-Reformation churches, wayside crosses, Scots pines, ponds, medieval moated sites, existing roads or green lanes, crossroads, wells, fords, even likely-sounding place-names (fig. 111). Based on the chronology of events in prehistory in use during the 1920s, this was proposing that a system of prehistoric pathways was traceable across the subsequent 3000 years of history. If so, then Watkins had a lot of explaining to do.

Watkins believed that the nomadic hunters of the Old Stone Age had begun the ley system. They piled up heaps of stones which were used as waymarkers, using the mountain peaks as direction-finders in their search for known sources of flint for tools. The ley system was then expanded and perfected in the subsequent Neolithic period. The principal mark points were natural features such as beacons and notches in hillsides, together with stones, mounds and ponds. 'Utility was the primary object' of these leys, but 'all down the ages the mark points of the tracks were assembly points for the people, for law, administration, religion, trade and recreation'.[4] Mark points became the sites of temples, and they also became burial places, which is why so many ley mark points are burial mounds. Later, as civilisation progressed, came wars and invasions, and so mounds were converted into defensive sites, by which time the ley system was in decline. The Romans built roads on the older straight tracks and churches were built on older sacred sites, while the ley system was slowly forgotten, with only remnants of it surviving in rural customs and traditions, and some place-names. Indeed the ley system was almost obsolete as soon as it was established – 'it belongs to a nomad life and civilisation destroyed it' – but it did not signify a Golden Age. Leys were the work of 'uncivilised man'.[5]

The idea might be beautiful in its simplicity, but it departed from conventional wisdom in so many fundamental ways that it is difficult to know where to begin. Archaeologists in the 1920s were beginning to develop a geographical approach to their subject, based on the distribution of monuments, and the premise that Neolithic technology would only allow certain land to be ploughed and cultivated. As technology developed throughout prehistory the heavier lowland soils were gradually exploited, with the pattern of settlement within the landscape changing radically over time. Watkins argued the opposite: that the same places had been used and reused over thousands of

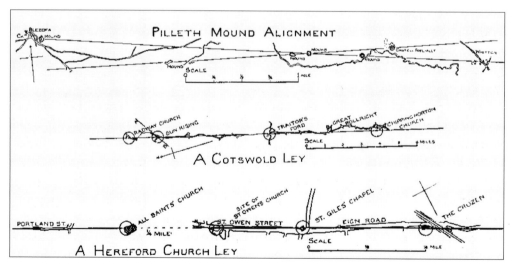

FIGURE 111. Typical Watkins leys are a reassuring perambulation through rural England.

years. Although the conventional archaeological model was the more sophisticated, it was not intrinsically more valid. Nor was the contention that Britain remained densely forested until it could be cleared for agriculture – dense forest would have precluded the kind of visible mark points that Watkins was advocating.

Few archaeologists paid attention to site evolution, in fact many would have considered site evolution a non-existent concept, but it is crucial to Watkins' theory, given that so many later prehistoric and historic features stand on leys. Watkins naively stated that 'it is the task of other branches of archaeology to work out the full chronology of the matter',[6] but he offered some evidence of his own. In the case of defended sites Watkins could argue that the location of forts and castles was dependent upon the local topography: they naturally chose the same places that had been so important to the ley system. In the case of churches Watkins quoted Pope Gregory's letter to Abbot Mellitus about the Christianisation of pagan sites. For actual examples he referred extensively to Walter Johnson's book *Byways in British Archaeology*, published in 1912, which devotes considerable space to proving that churches were built on older sites. Watkins accepted this evidence uncritically: places where medieval churches cluster in small areas, such as Bristol and Oxford, gave him a suspiciously large number of prehistoric alignments.

Leys are straight and Watkins believed they could only have been sighted accurately by trained surveyors, using surveying rods and beacon fires as directional aids. He coined the terms 'coleman' and 'dodman' to describe these surveyors, but the names were less significant than the implications of their existence. Having described leys as the work of 'uncivilised man', he then posited an organised, universal system of trackways throughout the whole country, which implied an organised, universal society. While really this was no more controversial than Lockyer's astronomer-priests, it contradicted the prevailing notion of a primitive society.

Having established that ancient sites form straight alignments, Watkins was saddled with the task of proving it. Might not such alignments occur by accident? Watkins thought not because there were so many of them, and the idea of imposing statistical tests on his data would have been alien to him. Once he had formulated his theory he never wavered from his conviction. This was surely one of his limitations, because proof by rational discourse was elusive. *The Old Straight Track* contains many speculative chapters encompassing folklore, place-names, the Bible, Greek mythology and ethnographic parallels, in an attempt to overcome the absence of any written reference to the ley system, not even by the Romans who would have known of it because they incorporated it into their own road network.

His excursions into philology were not very successful. For example he seemed to think that the Cornish circles known as Dawns Men signified 'men at daybreak', and his terms 'cole', 'dod' and 'ley' were never very satisfactory. As to the Bible, Watkins found many suggestive passages. 'I will go before thee, and make the crooked places straight', declares the Prophet Isaiah, while Luke urges us to 'prepare ye the way of the Lord, make his paths straight', which was hardly a topographical point. Nor is the following passage from Proverbs: 'Let thine eyes look right on, and let thine eyelids look straight before thee. Ponder the path of thy feet, and let all the ways be established, turn not to the right hand, nor to the left.' However, here Watkins would have found a suggestion that straight paths had in fact existed. He claimed that some ethnographic parallels bore this out. Natives of Uganda, Texas and Gaza, and the Bedouins of Egypt, all apparently travelled in straight lines from one landmark to the next, although Watkins was unable to say whether these landmarks were all laid out in the same straight line. Then there was a muddled attempt to interpret the role of Hermes the messenger in terms of leys, linking him with a Celtic god called Toutates, which was corrupted into alignment place-names incorporating Toot, Tute, Twt or Tot. It is not the most coherent chapter in his book.

The case was weak, yet the existence of so many alignments across the countryside was proof enough for Watkins, and for others. Watkins quotes many endorsements from members of the public which read like a sales pitch. 'I was frankly sceptical concerning the conclusions you arrive at', a Mr Darr wrote to him from Leicester, 'so I set about testing your remarkable theory to see if it could be substantiated here in Leicestershire. You will be pleased to hear that my own investigations entirely support your results, and the trackway lines I have obtained even so far are amazing.' In the *Westminster Gazette*, a Mr C. L. Davies wrote: 'I am no antiquarian but sufficiently interested to see whether support for Mr Watkins' contentions can be obtained from my local map. The results are rather remarkable . . .'[7]

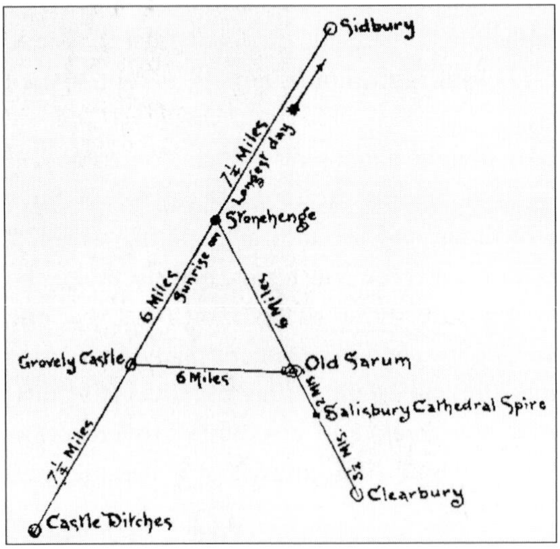

FIGURE 112. Watkins adopted Lockyer's Stonehenge equilateral triangle as three leys, the only leys in *The Old Straight Track* to pass through a stone circle.

The interpretation still had its problems. Beacons were terminal points of many leys, and so as trackways they made little practical sense. Then there was the problem of Lockyer's astronomical alignments, given that Lockyer had found and published examples of leys long before Watkins had even coined the term (fig. 112). Although Watkins acknowledged that some leys were astronomical in function, the whole issue was rather fudged: 'Whether the sun alignments were originally distinct from utility (trackway) alignments I cannot say, but they certainly became linked together in Britain.'[8]

Despite these anomalies, the old straight track was presented as an all-embracing explanation that offered little scope for development but plenty of opportunity for confirmation. Leys were about ley hunting, which was about fieldwork, and anyone with a map and a pair of walking boots could do it. Its appeal is encapsulated in Robert Louis Stevenson's quote, which Watkins cites at the beginning of his book. As John Michell later wrote, 'even those with no particular interest in antiquities and ancient history have enjoyed *The Old Straight Track* for the delightful account of a quest, which led Watkins through many curious byways both in his native landscape and in the realm of scholarship'.[9] Vita Sackville-West described ley hunting as 'a new sort of game one can play with oneself. I can imagine no more entertaining way of spending a summer holiday'. But it also required certain standards, so Watkins' *The Ley Hunter's Manual* of 1927 was written with the express purpose of helping others to add to the corpus of ley knowledge (fig. 113). This was based on his own working methods.

Watkins insisted on the use of Ordnance Survey maps, for without maps there would be no ley theory. The various kinds of mark points would be ringed on the map and then it was a case of carefully applying a straight edge to see if any alignments occurred. Three mark points in alignment were insufficient proof of a ley, four was the minimum. Map work alone was, however, not enough. It was necessary to test it by walking along the old straight track itself, during which Watkins suggested, from his own experience, that more confirmatory mark points would appear. With commendable optimism Watkins suggested that even this was not the ideal way of proving an alignment: 'the method in the future is an aeroplane flight along the ley'.

Watkins' theory was popular from the outset, with the Straight Track Postal Portfolio Club being formed in 1926. It allowed enthusiastic amateurs to exchange information by post, and

FIGURE 113. Leys were about ley hunting. Watkins published this guide for his disciples in 1927. (*Fortean Picture Library*)

it also introduced members who were offering different explanations of the straight line phenomenon. Boyle Somerville was principally interested in astronomy. In a book called *The Geometric Arrangement of Ancient Sites* published in 1939, Major F. C. Tyler argued that ancient sites had been arranged in concentric circles. In the same year Arthur Lawton published *Mysteries of Ancient Man*, in which he introduced the notion that leys were associated with some kind of terrestrial current. But this is looking far into the future. The image of the Old Straight Track Club in the 1930s is an innocuous one, of outings to selected ley points, of ladies and gentlemen with picnic hampers (fig. 114). Watkins

FIGURE 114. The Straight Track club on an outing to Stonehenge in the 1930s. (*Hereford and Worcester County Libraries*)

struck a chord with these people when he wrote, 'out from the soil we wrench a new knowledge, of old, old human skill and effort, that came to the making of this England of ours'.[10] Watkins died in 1935, and the culture that inspired those last words died in 1939, although the Straight Track Club was not formally wound up until 1948. Yet this was not the end of leys, only the end of the beginning.

Leys achieved no intellectual credibility among archaeologists, most of whom either ignored or were unaware of the issue. Indeed Watkins' style comes from another age, of the antiquary rather than the archaeologist. At a time when archaeologists were interested in what evidence lay beneath the barrows, Watkins was only interested in their topographical aspects, a highly unfashionable subject in the 1920s. His excursions into folklore, the Bible and place-names must have seemed very innocent and amateurish when the era of the professional had just dawned. For a book about prehistoric trackways, *The Old Straight Track* devotes little space to actual prehistoric sites, and this was unacceptable. Moreover, given that Watkins inspired a theory about the purpose of stone circles, it is strange to see only Stonehenge standing on a ley. Watkins was a Herefordshire man, a county with no stone circles and few megalithic remains of any consequence, and it was the Herefordshire countryside that inspired the ley theory.

As far as ley hunters were concerned the *bête noire* of the archaeological establishment was O. G. S. Crawford. In his *Archaeology in the Field* of 1953 he could find only disdain for Watkins' cult classic: 'the author found that, if he drew a straight line on a small-scale map with a broad pointed nib it passed through a number of objects on the ground, such as haystacks, cathedrals, ponds and large stones'.[11] This kind of distortion of ley theory would be replicated many times in future years. Crawford, the founder and editor of the independent archaeological magazine *Antiquity*, first published in 1927, refused to print a paid advertisement for *The Old Straight Track*. There was a great irony in this because Crawford also had a day job: he was Archaeology Officer with the Ordnance Survey.

22

John Michell and
The View over Atlantis

Arguably the most important and influential ley book ever published was John Michell's *The View over Atlantis*, which first came out in 1969. It presented the kind of radical and provocative vision of ancient Britain not seen since Stukeley, but it did not emerge out of a vacuum. Michell based his work on Watkins' leys, but also incorporated many other strands of fringe thought which had been gathering pace ever since the 1920s. Although many of these theories could be seen to contradict each other, Michell saw them as a cumulative awareness toward a more complete realisation of ancient Britain (fig. 115).

Leys of a sort were being studied in inter-war Germany, although the alignments were not old straight tracks. Thanks to Wilhelm Teudt these studies became tangled up in National Socialism, so that when the finger of shame was pointed at Germany after the war Teudt's ideas were understandably in disgrace. Teudt found 'holy lines' which linked special places in the landscape — hills, earthworks and pagan sacred sites later appropriated by Christianity — to astronomical events. He was also director of an SS project under the auspices of Deutsche Ahnenerbe (German Ancestral Heritage), which created a Nazi cult centre at the famous Externsteine rocks in Lower Saxony. A hilltop chapel here was said to be the focus of many alignments, and the place had already been mythologised as the sacred heartland of Germany. Teudt was seemingly unaware of Watkins and his leys but, in

FIGURE 115. John Michell inspects a divining rod at the 1977 Ley Hunters' Moot on Hampstead Heath in London. (*Fortean Picture Library*)

any case, the two men were poles apart. Watkins was a proud and patriotic Englishman with a sentimental attachment to the old shires. Teudt was an active Nazi sympathiser, studying holy lines as proof that astronomy and science began not in Babylon but in Germany.

When Dr Wilhelm Reich's *The Discovery of the Orgone* was published in New York in 1942, this Austrian psychologist could have had no premonition that his work would be made relevant to ancient history. Even though the scientific establishment dismissed his claims, Reich believed he had discovered 'orgone energy', which was the medium through which magnetic and gravitational forces manifested themselves. By building an 'orgone accumulator' – a chamber covered with alternate layers of steel wool and rock wool – a person could receive an increased orgone flow, leading to a heightened state of being. Michell likened these alternate layers to organic and inorganic material. He claimed that barrows had been built with such alternate layers, and that therefore 'it is difficult not to suspect that this form of energy was known and controlled in prehistoric times'.

Newgrange and Knowth, the great chambered tombs of Ireland, are cited by Michell as being 'covered with a layer of turf and with successive layers of clay and sod'. The significance of this may be arguable, but the evidence is incontrovertible, unlike certain other personal opinions which are purely subjective. These included the psychometric revelations of Miss Olive Pixley and John Foster Forbes. Miss Pixley, who came from a military background, was described by her friends as a large, bustling woman, dressed in uncompromising tweed suits, the stern, no-nonsense type. But she also had mystical experiences. In a book called *The Trail*, published in 1934, she wrote of the Stonehenge builders: 'They not only worshipped the Light, but they knew how to draw the rays of the Sun into their very being. They did not just worship with their minds. Their ritual included the knowledge of how to draw into their bodies the creative energy of the Sun Force.'[1] Silbury Hill, however, told her a different story. It was the site of a stone circle where black magic had been practised, so the mound was built to cover the circle and bury its evil atmosphere. Miss Pixley's friend, John Foster Forbes, was equally interested in psychometry, the process of gaining knowledge about the past by being susceptible to the psychic qualities of a thing or place. Forbes grew up in Aberdeenshire, where he became familiar with the Recumbent Stone circles and with the theories of the astronomical fraternity. In his aptly titled book of 1938, *The Unchronicled Past*, he writes that stone circles were built 'not only in conjunction with astronomical observation by the advanced priesthood, but that the actual sites should serve in some measure as receiving stations for direct influences from heavenly constellations that were known and appreciated by the priesthood'.[2]

Arthur Lawton's claim that leys were some form of earth energy was given a new lease of life during the 1950s, prompted by the French ufologist Aimé Michel. Michel

noticed from reports of UFO sitings that they tended to travel in straight lines, which
he called 'orthotenies'. An ex-RAF pilot, Tony Wedd, suggested instead that the UFOs
were following leys, which were lines of magnetic current. Wedd's pamphlet, privately
printed in 1961, called *Skyways and Landmarks*, was the beginning of a new era of ley
studies. In 1962 the Ley Hunter's Club was established by a group of ufologists, and
in 1965 a new magazine called *The Ley Hunter* was founded, although only seven issues
were printed before it folded the following year.

When Lawton published his *Mysteries of Ancient Man* in 1939 he suggested that one
way his proposed terrestrial energy could be detected was by dowsing. Dowsers have
been divining earth energies ever since. Chief among the pioneers was Guy Underwood,
a solicitor from Bradford-on-Avon, whose book *The Pattern of the Past* was posthumously
published in 1969, just in time for Michell to incorporate its ideas into *The View over
Atlantis*. Underwood spent many years dowsing at ancient sites, coming to the conclusion
that stone circles and the altars of pre-Reformation churches stood above strong sources
of energy called blind springs, and that standing stones mark the course of underground
streams. He also claimed to have detected some mysterious natural force flowing across
the Earth's surface. He called these energy flows 'aquastats' and 'track lines'. They linked
up all sorts of ancient sites, but in this case the lines were not straight.

Another well-known dowser was the archaeologist Tom Lethbridge, whose *The
Legend of the Sons of God* was published in 1972. While Lethbridge came to a completely
different conclusion to Underwood, he did find that stone circles possessed an energy
which he called 'bio-electricity'. It was created by the exertions of dancers inside the
ring of stones and was used to power alien spacecraft. At the Merry Maidens stone
circle in Cornwall Lethbridge recounted a curious incident in his attempt to date the
circle: 'On a fine day I went up to the circle, set the pendulum at thirty inches, which
is the rate for age, put my hand on top of a stone and set the thing swinging.' Each
turn of the pendulum was to count for ten years, but 'as soon as the pendulum started
to swing, a strange thing happened. The hand resting on the stone received a strong
tingling sensation like a mild electric shock . . . The stone itself which must have
weighed over a ton, felt as if it were rocking and almost dancing about. This was quite
alarming but I stuck to my counting.'[3] After 451 turns it stopped, and so Lethbridge
dated the Merry Maidens to 2450 BC, plausible at the time but now considered a few
hundred years too early.

There is an obvious tendency to dismiss personal experiences such as psychometry
and dowsing as having no relevance to archaeological interpretation. The information
described above is well-nigh impossible to authenticate by rational means. The subjectivity of the claims has led to a belief that people find only what they want or expect
to find, and that therefore their claims cannot exist exterior to contemporary experience.
However, as Michell would argue, even if the individual can be wrong a combination

of many individuals coming to the same conclusions has to be taken seriously. For example, there are errors and absurdities in Lockyer's work, yet the publication of Thom's first book, in 1967, showed that Lockyer's approach had been valid. Michell, quicker than the archaeologists to assimilate Thom's hypothesis, orchestrated a scattered range of evidence, drawn from astronomy, leys, psychometry, dowsing, orgone energy, folklore and more (but not archaeology), to create something new and original.

The Britain of the stone circle builders was part of a universal civilisation whose people discovered that the Earth is a living being possessing natural energy. The wisdom embodied in the ley system was 'a fusion of the terrestrial spirit with the solar spark, by which this energy could be disposed to human benefit'. Springs, wells, certain rocks and hills, all 'places of inherent sanctity', were natural centres whence the sacred current flowed, a flow which was manipulated by the spiritual irrigation of the landscape. Stone circles, standing stones and mounds of various types were all positioned to make maximum use of the 'terrestrial life current'.

The intensity of the current varied according to the phases of the sun and moon, hence the seemingly obsessive interest in astronomy (fig. 116). The most dramatic astronomical event was an eclipse: 'when this takes place, the magnetic activity normally stimulated by the eclipsed body greatly diminishes, with considerable effect on the regular flow of terrestrial current'.[4] Folklore worldwide tells us that an eclipse is an event to be feared, so Michell supposed that astronomers had to calculate when they would occur, so that people could take precautionary measures to safeguard against the interruption of the magnetic flow.

How and why the universal civilisation declined is unclear. One manifestation of it was the practice of human sacrifice, which is documented across the world – among the Aztecs for instance – and among the pre-Roman Druids. Michell blamed the priests for gaining but then abusing their powers. But he also cited evidence that in some

FIGURE 116.
Boscawen-un in
west Cornwall
was the focal
point of many
leys, which
Michell argued
were extensions of
the astronomical
orientations pro-
posed earlier in
the century by Sir
Norman Lockyer.

remote parts of the world a knowledge of the old magical system has been preserved. The Aborigines of Australia believe that the world was created during the Dreamtime by gods who traversed the country along 'songlines'. The people carve churingas, stone tablets with concentric circles and lines, which represent the sacred paths and centres of the Australian landscape and are used in divination. They also visit sacred centres on a seasonal basis and by performing a ritual release the life essence of particular plants and animals, thereby increasing their fertility.

Michell's most persuasive evidence, however, came from China. Like many ley researchers who came after him, he refers extensively to a book by Ernest Eitel, originally published in 1873, called *Feng-shui, or the Rudiments of Natural Science in Old China*. Here, for a western readership, was an account of the ancient Chinese practice of geomancy. Interest in it had been prompted by the disbelief of European businessmen in China who, when they were planning roads, railways and factories, were continually told to take only certain routes, or occupy only certain locations, which made no social, economic or utilitarian sense.

Feng-shui – wind and water – recognises that lines of magnetism run over the surface of the Earth, and are of two kinds: yin and yang. The task of the geomancer is to detect these currents and interpret their influence. The most favourable positions are where the two currents meet, but then the geomancer has to consider the astrological properties of the place, because every part of the Earth falls under a particular planetary influence. In former times the geomancers were especially concerned with finding the best locations to build tombs, but in effect every building was placed according to geomantic rules. Thus the entire landscape was harmoniously contrived according to this magic system. Feng-shui avoids straight lines. According to Eitel, 'straight lines of ridges or chains of hills are supposed to produce malign influences', and 'tortuous, crooked lines are the indications of a beneficial breath'. This is not the only fundamental difference between British and Chinese geomancy: 'another indication of the existence of a malign breath are detached rocks and boulders'. Notwithstanding these contradictions the current, *lung-mei*, was rendered as 'dragon current' in English. Assuming that leys were laid out using the same geomantic principles, Michell looked for dragons in popular belief as confirmatory evidence of their existence.

According to Michell, Stukeley nearly found the truth when he saw Avebury as a symbolic serpent with wings. As for dragon lore, it is not as universal as Michell supposed. Somerset has many dragon-slaying legends, although few megalithic sites, while Cornwall has many megalithic sites, but no dragon legends. However, references to dragons occur everywhere in some form or other, especially connected with Christianity: carved on fonts and bench ends, and depicted in stained glass, where they are usually being slain by Saints Michael, George and Margaret. The fact that hilltop churches in Britain and elsewhere are usually dedicated to Saint Michael was not lost

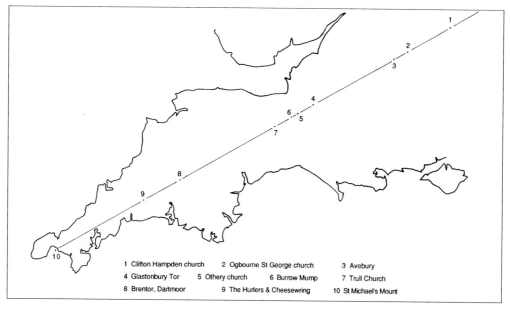

1 Clifton Hampden church   2 Ogbourne St George church   3 Avebury
4 Glastonbury Tor   5 Othery church   6 Burrow Mump   7 Trull Church
8 Brentor, Dartmoor   9 The Hurlers & Cheesewring   10 St Michael's Mount

FIGURE 117. John Michell's St Michael's Line from St Michael's Mount to Avebury is the most famous ley ever claimed. Unfortunately, it was later shown to be inaccurate. *(After Michell, 1969)*

on Michell, and indeed St Michael associations provided him with his most impressive looking ley, travelling nearly 400 miles across southern England (fig. 117).

The line was set up between two Somerset hills which are topped with St Michael chapels: Glastonbury Tor and Burrow Mump. To the east the line passes through Avebury, and then continues on to the east coast where it meets the sea near Lowestoft. On its way it passes through many *bona fide* ley points, including the abbeys of Glastonbury and Bury St Edmunds, 'the two greatest abbeys of mediaeval England'. To the south west the line passes over Dartmoor, including Brentor with its hilltop church of St Michael, and then to Bodmin Moor where mark points include the Hurlers stone circles and the Cheesewring, before it continues westwards and ends at St Michael's Mount near Penzance. Although Michell claims that the ley 'is remarkable for its length and accuracy', accurate it is not.

Nor are some of Michell's other claims. When he says that 'several alignments of ancient sites in Cornwall terminate on the coast at logan stones', and of such stones that 'many are heavily scored with cup marks', he neglects to say that at the time of writing there was only one of these stones left in Cornwall. Similarly, the top stone of the Cheesewring is apparently 'carefully inscribed with prehistoric markings', which is merely repeating an unsubstantiated and highly dubious claim made by William Borlase in the eighteenth century. Logan stones and rock piles evidently 'played an important part in the generation of terrestrial current' because they are 'associated by tradition with the invocation of fertility'.[5] This again is a dubious assertion, but in any case this breaks one of the cardinal rules of Feng-shui – the avoidance of bare rocks.

There are other inconsistencies and inaccuracies in Michell's work, not that casual readers, swept off their feet by the author's breathtaking display of erudition, notices them. *The View over Atlantis* is persuasive, beautifully written and, whether you agree with it or not, highly significant in its attitude to scholarship. Michell does not embrace the modern belief system called science because he believes in alchemical or magical science rather then the modern technological form. One consequence of this is an absence of rigorous critical analysis in his book, which many would argue is highly convenient for the author. Michell believes that 'revelation comes to those who invoke it through intense studies and a lively curiosity of mind'. Such revelations came to Watkins and William Stukeley. Michell champions Stukeley as the last of 'the scholars in the old tradition, in the archaic study of sacred history and cabalistic science'.[6] This was the traditional path to enlightenment, and Michell is trying to revive it. He believes in wise men and visionaries, not clever people, and the wisest of them all were the ancients. In former times 'certain incommunicable knowledge' was gained 'through a course of study in preparation for induced moments of perception, in which aspects of the hidden universe stand out clear and orderly to the inner mind'.[7] These same perceptions illuminated the work of Pythagoras, Plato, the Hebrew Cabalists and the Gnostics of the Christian Church, and were embodied in the ley system. Science destroyed it: 'the earth is slowly dying of poison, a process whose continuation is inevitably associated with many of the fundamental assumptions of the modern technological civilisation'.[8]

Michell contrasts the spiritual nothingness of modern materialism with the Golden Age of ancient, and not so ancient, Britain. There is virtually no archaeology in *The View over Atlantis* because Michell thinks its techniques are inadequate and, like most ley books, churches feature more often than stone circles. This is because Watkins, Michell and their followers are studying not ruins in the landscape but a landscape in ruins. Using words, Michell tries to restore it. In one passage he writes of leys, here used as pathways: 'to travel along these lines was to pass secretly through the country by tree-lined passages, shaded from the sun by branches meeting overhead. The endless soft, flickering light deepened the dream within which the traveller moved.'[9] This sounds more like landscape gardening than Arcadia. Elsewhere the pastoral idyll turns reassuringly into good old-fashioned nostalgia: 'Country people in the days of Thomas Hardy still found their way from village to village by following the old landmarks, stones and church towers.' As they did so, 'for the last time the landscape could be seen in its old form, harmoniously laid out according to the rules of terrestrial geometry'.[10] For William Blake, writing a century before Hardy, the dark, satanic mills had already poisoned his beloved Albion. Michell hailed Blake's vision of the New Jerusalem descending on England. In his later work Michell has found that Stonehenge and Glastonbury embody the ancient cosmological diagram of New Jerusalem. Thus Stonehenge and Glastonbury has each become an omphalos of the New Age cult.

Another prophet was the psychoanalyst Carl Jung. In a book published in 1959, called *Flying Saucers: A Myth of Things Seen in the Skies*, he interpreted the sudden increase of UFO sightings as a portent. They signified 'changes in the constellation of psychic dominants . . . which bring about or accompany long lasting transformations of the collective psyche'. Humanity was on the verge of a fundamental change. Such great changes are astrologically determined, and take place as the sun enters a new sign of the zodiac, traditionally every 2160 years. The birth of Christianity coincided with the Age of Pisces, which is now giving way to a new age, the Age of Aquarius. Here is the urgency in *The View over Atlantis* and its imitators: modern materialism has abused the Earth, a process which cannot go on indefinitely, and it is time to restore 'our promised and potential natural paradise'. The solution is simple, and leys are at the heart of it: 'Through the rediscovery of access to divine law . . . the principles of true spiritual science may be re-established.'[11]

23

Mysterious Britain

John Michell's first articles on leys as energy lines were published in an anarchist paper, the *International Times*. It was 1967, the psychedelic year, the dawning of a New Age when anything could happen, and often did. In 1968 the *IT* printed an article called 'The Code of the Sacred Islands' which completely rewrote the annals of prehistoric Britain. Its author is known only by his or her nom de plume, 'Karana', which is possibly just as well: 'The wise men of the Stone, Bronze and Iron Ages of Britain were masters in the art of consciring [a special form of deep meditation]. Others took the trip after drinking from the Cauldron of Wisdom a potion brewed from *Amanita muscaria* [an hallucinogenic mushroom] and four herbs.' It's that word 'trip' that does it, and you will not be surprised to know that Karana is acquainted with 'the disciplined use of LSD'. Men and women were 'living on the edge of a dream', whatever that means, and 'because they were able to retain and put their inner experiences into practice, life became a poem. The music of the spheres was a reality. For them the cosmic life was expressed joyously in wind and sailing clouds and in a glory which shone in all living things.'[1]

Similar utopian fantasies colour Paul Screeton's *Quicksilver Heritage* of 1974. Even the title is pseudo-mystical. Screeton believes that 'the seeker after the truth of leys' can attain a level of consciousness where everything is possible:

As he gazes towards Orion's Belt he will become an astronaut of inner space, becoming calm, becoming at one with the cosmos, expanding into a timeless consciousness where the truths of man's unbreakable link with the heavens enfold untold centuries, and he will withdraw facts as intuitions and truth as comprehension. There are no barriers to time, only those we pretend exist, and leys offer us the positive negation of time in that they are, were and always will be. They are there. They were there a long, long, long time ago.[2]

We can laugh – it's irresistible – at this and Karana's acid-dropping, dope-smoking verbal diarrhoea, but Screeton's alienation from modern materialism is a serious issue, however feeble his Arcadian dreams turn out to be: 'We are far from the end of The Old Straight Track. But it has given me a new insight into many subjects and into deeper consciousness, yet it has not reached the politicians, the armament manufacturers, the military, the racial extremists', and so on. Ley hunters were 'but nightingales singing in a midnight thunderstorm', a suitably dainty image.[3]

In 1969 Paul Screeton revived *The Ley Hunter*, which he edited until 1976. The magazine and the movement thrived partly because its simple message offered an antidote to modern urban decadence, but also because it rejected the Savagery-Barbarism-Civilisation dogma of orthodox archaeology, which could be seen to justify modern western achievements. Stonehenge was ours, and yet it was innocent of the crimes and ills of modern humanity, such as exploitation of the land, imperialism, warfare and the rest. The ley vision was an unashamedly romantic, alternative Britain, and was fundamentally about the countryside. It therefore inspired a range of topographical musings, all of which were forms of escapism (fig. 118). In *The Ley Hunter's Companion* of 1979 Paul Devereux and Ian Thomson describe ley hunting as ideal for 'people who want to get away from it all'.[4] Paul Screeton, meanwhile, wrote with a purple pen: 'He [the ley hunter] will walk through sunlit glades, meditate under gospel oaks, rest his weary feet on special mounds while listening to high flying skylarks, pass by duckponds swarming with tadpoles' and more, but this is a countryside myth tailored to people brought up in towns.[5]

FIGURE 118. Kits Coty, in Kent, is less than an hour from London, proving that Britain can be mysterious even in the Home Counties.

Anthony Roberts connected the British countryside, or parts of it, with Atlantis. His 1975 *Atlantean Traditions in Ancient Britain* told of voyagers from Atlantis colonising Ireland and south-western England. In Cornwall contemplation of nature reached a crescendo:

> Standing on the moor at sunset, the images change and a mental alchemy takes place in the mind of the beholder. The sky shines with wonder. The power of the earth surges into the body, and from the depths of the mind the blazing giants of Atlantis seem to sweep in from the Western sea and dissolve into the darkening face of the landscape.[6]

The countryside made strange was the theme of Janet and Colin Bord's eclectic and popular *Mysterious Britain*, which was published in 1972. It dips into prehistoric monuments, churches, mazes, wells, King Arthur, folklore, ghosts, the Loch Ness monster, UFOs and Morris dancing. Mysteries are constructed but not resolved (that would ruin them); seemingly unrelated places like Glastonbury, Avebury, the Rock of Cashel and the Tower of London rub shoulders amicably. The book spawned a range of coffee-table books on Britain which had the word 'Secret' or 'Hidden' or 'Mysterious'

somewhere in their titles. Leys are an integral part of *Mysterious Britain*. The Bords
invite readers to test the theory for themselves, whence 'a realisation of how much the
encroachments of the twentieth century are changing our beautiful land grows very
strong'.[7]

The Bords main contribution to ley literature was in the interpretation of folklore.
They published a book on the subject in 1976, called *The Secret Country*, which was
billed as a sequel to *Mysterious Britain*. It took a miscellaneous collection of traditions
and customs and interpreted them as 'folk memory' proving the former existence of
leys and their telluric force. The custom of beating the bounds was interpreted as 'the
remnants of rituals which were carried out on special days in order to intensify, build
up, store or release the earth currents', rather a novel justification for smacking someone's
bottom.[8] Numerous traditions of moving churches, where the parish started to build
in one place only for the Devil mysteriously to move it elsewhere, become the necessity
of building churches where the ley current passes. Stories of moving stones suggest that
they were actually alive, and so were 'live' with terrestrial energy (fig. 119). But this
is a facile interpretation. The Bords looked at folklore and tried to dig up facts where
there are only meanings: stones were considered to be animate, but to claim that they
moved around in the literal sense misses the point.

FIGURE 119.
St Lythans
chambered tomb,
near Cardiff.
According to
folklore the stones
become animate
on midsummer's
night, which was
interpreted by ley
writers as folk
memory that the
stones were once
live with
terrestrial energy.

Anthony Roberts fared little better in an examination of giants in myth and history, called *Sowers of Thunder*, published in 1978. Giants are here regarded as titans in the physical and metaphysical sense. Richard Carew's description of the unearthing of a giant near Land's End is cited as one of the four definite discoveries of giants in barrows. Typically, the account was written in the sixteenth century and was based on hearsay. Written accounts of barrow excavations, from the eighteenth century to the present day, never record such findings, but this is because the bones of giants 'were ignored, disrupted or deliberately destroyed' in a conspiracy by archaeologists to sustain their theories of linear progress. However, the gist of the book revolves around a quote from William Blake: 'The Giants who formed this world into its sensual existence, and now seem to live in it in chains, are in truth the causes of its life and the sources of all activity.' These giants were the ley geomancers, who 'expertly married the subtle techniques of cosmic perception with the practical reality of ecological balance'. This is the alternative Britain that he trumpets as Albion, 'the hidden soul of Britain'. Roberts also misquotes Blake's 'All things begin and end at [sic] Albion's Ancient, Druid, Rocky Shore' to show that Blake was a prophet of the New Age to come.

Much of this was just an elaboration of Michell's work. So was the Bords' flirtation with the paranormal in *Mysterious Britain*. Here the revelations of John Foster Forbes and Miss Pixley get a good airing, as does a psychometric interpretation of Castlerigg made by Iris Campbell in 1944. Castlerigg was 'a central Meeting Place where Priests would come from surrounding Centres – but of a funereal nature; performing their funeral rites by weaving different cosmic colours around the bier in order to speed the departure of the passing Soul'.[9] Another of Michell's asides was telekinesis, the ability to move objects by thought power, which is introduced by the Bords as a possible method of erecting Stonehenge. This is seen as preferable to the standard explanation: 'gangs of sweating barbarians' defiled their image of the place, even though gangs of sweating labourers might seem more human than a gang of superminds exercising control over nature without moving a muscle.

Unlike the majority of ley hunters, dowsers concentrated their efforts on prehistoric stones, although their interpretations differed (fig. 120). The work of John Williams, a solicitor from Abergavenny, is little known, principally because he did not ally his work to leys. He claimed, with statistical back-up, to have discovered alignments, but he only used prehistoric sites. The alignments were known as SCEMB lines, from the initials of the sites involved: Standing stones and circles, Camps and cairns, Earthworks, Mounds and pre-Roman moats, and Barrows. Williams found that some stones, when touched in the right place, gave him a twisting sensation in the spine, or even produced a shock so violent that he was thrown off the stone altogether. A fellow Abergavenny dowser, Bill Lewis, believed there was a link with megalithic sites and underground

FIGURE 120.
The Blind Fiddler
standing stone in
west Cornwall, a
favourite among
ley hunters. The
stone has twitched
many a dowsing
rod.

water. He passed his knowledge on to Tom Graves, who began dowsing because of
his interest in leys.

At the Rollright Stones, Graves divined 'a spin of energy or power' around the
circumference of the circle and surface 'flows' of power travelling from the circle in
straight lines. Graves called these lines 'overgrounds', and suggested they might have
been 'the non-physical reality' behind the ley system. In his 1978 book *Needles of Stone*
he likened prehistoric stones, linking the Earth's energies, to a kind of Earth acupuncture,
another of Michell's ideas. Graves suggested that this acupuncture should still be practised
and so began hammering copper-topped poles into the Earth at certain places. This
modern geomancy was deemed a useful palliative against the relentless onslaught on
nature by western civilisation.

Francis Hitching used the evidence of dowsers, as well as Thom's theories and
traditional ley thought, in his 1976 book *Earth Magic*, which attempted to channel
alternative and orthodox data into one version of prehistory. There are shades of Watkins
in the way he envisaged the ley system being created from the time the first nomads
peopled Britain after the Ice Age. They became aware of a mysterious force, the kind
detectable by dowsers, in certain rocks and certain places, and gradually this discovery
was manipulated. The most important stage was 'the realisation that some wells of water
and some stones, drunk or touched or embraced in a certain way, could be used to
regenerate and revitalise', and that this mysterious form of energy was related to the
heavenly bodies. The manipulation of Earth magic through the ley system eased the
transition from a nomadic to a sedentary life; also 'for the earliest communities the
power in a stone circle would have been invoked to increase fertility, cure sickness and
prolong life'.[10] *Earth Magic* is a modified and more moderate version of *The View over
Atlantis*. It tries to avoid the incredible, such as Screeton's claim that four harvests a
year were possible by manipulating leys.

The archaeological establishment could not have cared less about Hitching's attempt at arbitration. Archaeologists mainly ignored the alternative scene, even though some of its younger practitioners joined the mainstream after flirting with the fringe. Ley hunters tended to enjoy their heretical status, exaggerating it in the process. John Michell talked of 'much ill-natured abuse' directed against Watkins, as if the poor man was too feeble to take it. Glyn Daniel, the editor of *Antiquity*, refused to print an advertisement for *The Ley Hunter*, from which Paul Screeton derived plenty of kudos. During the 1970s the term 'lunatic fringe' entered the archaeologist's vocabulary, with leys lumped together with likes of Erich von Daniken, 'pyramidiots' and anyone else with an exotic view of the past. Meanwhile Watkins' employment as a salesman in the brewing trade was an irresistible opportunity to speculate on the origins of his strange theories. This was a good excuse not to address the issue. Peter Lancaster Brown, an astronomer and not an archaeologist, described John Michell as 'a self-confessed flying saucer enthusiast', as though this were sufficient for men in white coats to come and take him away. Among the academic disciplines those with the most legitimate reason to be annoyed with leys were the landscape historians, given that their territory was being so blatantly trespassed. Richard Muir, in his *Shell Guide to Reading the Landscape* of 1981, therefore singled out ley hunters for special treatment: 'A corner of the human psyche craves for fantasy and the bizarre in this demystified age of computerised certainties. We need our Loch Ness monsters, UFOs and abominable snowmen – perhaps they even exist. But we could do without leys.'[11]

The overall situation was summed up by Paul Devereux and Ian Thomson, who wrote in 1979, 'we are hard pressed to find any meaningful public discussion about leys (either for or against) on the part of the archaeologists'.[12] Richard Atkinson did take up the challenge, arguing the case against in *The Ley Hunter*, but a comprehensive examination of the subject by archaeologists had to wait until 1983, when *Ley Lines in Question* by Tom Williamson and Liz Bellamy was published. Unfortunately it came a little late, as it mainly tackled the sensationalist claims of the 1970s. The authors picked off some easy targets, such as the quaint literary style, the slipshod methods, the fallibility of intuition and the falsification of evidence. The seventies had produced plenty of ephemeral literature which was out of date by the time each book appeared, but some of their criticisms were valid, particularly with regard to statistics.

Statisticians had looked at leys long before the archaeologists. As early as 1965 Peter Furness contributed an article on the subject to *The Ley Hunter*, in which he calculated that if leys were due to chance a seven-point ley would occur only once in a thousand one-inch OS maps. In the 1970s Robert Forrest declared the Furness approach inadequate because it was based on map data, which could allow a ley width of up to one hundred metres. He also argued that four-point alignments were not statistically significant. Michael Behrend's despairing remark that 'the facts may be against us' was one reason why ley hunters gave statistics such a lukewarm response. Many people had researched leys in the sixties and seventies, some more assiduously than others, but the statisticians gave them a rude awakening. The most incredible ley ever claimed must be 'The Belinus Line' which was described in Guy Raglan Phillips' *Brigantia* of 1976. This began at Lee on Solent, passed through such famous megalithic sites as Winchester, Birmingham, Manchester, Carlisle, and continued up through Inverness to Inverhope. One of his mark points along the ley was a line of gorse bushes. This is an extreme example, and not all ley hunters accepted it, but it is an illustration of why alignment theories could be ridiculed by archaeologists at their leisure. If ley hunters were to present a convincing case then they would have to employ much higher critical standards.

In *The Ley Hunter's Companion* Devereux and Thomson presented a selection of leys, all of which had previously been published in books, magazines or *The Ley Hunter*. They took fifty acceptable map leys and then studied the alignments in the field, during which some of the lines were found to be inadequate. Their book included forty leys, none of which had less than five mark points, with an average length of just over ten miles. These included Lockyer's alignment linking Stonehenge, Old Sarum and Salisbury Cathedral. There were also leys around Avebury, Glastonbury, London and Hereford-shire. There were several seven and eight point leys, even a ten point ley running through Cambridge. If alignments occurred only by chance, these leys should not exist. However, only one of them was made up solely of Neolithic and Bronze Age sites: at Corfe in Dorset, which has a stone circle, five barrows and the hill on which Corfe Castle was later built.

The use of so many later sites was unacceptable to archaeologists. Tom Williamson and Liz Bellamy patiently worked through the claims for site continuity offered by the ley hunters and found them wanting. There are cases where continuity can be established but these are exceptions. They cite the excavation of a variety of sites, such as mottes, castles, churches, Iron Age fortifications and settlements, where no evidence of earlier activity was found. Their conclusion seems perfectly reasonable: why should archae-ologists believe a church was a site of Neolithic activity if an excavation yields no evidence?

This was always a primary argument against leys. John Michell attempted to counter it in a book called *The Old Stones of Land's End*, published in 1974, which was a study of alignments in West Penwith. To avoid controversy Michell decided to consider only standing stones, stone circles and chambered tombs, with later features used 'for confirmation only'. It was not a systematic study of the area because Michell had clear ideas about the purpose of leys and where these lines should run. Many of the impressive alignments are therefore extensions of Lockyer's astronomical alignments.

Between fifty-three sites Michell found twenty-two alignments of 'rifle barrel accu-racy', many more than chance would predict. Yet though ley books invariably referred to it as incontrovertible proof of the ley system, the archaeologists disagreed. John Barnatt made a survey of Cornish monuments for his *Prehistoric Cornwall* of 1982. In his book Barnatt disputed some of Michell's criteria, although he suggested that further, more rigorous, research might be beneficial. However, Tom Williamson and Liz Bellamy savaged the whole enterprise. To begin with they noticed that later features, such as wayside crosses and churches, were being used for more than just confirmation. A visit to the sites found other deficiencies. Many small stones were crucial to the alignments because Michell argued that 'a stone was often placed at the extreme limit of visibility so that only its tip showed above the horizon. No stone was taller than it had to be.'[13] Williamson and Bellamy did not agree that these stones were prehistoric; nor did John Barnatt, and nor did Vivien Russell, who had recently made her own archaeological survey of the district. The stones were small, unlike the other standing stones in the district, and were either rubbing-posts for cattle or big stones in field walls; one was even standing in an Iron Age 'round'. There were very many similar stones that Michell could have used but did not because they did not fall on the preconceived alignments. Therefore the proclaimed statistical significance of the alignments was nothing of the sort. Williamson and Bellamy's judgement is unforgiving: 'There could be no more appropriate illustration of the nature of ley methodology than the way in which these impressive results have been derived from doctored data.'[14]

Despite this convincing demolition job, *The Old Stones of Land's End* lives on in recent ley literature, although whether 'it continues to be the agony of sceptics', as Paul Devereux claims, is doubtful.[15] Some of the alignments, as well as Michell's St Michael's Line, redefined as the 'Dragon Path', were used as the basis for walks in Shirley Toulson's *The Moors of the South West* of 1982. This was a novel and appropriate way of popularising the concept. Another way was adopted by Colin Wilson in his book *Mysteries* of 1978, where leys were drawn into the wider arena of the occult. This is how they have passed into popular mythology, usually using the strictly incorrect term 'ley-lines'. One of the most bizarre ley-line manifestations took place in 1983 when various supernatural happenings occurred on the set of Granada Television's *Coronation Street*. According to an article in the *Sunday Mirror* the cast went down with colds and coughs, and were unable to concentrate, a situation blamed on the bands of energy which transmitted both good and evil forces. This of course undermines the serious study of leys, but that is the price of popularity. If you asked a random selection of the public what a megalithic yard or a henge is, very few people would know. But everybody has heard of ley-lines.

24

Earth Mysteries

The term 'Earth Mysteries' was first coined in the 1970s and is now the title given to alternative research which incorporates leys. Paul Devereux, its leading campaigner and spokesman, is unequivocal about its aims and principles. He describes the approach as multi-disciplinary, or holistic, as it draws ideas from many sources: archaeology, folklore, anthropology, geomancy, metrology, geology, geophysics, psychology, and direct human experience. This integrated approach is favoured above conventional archaeology, which he thinks has too narrow a frame of reference to tackle the fundamental issues. But it is not simply a question of being right: 'Earth Mysteries researchers do not study ancient monuments as a form of genteel antiquarianism, but to see if fundamental principles regarding harmony between mind, body, spirit and planet can be learned from ancient peoples; principles which can perhaps be adapted and applied to our modern condition.'[1]

Earth Mysteries has adopted a worldwide remit, even though the study of monuments in the British landscape remains one of its central concerns. Indeed stone circles were the key element in its most sustained research programme of the seventies and eighties, the Dragon Project. When Paul Devereux became editor of *The Ley Hunter* in 1976 he found that, although stone circles and related monuments were generally assumed to contain some form of energy, the different perceptions of this energy were rather vague and suffered from the problem of accountability. Dowsers and psychometrists were offering only 'soft' evidence. Francis Hitching grappled with this issue in his book and television documentary *Earth Magic.* The dowser Bill Lewis had suggested that the Llangynidr Stone near Crickhowell, in Breconshire, possessed some form of power, so Hitching arranged for Dr Eduardo Balinovski, of Imperial College, London, to take measurements at the stone using a gaussmeter, which reads static magnetic field strength. Balinovski *did* register a magnetic anomaly in the stone, but any celebrations were premature because further readings, taken by Professor John Taylor of King's College, London, gave contradictory results.

The Dragon Project was founded in 1977 to test the energy hypothesis more systematically. Progress might have been quicker had the project known precisely what kind of energy it was looking for, but it was also slow for financial reasons. Only limited outside funds were available, so the use of fancy equipment and the experts to operate it was somewhat constrained. In fact, early tests of possible magnetic fields around standing stones were made with shrimp sensitive to such fields. Later it proved possible to borrow magnetometers from universities, although ordinary compasses have identified 'magnetic' stones at a number of stone circles. A detailed magnetic survey of megalithic sites continues to be undertaken by the Dragon Project.

In its early days, the Dragon Project's main field base was the Rollright Stones, where a variety of other energy effects were sought, including ultrasound, radiation and electronic voice phenomena (EVP). What a bizarre spectacle this must have presented to early morning visitors, who would have seen geiger-counters, magneto-meters and the like being applied to a ring of gnarled old stones with religious solemnity. In the event, despite promising initial results, Rollright yielded nothing conclusive, but provided a lesson in the technical difficulties involved in such investigation. The project moved further afield in the 1980s, claiming a little more, if patchy, success. During 1983 and 1984 it took on volunteers from the Association for the Scientific Study of Anomalous Phenomena (ASSAP) to form the Gaia Programme. This was set up specifically to monitor radiation levels, which gave the Dragon Project its largest body of data.

Easter Aquorthies is a Recumbent Stone circle in Aberdeenshire, which was monitored for radiation by Cosimo and Ann Favaloro in 1987 (fig. 121). The readings were deliberately taken to coincide with the major lunar standstill because Aubrey Burl had argued that these circles had been oriented to the most southerly rising and setting of the moon. Over a twelve-hour period the Favoloros found that levels of natural radiation inside the ring were consistently higher than readings taken outside the ring, except for one short period that coincided with the setting of the moon.

The Easter Aquorthies circle is made up of granite stones, and other granite stones

FIGURE 121. Easter Aquorthies stone circle in Aberdeenshire, which was monitored for natural radiation by Cosimo and Ann Favaloro in 1987. (*Fortean Picture Library*)

have been found to be mildly radioactive. Among several stone circles on Machrie Moor in Arran one circle in particular, two concentric rings of stones occupying the highest ground, gave a significantly higher radiation count than the other circles. Moreover one of the stones, the tallest, gave a radiation count 33 per cent higher than normal. The same phenomenon was recorded at Long Meg where the granite stones in the north-west quadrant gave significantly high readings. If this sounds like the beginning of something really big, expectations floundered among the granite circles of Cornwall, where radiation levels within the ring tended to be lower than without. In other places energy anomalies were absent or frustratingly elusive, which may be the same as absent. Stonehenge, whose bluestones have been the object of so much speculation, proved a conspicuous disappointment.

A natural response to this mish-mash of information is: so what? The fact that granite sometimes emits higher than natural levels of radiation has no more bearing on its use at Easter Aquorthies than for the building of Aberdeen harbour. The basic premise of the project was also suspect in its search for anomalous forms of energy. The notion of 'anomalies' invested the work with a spurious significance, but ignored the fact that the Earth is buzzing with energy which might equally be regarded as inscrutable, in the wind, the rain, the soil, and receives cosmic energy from the sun and the moon.

The Dragon Project travelled the country looking for nebulous energy sources, alighting wherever they were found. Encouraging results could be obtained but, in the case of the Llangynidr magnetic anomaly and ultrasound at Rollright, these were not necessarily as significant as they seemed. Results frustrated Don Robins in his 1985 book, *Circles of Silence*, but five years later, in *Places of Power*, Paul Devereux felt confident enough to draw some general conclusions. Devereux believed that if an individual block of stone had special magnetic or radioactive properties these would have been known about. This is an article of faith rather than a scientific assessment. Even if Devereux were correct, there are still problems of interpretation. It appears that energy effects are related to actual stones rather than the intrinsic qualities of a place. This is important, because if energy exists in the stone then the place it is erected is shown not to be of primary significance, and it was place that defined the ley network. Devereux thought that stones possessing unusual magnetism could have been divined by applying 'a piece of magnetite on a thread; a lodestone'. The behaviour of such 'magic stones' would have signified the presence of spirit, but the stones were then, it seems, moved to another location.

In *Places of Power* the evidence for energy effects is swelled by reported sightings of 'earth lights', which Devereux described at length in his *Earth Lights Revelation* of 1989. Earth lights are his own explanation of mysterious light forms like will-o'-the-wisps, 'fairy lights' and corpse candles. Devereux claimed that they are not UFOs but a natural energy produced by a conjunction of certain geological and atmospheric conditions.

They occur in places where there are fault zones, rocky outcrops, inland waters or areas of mineral deposits. Certain earth lights sightings have also apparently been associated with stone circles, for which Devereux offers a reason. In his earlier *Earth Lights* of 1982 one of his collaborators, Paul McCartney, a geochemist, claimed that stone circles had been erected within a mile of either a surface fault or a geological intrusion.

In 1919 a Mr Sington wrote in the *English Mechanic and World of Science* of seeing 'a rapidly moving light as bright as the acetylene lamp of a bicycle' which was 'directly in the direction of the Druidical circle' of Castlerigg. Sington jumped to the irresistible conclusion, that if lights had occurred there from time to time then the early inhabitants 'would have attached great significance to them, and might then have selected the site as a place of worship'.[2] This is more or less what Devereux was claiming.

The most spectacular of recent earth lights events occurred in the vicinity of the Moel ty Uchaf circle (but also in the vicinity of many other things) in Clwyd in 1974, and had many witnesses. People saw red discs of light in the sky and heard a loud bang, but subsequent reconnaissance flights by the RAF failed to find the debris of a meteor. In Gwynedd, lights were reported near the Dyffryn Ardudwy chambered tomb in 1905; and in 1907 a ball of light was seen near the Mitchell's Fold circle in Shropshire. However, after the Dragon Project's insistence on hard data, it is surprising to read about an energy effect authenticated entirely by personal testimony. Paul Devereux is very defensive about this kind of evidence, presumably because he risks being labelled a crank for publicising it. So do some of his informants. He assures us that the woman who saw an orb of light at Avebury in 1983 is 'a solid, reliable countrywoman in her middle years', but he cannot name her because 'she is a very well-known member of that community'. His own interest in Earth Mysteries was aroused after witnessing an unexplained light phenomenon in the 1960s. He has recounted this experience on many occasions but usually, I think, in expectation of receiving a chorus of derision in return. Anyone who has read his books can have no grounds to doubt his seriousness.

Even archaeologists can have an earth lights experience. In 1979 John Barnatt had been surveying sites in Cornwall with Brian Larkman when, after dark, they both witnessed 'periodic short bursts of multicoloured light' in the claustrophobic interior of Chun Quoit (fig. 122). Devereux had an ingenious explanation for this: that the light may have been perceived by the quoit builders as the spirit of their ancestors. Not only does this suggest that the builders knew about earth lights, it also indicates that they knew how to contrive them. The plot thickened when the Dragon Project took their geiger-counters there in 1988. They recorded a natural radiation level inside the granite chamber 123 per cent higher than in the surrounding environment. What the connection is between radiation and multicoloured lights is anyone's guess.

In a recent book, *The New Ley Hunter's Guide*, Devereux has distanced himself from his earlier work on earth energies and their significance. At the same time he talks of

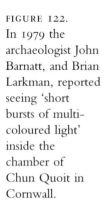

FIGURE 122. In 1979 the archaeologist John Barnatt, and Brian Larkman, reported seeing 'short bursts of multi-coloured light' inside the chamber of Chun Quoit in Cornwall.

a 'Great Divide' between serious Earth Mysteries research and New Age fantasists who, with their dowsing rods still twitching, continue to tune in and turn on to lines of terrestrial current. Hamish Miller, a dowser, has reinterpreted John Michell's famous St Michael's Line which, although it was long ago shown not to be straight, is still too exciting an idea to pass up. Miller accounted for its unstraightness by the fact that the current is sinuous. Indeed there are two proposed currents which, because of the patron saints of the churches they pass through, he has dubbed the Michael and Mary lines. With Paul Broadhurst he wrote an extraordinary book called *The Sun and the Serpent*, published in 1989, in which the reader is taken on a voyage of discovery across southern England. It now passes through many more places of historic interest than Michell could muster for his original line. The itinerary reads like a magical mystery tour dreamt up by the English Tourist Board, but what it proves is unclear, except perhaps that dowsing is believing.

During the 1980s the concept of leys underwent a thorough reexamination, stimulated to some extent by the discovery of alignments and landscape lines in the Andes. In 1978 Tony Morrison published *Pathways to the Gods*, which described an Amerindian trackway system in the Altiplano region of Bolivia. Here pathways run straight, regardless of terrain, for up to twenty miles, and link shrines, over which some Christian churches were later built. While the date of the system is unknown, it almost exactly replicates Watkins' old straight tracks. The Indians worshipped spirits at the shrines called *mal'ku*, translated by the anthropologist Alfred Metraux as 'spirit of place', or *genius loci*. The lines are still occasionally walked in what are now Christianised ceremonies.

Aerial photographs of the desert plains at Nazca in Peru show an amazing grid of lines which must have brought loud cheers from ley hunters when they first saw them. In addition to straight lines and geometric shapes, there are also animal, plant and spiral designs, all of which were laid out in the first millennium AD. The lines radiate from cairns and were etched into the landscape by removing the surface of the desert pavement to expose a lighter soil underneath. They became known to the western world after their discovery by Dr Maria Reiche, a German mathematician, in 1941. However, her theory that they were astronomical in function was not supported, or at least not entirely, by two American academics who made the most thorough investigation of them, Gerald Hawkins (of Stonehenge fame) and Anthony Aveni. So the Earth Mysteries group can still present them as an Earth Mystery.

Linear features in North America are equally enigmatic. The Hopewell Indians of Ohio, during the first half of the first millennium AD, laid out vast ritual landscapes which included long, straight linear earthworks. At Chaco Canyon in New Mexico the Anasazi Indians of prehistory left a system of 'arrow straight' roads, remarkable given that the people had neither horse nor wheel. In their book *Lines on the Landscape* of 1989 Nigel Pennick and Paul Devereux cite many other examples of linearity across the globe, but it is high time we returned home.

The landscape lines of prehistoric Britain – cursuses, stone rows and field boundaries known as reaves – were recognised and studied by archaeologists long before the Earth Mysteries group grasped their potential. The study of cursuses has a long enough history in the twentieth century, but the seventies ley hunters made no use of them. Aerial photography has recently discovered many more of these sites – over fifty are now known – providing archaeologists with the opportunity to give them serious attention. It was an archaeologist, Dr J. F. S. Stone, who first noticed that if the line of the Greater Stonehenge Cursus was extended eastwards it would pass over a solitary stone called the Cuckoo or Cuckold Stone, and then Woodhenge. The cursus is just over one and a half miles long, and the alignment to Woodhenge adds up to just over two and a half miles. Paul Devereux was understandably jubilant: 'Let us not mince words: *this is a ley*.'[3] The Dorset Cursus, at just over six miles, is the longest in Britain. In fact two linear earthworks joined together, both point to long barrows, so this is another case of the deliberate alignment of sites. At Rudston in Yorkshire there are four cursuses, one of which is aligned to the standing stone in the churchyard. Devereux has also noted other cursuses which are aligned to medieval churches: at Fornham in Suffolk to Bury St Edmunds Abbey; and at Lechlade in Gloucestershire to Southrop church.

The Dartmoor reaves are among a number of Bronze Age coaxial field systems – fields laid out systematically according to a major axis – discovered in Britain since the 1970s. The reaves survive as low stone banks, laid out in long lines, in a fashion that Andrew Fleming has described as 'terrain oblivious'. These field boundaries are obviously very difficult to date, although the south Dartmoor reave system may have been a single undertaking during the period 1700–1600 BC. It therefore seems to be part of a planned system of land division. To the ley hunter the reaves are evidence that lines could be surveyed with considerable skill by prehistoric communities, although Pennick and Devereux underemphasise the fact that they are not straight in the ley hunter's sense of the word. The slightly earlier stone rows of Dartmoor are not straight either, even if they are associated with other monuments in the way the cursuses are. The row on Stall Moor leads from a stone circle to a cairn. Devereux thinks that the initial, straight section of the row, leading from the circle, was aligned to the cairn. When the row was later extended to the cairn it was built in a less disciplined fashion.

For what it is worth, the Kennet Avenue at Avebury also appears to have been laid out in a succession of straight lengths, but this is hardly a convincing demonstration of Avebury as a geomantic centre. In fact the area has long been an Achilles Heel for ley hunters: there are a profusion of monuments but no obvious alignments. Paul Devereux agonised over this during several visits to the place, but his eventual discovery of a pattern in the landscape formed the basis of his book, *Symbolic Landscapes*, of 1992. Recent archaeological work at West Kennet long barrow has suggested that the original barrow was extended by the addition of a 'tail', producing the elongated mound we are familiar with today. Why was this done? Devereux thinks he has the answer because, standing at the western end of the tail, the view to the Windmill Hill causewayed enclosure is intersected by the ledge of Silbury Hill. This also means that the top segment of Silbury Hill stands clear of the horizon. Devereux then went to East Kennet long barrow, the Sanctuary, the Cove and the Obelisk, and Beckhampton long barrow, and discovered the same thing – the skyline intersects Silbury along the 'ledge'. Furthermore, from the Horslip long barrow, west of Avebury, the chamber of the West Kennet long barrow just touches the slope of Silbury. Silbury Hill is later than the long barrows and, presumably, the Sanctuary, and so Devereux's solution was that it had been raised 'with consummate skill' to form the centrepiece of Avebury's preexisting 'sacred geography'.

These sightlines at Avebury were not noticed earlier because nobody had looked for them. The tendency of archaeologists has been to study sites in isolation, a tendency reinforced by excavation which, so to speak, takes the site out of its landscape and puts it in a laboratory. In contrast, to Devereux the landscape provides the meaning to the monuments within it and, although this illustrates his affiliation with earlier ley hunting, he has taken the study to a more mature level. Ironically, archaeologists such as Richard Bradley and Christopher Tilley have recently adopted a similar technique in the study of monuments,[4] while Devereux in fact aired his Avebury hypothesis in the mainstream journal *Antiquity* in 1987. His theories have been developed in a series of recently published books, including *Lines on the Landscape* (1989), *Shamanism and the Mystery Lines* (1992) and *Symbolic Landscapes* (1992).

Devereux sees the British and American landscapes lines, as well as the Chinese Feng-shui, as a geomancy that linked the spiritual and mundane worlds. The individuals who orchestrated this landscape were the shamans, and here Devereux acknowledges his debt to the religious historian, Mircea Eliade. The shaman is the member of a community who has access to the spirit world. According to Eliade, he specialises in a trance, during which his soul is believed to leave his body and ascend to the sky or descend to the underworld. Drumming, trance dancing, special breathing methods and hallucinogenic substances were the means by which the trance was induced, and Devereux cites many examples around the world where such practices have been common. Mention of hallucinogenic substances provokes either indignation or a snigger in our present society, but Devereux suggests that Fly Agaric and Psilocybin mushrooms could have been used by shamans in Britain. He also argues that certain places where there is a higher than normal level of natural radiation could have augmented the effects of other methods. So presumably the shamans entered their trance states within stone circles.

Paul Devereux suggests that the lines on the landscape mark the out-of-body flights by the shamans in their journey to the spirit world. The world of spirits encompasses the dead, and cursuses are often aligned to burial mounds, so these linear earthworks may not have been for the procession of mourners but for the passing of spirits. A similar explanation is offered for the stone rows of Dartmoor: the rows, which usually have a cairn at one end, were spirit lines, while the stones set across their lines at the opposite ends were to block the passage of spirits (fig. 123).

For confirmation of this Devereux has offered a variety of new evidence that spirits travelled in straight lines. In Feng-shui it is malevolent spirits – including the spirits of the dead – which travel straight, the reason why Chinese geomancy avoids them. This in turn may be paralleled in the numinous 'fairy paths' of Irish folklore, on which it was considered unlucky to build a house. Then there is the case of 'ghost paths' in medieval Holland and Germany, which Devereux thinks may be a relic of Neolithic practice. Similar claims for straight ghost paths, also known as coffin lines and death roads, has recently emerged in Britain, relying on either the soft evidence of personal experience or on the dubious evidence of folklore. In Cornwall neither Robert Hunt, William Bottrell nor Margaret Courtenay ever found evidence of ghost paths when they were avidly collecting folklore in the nineteenth century. Therefore a certain scepticism is natural when Gabrielle Hawkes and Tom Henderson-Smith claim to have encountered oral traditions of ghost paths in 1990s Cornwall. Such new claims illustrate another tendency of Earth Mysteries research, which although it can reject leys as lines of power, and leys as old straight tracks, not to mention a host of other weird ideas, still needs to replenish its stock of enigmas. The sanctity of the straight remains untouchable.

Returning to Avebury, Devereux sees the sight line linking West Kennet, Silbury and Windmill Hill as a shamanic line. There is evidence for the use of bones from West Kennet for rituals at the Windmill Hill causewayed enclosure. They may possibly have involved the hallucinated voices of the ancestors heard through their skulls.

FIGURE 123. Merrivale stone row on Dartmoor. Paul Devereux has argued that such rows are spirit lines across the landscape.

Another possibility is that out-of-body trance journeys were taken by the shamans during rituals. Although the 'spirit path' is not formally marked on the landscape it is there symbolically. Later, when Silbury Hill had been raised, Devereux suggests that the summit was used by the shamans for their 'sitting out' because it stood at the centre of Avebury's spirit lines.

The essence of these ideas is that prehistoric monuments in Britain were the product of a consciousness alien to modern western thinking. The fact that parallels can be drawn between Britain and other parts of the world does not signify a universal civilisation, but some archetypal human awareness. We encountered a similar argument in the nineteenth century, in Lewis Morgan's theory of the 'psychic unity of man'; and in the work of William Gowland and Daniel Wilson, who both explained megalithic monuments in Europe and Asia as representing 'a similar development of the human mind'. To nineteenth-century archaeologists it was a stage in the progression from savagery to civilisation, but at the end of the twentieth century the agenda has changed.

Paul Devereux thinks, and there are many people who agree with him, that modern western civilisation is not the acme of human achievement. It is successful and arrogant but has a long casualty list. This is contrasted to an argument for the innate awareness of nature and its spiritual forces which has been lost in the west. Devereux tells the ley hunter that 'by peering into the layers of time covering our landscapes, we are simultaneously plumbing deep layers of our subconscious minds'.[5] He seems to want to reclaim contact with the nature-awareness we have apparently lost, but this is of course impossible. Our current mental habits and scientific arguments are too deeply engrained, and we are too cynical to put our trust in shamanism and all its potential for manipulation. Earth Mysteries is fed by its disaffection with the modern world, as was the ley hunting boom of the 1960s. Its goals are as unattainable as John Michell's New Jerusalem, and all the movement can do is prolong the journey by ever reinventing the subject. It may well be that 'we have forgotten about our inner life; we have forgotten that the land is sacred, and we have forgotten the interaction between them both'.[6] The pursuit of Earth Mysteries may offer personal fulfilment, but for society it is a consolation, not a solution.

25

Radiocarbon and Other Revolutions

There was a revolution in archaeology in the 1960s and its chief protagonist came, appropriately enough, from outer space. Its name was Carbon-14, a radioactive isotope formed in the Earth's upper atmosphere by cosmic radiation. Very slowly Carbon-14 decays at a constant, known rate, so that half of a given sample will have disappeared after a period of about 5700 years. Its decay is balanced by its creation through cosmic radiation, so the proportion of Carbon-14 to the ordinary Carbon-12 isotope in the atmosphere remains constant – for every Carbon-14 atom there are a million million Carbon-12 atoms. Carbon-14 enters the food chain when plants absorb carbon dioxide from the air during photosynthesis. It then passes into animals which eat plants, and finally into animals which eat animals which eat plants. So the proportion of Carbon-14 to Carbon-12 in all living organisms is the same as it is in the atmosphere. This balance is maintained until organisms die, when they cease to take in fresh supplies of Carbon-14, and the existing Carbon-14 decays.

In 1949 Professor Willard Libby of the University of Chicago announced that a knowledge of this process could be used to date archaeological remains. The principle of radiocarbon dating is to measure the proportion of Carbon-14 left in a given sample of organic matter (usually charcoal, wood, bone or antler) and to calculate how long the process of decay without replenishment has been going on – in other words to calculate when the organism died. The technique has its limitations because it can only give approximate dates for samples tested, expressed as a statistical margin of error, but in 1950 this was a small price to pay for an independent form of dating which no longer had to rely on historical dates from the Mediterranean world.

Archaeologists greeted radiocarbon with eager anticipation, but it soon confounded expectations. In 1952 a date of 2620 BC was calculated for an early Neolithic settlement at Durrington Walls near Stonehenge. Stuart Piggott, who in his *Neolithic Cultures of the British Isles*, written in 1951, placed the earliest Neolithic culture in Britain at 2000 BC, declared that the Durrington Walls date was 'archaeologically inacceptable'. So were the amazingly early dates for megalithic tombs in Brittany. When French laboratories started publishing figures earlier than 3000 BC, which was earlier than the Cretan round tombs they were supposedly derived from, many British archaeologists were publicly surprised and privately suspicious.

Nevertheless, with the publication of more and more radiocarbon dates during the 1950s, the Diffusionist chronology of Childe and his contemporaries looked increasingly creaky. Some archaeologists, although Childe was not one of them, responded by declaring that the scientists must have got it wrong. In the event radiocarbon dating *was* found to be significantly in error, but not in the direction preferred by reactionary diffusionists. Alarm bells had started ringing when the radiocarbon dates for ancient Egypt failed to match those of the Egyptian calendars. Elsewhere in Europe and the Near East radiocarbon dates were earlier than archaeologists expected, but in Egypt they were later. For a while the whole corpus of work on Egyptian chronology, reconstructed from written records, was cast in doubt, until it was shown that radiocarbon dates had to be calibrated before they could be expressed in calendar years.

One of the assumptions made by Libby when he developed the dating technique was that the concentration of Carbon-14 in the Earth's atmosphere had remained constant through time. This was found to be untrue when samples of the long-lived Bristlecone pine tree were submitted for testing. The Bristlecone pine grows in the White Mountains of California and can live for over 4000 years. It is also particularly suited to tree ring dating, or dendrochronology, because its annual growth rings are quite marked. In the early 1960s, when samples taken from these trees were radiocarbon dated, the dates failed to match the tree ring sequence. This was accounted for by the fact that the concentration of Carbon-14 in the atmosphere in prehistoric times was higher than it is today. Therefore the samples had a larger proportion of Carbon-14 than had been anticipated, and so gave misleadingly recent dates. In 1967 Professor Hans Suess, who had been testing Bristlecone pine samples in his laboratory in California, proposed that radiocarbon dates earlier than 1200 BC needed to be adjusted to calendar years. Although to date it is still not possible to produce a precise calibration chart for this, the essential validity of tree ring calibration has never been questioned.

Suess produced his own calibration chart which brought his dates for Egypt into broad agreement with the traditional historical dates. In north-west Europe the effects of this calibration were staggering. Stuart Piggott excavated the long barrow at Dalladies in Kincardineshire in 1970, which produced a date of 3240 BC. When this was calibrated it was pushed back to between 4200 and 4000 BC. The Neolithic period thus began more than 2000 years earlier than Piggott had proposed less than twenty years previously. Dalladies was by no means exceptional: Fussell's Lodge long barrow was also dated earlier than 4000 BC, Wayland's Smithy and Nutbane long barrows around 3500 BC, while Arminghall, one of the earliest henges, was dated 3300 BC, and the sarsen structure of Stonehenge 2120 BC. The earliest date for a megalithic tomb was Kercado, at Carnac in Brittany, dated at an astonishing 4800 BC.

The megalithic chambered tombs of Britain and Brittany were now recognised as being far earlier than the round tombs of Crete, their supposed ancestors. More than that, they were shown to be the earliest stone-built monuments in the world. For an earlier generation of archaeologists, who had painstakingly studied the tombs of Iberia and the Mediterranean for the origins of the British megaliths, this was a crushing blow. To a new generation these were exciting times, well expressed in Colin Renfrew's *Before Civilization* of 1973, where the challenges facing archaeologists were anticipated with undisguised enthusiasm.

Renfrew talked in terms of a Radiocarbon Revolution, but its arrival coincided with a more profound revolution in archaeology, one that was resisted with far greater force. Even before the full impact of radiocarbon had been felt, American archaeologists such as Lewis Binford were challenging the limits of archaeological inference proposed by Christopher Hawkes, Stuart Piggott and others in the 1950s. Archaeology had then adopted a limited range of conceptual models, such as the Three Age System, and a narrow range of possibilities to explain change (i.e. invasion). Drawing on work from other disciplines the Americans now used 'archaeology as anthropology', ecological and geographical models, and cybernetics to advance new ideas, most of which were concerned with explaining different levels of social complexity. They focused on social 'processes', hence the term 'processual archaeology'.

The leading British advocate of this new archaeology was David Clarke, a Cambridge don. Clarke argued for a new critical self-awareness on the part of archaeologists, pointing out that every archaeologist has a preconception which restricts archaeology to certain aims and methods of explanation, and demanded that these preconceptions be recognised. The act of critical self-awareness influenced methodology because the inductive approach, pioneered in archaeology by John Aubrey, whereby generalisations are made from accumulated data, was rejected as postulating an impossible objectivity, even if there are professional archaeologists who still subscribe to it. A new deductive approach demanded the formulation of hypotheses which could be tested against the data, which would then inform new hypotheses for testing, and so on.

Of all these new approaches cybernetics, better known as systems theory, had the most potential. It grew from the assumption that socio-cultural systems are integral whole units. Therefore material technology, economy, agriculture, social organisation, ideology and ecology are merely sub-systems extracted by the archaeologists for the convenience of study. Clarke described the socio-cultural system as 'a unit system in which all the cultural information is a stabilised but constantly changing network of intercommunicating attributes forming a complex whole'.[1] A change in one unit or sub-system would trigger changes in one or more others until a position of equilibrium was reached. A simplified example might be a society where land is scarce and there are property qualifications for marriage. This would cause marriage to be deferred until an otherwise eligible partner had accumulated sufficient property, causing fertility to be lowered and the population to decrease. Conversely, an increase in population may stimulate an advance in farming techniques such as irrigation, which in turn increases productivity and allows further growth of population.

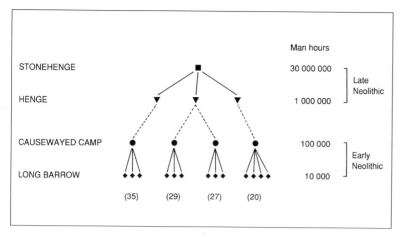

STONEHENGE

HENGE

CAUSEWAYED CAMP

LONG BARROW

(35)   (29)   (27)   (20)

Man hours

30 000 000

1 000 000

100 000

10 000

Late
Neolithic

Early
Neolithic

FIGURE 124. Renfrew's hierarchy of Wessex monuments, based on the work hours needed for their construction. Processual archaeology was perfectly suited to diagrammatic representation. (*After Renfrew, 1973*)

Systems theory is a dynamic and flexible model of society (fig. 124). In the 1970s it proved more useful in explaining change in prehistory than the outmoded Invasion Hypothesis, which presented cultures as essentially static entities. It established that society is structured by many competing elements, but also advanced the dubious idea that societies and the individuals within them obey immutable laws of human behaviour. This mechanistic view of society, where humanity is a slave to deterministic causal relationships, and where the individual is reduced to invisibility within the system, is perhaps just a different way of portraying the past in the image of the present. In its most extreme manifestation systems theory argued that, although archaeology can study only a fraction of sub-systems, since all sub-systems are interrelated it is therefore possible to reconstruct prehistoric societies in their entirety.

On the basis that 'theory is built by theorising', the search for a viable conceptual framework for archaeology has continued since the 1980s. A new tendency has emerged that rejects the 'cybernetic wasteland' of the processualists, taking the view that a social totality cannot be broken down into constituent parts. No single prehistory can be written because, as with history, experience is individual rather than collective. For example stone circles could be studied from the point of view of those admitted to the circle, or of those kept without; between the person at the front, the middle or the back of a procession; between men, women, old, young, and so on. In answer to the criticism that the nature of archaeological evidence permits only general statements to be made, it is argued that archaeologists only dig up specific events, not totalities.

'Post-processual archaeology' has derived its intellectual thrust from structuralism, semiotics and post-structuralism. Its leading advocates are probably more familiar with the work of French thinkers, such as Barthes, Bourdieu, Foucault and Derrida, than they are with Neolithic pottery. One of its aims is to break from the theoretical straitjacket of the social totality and social process, by emphasising the relationship between the individual and society, and to acknowledge that individuals have a creative influence over their own lives. These factors, it is argued, have become condensed into the archaeological record. An analogy drawn between material culture and language, and the observation that meaning in both is dispersed not via a single but through chains of signification, has spawned the cliché 'material culture as text', implying that the archaeological record can be read in the same way as a book. The control of meaning in material culture or written texts is achieved, according to Ian Hodder, by creating boundaries across which meaning is not dispersed, suggesting that human thought processes are highly contextualised, hence Hodder's 'contextual archaeology'.

A simple example of Hodder's thinking was offered in the case of Scandinavian chambered tombs, generally held to represent kinship groups held together by common descent from ancestors. However, the lineages would have had to exist before the tombs that represent them could have been constructed. The idea that megaliths represent lineages partly derives from the remains of large numbers of individuals contained within them, but long mounds were initially associated with single burials, being used as ossuaries only later. Hodder's explanation is that 'the initial use of the tombs for individual burial created a text which could be read in relation to the formation of lineages. The tomb itself creates the potential for the idea of a descent group linked to a common ancestor. The text had to be written before the tomb could be given new meaning and the lineages formed.'[2]

Only a minority of archaeologists work under the banner of Theory with a capital T. In 1982 Colin Renfrew remarked of his colleagues that 'discussions at many meetings in London . . . continue to focus upon matters of fact − that is to say upon scholarly assessments of accumulated data. Theoretical or processual issues are rarely discussed at such meetings.'[3] Ian Kinnes perhaps spoke for many of his colleagues when he argued that prehistory requires 'systematic explanations but not explanation by systems'. In fact systematic study, based on excavated evidence, was in the process of challenging Diffusionism even before the implications of radiocarbon had become clear.

The post-war expansion of the archaeological profession produced not only new archaeologists but more archaeologists. Pursuing their own specialisations, they embarked on a rigorous scrutiny of the archaeological record, with conclusions increasingly at odds with traditional explanations. Isobel Smith's work on Windmill Hill and Avebury is a good example, because she found 'continuity of concepts and practices first detectable in the earlier Neolithic period and extending forward into the Bronze Age'.[4] Another example came in the study of Scottish chambered tombs. Three tombs excavated by J. X. W. P. Corcoran in the early 1960s revealed evidence of more than one phase of construction. Tulach an t'Sionnaich in Caithness began with a single chamber covered by a circular cairn, which was later completely sealed beneath a heel-shaped cairn. Later still this was engulfed by a monumental long cairn. At Tulloch of Assery, also in Caithness, a small passage grave under a long cairn was enveloped by a new horned cairn with its own separate passage grave. Mid Gleniron, in Wigtownshire, revealed two cairns in tandem, each with its own chamber, which were later covered by a single cairn with a façade that allowed access to only one of the chambers. Nor was this evidence confined to Scotland: excavation of Dyffryn Ardudwy in North Wales and Wayland's Smithy also revealed more than one phase of building. By implication this work rejected the parallels which had been drawn between Scottish tombs and those of France and Iberia, although it was the radiocarbon calibration, which greatly expanded the Neolithic time scale, that established their validity.

Radiocarbon proved to be a watershed in the explanation of prehistory: all subsequent studies have been biased toward continuity rather than invasion. During the 1970s advocating the Invasion Hypothesis was like trying to sell meat to a vegetarian. There was an understandable reaction against 'invasion neurosis', as Grahame Clark now called it, and even the theory of a Beaker Folk was sorely tested. The evidence for an influx of migrants in the Early Bronze Age depended largely on the evidence of a round-headed people invading and superseding a long-headed people. But this was based on a small sample of burials in barrows, which in turn represented a small selection of prehistoric populations. The difference between the two skull types could therefore easily be explained as a genetic change over a long period of time. Meanwhile the appearance of beakers could be explained as forming part of a cult package just as easily as representing an invasion. However, diffusion of a sort did take place at one crucial time in British prehistory. The adoption of farming, using foreign strains of wheat and foreign breeds of cattle, proves that somebody had to sail over in a boat and exert influence from beyond these shores, but colonising Megalith Builders have fallen out of favour.

In 1969 Humphrey Case argued that establishing a farming economy, requiring the transport of seeds and livestock across the English Channel, and 'the long, hazardous and absorbing struggles needed at first to maintain the farming cycle', would have precluded the erection of large ritual works. The long barrows were therefore the product of 'stable adjustments', i.e. the fruits of an agricultural surplus. More recently this view has been challenged by, among others, Julian Thomas, who in his *Rethinking the Neolithic* of 1991 argued against treating the Mesolithic and Neolithic as if they are oil and water. Many prehistorians have pointed out that food surpluses were a feature of the hunter-gatherer way of life, and that in Australia a hunter-gatherer lifestyle produced a monument-building culture. Thomas also suggested that archaeologists have previously underestimated the degree of dependence on wild food resources in the early Neolithic, and that the early Neolithic lifestyle was substantially mobile. Moreover, taking Europe as a whole, many of the earliest monuments are to be found in the Atlantic margin, the very places where evidence for cultivation is least forthcoming. As soon as the axiom linking megaliths with farming is given up, then the transition between Mesolithic and Neolithic becomes far more interesting and suggestive of new interpretations. Indeed prehistory is increasingly seen as a continuum. The old invasion model, where one culture was superseded by another, has come to look curiously like the catastrophe theories of eighteenth-century geology.

The evidence for continuity was there all the time. In his *The Age of Stonehenge* of 1980 Colin Burgess pointed out essential similarities between long and round barrows which archaeologists had hitherto been conditioned not to see. Both reveal evidence of timber structures and, like the long barrows, those of the round barrows appear to have represented mortuary enclosures which were left open for a considerable time before a barrow was raised over them. This one example demonstrates the fallibility of archaeological interpretation, despite the accumulation of a mass of reliable information, and highlights a flaw in the empirical method of reconstructing prehistory on 'established facts'. The evidence must be questioned, but you only get answers to the questions you ask, so any reconstruction of prehistory will be distorted by contemporary preconceptions.

In 1976 Aubrey Burl published *The Stone Circles of the British Isles*, a book that was long overdue. Archaeologists had already published painstaking and detailed scrutinies of beakers and bronze axes; here at last was the first catalogue of all the known stone circles and an attempt to make sense of them. Although it was written after calibrated dates came into circulation, very few stone circles had been excavated recently enough to have provided samples for dating. This remains true today. Burl therefore projected known dates on to a relative chronology based on typological association. He established that the earliest circles, some of them perhaps earlier than 3000 BC, are the great open rings of Cumbria (Long Meg, Swinside, Castlerigg), Stenness in Orkney (fig. 125) and the Clava cairns of Inverness. The latter were the inspiration for the Recumbent Stone circles of neighbouring Aberdeenshire, probably built during the period 2500–2000 BC, when the majority of the better-known British circles were erected, including the enormous circles at Stanton Drew and Avebury. Burl, however, detected a general reduction in the scale of circles over time. He thought the majority of them, the small ones, were built after 2000 BC, perhaps until as late as 1200 BC. Given this 2000 year timespan, he thought it likely that the first stone circles had a purpose and meaning very different from the last.

The origin of the stone circle form is more difficult to explain. Some excavations – for example Balfarg in Fife by Roger Mercer and Croft Moraig in Perthshire by Stuart Piggott and Derek Simpson – have shown that the stones were preceded by timber circles. Two circles on Machrie Moor, excavated by Alison Haggarty in the 1980s, showed that the stones had been placed exactly where timber posts had stood, despite the fact that the ground had been ploughed in the intervening period. Far from explaining the origin of the stone circles, this evidence merely begs the question: where did the timber rings originate? The same is true in the case of the early henges of

FIGURE 125. The Stones of Stenness in Orkney. Radiocarbon dating has established it was erected before 3000 BC and is one of the earliest circles in Britain. (*Historic Scotland*)

southern and eastern Britain, which Burl saw as contemporary and analogous to the great open circles of Cumbria. While there may be no single, simple solution to explain the appearance of stone circles, there is an implication here that henges, timber rings and the earlier stone circles share an ultimate source, and that this may rest in hitherto overlooked characteristics of the circular chambered cairns.

Graham Callander's theory that stone circles evolved from the kerbstones of circular cairns was rejected by Burl on chronological grounds. At Callanish the small chambered cairn was raised inside the circle after the circle was built. A reappraisal of Hemp's excavation at Bryn Celli Ddu in Anglesey established that this too was built on top of an existing stone circle. Although in these cases the chambered cairn was apparently built much later than the circle, in others it is possible that the stone circle was intended to be the initial phase in the construction of a tomb. The earliest dated stone circle anywhere is Newgrange in Ireland, which produced radiocarbon dates averaging 3250 BC. It was probably erected before the great chambered tomb was built. At Knocklea near Dublin a stone circle was actually concealed under a cairn. Burl suggested that there may have been two stages in the building of such chambered tombs: the first dedicatory or propitiatory rites within a stone ring; followed up by completion of the tumulus.

Burl later looked for and found similar evidence in Britain. Beneath the mound of Callis Wold, one of a number of Neolithic round barrows on the Yorkshire Wolds, was a circular, ditched enclosure with a wooden mortuary house in the centre.

Excavation reports of similar Neolithic round barrows also hint of circular ditches, or rings of stones or posts, which originally stood open until concealed beneath the great covering mounds. Burl believes that in the Neolithic period 'death and the dead obsessed the living', and that 'needing to control these powerful and dangerous spirits, the people confined the bones inside "magic" rings of earth or stone'.[5]

More recently Tom Clare has tackled the same problem of origins, but in his case from the perspective of the henges. He has argued that stone circles should be seen as comparable not only to henges but also to the lesser-known ring banks and ring ditches. Each created a circular area within which ritual could be performed. Whether the circle was defined by stones, a bank, a ditch, a bank and ditch, or a combination of earthworks and stones, was a matter of local preference, not necessarily a differentiation or hierarchy of function. Like Burl, he sees the origins of such enclosures in the earlier Neolithic. There is an obvious connection made with causewayed enclosures, but Clare also added rectilinear enclosures associated with long barrows, and the forecourts of chambered tombs. He argued that timber mortuary enclosures were later enclosed within long mounds, that the raising of the mound may not have been the original intention, and that sealing an enclosure beneath a mound was similar to blocking the entrance to a megalithic tomb.

The sealed entrances to the megalithic tombs may be echoed in the Recumbent Stone circles of north-east Scotland. There are many examples where the entrance to an enclosure is defined either by raised banks or, in the case of stone circles like Castlerigg and Avebury, by the tallest stones in the ring. The Recumbent Stone circles have the largest stones standing beside the recumbent, so Clare suggested that the recumbent is reminiscent of the blocking stones of the chambered tombs. In these studies, Burl and Clare established that stone circles cannot be viewed as a separate species, as the astronomers had done, and that the stone circles cannot be understood without reference to the kinds of monuments that preceded them.

Current opinions on Neolithic burial monuments owe much to the pioneering excavations of the fifties and sixties. At West Kennet long barrow Stuart Piggott argued that its builders were practising an ancestor cult. At Wayland's Smithy Richard Atkinson suggested that a great totem pole had stood above the wooden mortuary house, implying that these tombs were not tombs, in the modern sense, but shrines to the ancestors. Evidence for the complex and convoluted treatment of the dead has merely reinforced this idea. The evidence for ritual activity in the forecourts may therefore not have resulted from funeral feasts, but from ceremonies essential to the living rather than the dead. Then there was Tulach an t'Sionnaich, the cairn which had been enlarged, then enlarged again on a grand scale, a spectacle in the physical as well as the ideological world of prehistoric people. The chambered tombs were, in Andrew Fleming's phrase, 'tombs for the living'.

26

Sex and the Dead

Sex and the dead, according to W. B. Yeats, are the only subjects worthy of a serious person's conversation. We can develop this to include fertility and death, love and death, the cradle and the grave, growth and decay, the future and the past, which all boil down to the essence of life, as fundamental today as it was 5000 years ago. So perhaps it is in terms of fertility and death that we should consider the great chambered tombs-cum-shrines and the stone circles. Analogies can be found in megalithic cultures across the world. On Malekula, in the New Hebrides, rings of stones were still being erected in the nineteenth century, where dances of death and rituals celebrating a creation myth were performed. In the Gambia stone circles raised up to a thousand years ago have been found, when excavated, to contain large cemeteries of skulls. Some villagers still hold seasonal festivals in them, where fertility cults celebrate sowing and harvesting. In Assam, where megalithic tombs were opened periodically to allow new interments, no work was allowed in the village when the tomb was open, in case the paddy should rot as the corpses in the grave had rotted. Closer to home, in Brittany certain stones connected with chambered tombs had the power to induce fertility in women.

In Neolithic Britain death came early. At the Hambledon Hill causewayed enclosure in Dorset most men were dead by thirty-six and women by thirty-one. Less than half of all children lived beyond the age of seven. At Isbister chambered tomb in Orkney the statistics are even grimmer: half of all children died in their first year, while most adults were dead before they were twenty. The chambered tombs were built by young people, many of them suffering malnutrition, osteoarthritis or loss of teeth, to say nothing of the hazards of childbirth. 'Death was no gentle stranger to these people. It was a house-guest.'[1]

This bleak vision of the lives of prehistoric people is the background to Aubrey Burl's reconstruction of prehistoric belief and ritual. Ambrose Bierce once described religion as 'a daughter of Hope and Fear, explaining to Ignorance the nature of the Unknowable'. Burl cites it to explain his own position: 'disease, accident and the frequency of death conditioned the rituals of people who could explain their troubles only by attributing them to forces that had somehow been offended, and had somehow to be controlled through the spirits of the ancestors'. This approach has been criticised for presenting too pessimistic an outlook, but Burl is not presenting an image of primitive barbarians, nor for that matter of noble savages. His Stonehenge people are recognisably human.

Burl's viewpoint is a personal one and his syntax is often decidedly poetic. Stonehenge is described variously as 'like a gaunt, wrecked cage of Time', and 'a dark place, oppressive as though Death were lurking in its shadows'. Death may have loomed large in Neolithic minds (although longevity is surely a relative concept). In a hostile world stone circles were places where 'rites of sexuality stated the need for a fertile land, and magical performances captured the image of the sun, human bones maintained ancestor cults, offerings were still made to the dead, broken pottery, broken arrowheads, broken twigs formed a "spirit" world in the fearful and imaginative minds of the people'.[2] Burl argued that death and fertility were integrated into one whole, so 'the fertility of the ground, the fecundity of women, the spirits of forebears that interceded with Nature on behalf of the living, the cold winter sunset and joyful summer sunrise, all these merged together in the animistic minds of these early farmers'.[3]

Fertility and death, then, is the theme of the stone circles. Burl has explored this idea in a number of books, especially *Prehistoric Avebury* (1979), *Rites of the Gods* (1981) and *The Stonehenge People* (1987). His criteria for study are the architecture of the stones, astronomy, ethnography and the artefacts uncovered by excavation. The last has involved him in a close reading of excavation reports, including the work of early investigators, from Hoare and Cunnington, back to Stukeley and even Inigo Jones. All their works provide valuable information if they are read critically. Burl has paid particular attention to artefacts which at the time of discovery were thought insignificant, things such as broken pottery, antlers, ox bones, pebbles and flints.

Winter was associated with death, and so was the moon: 'its very association with night may have symbolised darkness, cold and death in a way the appealed vividly to the allusive imagination of prehistoric man'.[4] In surveys of tombs and associated structures Burl detected orientations to the moon and the winter solstice, which led him to envisage nocturnal winter ceremonies. The Clava cairns in Scotland have lunar orientations, as do the neighbouring Recumbent Stone circles of Aberdeenshire. Many of the recumbent stones have cup marks, which Burl interpreted as lunar symbols, but they are oriented too far south to align on any rising or setting. However, at the major standstill the moon as seen in the north of Scotland barely rises above the horizon, so 'the low-rising moon would appear almost to float along the flat top of the recumbent itself'.[5]

At Avebury the Cove was oriented to the most northerly moonrise, while the lesser known Beckhampton Cove, later linked to Avebury by the Beckhampton Avenue, was oriented to midwinter sunrise. At Stonehenge Burl argued (as did Atkinson) that a wooden building preceded the stone circles. Assuming that its entrance was in line with the original entrance to the henge, it was oriented to the most northerly moonrise. The building was a mortuary house where the important dead were placed while their flesh decayed, before their bones were taken to one of the nearby long barrows. The argument for this is based on the lunar alignment plus two other important pieces of evidence.

Accounts of digging at the centre of Stonehenge in the seventeenth century talk of unearthing animal bones, including ox skulls, and ox skulls have been found at many long barrows. The Beckhampton Road long barrow near Avebury contained three ox skulls but no human remains. At Fussell's Lodge it appears that an ox hide, complete with hooves and skull, had been draped over the charnel house with the horned head above the entrance. The ox may have had a totemic significance, 'perhaps the epitome of strength, perhaps even as the emblem of a richer, more powerful member of the group', but the importance of these skulls was their association with death rites.

The only stone connected with the first phase of Stonehenge is the Heel Stone, standing outside the bank and ditch. In the succeeding phases there were also single pillars: the Slaughter Stone, one of the bluestones, but larger and standing apart from the concentric circles; and the Altar Stone, standing in the centre of the sarsen horseshoe. Single pillars or posts are also connected with chambered tombs, notably in the chamber at Bryn Celli Ddu, and in the forecourt at Cairnholy in Kirkcudbright, where the single pillar appears to have been the focus of ceremonial activity because a number of fires had been lit around it. There are many other cases of pillars or posts connected with long barrows, such as Giant's Hills in Lincolnshire, Wor Barrow, Thickthorn Down and Badshot Lea in Wessex. These were 'representations of the female guardian of the dead', and so 'stones outside henges and stone circles may also have been the embodiment of this protective spirit'.[6] The horseshoe of trilithons at Stonehenge is another echo of earlier times. A similar configuration of wooden posts was found by Grahame Clark in his excavation of Arminghall in the 1930s, and others are known from stone circles such as Croft Moraig and Loanhead of Daviot in Scotland. Burl likened them to the crescent-shaped forecourts of chambered tombs, but 'with the end of long barrow building, only a symbolic component of a megalithic tomb was constructed'.[7]

This interpretation of Stonehenge can also be applied to Avebury. Here the Sanctuary with its original wooden building is also seen as a mortuary house. Fragments of burnt sarsen recovered during Maud Cunnington's excavation in 1930 may be related to the scorched bones found in the West Kennet chambered tomb less than a mile away. The similarity between coves at Avebury and elsewhere, and the single chamber megalithic tombs, like the Cornish quoits, has long been recognised. Burl interprets the Avebury Cove as a symbolic burial chamber (fig. 126), while the Obelisk at the centre of the south circle was another single pillar signifying the protectress of the dead – 'an image of the ancestors and fecundity of the earth'. There was therefore a continuation of earlier practices, because the rites performed within stone circles were very similar to those enacted in the outdated tombs, but now executed in an open-air structure.

At Avebury Burl saw ceremonies where skulls and other bones were carried along

FIGURE 126. The Avebury Cove, possibly a symbolic burial chamber.

the Kennet Avenue for rituals at the Cove and Obelisk. The discovery of red ochre at the Sanctuary led him to suggest that these skulls, and the people carrying them, may have been painted. Rituals were led by witch-doctors, or shamans, for whom Burl accepts there is little primary but some secondary evidence. Two Bronze Age burials from different parts of Denmark were found accompanied by a witches' brew of oddities – claw of falcon, tail of snake, tooth of horse, jaw of squirrel, quartz pebbles – which were probably the paraphernalia of sorcery. Some curious and rare objects have also turned up in British barrows – strange pebbles, perforated ox bones that could have been used as whistles to summon up the spirits of the dead, small pieces of bone and chalk with star and lozenge patterns. Rock carvings in Scandinavia, made in about 1800 BC, show what are presumably priests, dressed in animal skins, or bird masks. Perhaps the witch-doctors at Avebury wore antler head-dresses or the hides of bulls. There were set times for performing ceremonies – 'primitive life is encircled by the year and its seasons' – and Burl argued that their annual feasts survived in the Celtic calendar, in festivals such as Beltane and Samhain. Equally likely, something that no archaeologist would have argued before the 1970s, is that the Druids described by classical writers were descended from the shamans of the circles, despite their superficial differences.

Ceremonies at the stone circles had three main elements: human bones; offerings to the Earth; and sexuality. The male/female symbolism of the Kennet Avenue stones, and the long broken up, perforated Ring Stone may have represented 'ritual mating at the time of sowing'. Death and fertility were also expressed in material offerings to the Earth. Pits were dug near the Obelisk into which fertile, brown earth was deposited. Antlers are found in the ditches at Stonehenge and Avebury, and in round barrows, but not always as worn out tools used in the excavating of earthworks. Many are undamaged, 'symbols of growth and rebirth', and can be viewed alongside the human remains found in the ditches. The burial of three women, one at the Sanctuary, one in the ditch at the southern entrance to Avebury, and another at Woodhenge, may have been 'personifications of the [death] "goddess" herself, acting as surrogates for an Other-World presence'.

FIGURE 127. The outer circle and ditch at Avebury. Aubrey Burl has interpreted the ditch as a magical as well as a physical boundary.

The idea of the huge Avebury ditch (fig. 127) may have come from a desire 'to penetrate the core of the earth in order to bury their antler picks as dedications that would give magical protection to the stone circles'.[8] This takes up a point made by Roger Mercer after his excavations at Hambledon Hill, that the placing of skulls on the ditch bottom 'was quite deliberate and in some way reinforced the physical or psychological strength of the boundaries'. In the Kennet Avenue were deposits of deliberately smashed pots, waste flints, earth, hazelnuts and the twigs of fruit bearing trees, which Burl interpreted as 'offerings of thanks and appeasement to the forces controlling the destinies of the men and women with whom the dead could speak'.

Burl has examined the theme of fertility and death, using the latter as his point of departure. There are two, equally personal, studies of the subject which have taken the opposite starting point. Michael Dames explored the theme of symbols – in objects, architecture and landscape – in two books, *The Silbury Treasure* (1976) and *The Avebury Cycle* (1977). Although a graduate in archaeology and geography, Dames was a lecturer in art history at the time he undertook his research. It was prompted initially by witnessing the anti-climax of the Silbury Hill excavations of the 1960s, which led him to believe that archaeologists had asked the wrong questions of prehistoric monuments and had therefore failed to make sense of them. He criticised conventional wisdom because of its tendency to 'fragment prehistory in the name of scientific analysis', and based his approach on the premise that the study of symbolic structures is a work of integration, not reduction.

Dames argued that a female divinity was worshipped in the Neolithic, and that 'the religion of the Great Goddess . . . was concerned with the three great realities of birth, marriage and death'.[9] In the Avebury district he tried to show how the landscape and its monuments could have been read as symbols of this goddess in various forms. For example Silbury Hill represented the goddess in labour, the hill being the womb, the quarry ditch being her body (fig. 128), while West Kennet long barrow was the goddess in old age. The Avebury monuments as a whole were a symbolic figure of the life cycle. Here a year-long religious drama was staged, 'with each edifice offering in turn a special setting for the celebration of a particular event in the farming year, matched by the corresponding event in the human life cycle'.[10] Dames believes that there is 'a common urge to identify the human life cycle with the seasons'.

FIGURE 128. According to Michael Dames, Silbury Hill represented the womb of the Great Goddess. The Avebury monuments as a whole were a symbolic figure of the life cycle.

The Silbury Treasure and *The Avebury Cycle* had more impact on Earth Mysteries research than they did on conventional archaeology. If they had read it, archaeologists would have had little difficulty dismissing the minutiae of his argument, but some of Dames' preoccupations, such as the way monuments were perceived in terms of a cultural landscape, prefigured some of the concerns of post-processual archaeologists. Dames interpreted Silbury as a 'harvest hill', an idea taken up by another geographer, Rodney Castleden, in his book *The Stonehenge People* of 1987. Despite the coincidence of their titles, Castleden and Burl have opposing views of Neolithic Britain. Castleden's book has a golden tinge to it: 'With something approaching ecological balance and communities as a matter of routine living peacefully within their means, it is possible to see in the Neolithic culture an object lesson for modern industrial economies and societies in the west.'[11]

It is perhaps inevitable that 'outsiders' such as Dames and Castleden should emphasise fertility over death, given that access to the archaeology of death is generally restricted to the professionals. Death does not make the same impact on visitors to chambered tombs as it does on the archaeologists who excavate them, and who are required to record meticulously and interpret the location of each fragment. Indeed the careful removal of bones from a tomb to some extent mirrors the care devoted to their original deposition. Therefore in their study of what part the dead played in the lives of the living archaeologists approach their subject from a different perspective.

Isbister chambered tomb on South Ronaldsay was partially excavated in 1958, and then again in the 1970s by Ronald Simison and John Hedges. It yielded over 16,000 human bones or fragments of bone (fig. 129). Isbister has a complicated tomb layout but is essentially a stalled cairn: it has an elongated passage which is divided into sections, or stalls, by paired vertical slabs which project slightly from the chamber walls. At Isbister an entrance passage is at right angles to the stalled chamber, which has wider end stalls and three side cells leading off it. Within this architectural configuration the bones were found to conform to an ordered deposition with 'little piles containing a skull and other bones along the sides of the main chamber, skulls in the side cells and residual bones under, and perhaps on, the shelves of the end stalls'.[12] The bones were often bleached and weathered, indicating that they had been exposed to the elements before their deposition within the tomb. Hedges argued that, after the process of excarnation was completed, the bones were initially deposited in a pile within the main chamber, and at this stage the bones were 'treated as being representative of a person'. Later, the piles of bones were sorted, 'with skulls being placed in one context and the post-cranial bones in another', and 'this was done with evident care'. In other words the dead ceased to exist as individuals. By sorting, dispersing and repositing the bones elsewhere within the tomb their individuality was subsumed. They had become 'the ancestors'.

FIGURE 129. Isbister chambered tomb in Orkney was excavated in the 1970s, yielding over 16,000 human bones. (*John Hedges*)

The bones within the tomb were not all human, and of particular significance were the numerous bird carcasses, fish bones and joints of meat. Hedges also pointed out that there were other potential foodstuffs which would not have left any archaeological trace, although he did recover 303 seeds, predominantly of barley. These deposits were painstakingly compared with other Orcadian tombs – of which only Quanterness, excavated by Colin Renfrew in the 1970s, yielded the same quantity and quality of evidence – which established distinct preferences for particular birds and animals. At Isbister, together with Quanterness, Blackhammer and Knowe of Rowiegar chambered tombs, mutton or goat was the favoured meat, while at Mid Howe it was beef and at Knowe of Ramsay and Knowe of Yarso it was venison. The early excavations of Orkney tombs failed to recover fish bones, but at Isbister and Quanterness there were quantities of small fish from local waters, and a small amount of shellfish. However, the settlement of Knap of Howar yielded large numbers of fish taken from further out to sea, while sea shells occur in tens of thousands on other contemporary habitation sites.

Hedges decided that these differences were not due to chance, but were the results of deliberate selection. The same was true of other organisms which he thought were deliberately placed within the tombs but which could not be classed as foodstuffs. At Quanterness there were significant numbers of bones from small song-birds, at Cuween on the chamber floor were twenty-four dog skulls, while at Isbister the predominant species was the white-tailed sea eagle.

What does all this mean? The distribution of certain foodstuffs and carcasses within strictly defined areas of the tombs of Orkney signalled to Hedges 'a dominant pan-tribal cultural homogeneity'. But within this homogeneity each tribe expressed its individuality in the form of totems and taboos. Ethnography has shown that tribes distinguish themselves from others by certain dietary restrictions, or taboos, which explains the diversity of meat found within the Orkney tombs. The better-known device for distinguishing tribal subgroups is the totem, which in anthropological case studies has usually been animal or bird species. Such birds or animals are seen as having an influence over the well-being of the tribe, who treat them with special respect or reverence. Hedges declared that there was evidence for the use of totems in Neolithic Orkney. In the case of Isbister, and the community which built and used it, it was the white-tailed sea eagle, hence the title of Hedges' book, the *Tomb of the Eagles*.

Evidence for the treatment of the dead at Hazleton North in Gloucestershire, which was excavated between 1979 and 1982 by Alan Saville, differed from the evidence at Isbister. Saville discovered evidence for the 'successive interment of whole corpses' which involved the disruption of previous interments. Meanwhile he thought that disarticulated long bones, and possibly skulls, had been removed, just as they were at West Kennet. Perhaps the most interesting aspect of the excavation was evidence for prior occupation of the site, and the relatively short duration of the life of the tomb. At Isbister there was evidence for burials at the site before the tomb was built. Beneath the mound at Hazleton North, Mesolithic flints indicated the use of the site as a small hunting station, while there was also a Neolithic dwelling, hearth and midden. The tomb itself was open for a short period of time, perhaps between 150 and 300 years, before it was sealed up. This is in sharp contrast to Isbister, which seemed to have been in use for around 800 years for the deposition of eagle carcasses, although it was used intensively as an ossuary for perhaps only 160 years.

Wayland's Smithy, on the Ridgeway in Oxfordshire, is comparable with Hazleton North in the sense that it is a Cotswold-Severn type tomb, but otherwise it was the product of a markedly different sequence of events. While it has long been recognised that the tomb was built on top of an earlier long barrow, Alasdair Whittle has produced a reinterpretation of the excavations carried out in 1962–63 by Professors Piggott and Atkinson which argues for a protracted series of distinct phases. He argues that the monument began as a shrine in the form of large wooden posts. Later a mortuary enclosure was built, defined by steep-sided banks of stones, possibly framed in wood, and possibly also covered with a flat wooden roof, to which access was possible over a long period.

Atkinson, in his summary of the excavations, published in *Antiquity* in 1965, suggested that excarnation had been practised, and that the bones were not placed within the mortuary structure until they were at least partly disarticulated. Drawing on the evidence from other tombs, Whittle suggested an alternative, which would fit the evidence just as well, that complete bodies may have been introduced into the enclosure, and that once the flesh had decayed the bones were sorted and sometimes robbed. In this interpretation 'the dead may have been actively tended' and 'the community of ancestors would have had a very prominent and widespread role among the living', but it was not a monument in the usual sense of the word. Monumentality came later, and 'it is possible to regard the construction of the barrow as equally radical an event, which profoundly changed the nature of the site'. Whittle wondered whether the construction of the secondary monument – the chambered tomb – was intended to replace or enhance the primary monument. Its erection marked a subtle change in the way the monument was perceived, because when it was built it was provided with a façade of stones which are integral with the chambers: 'façade, chambers and the larger proximal kerb stones all emphasise now the external appearance of the monument. It is this change which may have distanced now the dead from the living.'[13]

I have taken three chambered tombs – Isbister, Hazleton North and Wayland's Smithy – as an example of how such detailed scrutiny of excavated evidence informs, and is in turn informed by, a broader interpretation of the Neolithic period. In the case of Isbister Hedges sought to show how the tomb could have been used by a territorially defined tribal sub group, whose culture was expressed in terms of totem and taboo, and whose territorial allegiance was symbolised by the tomb. The active life of the tomb, and perhaps also the social function it was intended to serve, was in the region of 800 years, more than twice the life of Hazleton North, which after a short period of use was blocked up, as if over and done with. This contrasts again with Wayland's Smithy, whose physical nature changed radically over a long period of time, from shrine to mortuary chamber, long barrow and chambered tomb. In these three tombs we have the raw material for the broader concerns of the archaeology of monuments – their place in culture and society.

27

Landscape, Culture, Society

During the 1970s archaeologists used monuments to reconstruct social organisation in prehistory. They tried to demonstrate that changes in the form of monuments – crudely speaking the change from chambered tombs to henges and stone circles – did not merely reflect but expressed the transformation of society through time. The key factors in elucidating this social role are the visibility and distribution of monuments in the landscape.

The two regions of Britain where this geographical approach was most effectively employed are Wessex and Orkney. The Wessex monuments have long been known and investigated, but until recently Orkney has been comparatively underresearched. During the 1970s there were major excavations at the chambered tombs of Quanterness on the mainland by Colin Renfrew, and Isbister on South Ronaldsay by John Hedges and Ronald Simison; the Stones of Stenness was excavated by Graham Ritchie; and a re-excavation of Skara Brae village was directed by David Clarke. Colin Renfrew and David Fraser studied the islands in terms of their social geography, Audrey Henshall scrutinised the chambered tombs and their contents, while Alexander Thom's detailed astronomical research proposed that the Ring of Brodgar was a lunar observatory.

In his *Before Civilization* of 1973 Colin Renfrew considered the distribution of the thirteen known chambered tombs on Rousay. He noticed that the tombs were spread out, mainly around the coast, and that their distribution corresponded roughly with the distribution of the crofts and farming settlements of the nineteenth century. The important point seemed to be that the tombs tended to be spaced out rather than clustered in one place, which encouraged him to think of each tomb defining a single territory. They represented discrete social units which were classified as 'segmentary societies'. Even though Childe had previously noted the correlation on Rousay between the tombs and the crofts, Renfrew gave it an added dimension. By the time of his *Investigations in Orkney* of 1979 the cairn was seen as a territorial marker, because it often 'looks out over the arable land of the local group which tilled it'. The cairns were therefore 'signalling devices, signifying group identity and territorial legitimacy'.[1]

This became an orthodox view of British chambered tombs: they were communal and a focus of territorial loyalty; they expressed and reinforced social cohesion, and legitimised the tenure of the resident community. In a doctoral thesis by David Fraser, published in 1983 as *Land and Society in Neolithic Orkney*, it was argued that the cairns occupied focal points in the landscape. Fraser showed how the tombs tended to be built close to a supply of building stone, in places where they commanded a view of the surrounding territory, either on or near farming land. Fraser called them 'community centres'. Because they were located on land frequented on a daily basis for farming purposes 'it is easy to envisage the monument becoming a convenient place to shelter from the wind, from where to watch over domesticated animals, and to hold all kinds of meetings and discussions'.[2]

Radiocarbon dating has established the beginning of the Neolithic in Orkney at around 3800 BC. Some of the tombs were built considerably later than this – Quanterness before 3400 BC and Isbister before 3200 BC – culminating with Orkney's latest and greatest chambered tomb, Maes Howe (fig. 130). Renfrew's excavation through its encircling ditch produced two radiocarbon dates of 2553 BC and 2985 BC, and he suggested it was built shortly before 2800 BC. Two radiocarbon dates for the Stones of Stenness, 3036 BC and 2891 BC, suggest it might have been built earlier but, given the statistical margin of error in the radiocarbon technique, Renfrew was unconvinced. Since the Ring of Brodgar (fig. 131) is broadly contemporary with Maes Howe, the emergence of the three largest monuments within a short timespan, and within a small geographical area, was interpreted as evidence for the 'centralising tendency' of society in Orkney.

By 1985 seventy-seven chambered tombs were known in the islands, although the original number must have been higher, but the Ring of Brodgar and the Stones of Stenness are the only stone circles. They stand a mile apart, on either side of the narrow stretch of land that joins the Loch of Harray and the Loch of Stenness. They command the same distant views of land and water, suggesting that the surrounding landscape

FIGURE 130.
Maes Howe, Ork-
ney's latest and
greatest cham-
bered tomb, with
a radiocarbon date
of approximately
2800 BC, showing
it to be broadly
contemporary
with the neigh-
bouring Ring
of Brodgar and
the Stones of
Stenness.
(*Historic Scotland*)

FIGURE 131. The Ring of Brodgar, on the shore of the Loch of Stenness and near the Stones of Stenness and Maes Howe, was interpreted by Colin Renfrew as representing the centralisation of power in Neolithic Orkney. (*Crown Copyright: RCAHM Scotland*)

was part of the statement they were making. They also required a far greater investment of labour than any of the cairns. Renfrew argued that with their appearance 'we can see the emergence of a larger social formation, to which the population of the whole mainland may have owed allegiance. Only by the support of the population as a whole, which may have been some 5000 strong, could this investment of labour have been organised.'[3]

The mobilisation and control of a large labour force indicates that centralisation has occurred, the same argument used by Atkinson for the building of Stonehenge and adopted by Renfrew as a model for the earlier Wessex monuments. Although the area has the two most famous of British stone circles, it has long been obvious that they cannot be understood without reference to the many earthwork constructions in the region. In 1973 Renfrew proposed a model for Wessex of 'chiefdom' societies to explain the different forms of monumental construction. The basis of his argument was that an increase in the scale of the works was a product of the increasing centralisation of power. The long barrows, therefore, were the earliest phase and represented the smallest social units, that is segmentary societies. However, contemporary with the long barrow period are the causewayed enclosures, whose distribution across Wessex suggested the emergence of five regions. Because of the work effort involved in their construction, Renfrew characterised them as indicating 'emerging chiefdoms'. The later Neolithic period saw the construction of the first henges, but there are five henges in Wessex which are significantly larger than the norm. Moreover, their distribution corresponds roughly to the distribution of the earlier causewayed enclosures, which led Renfrew to propose 'an increased population and a more developed social hierarchy'. Of these giant henges Avebury, close to the Windmill Hill causewayed enclosure, is the best known (fig. 132), while three of the others – Mount Pleasant (near Maiden Castle) and Marden (near Knap Hill) in Dorset, and Durrington Walls (near Robin Hood's Ball) in Wiltshire – contained large wooden

FIGURE 132. Avebury is one of the superhenges of Neolithic Wessex and was interpreted by Renfrew as symbolising a territorially-defined chiefdom.

buildings. The work effort involved was drastically increased – to about a million work-hours, compared with the hundred thousand work-hours for the causewayed enclosures. Silbury Hill, requiring around eighteen million work-hours, might indicate 'the five Wessex chiefdoms coalescing into one greater chiefdom with five constituent tribes'.

This model was partly suggested after Geoffrey Wainwright's excavation at three of the large henges – Marden, Mount Pleasant and Durrington Walls – between 1966 and 1971. These revealed post holes of large, circular wooden buildings, which Wainwright interpreted as social and ceremonial centres of developed chiefdoms, drawing a parallel with the 'council houses' of the Creek Indians of Georgia which were described in the eighteenth century. In a review of his excavations, published in 1989 as *The Henge Monuments*, he described these massive monuments as 'the summation of a process that had been underway for nearly a millennium'. This was very much a long-distance view of the issue.

In his *The Social Foundations of Prehistoric Britain* of 1984 Richard Bradley reappraised this model, arguing that access to the supernatural could have been one route to political power, and that this power was initially enforced through ritual and ceremonial rather than political coercion. The henge monuments were therefore part of a process of political change, rather than merely the product of it. Bradley thought that the erection and use of large monuments performed a communal function, but that it probably also concealed the power of a small elite. Subsequently the use of these ceremonial centres may have emphasised the separation of an elite and its rituals from the rest of the population.

Renfrew's initial model did not account for the cursus monuments. The relationship between long barrows and causewayed enclosures is also not entirely resolved, partly because the purpose of the enclosures has always been a matter for debate. In 1974, when Roger Mercer began digging at the Hambledon Hill causewayed enclosure in Dorset, it became clear that he was studying not a single site but a Neolithic landscape, because of the presence of outworks. These included an enclosure, defined by a timber palisade, which was possibly a settlement. If so it may have come to a violent end because there was evidence that the palisade had been burned down. Mercer also found the skeleton of a young man with an arrowhead in his chest.

As to the main causewayed enclosure, Mercer excavated 20 per cent of its ditch and unearthed the remains of seventy individuals, of whom 60 per cent were children. The corpses had been exposed elsewhere before their final deposition, and Mercer presumed this exposure had taken place inside the enclosure. He therefore described it as 'a vast, reeking open cemetery, its silence broken only by the din of crows and ravens'.[4] The structure of the dead population, with its high proportion of children, did not seem to Mercer to be inconsistent with the entire population of a subsistence economy.

However, adjacent to the enclosure was a long barrow, unfortunately bulldozed in the 1960s, although Mercer's excavation recovered scattered human remains which may have been those of one man.

In his *The Stonehenge People* Aubrey Burl used the long barrows to demonstrate an individualising tendency in society, relying on radiocarbon dates and accounts of previous excavation work. Fussell's Lodge near Salisbury was dated earlier than 4000 BC and must therefore be one of the earliest long barrows. It contained fifty-seven burials, well above the average, and Burl has described it as 'a family mortuary house used by a group of a dozen or more people and their descendants for a century or more'.[5] However long barrows were built over a thousand year period. Lambourn in Berkshire is dated 4260 BC and Beckhampton Road near Avebury produced two dates, 3265 BC and 2980 BC. During this time the number of burials declined: Nutbane (3510 BC) in Hampshire contained four burials; Wor barrow in Dorset six; while others, such as the Winterbourne Stoke Crossroads long barrow near Stonehenge, excavated by John Thurnam, contained only a single male. 'Sepulchres for communal family burials' had changed into 'prestigious monuments for the burial of a single, adult male'.[6] Moreover, some of these long barrows are real monsters – Old Ditch barrow near Tilshead is fifteen times the size of Fussell's Lodge.

Burl followed Mercer in ascribing a variety of functions, such as settlement, defence, ritual and burial, to the causewayed enclosures, which were built from about 3500 BC. During their period of use Burl detected (some others do not) a crisis in Neolithic society because of a rise in the population and exhaustion of the soil. During this unsettled period ancestor cults developed, people killed other people (as at Hambledon Hill), and leaders emerged who were 'engaging in ever-more grandiloquent projects to proclaim the permanence of their society in an unstable world'.[7] Burl dated the Stonehenge Cursus at 3500 BC and gives it a funerary function, part of the protracted rites which saw the leaders of society buried in their own long barrow, sixteen of which are known within a three-mile radius of Stonehenge. The first phase of Stonehenge, the bank and ditch, is dated 3200 BC, but Burl believes that a wooden building had long been standing in the centre, a mortuary house for a privileged minority. The power of the minority was therefore expressed not merely in their excessively large barrows but in the great communally built Cursus and the appearance of the first henges.

This is all very well, but so far archaeologists have talked around the subject of monuments with little real penetration. Territoriality and social stratification present the monuments as signs conveying a narrowly-defined message. They tell us little of the way people interacted with them. If the social role of monuments was the principal concern of processual archaeology then the chief preoccupation of post-processual archaeology has been with their cultural role.

Richard Bradley has described the building of the first prehistoric monuments as a crucial moment in human history because 'their creation involved a subtle change in the relationship between culture and nature'. As the title of his book of 1993 says, monument builders were *Altering the Earth*. These chambered tombs and long barrows, and later the stone circles, cursuses and henges, were self-evidently the most conspicuous features in the prehistoric landscape. Given that for their builders monuments were an embodiment of ideas, Bradley has argued for a move 'away from a Neolithic which is defined by its subsistence economy to one which is much better characterised by monuments: a Neolithic that is more securely based on cultural practice'.[8] For example, he sees the orientation of monuments to astronomical events as bringing the timeless order of nature into the world of human culture, which would have put the structures, and the people invested with authority thereby, 'beyond any kind of challenge'. Bradley has also introduced the concept of monuments in the landscape, which is perhaps where post-processual based archaeology has made its most significant contribution to the study of monuments. Before we look at this further, this is an appropriate moment to examine one of the more recent myths of landscape history.

In 1955 W. G. Hoskins published *The Making of the English Landscape*, a pioneering attempt to understand the evolution of the English countryside. Hoskins cast an analytical eye over the landscape, but despite writing a chapter on prehistory he did not draw attention to a single prehistoric monument. He could see evidence for Celtic field systems and settlements, but such conspicuous features as Avebury and Stonehenge fail to merit a single mention. In hindsight this might seem a peculiar notion, but Hoskins was a medievalist who applied an economic model to the landscape. His excursion into prehistory was guided by contemporary archaeologists who interpreted the prehistoric landscape primarily in terms of subsistence. The recent discovery of cursuses and other forms of cultural geography have helped to render these ideas obsolete but, such is Hoskins' venerable status, his ideas on prehistory have remained in circulation long after they have outlived their usefulness. As recently as 1988 Christopher Taylor could write of 'the great ritual and burial monuments' that 'while these are of considerable archaeological importance they seem to have little significance in the wider history of the landscape'.[9] Richard Muir, in his 1981 *Reading the Landscape*, explained why: 'The greatest achievements of these peoples was not the erection of awesome ritual monuments – impressive as these may be – but the systematic and relentless pacification, working and remoulding of the land which Nature provided.'[10]

Aside from the fact that archaeologists no longer judge the 'achievements' of prehistoric people, this is a classic example of imposing contemporary experience and values on to past peoples. Hoskins' followers can perceive the landscape in purely functional terms because in our own urban society the agricultural and cultural landscapes are so clearly distinguishable, but 6000 years ago these lines of demarcation may not have existed. In fairness, archaeology has in the past been equally guilty of this tendency, especially in its use of environmental archaeology which has studied the landscape specifically in terms of subsistence economies.

The landscape as a symbolic entity is not a new idea: 'Megalithic sites should not be studied individually in isolation, but in relation to their each other and to the local landscape.'[11] This is a rather mild statement and yet it was made as long ago as 1974 by John Michell, who can hardly be described as the archaeologist's friend. Archaeologists who have developed the idea of landscape in their work have come to display some alarming similarities to the work of Earth Mysteries group. For example, Barbara Bender noticed the alignment of the Stonehenge Cursus to the Cuckoo Stone and to Wood-henge, although she has found it 'difficult to interpret'. Richard Bradley toured the Kilmartin Valley in Argyll, where he found standing stones, a henge, a linear barrow cemetery, rock art sites and the Temple Wood stone circle. His description of it could have been written by Paul Devereux:

> Standing stones . . . are positioned in relation to topographical features, but they are also erected in relation to one another, so that they can form short alignments extending across the landscape. Sometimes those alignments are directed towards other features: prominent points in the terrain, or the movements of the sun and moon.[12]

These uncanny resemblances between Earth Mysteries and the archaeological establishment can be overplayed. I have drawn attention to them here to demonstrate that archaeology does not have a monopoly of the right ideas, and to emphasise that in adopting this new approach it can be seen how previous techniques limited the range of possible interpretations. In taking an individual monument as the unit of analysis, interpretation has been confined to questions such as date and function; and excavation has been the chief criterion for answering such questions. Richard Bradley has admitted that 'such a timid approach to the archaeology of monuments reflects badly on the subject as a whole'.[13]

The way in which monuments and the landscape were perceived by their builders may seem totally beyond reach of the archaeologist, but different methods have been adopted to try to understand how such places *could* have been seen. Barbara Bender has used analogies from prehistoric Greece and Aboriginal Australia to demonstrate that the landscape is anthropomorphised and mythologised: in so doing people render nature and culture indivisible. The folklore of Britain teaches the same lesson, although the subject appears out of bounds to archaeologists; instead Bender has had to travel the globe and cite the highly-fashionable Aborigines to make her point. Bender also suggests the gendering of monuments (the opposition of the cursus and the circle) and artefacts. In Arnhem Land in Australia and elsewhere bone and stone are symbols of persistence and immortality, in contrast to the Earth and its fragile plant life. Therefore stone was perceived as a male phenomenon, while the Earth is female: 'Here we find one of those ritual elisions through which processes of social reproduction (the male "stone") come to encompass . . . biological reproduction (female "earth").'[14]

A more beneficial approach to the landscape might be to spend some time in it. This may seem an obvious point, but archaeologists have previously conceived landscapes in a very abstract way. In developing the theory of tombs and territoriality the processualists drew maps with polygonal zones around the tombs, simulating boundaries. But the landscape was never perceived in this map-like way, it was traversed on foot in the one-dimensional form of paths. Christopher Tilley bought a pair of walking boots and set off to explore monuments in south-west Wales, searching for insights into how the monuments could have been seen and used in the context of the contemporary landscape. The results of his excursions in Pembroke-shire, the Black Mountains and Cranborne Chase, and the familiarity gained by repeated visits to these places, informed the ideas in his 1994 book *A Phenomenology of Landscape*. He pointed out that once the car is left behind, and a monument is approached on foot from several different directions, then 'it is possible to observe in a much more subtle manner the way in which it is related to its physical surroundings, the lie of the land'. In south-west Wales Tilley found that not all of the monuments were located in prominent positions; nor did intervisibility seem to be the important determining factor in their location, as it had seemed to be in Orkney. In fact he thought that some were 'only meant to be seen, or approached, from certain directions'. He also suggested that the dominant points in the landscape of Pembrokeshire were not chambered tombs, which in terms of cultural geography were subordinate and referenced to rock outcrops, which he described as 'non-domesticated "megaliths"':

> The outcrops key the monuments into the landscape, drawing attention to their location and making them special places. At a distance the outcrops indicate where to look for or expect to find a monument. They both mark out monument locations and hide them from the eye. They are all in places up to which one has to climb from surrounding lower areas, suggesting their ritual liminality and removal from day-to-day existence.[15]

The Gwal y Filiast dolmen is on a forested slope on the edge of the Prescelly mountains, and its chamber entrance faces down a slope towards a stream. Both upstream and downstream from this point the River Taf is calm, but where the monument is located there are rapids. Tilley suggests that the white water determined the location of the tomb, bearing in mind 'the importance of rapids in rivers in many systems of mythological thought as constituting doors or openings to the underworld'.[16]

The Pembrokeshire cromlechs have yielded few artefacts in excavation, and therefore are unlikely to have served for successive interments. Nor does the theory of territorial markers have much to recommend itself here. Tilley argues that 'they seem to have acted primarily as symbolic reference and ritually important ceremonial meeting-points on paths of movement, drawing attention to the relationship between local groups and the landscape'.[17]

This kind of personal approach to monuments in the landscape is always vulnerable to the criticism that people inevitably find the patterns they are looking for. Astronomers are particularly adept at this, but Tilley and others have a different and far less narrow agenda. Since there is no demonstrable link between the building of monuments and the creation of an agricultural surplus, the creation of the first monuments can be seen in a wider context of the continuity between Mesolithic and Neolithic ways of life. In his *Rethinking the Neolithic* of 1991 Julian Thomas argued that wild food resources were an important constituent of food supplies, and that social and subsistence life was centred on a seasonal cycle of movement. Richard Bradley has cited the example of the Aboriginal hunter-gatherers of Australia, who although they were mobile across a large area were in fact monument builders. The synchronism of farming and tomb-building need not necessarily be explained in functional terms:

> The common element is that in both cases the population was making a radical break with what they had known before. They were changing their attitudes to nature and the wild by domesticating plants and animals, and they were changing their whole conception of place by building megalithic tombs. Both attest a similar change of attitude, but the link was in the mind, not in the ploughsoil.[18]

It is the routes of mobility – paths – which are seen as determining factors in the building of the first monuments, and thus they can be seen to belong to mobile populations rather than sedentary farmers. This is the crux of Tilley's argument in south-west Wales, which is partly informed by work on the origins of monuments in Wessex. John Barrett has interpreted the first Wessex burial monuments as situated on a network of paths 'which fixed places of ancestral veneration on the landscape'. There are three long barrows in the vicinity of Avebury (Horslip, Beckhampton Road and South Street), which yielded no evidence of burials when they were excavated in the 1960s. There were, however, traces of apparently inconsequential activity at these places before the mounds were built. Barrett explains this activity as the remains of meetings and exchanges by which means they acquired their significance. There is also circumstantial evidence that the chambers of the West Kennet long barrow were set within a pre-existing mound, and that mortuary and ancestral rites here only came into being after the place had acquired its significance. This has raised the question of what the mound builders were up to if not commemorating their dead,

FIGURE 133. The Kennet Avenue, Avebury, was a formalised path that structured movement through the landscape.

except perhaps 'the creation of a cultural geography in terms of time and place' (fig. 133).

According to Barrett the formal demarcation of paths is expressed in the cursus monuments, which must be the ultimate statement of cultural geography. The Dorset Cursus is six miles long. It therefore had a greater impact on the landscape than any stone circle, although once it had been dug the ditches were never maintained. Richard Bradley has argued that 'its overall design makes little sense except to those inside it'. Its lack of formal entrances reinforces his opinion that part of its purpose was to exclude outsiders. Long barrows cluster in the vicinity of it, with two aligned on its terminals, while two others encroach upon it. There was an emphasis on the dead, or 'the ancestors'. One of its sections is aligned on the midwinter sunset. Bradley has argued that by relating the monument to the movement of the heavens its architects made the cursus appear part of nature and thus above any kind of challenge, as well as making the dead seem part of the unchanging world of nature.

In the second millennium BC there is similar evidence for the ordering of the landscape on non-functional terms. John Barnatt came to this conclusion after a survey of monuments and settlements on Bodmin Moor for his *Prehistoric Cornwall* of 1982. The Stannon circle, for example, stands in its own territory, between two streams, where there is no evidence of dwellings or field systems, and midway between two extensive settlements. Another separate area contained fifteen cairns. If these observations reflected a real pattern, then to Barnatt it was evidence that a distinction was made within the landscape between sacred and functional areas.

Spanning the period between the fourth and second millennia is the district around Stonehenge, which has traditionally only been studied in terms of its ritual monuments. In 1979 the Royal Commission on the Historical Monuments of England published *Stonehenge and its Environs*, containing an evaluation of the archaeological monuments in the area and recommendations for future research. A year later the Stonehenge Environs Project was set up by the Trust for Wessex Archaeology. One of its aims was to study the settlement and environment of the area because the wealth of monuments, most of which are funerary, may have led to a biased view of the area as being wholly devoted to ritual. Furthermore, by studying the landscape of the district the project was able, among other things, to put the various phases for the building of Stonehenge into a wider context. Two books by Julian Richards, *The Stonehenge Environs Project* of 1990 and the *English Heritage Book of Stonehenge* of 1991, have considerably enhanced our knowledge of the great stone circle. These have since been complemented by *Stonehenge: In Its Landscape*, published by English Heritage in 1995, reporting fully on the various excavations at Stonehenge during the twentieth century.

The Stonehenge Environs is an area of roughly fifteen square miles. Apart from Stonehenge it contains four other henges. Of these Coneybury and Woodhenge are classic henges; a small site known as Fargo Wood has been called a mini-henge; and Durrington Walls is a massive 'henge enclosure'. Stonehenge is the earliest of them, and no one now seriously doubts that it originally contained a wooden building. However, the site may have been abandoned after only a short period of use. Recent environmental work has suggested it was soon overgrown with long grassland scrub, a state in which it stayed for a considerable length of time.

A mile south east of Stonehenge is the Coneybury henge. The earthwork has long been ploughed out and at one time it was thought to have been a round barrow, until aerial photography revealed it to be an oval enclosure with an entrance to the north east. Excavations were carried out by the Stonehenge Environs Project in 1980, when a radiocarbon date suggested the ditch was dug about 2750 BC. Excavation of the interior showed that stakes had been arranged in a ring around the perimeter, with six radial lines of posts emanating from the centre. Environmental evidence suggested that the site was situated in a small woodland clearing, which again was abandoned after a brief period of use, when it became overgrown. Later the focus of activity in the area shifted two miles east of Stonehenge, to Durrington Walls and Woodhenge, both by the River Avon. It is also perhaps significant that, unlike Stonehenge, Durrington Walls and Woodhenge stand in an area not cluttered by reminders of the past, such as the long barrows and Cursus.

Durrington Walls, by far the biggest of the henges, is dated roughly 2600 BC, its near neighbour Woodhenge 2500 BC. During their prominence the first beakers, now read in terms of status rather than invasion, appear in the archaeological record. However, both sites went into decline in the latter part of the third millennium BC (as did Avebury). At the same time the long abandoned Stonehenge earthwork, in the middle of an ancient landscape of long barrows and cursuses, was being reclaimed.

Stonehenge was rebuilt in stone and became the ceremonial focus of what Julian Richards has described as a 'highly structured funerary landscape'. Within a three-mile radius of the monument are over 300 round barrows. The latter have long been recognised as forming certain clusters, now called barrow cemeteries. The Normanton Down barrows to the south, and the Cursus barrows to the north, stand in line on the crests of low ridges, so that from Stonehenge their larger mounds are silhouetted against the sky. At Winterbourne Stoke Crossroads, two miles to the west, the barrows form a linear series in line with a long barrow which had stood for over a thousand years before the first round barrow was raised. Richards has suggested that the King Barrows, to the east and about midway between Stonehenge and Durrington Walls, acted as a boundary, cutting off the old ideological territory and marking the limit of the ceremonial zone around Stonehenge. Although they have never been excavated, the roots of fallen trees exposed the cores of some of these mounds, which were examined in 1990. They revealed that some of the larger barrows were substantially turf built, which is unusual, and would have involved stripping large areas of land, so Richards suggested that the barrows might have been 'a form of physical, if not symbolic "sterilisation"'.

Environmental work by the Stonehenge Environs Project suggests that the vicinity of Stonehenge in 2000 BC was open grassland. Sheep and goats may well have grazed on it but Richards suggests that 'taboos may have operated to prevent either settlement or cultivation, in a form of "ritual exclusion zone"'. Only three possible settlement sites were found, but even these may just as easily have been the remains of ploughed out burials. Slightly further afield there is evidence for some arable farming, with the creation of field boundaries in the Later Bronze Age, after about 1500 BC, during which time the Stonehenge Avenue was extended toward the River Avon.

Stonehenge was apparently the last prehistoric monument to go out of use, so it is an appropriate place for us to finish. Richard Bradley has drawn a distinction between monuments which were an event, and those which were part of a process. For example, Hazleton North was in use between about 3800 and 3500 BC. After this intense activity there was no further monument building in the district. Bradley therefore interprets it

FIGURE 134. Stonehenge: constructed as a myth about the past to justify the present?

as an 'event'. West Kennet has the opposite history: it was part of a process because formal deposits are ranged over a period of about a thousand years, and the chambered tomb later became part of a monument complex, which Hazleton North did not. A different sort of process is visible at Maiden Castle in Dorset, where a bank barrow was superimposed on an earlier causewayed enclosure 'as if to subvert the existing meaning of a particular construction'. This process is not always confined within prehistory, because we could include places which have been reinterpreted more recently, like the henge at Knowlton or the stone circle at Midmar, whose churches added another layer of meaning to the site.

Stonehenge and the barrows ranged around it are the classic example of the reworking of a place over a long period of time. There is a consensus of opinion that the sarsen circle and horseshoe symbolically reproduce the wooden structure that had been built here over a thousand years previously. Thus the builders of the sarsen Stonehenge were reinterpreting the past, and they did so from a contemporary perspective. According to Bradley, 'new developments are more secure when they are invested with the authority of the past. That is why origin myths are so important and yet so malleable'.[19] In this at least the building of Stonehenge, and its subsequent reinterpretation by antiquaries and archaeologists, share some common ground. These parallels can be exaggerated, but the important point is that the communities who built the first monuments inscribed their presence on the landscape. Thereafter the landscape had a history written into it. This is the context in which Stonehenge was reworked in stone and in which archaeologists reconstruct the past (fig. 134). The interpretations of Stonehenge given by Geoffrey of Monmouth, William Stukeley and John Michell may be dismissed as bogus, but was not the sarsen Stonehenge also a myth about the past contrived to give authority and meaning in the present?

28

Epilogue

With hindsight, it is clear that in writing about the monuments each generation has said as much about itself as it has about prehistory. At the most basic level, the megaliths have offered plenty of scope for self-glorification, to which Stukeley, Lockyer, Hawkins and other lesser fry have succumbed. Others have had a particular axe to grind, using the past in a political sense. Geoffrey of Monmouth allowed his chauvinism free reign in his *History of the Kings of Britain*, while William Stukeley used his study of Avebury and Stonehenge to assert the moral authority of the Church of England. In more recent times John Michell and his followers have used ancient monuments as a benign weapon against the excesses of consumer society.

Contemporary preoccupations are betrayed in less obvious ways. John Aubrey's view of the Ancient Britons was informed by his reading of the classical authors, and if he conceived them as primitive then this was at least partly engendered by the optimism of his times, symbolised by the progressive outlook of the Royal Society. By the eighteenth century the agenda had changed. It is hardly insignificant that of the leading eighteenth-century scholars – Stukeley, Borlase, Rowlands and Wood – only John Wood was not a clergyman. For Wood the stone circles were the work of philosophers, and his work on Stanton Drew was complementary to his claims for the exalted origins of Bath, the object of his architectural ambitions. For Stukeley, Borlase and Rowlands the subject of antiquities was primarily the study of ancient religion, and the most authoritative book on religion was the Bible. Consequently, they were writing about a subject on which they already had strong beliefs.

Although the theories of the antiquaries managed to outlive the eighteenth century, the nineteenth century is characterised by the barrow diggers rather than the dregs of the Stukleyite genre. Generally the subject was dominated by educated men with plenty of spare time for leisurely pursuits, although there was a preponderance of clergymen in early barrow digging. Ironically, archaeology was part of a growing debate on the origins of the world and of mankind, the outcome of which was to undermine the authority of biblical history. Lyell's *Principles of Geology* and Darwin's *Origin of Species* certainly made more impact on the intellectual world than the excavation of barrows, which could rarely be accorded intellectual credibility. Nor was it from barrow digging that the big idea in nineteenth-century archaeology evolved: the Three Age System came from abroad. But excavation of barrows and cairns made a significant contribution to the nineteenth-century understanding of evolution and progress. The barrows and stone circles were raised by people who had only primitive tools, from which came the assumption that they must also have had primitive minds. This outlook was also conditioned by the rise of the British Empire, and the belief that the human races are not all equal. However odious this may seem today, it may be that the early archaeologists, most of whom came from the ruling classes, were trapped by their cultural backgrounds and could not think about the world in any other way.

Not until the 1960s were the suppositions of previous generations rejected wholesale. The new archaeologists were a different breed, brought up in the last days of the Empire, in a new sociological configuration and very often with an education in the sciences. Archaeology had hitherto belonged to the humanities but, to the new generation, its future lay increasingly in statistics, environmental archaeology and the new geography. Archaeologists like David Clarke seemed to take pleasure in their radical stance and their scientific newspeak, and if the new archaeology irritated some of the older archaeologists this was a cause for satisfaction rather than rapprochement.

The 1960s was also a turning-point in archaeology because with it came the new critical self-consciousness of archaeologists, many of whom came to recognise that their prejudices were inexorably embedded in their ideas about the past. If science was an effort to overcome this, the brave new world of social systems merely conceived the past in terms susceptible to scientific procedures. In fact, its recreation of past communities is to some extent mirrored by the way that planners envisaged future communities in new towns, with all material, social and cultural needs prescribed. Both failed to cater for the creative, destructive and unpredictable elements in society, which allowed the humanities to fight back and to emphasise the cultural life of people rather than merely their modes of subsistence and social stratification. This quest for the individual in prehistory is itself perhaps a reflection of the multi-cultural Britain where nearly everybody is entitled to a voice, be they women, black, gay, Jewish, whatever.

The two areas where the reconstruction of the past has departed from mainstream thinking – astronomy and leys – emphasise the romantic side of archaeology, but are otherwise still firmly rooted in the times that created them. The astronomers and ley hunters were also the pied pipers of popular archaeology: their theories were persuasive and easy enough to assimilate, which perhaps accounts for their widespread appeal. Archaeo-astronomy began in earnest in the first decade of the twentieth century with Sir Norman Lockyer, whose self-glorification, in the guise of the noble astronomer, informed his reconstruction of stone circles and the origin of civilisation. This origin he traced directly to Egypt in a hyperdiffusionist concept which was soon to show its ugly face as an essentially fascist outlook. Even in the early twentieth century hyper-diffusionism was considered by many a simplistic and amateurish concept. The later astronomical work of Hawkins and Hoyle, which in its pomp might have seemed to be taking our understanding of the past to the brink of a revolutionary new consciousness, now seems little more than an exercise in sensationalism by academics with only a passing interest in the ancient world. Their glib, over-confident analyses summed up the arrogance of the scientists and the gullible nature of the society that lapped their ideas up. Such work would not be accepted so uncritically in the 1990s. Science fiction is the genre in which Hawkins and Hoyle now fit most comfortably.

Alfred Watkins was born in 1855 and lived through a period of irreversible encroachment by the industrial revolution on rural communities. The influence of industrialisation on Watkins' theory was primarily nostalgic, a yearning for an England of the Shires which he perceived as rapidly in decline. While hardly a new idea, it received added significance during Watkins' lifetime, when the countryside lost so many people to the towns and the trenches. The ley movement has always be prone to a similar nostalgia. In the 1970s writers like Paul Screeton and Janet and Colin Bord betrayed a townie's love of the countryside, while seventies ley writers regularly expressed their faith in old country ways, conceived as innocent of the ills of modern society. Ironically, some of these writers who advocated a closer relationship with nature inadvertently emphasised just how far they have travelled from it.

None of this is worthy of rebuke. Each generation has reconstructed a past which is meaningful to them. Its list of choices has never been infinite. To the antiquarian clergymen of the eighteenth century the choice was between the true religion revealed by God and the idolatries of the Gentiles. Nothing else would have made sense. This is surely true of the nineteenth-century diggers as well: they lived in a world where progress was unstoppable. And as for Watkins and his followers, nostalgia is a natural reflex which needs no introduction in modern society.

This tendency to reconstruct the past in terms that are familiar or reassuring to us is a product not only of our preconceptions, but also of the methods we use to study it. We saw that Alexander Thom postulated a society of astronomer-mathematicians who bore a suspicious resemblance to professors of civil engineering. People find the patterns they are looking for. In Thom's case his primary tool was the theodolite, a device for precision surveying. The conclusion of his surveys was that the stone circle builders also engaged in precision surveys. Only a theodolite could have shown him this, which is a circular argument. Similarly Thom, as well as Stukeley and Flinders Petrie, assumed that the stone circle builders used an exact unit of length; in such cases the pattern is inevitably found. In the same way, if a map is used to look for a pattern in the landscape, then a pattern will inevitably emerge, as ley hunters have demonstrated time and time again. All of these are self-fulfilling prophecies.

Archaeology has also been constrained by its principal mode of operation, the excavation. We are not concerned here with the kind of typological classifications and the use of stratigraphy to place artefacts and sites within a relative chronology. Even when such practices are based on sound principles, they provide only a certain kind of information. In the explanation of prehistoric life there is more room for manoeuvre. Excavation focuses the archaeologist's mind on what lies below the ground, so that the unit of analysis becomes the archaeological site. By doing so, options for understanding a particular place are dramatically reduced, which is precisely why the most recent archaeological approaches have tried to encompass a wide range of methods and concepts. After all, the same data has been used by diffusionists, processualists and post processualists, yet they have created different versions of prehistory.

It is said that while there can never be such a thing as complete objectivity, neither can there ever be complete subjectivity. It is also true to say that while archaeologists have consistently projected their own views on to the past, it does not follow that they can say nothing meaningful or truthful about it. In fact archaeology has made steady progress in understanding the megaliths by adopting certain ideas of previous generations, and by rejecting others. While the break between the new archaeology of the late 1960s and its diffusionist predecessor may have seemed radical and complete, the understanding of the chambered tombs as ancestral burial places was a direct consequence of the excavations of the 1950s, which advocated the practice of ancestor cults. Indeed the idea of ancestral burial places has even outlived the notion of 'segmentary societies' and cybernetics. Other ideas have a much longer vintage and are arguably universal, if rather general. Aubrey Burl has interpreted stone circles in terms of death and regeneration; Stukeley came to a similar conclusion at Avebury in 1743, a place where the connection between fertility rites and death was also made in the 1930s during Alexander Keiller's excavations.

Each generation has posed particular questions, or at least it has imposed upon itself certain problems to be resolved. The one exception is perhaps the seventeenth century. Aubrey's work was a process of finding out about the monuments. Indeed his empirical approach was inevitable and necessary at that stage. The hypothesis-forming deductive approach could not operate until certain knowledge had been gained by empirical means. It was in the eighteenth century that antiquaries first came to the subject with specific questions, although most of these were rendered obsolete in the nineteenth century by geology and evolution. In the 1950s Christopher Hawkes' ladder of inference — technology, economy, society and religion — was a different way of structuring interpretation, which served his generation well. Now that it has been superseded, the separation of these four elements encompassing the world of the monument builders looks closer to twentieth-century Britain than to prehistory. The diffusionists only asked certain questions, as did processual archaeology, as did for that matter astronomers, barrow diggers and antiquaries, which brings us to the crux of the matter. In what ways is the past to be studied?

If archaeology is not a science, it is at least a discipline, with recognised procedures for conducting its business. It is the formulation of procedures that has occupied theorists since the 1960s, in recognition of the fact that our understanding of the past is directly related to the questions we ask and the way we go about answering them. We have seen that the astronomers adopted too narrow a conception of megaliths, and that Earth Mysteries research, despite using a greater range of techniques than conventional archaeology, still narrows its range of understanding by presenting the past as mysterious.

Of all the methods ever employed to study the monuments, most were first tried out in the eighteenth century, arguably the most interesting period of archaeological study. Stukeley, for example, used astronomy, excavation, survey and his personal impressions of place to create his vivid picture of Avebury and Stonehenge. In reconstructing ritual activity at Stonehenge, drawing a distinction between the multitudes who were kept outside the sacred precinct and the 'priests and chief personages' who were allowed in, he was adopting the very same methods now in favour among postprocessual archaeologists, even though his database was less secure. The same is true of Borlase and the connection he perceived between the monuments and other features in the landscape. His rock idols, for a long time considered to be an unfortunate aberration in his otherwise excellent work, might now be redefined as 'non domesticated megaliths'. In future this interpretation of monuments within the landscape, and in relation to natural landmarks within it, is unlikely to be dismissed as an imaginative conceit. It is more likely to become a perfectly valid, indeed normal approach.

The future of monument archaeology is surely in adopting a wide range of approaches if it is not to be frustrated by limited ambitions. Although our understanding of prehistory may always be constrained by contemporary experiences and outlooks, we can pose questions, at the same time imposing certain intellectual standards on our interpretations, which will render the monuments coherent and meaningful, even if future generations decide to pose different questions. The new wave of approaches, particularly the relationship between monuments and the natural world, and the concept of sacred landscapes pioneered in Earth Mysteries research, has presented opportunities for studying certain kinds of monument which have hitherto been marginalised in archaeological thinking. These are rock art sites and solitary standing stones. The study of petroglyphs in south-west Scotland by Richard Bradley and others has taken as its starting-point the idea of a mobile pattern of land use in the early Neolithic. Although the carvings are impossible to 'translate', they can nevertheless be studied in terms of their relationship with the surrounding topography, and the ways in which they may have influenced the use and exploitation of the land at a time when field boundaries did not exist. A similar approach could be adopted for the study of menhirs, which have hitherto not generated much interest among archaeologists.

These non-intrusive forms of archaeological study are likely to come more to the fore in an economic climate where excavation is prohibitively expensive. Indeed it may be that the emptying of chambered tombs in the name of science will be frowned upon by future generations. For a long time now archaeology has thrived on fresh discoveries provided by digging. Whether its primary aim should be to continue to accumulate yet more objects and more data is debatable. Ethnography has contributed much to the understanding of prehistory and has cost the archaeologist nothing in terms of exploiting the finite archaeological resource. The same might be true of folklore if it is ever taken seriously by prehistorians.

Earth Mysteries researchers have never taken anything away from the monuments, and much of what they have brought to them has been appropriated now by the mainstream. Equally, astronomy has come and gone without leaving a trace, although the techniques of astronomers have always been alien to archaeologists, one of the reasons they were so vulnerable to the inroads of Gerald Hawkins and Alexander Thom. It will be interesting to see how astronomy fares in the future. John North's recent *Stonehenge: Neolithic Man and the Cosmos* (1996) offers the requisite helping of radicalism in its interpretation, not only of Stonehenge but of the earlier long barrows as well. Like any good contextual archaeologist, North has criticised previous workers in the field for their predisposition to work only in two dimensions. To understand the observation techniques that could have been used at stone circles or long barrows, it is necessary to think in three dimensions. For example, he has interpreted the Aubrey Holes at Stonehenge as a ring of posts with lintels, rather like the later sarsen circle, which acted as an artificial horizon for celestial observation. The basis of his argument is that stellar alignments were achieved in the early Neolithic, to be followed by widespread observation of the sun and moon. North, a historian of science, may be open to the usual criticism of having too narrow an agenda, but he argues that the monuments of prehistory form the physical remains of an intellectual culture; the fact that this culture has not been written about in the same way as Egyptian or Babylonian astronomy does not make it any less real.

North has made liberal use of published excavation reports, yet it remains doubtful that his thesis will enter the mainstream: while the astronomer can appropriate archaeological evidence, archaeology is still largely unable to come to terms with astronomical data, and is slow to accept methods which fall outside its own rather limited scope. Scholars of artefacts have slowly turned their attention to the ideology of monuments and to the physical world they inhabited. The time must come when the night sky is accepted as integral to these ideological and physical worlds.

To most of its practitioners archaeology is a practical rather than a cerebral activity. The natural tendency of most archaeologists is therefore to want new excavations to answer specific questions. One of the most exciting prospects for the future of monument study comes from recent work in the Avebury district. This is the prelude to a future reinterpretation of the area's 'sacred geography'. It is based on investigating new areas and reexamining previous excavations. Joshua Pollard has reinterpreted the evidence of

Maud Cunnington's excavations at the Sanctuary near Avebury in 1930. He has suggested that the stone and timber settings may have belonged to a single phase of construction in about 2500 BC, and that it was contemporary with the main Avebury henge and the Kennet Avenue that links them. Pollard suggested that the configuration of stones and posts at the Sanctuary was evidence for the formalised movements around the structure: one along the corridors to and from the central area; and the other, circular movement around the individual rings of posts. This idea that monuments incorporated a functional demarcation of space which structured ritual and ceremonial activity has been rehearsed elsewhere, but it provides an added dimension to the study of the Avebury monuments.

Nearby, between the Kennet Avenue and the West Kennet chambered tomb, Alasdair Whittle has recently excavated a palisade enclosure and a double circular timber structure, both of which may have been sacred precincts. Another possible circular structure defined by wooden posts was found by Andrew David in a resistivity survey within the henge itself. Added to this are the full publication of the Silbury Hill excavations of the 1960s; and the first radiocarbon dates for Avebury, only recently published, taking finds from previous excavations for analysis. These radiocarbon dates have supported the views of Isobel Smith and Aubrey Burl that Avebury was essentially a unitary construction, although it may have taken longer to build than the 300 years envisaged by Burl. A further twist has been added by the discovery of an excavation notebook, relating to a trench dug through the bank by Henry Meux in 1894, which suggests that an earlier bank preceded the present one. Similar evidence was revealed in a trench cut through the bank by Faith Vatcher in 1969. While this evidence was taken seriously by Alasdair Whittle and Michael Pitts in their recent survey of the Avebury sequence, they recommended that further excavation would be needed to clarify the situation. This is what keeps archaeology moving: new information prompts new ideas, which inform new investigations. It is a perpetual intellectual riddle that thrives on the desire to know more.

Gazetteer

The following list covers the most important megalithic sites in Britain. Most of them are well signposted, although an Ordnance Survey map is often required. Adventurous explorers can find more comprehensive gazetteers in Nicholas Thomas, *A Guide to Prehistoric England* (London, 1960); Christopher Houlder, *Wales: An Archaeological Guide* (London, 1974); Euan Mackie, *Scotland: An Archaeological Guide* (London, 1975); and R. Feachem, *A Guide to Prehistoric Scotland* (London, 1963).

England

Arbor Low, Derbyshire (SK 160 636). Stone circle.
Five miles west of Bakewell in the Peak District, beside a minor road off the A515. A circle of recumbent stones inside a henge. To the south west is a large Bronze Age barrow known as Gib Hill.

Arthur's Stone, Herefordshire (SO 318 431). Chambered tomb.
Beside a minor road north of Dorstone. The monument is dominated by a large capstone, but traces of a former passage are also visible.

Avebury, Wiltshire (SU 103 700). Stone circle and avenue.
Reached from the A4 west of Marlborough. The largest megalithic ruin in Britain, the stone circle with its inner rings stands with the village inside a henge. On the south side the Kennet Avenue leads to the Sanctuary on Overton Hill (SU 118 679), where the positions of the former stones are marked in concrete.

Belas Knap, Gloucestershire (SP 021 254). Chambered tomb.
Reached by a long walk from a minor road south of Winchcombe. The burial chambers are in the long sides of the mound. At the north end is a false entrance with forecourt.

Boscawen-un, Cornwall (SW 412 274). Stone circle.
On the south side of the A30 between Penzance and Land's End. Nineteen stones make up the ring, with a taller stone in the centre.

Carn Gluze, Cornwall (SW 355 313). Bronze Age barrow.
On the South West Coast path, or alternatively reached from a minor road west of St Just. Also known as Ballowall barrow. The site is at the top of the cliffs, commanding a fine view over the Atlantic.

Castlerigg, Cumberland (NY 292 236). Stone circle.

Beside a minor road one mile east of Keswick. Sometimes known as Carles, the stone circle has fine views of Blaencartha and Skiddaw.

Chun Quoit, Cornwall (SW 402 339). Chambered tomb.
Reached on foot from Chun Farm, off a minor road between Morvah and Penzance. The quoit resembles a granite mushroom and overlooks the Atlantic to the north. Close by is the Iron Age Chun Castle.

Devil's Arrows, Yorkshire (SE 391 666). Standing stones.
On the west side of Boroughbridge, close to the A1. Three tall standing stones.

Druid's Temple, Yorkshire (SE 174 787). Folly.
Reached from a minor road to the south west of Masham. The folly, built in the 1820s, is in the middle of a forestry plantation and contains a fanciful version of Stonehenge, with dolmens and rockpiles added for good measure.

Hetty Pegler's Tump, Gloucestershire (SO 790 001). Chambered tomb.
Reached from the B4066 north of Uley. Also known as Uley long barrow. The site is perched high above the Severn valley.

The Hurlers, Cornwall (SX 258 714). Stone circles.
On the west side of Minions, on Bodmin Moor. Three stone circles in a bleak landscape of mining ruins. The famous Cheesewring is visible and easily accessible from here.

King Arthur's Round Table, Cumberland (NY 523 284). Henge.
One mile south east of Penrith and close to Mayburgh henge.

Kits Coty, Kent (TQ 745 608). Chambered tomb.
On the North Downs and reached from a minor road east of Burham. The three uprights and a capstone stand in a field, comically enclosed in a metal fence.

Knowlton, Dorset (SU 025 100). Henges and ruined church.
Reached from a minor road to the west of the B3078 north of Wimborne Minster. A line of three henges, in the centre of the middle henge is a ruined Norman church.

Long Meg and her Daughters, Cumberland (NY 571 373). Stone circle.
Reached from a minor road from Little Salkeld, about seven miles north east of Penrith. The largest circle in northern England. Standing apart from the seventy-seven stones of the circle is Long Meg, a solitary standing stone.

Maiden Castle, Dorset (SY 669 884). Bank barrow, causewayed enclosure and hillfort.
South west of Dorchester. Best known as the most spectacular of Iron Age hillforts, the remains of a Neolithic bank barrow can be seen inside the hillfort, which itself was built over an earlier causewayed enclosure. From the summit of the hillfort several prominent Bronze Age barrows can be seen.

Mayburgh, Cumberland (NY 519 285). Henge.
One mile south east of Penrith. A large henge with a tall standing stone in the centre.

Men-an-tol, Cornwall (SW 427 349). Holed stone.

Reached from a minor road between Morvah and Penzance. This is a site to participate in, as it is essential to crawl through the hole.

Merrivale, Devon (SX 553 746). Megalithic landscape.
On Dartmoor, beside the B3357 between Tavistock and Two Bridges. Similar to but more accessible than Shovel Down, it has a variety of sites: two stone rows, a stone circle and a tall standing stone.

Merry Maidens, Cornwall (SW 433 245). Stone circle.
Beside the B3315 south west of Newlyn. Nearby are two tall standing stones known as the Pipers.

Mitchell's Fold, Shropshire (SO 304 983). Stone circle.
Reached from a minor road off the A488 south west of Shrewsbury. The site is close to the Welsh border and has fine views into Montgomeryshire.

Nine Ladies, Derbyshire (SK 249 635). Stone circle.
On Stanton Moor in the Peak District, about five miles south of Bakewell. A small stone circle stands in a rich landscape of cairns and barrows, a standing stone and several denuded circles.

Nine Stones, Winterborne Abbas, Dorset (SY 610 903). Stone circle.
Beside the A35 Dorchester to Bridport road. A small but well-preserved stone circle.

Rollright Stones, Oxfordshire (SO 296 309). Stone circle, chambered tomb, standing stone.
By the side of a minor road off the A3400 near Long Compton. The site consists of a stone circle (the King's Men), to the south east of which is a chambered tomb known as the Whispering Knights. On the other side of the road is the King Stone.

Rudston, Yorkshire (TA 097 677). Standing stone.
On the B1253 west of Bridlington. The tallest standing stone in Britain stands in the churchyard.

Shovel Down, Devon (SX 655 506). Megalithic landscape.
On the north-east side of Dartmoor, reached from a minor road west of Chagford. Shovel Down has several stone rows, a stone circle, and a group of cairns.

Silbury Hill, Wiltshire (SU 100 685). Earthen mound.
On the A4 south of Avebury. Silbury is the largest prehistoric mound in Europe.

Spinsters' Rock, Devon (SX 700 908). Chambered tomb.
Near Drewsteignton on the north-east side of Dartmoor, reached by minor roads south of the A30. A burial chamber consisting of three uprights and a capstone.

Stanton Drew, Somerset (ST 601 634). Stone circles.
In a village about six miles south of Bristol. The stone circles are in the fields behind the village. Beside the Druids Arms are three stones known as the Cove.

Stonehenge, Wiltshire (SU 123 422). Stone circle.

On the A344 two miles west of Amesbury. Overcrowded, and with inadequate facilities, alas.

Stoney Littleton, Somerset (ST 735 572). Chambered tomb.
About five miles south of Bath, reached from a minor road south of Wellow. A typical Cotswold-Severn type tomb with drystone walling around its forecourt.

Trethevy Quoit, Cornwall (SX 259 688). Chambered tomb.
On the south side of Bodmin Moor, the site is reached from minor roads north west of St Cleer. A typical Cornish quoit with a curious aperture in the capstone.

Wayland's Smithy, Berkshire (SU 281 854). Chambered tomb.
On the Ridgeway. The site is reached on foot from Uffington Castle and White Horse, on a minor road south of the B4507 west of Wantage. A restored chambered tomb with an impressive façade.

West Kennet, Wiltshire (SU 104 677). Chambered tomb.
On the south side of the A4 close to Silbury Hill. The restored tomb is perhaps the most impressive in southern Britain.

Zennor Quoit, Cornwall (SW 469 380). Chambered tomb.
On moorland on the south east of Zennor village, the site is reached by a walk from the B3306. Five upright slabs and a slumped capstone make up the chamber of a large tomb.

Wales

Arthur's Stone, Glamorgan (SS 491 905). Chambered tomb.
On the north side of the B4271 in the Gower peninsula. The chamber is beneath a twenty-five-ton glacial boulder raised up on smaller stones. The site has fine views north over the Loughor estuary.

Barclodiad y Gawres, Anglesey (SH 329 708). Chambered tomb.
On the coast, and close to the A4080 between Llangadwaladr and Llanfaelog. A chamber set in a large round cairn.

Bryn Celli Ddu, Anglesey (SH 507 702). Chambered tomb.
Close to the A4080 south west of Menai Bridge. A chambered tomb built over an earlier stone circle. The chamber is reached by a long, roofed passage.

Carreg Samson, Pembrokeshire (SM 864 334). Chambered tomb.
On the Pembrokeshire Coast Path south of Strumble Head. Seven uprights with a capstone perched precariously on top.

Harold Stones, Monmouthshire (SO 496 052). Standing stones.
At Trellech on the B4233 Chepstow to Monmouth road. An alignment of three standing stones is on the south side of the village.

Pentre Ifan, Pembrokeshire (SN 099 370). Chambered tomb.

Reached from a minor road off the B4329 at Brynberian. Perhaps the finest megalithic chambered tomb in South Wales, consisting of capstone perched on exposed uprights.

St Lythans, Glamorgan (ST 101 723). Chambered tomb.
A mile south of Tinkinswood, at the side of a minor road. A denuded cairn has left the uprights and capstone fully exposed.

Tinkinswood, Glamorgan (ST 092 733). Chambered tomb.
Reached from a minor road off the A48 at St Nicholas, five miles west of Cardiff. The tomb has a forecourt with drystone revetment and the chamber is enclosed by a forty-ton capstone.

Ysbyty Cynfyn, Cardiganshire (SN 752 791). Stone circle.
On the A4120 north of Devil's Bridge. A church built inside a stone circle, with original stones now in the churchyard wall and forming gateposts.

Scotland

Ballochroy, Argyll (NR 731 524). Standing stones.
On the west coast of Kintyre, off the A83 south of Tarbert. Three aligned standing stones with views to Islay and Jura.

Blackhammer, Rousay (HY 414 276). Chambered cairn.
A stalled cairn on the south side of the island.

Cairnholy, Kirkcudbright (NX 517 538). Chambered cairns.
Four miles south east of Creetown, and a mile's walk from the A75. There are two chambered cairns here, both of which have horn-shaped forecourts. The site overlooks Wigtown Bay.

Cairnpapple, West Lothian (NS 987 717). Cairn.
Reached from a minor road south east of Torpichen on the B792. A large cairn formerly surrounded by a ring of stones, the positions of which are marked with concrete posts.

Callanish, Lewis (NB 213 330). Stone circle and alignments.
Reached from the A858 to the west of Stornoway. There are seven stone circles around Loch Roag on the west side of the island, of which Callanish is the most impressive. It consists of a circle of tall stones with a cairn in the centre. From the circle there are single lines of stones on the east, south and west sides, with an avenue to the north.

Camster, Caithness (ND 260 440). Chambered tombs.
Beside a minor road from Lybster to Watten. Bleakly situated, the two chambered tombs are known as the Grey Cairns.

Cnoc Fillibr, Lewis (NB 225 335). Stone circle.
South of the A858 Stornoway to Callanish road, nearly a mile from the main monument. Sometimes known as Callanish III, it consists of a double ring of stones.

Dwarfie Stane, Hoy (HY 243 004). Chambered tomb.
Reached from a minor road on the north-west side of the island, south of Linksness.
A rock-cut tomb.

Easter Aquorthies, Aberdeenshire (NJ 733 208). Stone circle.
Reached from a minor road on the west side of Inverurie. A typical Recumbent Stone
circle.

Holm of Papa Westray (HY 509 518). Chambered cairn.
A large cairn now protected under a concrete roof. It has zig-zag, circle and rectangular
motifs carved on to the stones.

Loanhead of Daviot, Aberdeenshire (NJ 747 288). Stone circle.
Beside a minor road on the north side of Daviot. Recumbent Stone circle.

Machrie Moor, Arran (NR 912 324). Megalithic landscape.
Inland from Tormore, Machrie Moor has a number of megalithic remains including an
elliptical ring of stones.

Maes Howe, Orkney (HY 318 127). Chambered tomb.
Reached from the A965 west of Kirkwall. Grouped with the Stones of Stenness and
the Ring of Brodgar, this is perhaps the most impressive megalithic landscape in Britain.
Maes Howe itself is undeniably Britain's finest chambered tomb. The chamber is reached
from a passage constructed of large stone slabs. The chamber itself has a corbelled roof
with monoliths supporting the corners.

Mid Clyth, Caithness (ND 294 384). Stone fans.
Inland from Clyth, off the A9 south west of Wick. The stone fans are without parallel
in Britain.

Mid Howe, Rousay (HY 372 306). Chambered cairn.
On the north-west coast. The largest of Orkney's stalled cairns.

Ring of Brodgar, Orkney (HY 294 134). Stone circle.
By the B9055, on a neck of land on the opposite shore of the two lochs to Stenness.
The largest stone circle henge in Britain.

Stones of Stenness, Orkney (HY 306 125). Stone circle.
Close to the shores of the Lochs of Harray and Stenness, near the B9055 west of Kirkwall.
The stone circle is now much despoiled, but its tall thin slabs of stone are striking in
appearance. To the west of the circle, close to the bridge over the two lochs, is the tall
Watchstone.

Temple Wood, Argyll (NR 826 979). Megalithic landscape.
On the south side of Kilmartin, close to the A816. Sites include a stone circle, an
X-shaped configuration of standing stones and several cairns.

Unival, North Uist (NF 800 669). Chambered cairn.
On the south side of Unival Hill, about an hour's walk from the A865.

England

Berkshire	Wayland's Smithy
Cornwall	Boscawen-un
	Carn Gluze
	Chun Quoit
	The Hurlers
	Men-an-tol
	Merry Maidens
	Trethevy Quoit
	Zennor Quoit
Cumberland	Castlerigg
	King Arthur's Round Table
	Long Meg and her Daughters
	Mayburgh
Derbyshire	Arbor Low
	Nine Ladies
Devon	Merrivale
	Shovel Down
	Spinsters' Rock
Dorset	Knowlton
	Maiden Castle
	Nine Stones
Gloucestershire	Belas Knap
	Hetty Pegler's Tump
Herefordshire	Arthur's Stone
Kent	Kits Coty
Oxfordshire	Rollright Stones
Shropshire	Mitchell's Fold
Somerset	Stanton Drew
	Stoney Littleton
Wiltshire	Avebury
	Silbury Hill
	Stonehenge
	West Kennet
Yorkshire	Devil's Arrows
	Druid's Temple
	Rudston

Wales

Anglesey	Barclodiad y Gawres
	Bryn Celli Ddu
Cardiganshire	Ysbyty Cynfyn
Glamorgan	Arthur's Stone
	St Lythans
	Tinkinswood
Monmouthshire	Harold Stones
Pembrokeshire	Carreg Samson
	Pentre Ifan

Scotland

Aberdeenshire	Easter Aquorthies
	Loanhead of Daviot
Argyll	Ballochroy
	Temple Wood
Arran	Machrie Moor
Caithness	Camster
	Mid Clyth
Kirkcudbright	Cairnholy
Lewis	Callanish
	Cnoc Fillibr
North Uist	Unival
Orkney	Blackhammer, Rousay
	Dwarfie Stane, Hoy
	Holm of Papa Westray
	Maes Howe, Mainland
	Mid Howe, Rousay
	Ring of Brodgar, Mainland
	Stones of Stenness, Mainland
West Lothian	Cairnpapple

Notes

Note to Chapter 1, Introduction

1. D. L. Clarke, 'Models and Paradigms in Contemporary Archaeology', in D. L. Clarke (ed.), *Models in Archaeology* (1972), p. 43.

Notes to Chapter 2, Pagan Traditions

1. Unless otherwise stated, the folklore of the monuments in this chapter is drawn from L. Grinsell, *Folklore of Prehistoric Sites in Britain* (1976).
2. M. Courtenay, *Cornish Feasts and Folklore* (1890), p. 102.
3. R. Hunt, *Popular Romances of the West of England* (1923), p. 90.
4. R. Carew, *Survey of Cornwall* (1969), p. 211.
5. C. Morris (ed.), *The Journeys of Celia Fiennes* (1949), p. 201.
6. Hunt, *Popular Romances*, p. 176.
7. Courtenay, *Cornish Feasts and Folklore*, p. 161.
8. A. Burl, *The Stonehenge People* (1987), p. 220.
9. W. Borlase, *Antiquities, Historical and Monumental, of the County of Cornwall* (1769), p. 179.

Notes to Chapter 3, The Church and the Devil

1. C. Weatherhill, *Belerion: Ancient Sites of Land's End* (1981), p. 70.
2. Unless otherwise stated, I have drawn the material for this chapter from L. Grinsell, *Folklore of Prehistoric Sites in Britain* (1976), and G. Daniel, *Megaliths in History* (1972).
3. A. Burl, *Prehistoric Avebury* (1979), pp. 37, 39.
4. R. Carew, *Survey of Cornwall* (1969), p. 203.
5. R. Hunt, *Popular Romances of the West of England* (1923), pp. 177–78.

Notes to Chapter 4, In Medieval Literature

1. P. Ucko *et al.*, *Avebury Reconsidered* (1991), p. 9.
2. C. Chippindale, *Stonehenge Complete* (1994), pp. 27–28.

Notes to Chapter 5, The Wonder of Britain

1. L. T. Smith (ed.), *The Itinerary of John Leland in or about the Years 1535–43* (1907–10), i, pp. xxxvii, xliii.
2. S. Piggott, *Ancient Britons and the Antiquarian Imagination* (1989), p. 18.
3. Ibid., p. 17.
4. Smith, *Itinerary*, v, p. 81.
5. Ibid., p. 85.
6. W. C. Borlase, *Naenia Cornubiae: A Descriptive Essay, Illustrative of the Sepulchres and Funeral Customs of the Early Inhabitants of the County of Cornwall* (1872), p. 163.
7. I. Jones, *The Most Notable Antiquity of Great Britain, Vulgarly Called Stone-heng on Salisbury Plain* (1655), pp. 8–9.
8. Ibid., p. 3.
9. Ibid., p. 40.
10. Anon., *A Fool's Bolt Soon Shott at Stonage* (1725), pp. 18–19.
11. J. Fowles and R. Legg (eds), *Monumenta Britannica, John Aubrey, 1626–97* (1980), i, pp. 19–20.

Notes to Chapter 6, John Aubrey and Friends

1. J. Fowles and R. Legg (eds), *Monumenta Britannica, John Aubrey, 1626–97* (1980) i, p. 17.
2. Ibid., pp. 18–19.
3. W. Camden, *Britain: or A Chorographicall Description of the Most Flourishing Kingdomes, England, Scotland and Ireland* (1610), p. 255.
4. Fowles and Legg, *Monumenta Britannica*, i, p. 21.
5. Ibid., p. 34.
6. Ibid., p. 38.
7. Ibid., pp. 25–26.
8. Ibid., p. 32.
9. Ibid., p. 24.
10. S. Piggott, *Ancient Britons and the Antiquarian Imagination* (1989), p. 74.
11. G. Daniel, 'Edward Lhwyd: Antiquary and Archaeologist', *Welsh History Review*, 3 (1967), p. 352.
12. Fowles and Legg, *Monumenta Britannica*, i, p. 25.
13. Ibid.
14. A. Burl, *The Stone Circles of the British Isles* (1976), p. 168.
15. J. Garden, 'A Copy of a Letter from the Reverend Dr James Garden, Professor of Theology in the King's College, at Aberdeen, to — Aubrey, Esquire', *Archaeologia*, 1 (1766), p. 317.

16. W. Borlase, *Antiquities, Historical and Monumental, of the County of Cornwall* (1769), p. 194.
17. Daniel, 'Edward Lhwyd', p. 356.

Notes to Chapter 7, William Stukeley

1. S. Piggott, *William Stukeley: An Eighteenth Century Antiquary* (1985), p. 94.
2. A. Burl, *Prehistoric Avebury* (1979), p. 50.
3. Piggott, *William Stukeley*, p. 34.
4. Ibid., p. 38.
5. W. Stukeley, *Stonehenge: A Temple Restored to the British Druids* (1740), p. 43.
6. Ibid., pp. 44–45.
7. Ibid., p. 46.
8. Piggott, *William Stukeley*, p. 90.
9. P. Ucko *et al.*, *Avebury Reconsidered* (1991), p. 89.
10. H. Rowlands, *Mona antiqua restaurata: An Archaeological Discourse on the Antiquities, Natural and Historical, of the Isle of Anglesey* (1766), pp. 45–46.
11. Ibid., p. 68.
12. S. Piggott, *The Druids* (1974), p. 120.
13. Rowlands, *Mona antiqua restaurata*, p. 48.
14. W. Stukeley, *Abury: A Temple of the British Druids* (1743), p. iv.
15. It has subsequently been established that, although the magnetic declination has a regular annual shift, it does not conform to any pattern or repeated cycle.
16. Stukeley, *Stonehenge*, p. 5.
17. Stukeley, *Abury*, p. 53.
18. Stukeley, *Stonehenge*, pp. 35, 53.
19. Ibid., p. 41.
20. Ibid., p. 34.
21. Ibid., p. 21.
22. Stukeley, *Abury*, p. 23.
23. Ibid., p. 13.
24. Ibid., p. 41.
25. Ibid., p. 2.
26. Ibid., p. 54.
27. Stukeley, *Stonehenge*, preface.
28. Piggott, *William Stukeley*, p. 97.
29. Piggott, *The Druids*, p. 119.
30. Piggott, *William Stukeley*, p. 104.
31. Stukeley, *Stonehenge*, p. 1.

Notes to Chapter 8, William Borlase

1. D. Defoe, *A Tour Through the Whole Island of Great Britain* (1974), p. 242.
2. P. Pool, *William Borlase* (1986), pp. 127–28.
3. Ibid., p. 54.
4. W. Borlase, *Antiquities, Historical and Monumental, of the County of Cornwall* (1769), p. 172.
5. Ibid., p. 53.
6. Ibid., p. 136.
7. Ibid., p. 169.
8. Ibid., pp. 173–74.
9. Ibid., p. 180.
10. Ibid., p. 182.
11. Ibid., p. 178.
12. Ibid., p. 176.
13. Ibid., p. 179.
14. Ibid., p. 205.
15. Ibid., pp. 191–92.
16. Pool, *William Borlase*, p. 129.

Notes to Chapter 9, Romantic Druids and the Picturesque

1. J. Wood, *An Essay towards a Description of Bath* (1749), i, p. 148.
2. Ibid., p. 3.
3. Ibid., p. 154.
4. Ibid., p. 159.
5. W. Stukeley, *The Family Memoirs of the Rev. William Stukeley* (1887), iii, pp. 275–76.
6. E. Duke, *The Druidical Temples of the County of Wilts* (1846), p. 7.
7. Cited in W. Long, 'Abury', *Wiltshire Archaeological and Natural History Magazine*, 4 (1858), p. 352.
8. Ibid.
9. Duke, *Druidical Temples*, p. 178.
10. J. Kemble, 'Notices of Heathen Interment in the Codex Diplomaticus', *Archaeological Journal*, 14 (1857), p. 134.
11. W. Borlase, *Antiquities, Historical and Monumental, of the County of Cornwall* (1769), p. ix.
12. A. Herbert, *Cyclops Christianus* (1849), p. 1.
13. W. Wordsworth, 'Guilt and Sorrow' (1794), stanza 14.
14. W. Wordsworth, 'The Monument Commonly Called Long Meg and her Daughters near the River Eden' (1821).
15. S. Piggott, *The Druids* (1974), p. 142.

16. Cited in G. F. Tregelles, 'Stone Circles', in W. Page (ed.), *The Victoria History of the County of Cornwall* (1906), i, p. 381.
17. G. Hawkins, *Stonehenge Decoded* (1970), p. 202.
18. C. Chippindale *et al.*, *Who Owns Stonehenge?* (1990), p. 105.

Notes to Chapter 10, Richard Colt Hoare and William Cunnington

1. L. V. Grinsell, 'A Visit to William Cunnington's Museum at Heytesbury in 1807', *Antiquity*, 43 (1969), p. 62.
2. B. Marsden, *The Early Barrow Diggers* (1974), p. 2.
3. S. Piggott, *Ancient Britons and the Antiquarian Imagination* (1989), p. 122.
4. R. H. Cunnington, *From Antiquary to Archaeologist: A Biography of William Cunnington, 1754–1810* (1975), p. 20.
5. Ibid., p. 60.
6. K. Woodbridge, *Landscape and Antiquity: Aspects of English Culture at Stourhead, 1718–1838* (1970), p. 225.
7. R. C. Hoare, *The Ancient History of South Wiltshire* (1812), p. 21.
8. Ibid., p. 121.
9. Ibid., p. 76.
10. Ibid., p. 2.
11. R. C. Hoare, *The Ancient History of North Wiltshire* (1819), p. 106.
12. Cunnington, *Antiquary to Archaeologist*, p. 76.
13. Woodbridge, *Landscape and Antiquity*, p. 211.
14. Hoare, *South Wiltshire*, p. 20n.
15. Ibid., p. 152.
16. Ibid., pp. 152–53.
17. Hoare, *North Wiltshire*, p. 71.
18. Ibid., p. 91.
19. Ibid., p. 122.
20. G. Daniel, *A Hundred and Fifty Years of Archaeology* (1975), p. 31.

Notes to Chapter 11, The Barrow Diggers

1. B. Marsden, *The Early Barrow Diggers* (1974), p. 29.
2. F. W. L. Thomas, 'Account of Some of the Celtic Antiquities of Orkney', *Archaeologia*, 34 (1852), p. 110.
3. Marsden, *Barrow Diggers*, pp. 25–26.
4. W. C. Borlase, *Naenia Cornubiae: A Descriptive Essay, Illustrative of the Sepulchres and Funeral Customs of the Early Inhabitants of the County of Cornwall* (1872), pp. 156–57.
5. Marsden, *Barrow Diggers*, p. 49.

6. K. Woodbridge, *Landscape and Antiquity: Aspects of English Culture at Stourhead, 1718–1838* (1970), p. 211.

7. Borlase, *Naenia Cornubiae*, p. 8.

8. G. Petrie, 'The Picts' Houses in the Orkneys', *Archaeological Journal*, 20 (1863), p. 33.

9. W. Greenwell, 'Notices of the Examination of Ancient Grave-Hills in the North Riding of Yorkshire', *Archaeological Journal*, 22 (1865), p. 107.

10. J. R. Mortimer, *Forty Years' Researches in British and Saxon Burial Mounds of East Yorkshire* (1905), p. xxiv.

11. J. Thurnam, 'On Ancient British Barrows: Part I, Long Barrows', *Archaeologia*, 42 (1869), p. 185.

12. W. Greenwell, *British Barrows: A Record of the Examination of the Sepulchral Mounds in Various Parts of England* (1877), pp. 119–20.

13. Ibid., p. 57.

14. J. Thurnam, 'On Ancient British Barrows: Part II, Round Barrows', *Archaeologia*, 43 (1871), p. 488.

Notes to Chapter 12, Stone Circles and Stone Age Man

1. H. Callender, 'Notice of the Stone Circle at Callernish, in the Island of Lewis', *Proceedings of the Society of Antiquaries of Scotland*, 2 (1857), p. 380.

2. J. Peter, 'Notice of Stone Circles, in the Parish of Old Deer', *Proceedings of the Society of Antiquaries of Scotland*, 19 (1885), p. 370.

3. J. N. G. Ritchie, 'The Stones of Stenness, Orkney', *Proceedings of the Society of Antiquaries of Scotland*, 107 (1976), p. 5.

4. Peter, 'Notice of Stone Circles', p. 375.

5. W. C. Lukis, 'Report on the Prehistoric Monuments of Wilts, Somerset, and South Wales', *Proceedings of the Society of Antiquaries of London*, 9 (1883), p. 352.

6. C. W. Dymond, 'The Megalithic Antiquities at Stanton Drew', *Journal of the British Archaeological Association*, 33 (1877), p. 304.

7. C. W. Dymond, 'A Group of Cumbrian Megaliths', *Journal of the British Archaeological Association*, 34 (1878), p. 32.

8. S. Seyer, *Memoirs Historical and Topographical of Bristol and its Neighbourhood* (1821), p. 100.

9. D. Wilson, *The Archaeology and Prehistoric Annals of Scotland* (1851), pp. 110–13.

10. R. N. Worth, 'The Stone Rows of Dartmoor', *Transactions of the Devon Association for the Advancement of Science*, 24 (1892), p. 416.

11. J. Simpson, 'On Ancient Sculpturings of Cups and Concentric Rings &c', *Proceedings of the Society of Antiquaries of Scotland*, 6, appendix volume (1867), p. 104.

12. C. W. Dymond, 'Notes on the Men-an-tol and Chywoon Quoit, Cornwall', *Journal of the British Archaeological Association*, 33 (1877), p. 178.

13. G. F. Tregelles, 'Stone Circles', in W Page (ed.), *The Victoria History of the County of Cornwall* (1906), i, pp. 406–7.

14. A. J. Evans, 'Rollright Stones', *Transactions of the Bristol and Gloucestershire Archaeological Society*, 16 (1891), pp. 39–40.

15. Dymond, 'Cumbrian Megaliths', p. 36.

16. C. Dalrymple, 'Notes of the Excavation of the Stone Circle at Crichie, Aberdeenshire', *Proceedings of the Society of Antiquaries of Scotland*, 18 (1884), pp. 322–23.

17. J. Bryce, 'An Account of Excavations within the Stone Circles of Arran', *Proceedings of the Society of Antiquaries of Scotland*, 4 (1862), pp. 523–24.

18. W. C. Lukis, 'On Some Megalithic Monuments in Western Cornwall', *Journal of the British Archaeological Association*, 33 (1877), p. 294.

19. R. J. C. Atkinson, 'Silbury Hill', *Antiquity*, 41 (1967), p. 259.

20. A. C. Smith, 'Excavations at Avebury', *Wiltshire Archaeological and Natural History Magazine*, 10 (1867), p. 216.

21. F. Petrie, *Stonehenge: Plans, Descriptions and Theories* (1880), p. 33.

22. Smith, 'Excavations at Avebury', p. 211.

23. H. St George Gray, 'The Avebury Excavations 1908–22', *Archaeologia*, 84 (1935), p. 161.

24. W. Gowland, 'Recent Excavations at Stonehenge', *Archaeologia*, 58 (1902), pp. 84, 86.

25. Ibid., p. 84.

26. Ibid., p. 87.

27. Ibid., p. 89.

Notes to Chapter 13, Diffusionism

1. G. Daniel, *A Short History of Archaeology* (1981), p. 150.

2. V. G. Childe, *What Happened in History* (1954), p. 24.

3. V. G. Childe, *Prehistoric Communities of the British Isles* (1940), p. 2.

4. C. F. C. Hawkes, 'Archaeological Theory and Method: Some Suggestions from the Old World', *American Anthropologist*, 56 (1954), pp. 155–68.

5. S. Piggott, *Approach to Archaeology* (1959), p. 95.

6. R. J. C. Atkinson, *Stonehenge* (1979), p. 13.

Notes to Chapter 14, Megalith Builders

1. G. Daniel, *The Prehistoric Chamber Tombs of England and Wales* (1950), p. 174.

2. V. G. Childe, *Prehistoric Communities of the British Isles* (1940), p. 77.

3. Ibid., p. 74.

4. Ibid., p. 77.

5. R. J. C. Atkinson, 'Neolithic Engineering', *Antiquity*, 35 (1961), p. 298.

6. Ibid., p. 299.
7. J. and C. F. C. Hawkes, *Prehistoric Britain* (1947), p. 43.
8. G. Daniel, *The Megalith Builders of Western Europe* (1958), p. 128.
9. Childe, *Prehistoric Communities*, p. 53.
10. Ibid., p. 39.
11. S. Piggott, *The Neolithic Cultures of the British Isles* (1954), p. 42.
12. W. F. J. Knight, 'Maze Symbolism and the Trojan Game', *Antiquity*, 6 (1932), p. 457.
13. Piggott, *Neolithic Cultures*, p. 166.
14. Daniel, *Prehistoric Chamber Tombs*, pp. 112–13.
15. Hawkes, *Prehistoric Britain*, p. 47.
16. R. J. C. Atkinson, 'Wayland's Smithy', *Antiquity*, 39 (1965), p. 130.
17. J. F. S. Stone, 'The Stonehenge Cursus and its Affinities', *Archaeological Journal*, 104 (1947), p. 19.
18. Hawkes, *Prehistoric Britain*, pp. 58–59.

Notes to Chapter 15, Beaker Folk

1. S. Piggott, 'Timber Circles: A Re-Examination', *Archaeological Journal*, 96 (1940), p. 210.
2. J. G. D. Clark, 'The Timber Monument at Arminghall and its Affinities', *Proceedings of the Prehistoric Society*, 2 (1936), p. 13.
3. V. G. Childe, *Prehistoric Communities of the British Isles* (1940), pp. 108–9.
4. W. F. Grimes, 'The Megalithic Monuments of Wales', *Proceedings of the Prehistoric Society*, 2 (1936), p. 109.
5. H. E. Kilbride-Jones, 'An Account of the Excavation of the Stone Circle at Loanhead of Daviot, and of the Standing Stones of Cullerlie, Echt, both in Aberdeenshire', *Proceedings of the Society of Antiquaries of Scotland*, 69 (1935), p. 195.
6. V. G. Childe, 'Final Report on the Excavation of the Stone Circle at Old Keig, Aberdeenshire', *Proceedings of the Society of Antiquaries of Scotland*, 68 (1934), p. 388.
7. Childe, *Prehistoric Communities*, pp. 101–2.
8. J. and C. F. C. Hawkes, *Prehistoric Britain* (1947), p. 59.
9. I. F. Smith, *Windmill Hill and Avebury: Excavations by Alexander Keiller, 1925–1939* (1965), p. 251.
10. Ibid.
11. Ibid.
12. C. Fox, *Life and Death in the Bronze Age* (1959), p. 173.

Notes to Chapter 16, Stonehenge and the Wessex Culture

1. *The Times*, 5 August 1927.
2. R. J. C. Atkinson, *Stonehenge* (1979), p. 171.
3. Ibid., p. 177.
4. Ibid., pp. 164–65.
5. Ibid., p. 166.
6. Ibid., p. 181.
7. Ibid., p. 167.
8. *Antiquity*, 40 (1966), pp. 256–57.

Notes to Chapter 17, The Sun and the Stars

1. H. Callender, 'Notice of the Stone Circle at Callernish, in the Island of Lewis', *Proceedings of the Society of Antiquaries of Scotland*, 2 (1857), p. 382.
2. A. L. Lewis, 'Stone Circles of Britain', *Archaeological Journal*, 49 (1892), pp. 136–54.
3. A. L. Lewis, 'The Stone Circles of Scotland', *Journal of the Anthropological Institute*, 30 (1900), pp. 56–73.

Notes to Chapter 18, Sir Norman Lockyer and his Followers

1. Lockyer's calculation was based on tables of the Obliquity published in 1873, which later computations showed to be inaccurate. The date should have been 1840 BC ± 200 years.
2. The Reverend J. Griffith, in N. Lockyer, *Stonehenge and Other British Stone Monuments, Astronomically Considered* (2nd edn, 1909), p. 335.
3. B. Somerville, 'Instances of Orientation in Prehistoric Monuments of the British Isles', *Archaeologia*, 73 (1923), p. 224.
4. J. Patrick, 'Midwinter Sunrise at Newgrange', *Nature*, 249 (1974), pp. 517–19; M. J. O'Kelly, *Newgrange: Archaeology, Art and Legend* (1982).
5. Lockyer, *Stonehenge*, p. 447.
6. B. Somerville, 'Orientation', *Antiquity*, 1 (1927), p. 40.
7. F. Stevens, *Stonehenge: To-Day and Yesterday* (1919), p. 66.
8. R. E. M. Wheeler, *Prehistoric and Roman Wales* (1925), p. 106.
9. V. G. Childe, *The Bronze Age* (1930), p. 164.
10. V. G. Childe, *Prehistoric Communities of the British Isles* (1940), pp. 100–1.

Notes to Chapter 19, Stonehenge Decoded

1. G. S. Hawkins, *Stonehenge Decoded* (1970), pp. 185–86.
2. R. J. C. Atkinson, 'Moonshine on Stonehenge', *Antiquity*, 40 (1966), p. 213.

3. J. Hawkes, 'God in the Machine', *Antiquity*, 41 (1967), p. 174.
4. G. Daniel, 'Editorial', *Antiquity*, 40 (1966), pp. 169–71.

Notes to Chapter 20, Pi and Pythagorean Triangles

1. J. Michell, *A Little History of Astro-Archaeology: Stages in the Transformation of a Heresy* (1989), pp. 118–19.
2. A. Thom, *Megalithic Lunar Observatories* (1971), pp. 45–51.
3. Ibid., pp. 91–105.
4. A. Thom, *Megalithic Sites in Britain* (1967), p. 27.
5. D. Heggie, *Megalithic Science* (1981), p. 11.
6. A. Burl, *Rings of Stone: The Prehistoric Stone Circles of Britain and Ireland* (1979), p. 70.
7. Thom, *Lunar Observatories*, p. 12.

Notes to Chapter 21, Alfred Watkins and the Old Straight Track

1. Quoted in A. Watkins, *The Old Straight Track* (1925), p. 14.
2. N. Pennick and P. Devereux, *Lines on the Landscape* (1989), pp. 39–40.
3. W. H. Black, 'An Address to the Congress at Hereford, 1870', *Journal of the British Archaeological Association*, 27 (1871), p. 270.
4. Watkins, *Old Straight Track*, pp. 215–16.
5. Ibid., p. 207.
6. Ibid., p. xx.
7. Ibid., p. 193.
8. Ibid., p. 215.
9. J. Michell, 'Alfred Watkins: A Note', in A. Watkins, *The Old Straight Track* (1970), pp. xvi–xvii.
10. Watkins, *Old Straight Track*, p. 218.
11. O. G. S. Crawford, *Archaeology in the Field* (1953), p. 269.

Notes to Chapter 22, John Michell and *The View over Atlantis*

1. J. Michell, *The New View over Atlantis* (1983), p. 207.
2. Quoted in J. and C. Bord, *Mysterious Britain* (1974), p. 36.
3. T. C. Lethbridge, *The Legend of the Sons of God* (1972), pp. 14–15.
4. Michell, *View over Atlantis*, pp. 86–87.
5. Ibid., pp. 74–75.
6. Ibid., pp. 13–14.
7. Ibid., p. 16.
8. Ibid., p. 97.
9. Ibid., p. 53.

10. Ibid., p. 50.
11. Ibid., p. 97.

Notes to Chapter 23, Mysterious Britain

1. Quoted in P. Screeton, *Quicksilver Heritage: The Mystic Leys, Their Legacy of Ancient Wisdom* (1974), p. 210.
2. Ibid., p. 19.
3. Ibid., p. 265.
4. P. Devereux and I. Thomson, *The Ley Hunter's Companion: Aligned Ancient Sites* (1979), p. 11.
5. Screeton, *Quicksilver Heritage*, p. 19.
6. A. Roberts, *Atlantean Traditions in Ancient Britain* (1975), p. 20.
7. J. and C. Bord, *Mysterious Britain* (1974), pp. 182–83.
8. Ibid., p. 22.
9. Ibid., p. 40.
10. F. Hitching, *Earth Magic* (1977), pp. 171–73.
11. R. Muir, *Shell Guide to Reading the Landscape* (1981), p. 116.
12. Devereux and Thomson, *Ley Hunter's Companion*, p. 43.
13. J. Michell, *The Old Stones of Land's End: An Enquiry into the Mysteries of Megalithic Science* (1974), p. 112.
14. T. Williamson and L. Bellamy, *Ley Lines in Question* (1983), p. 107.
15. N. Pennick and P. Devereux, *Lines on the Landscape* (1989), p. 213.

Notes to Chapter 24, Earth Mysteries

1. C. Chippindale *et al.*, *Who Owns Stonehenge?* (1990), p. 37.
2. P. Devereux, *Earth Lights Revelation* (1989), pp. 106–8.
3. N. Pennick and P. Devereux, *Lines on the Landscape* (1989), p. 54.
4. R. Bradley, *Altering the Earth: The Origins of Monuments in Britain and Continental Europe* (1993); C. Tilley, *A Phenomenology of Landscape: Places, Paths and Monuments* (1994).
5. P. Devereux, *The New Ley Hunter's Guide* (1994), p. 104.
6. Pennick and Devereux, *Lines on the Landscape*, p. 262.

Notes to Chapter 25, Radiocarbon and other Revolutions

1. D. L. Clarke, *Analytical Archaeology* (1978), p. 42.
2. I. Hodder, 'Material Culture Texts and Social Change: A Theoretical Discussion and Some Archaeological Examples', *Proceedings of the Prehistoric Society*, 58 (1988), p. 72.

3. C. Renfrew and S. Shennan, *Ranking, Resource and Exchange: Aspects of the Archaeology of Early European Society* (1982), p. 141.
4. I. F. Smith, *Windmill Hill and Avebury: Excavations by Alexander Keiller, 1925–1939* (1965), p. 252.
5. A. Burl, *Prehistoric Stone Circles* (1983), p. 10.

Notes to Chapter 26, Sex and the Dead

1. A. Burl, *The Stonehenge People* (1987), p. 13.
2. A. Burl, *Prehistoric Avebury* (1979), p. 142.
3. Ibid., p. 84.
4. A. Burl, 'By the Light of the Cinerary Moon: Chambered Tombs and the Astronomy of Death', in C. L. N. Ruggles and A. W. R. Whittle (eds), *Astronomy and Society in Britain during the Period 4000–1500 BC* (1981), p. 268.
5. A. Burl, 'Science or Symbolism: Problems of Archaeo-Astronomy', *Antiquity*, 54 (1980), p. 196.
6. Burl, *Stonehenge People*, pp. 79–80.
7. Ibid., p. 212.
8. Burl, *Avebury*, p. 213.
9. M. Dames, *The Silbury Treasure: The Great Goddess Rediscovered* (1976), p. 52.
10. M. Dames, *The Avebury Cycle* (1977), p. 9.
11. R. Castleden, *The Stonehenge People: An Exploration of Life in Neolithic Britain, 4700–2000 BC* (1987), p. 260.
12. J. Hedges, *Tomb of the Eagles: A Window on Stone Age Tribal Britain* (1984), p. 133.
13. A. W. R. Whittle, 'Wayland's Smithy, Oxfordshire: Excavations at the Neolithic Tomb in 1962–63 by R. J. C. Atkinson and S. Piggott', *Proceedings of the Prehistoric Society*, 57 (1991), p. 98.

Notes to Chapter 27, Landscape, Culture, Society

1. C. Renfrew, *Investigations in Orkney* (1979), pp. 216, 222.
2. D. Fraser, *Land and Society in Neolithic Orkney* (1983), ii, p. 423.
3. Renfrew, *Investigations in Orkney*, p. 218.
4. R. Mercer, *Hambledon Hill: A Neolithic Landscape* (1980), p. 63.
5. A. Burl, *The Stonehenge People* (1987), p. 16.
6. Ibid., p. 19.
7. Ibid., p. 42.
8. R. Bradley, *Altering the Earth: The Origins of Monuments in Britain and Continental Europe* (1993), p. 74.
9. C. Taylor, 'Introduction and Commentary', in W. G. Hoskins, *The Making of the English Landscape* (1988), p. 16.

10. R. Muir, *Shell Guide to Reading the Landscape* (1981), p. 31.
11. J. Michell, *The Old Stones of Land's End: An Enquiry into the Mysteries of Megalithic Science* (1974), p. 110.
12. Bradley, *Altering the Earth*, p. 45.
13. Ibid., p. 46.
14. B. Bender, 'Theorising Landscapes, and the Prehistoric Landscapes of Stonehenge', *Man*, 27 (1992), p. 744.
15. C. Tilley, *A Phenomenology of Landscape: Places, Paths and Monuments* (1994), p. 99.
16. Ibid., p. 109.
17. Ibid.
18. Bradley, *Altering the Earth*, p. 17.
19. Ibid., p. 116.

Bibliography

Adams, J., 1856, 'The Opening of Veryan Beacon', *Thirty-Seventh Report of the Royal Institution of Cornwall*, 23–26.

Anderson, James, 1779, 'An Account of Ancient Monuments and Fortifications in the Highlands of Scotland', *Archaeologia* 5, 241–66.

Anderson, Joseph, 1867, 'Of the Chambered Cairns of Caithness', *Proceedings of the Society of Antiquaries of Scotland* 6, 442–51.

Anderson, Joseph, 1886, *Scotland in Pagan Times: The Bronze and Stone Ages*. Edinburgh: David Douglas.

Anon, *A Fool's Bolt Soon Shott at Stonage*. Facsimile of first printing (1725) in R. Legg, 1986, *Stonehenge Antiquaries*. Milborne Port: Dorset Publishing Co.

Ashbee, Paul, 1960, *The Bronze Age Round Barrow in Britain*. London: Phoenix House.

Ashbee, Paul, 1966, 'The Fussell's Lodge Long Barrow Excavations', *Archaeologia* 100, 1–80.

Ashbee, Paul, 1970, *The Earthen Long Barrow in Britain*. London: Dent.

Ashbee, P., Smith, I. F., and Evans, J. G., 1979, 'Excavation of Three Long Barrows near Avebury, Wiltshire', *Proceedings of the Prehistoric Society* 45, 207–300.

Atkinson, R. J. C., 1961, 'Neolithic Engineering', *Antiquity* 35, 292–99.

Atkinson, R. J. C., 1965, 'Wayland's Smithy', *Antiquity* 39, 126–33.

Atkinson, R. J. C., 1966, 'Moonshine on Stonehenge', *Antiquity* 40, 212–16.

Atkinson, R. J. C., 1967, 'Silbury Hill', *Antiquity* 41, 259–62.

Atkinson, R. J. C., 1969, 'The Date of Silbury Hill', *Antiquity* 43, 216.

Atkinson, R. J. C., 1970, 'Silbury Hill 1969–70', *Antiquity* 44, 313–14.

Atkinson, R. J. C., 1979, *Stonehenge: Archaeology and Interpretation*. Harmondsworth: Penguin.

Atkinson, R. J. C., Hawkins, G. S., Newall, R. S., Newham, C. A., Sadler, D. H., and Thom, A., 1967, 'Hoyle on Stonehenge: Some Comments', *Antiquity* 41, 91–98.

Aubrey, John, 'Monumenta Britannica, or a Miscellanie of British Antiquities', vol. 1. Bodleian Library MS Top. Gen. c 24.

Aubrey, John, 'Monumenta Britannica, or a Miscellanie of British Antiquities', vol. 2. Bodleian Library MS Top. Gen. c 25.

Barnatt, John, 1982, *Prehistoric Cornwall: The Ceremonial Monuments*. Wellingborough: Turnstone Press.

Barnatt, John, and Moir, Gordon, 1984, 'Stone Circles and Megalithic Mathematics', *Proceedings of the Prehistoric Society* 50, 197–216.

Barrett, John C., 1994, *Fragments from Antiquity: An Archaeology of Social Life in Britain, 2900–1200 bc.* Oxford: Blackwell.

Barrett, John C., Bradley, Richard, and Green, Martin, 1991, *Landscape, Monuments, and Society: The Prehistory of Cranborne Chase.* Cambridge: Cambridge University Press.

Bateman, Thomas, 1861, *Ten Years Digging in Celtic and Saxon Grave Hills in the counties of Derbyshire, Staffordshire and Yorkshire from 1848 to 1858.* London: George Allen & Sons.

Bede, *A History of the English Church and People*, translated by Leo Sherley-Price. Harmondsworth: Penguin, 1955.

Bender, Barbara, 1992, 'Theorising Landscapes, and the Prehistoric Landscapes of Stonehenge', *Man* 27, 735–55.

Beowulf, translated by Michael Swanton. Manchester: Manchester University Press, 1978.

Binford, Lewis R., 1972, *An Archaeological Perspective.* London: Seminar Press.

Black, W. H., 1871, 'An Address to the Congress at Hereford, 1870', *Journal of the British Archaeological Association* 27, 268–70.

Black, W. H., 1872, 'Notes on Wareham and on Early Customs and Monuments in Dorset', *Journal of the British Archaeological Association* 28, 230–37.

Blake, William, *Complete Writings.* Oxford: Oxford University Press, 1966.

Bord, Janet and Colin, 1974, *Mysterious Britain.* St Albans: Granada.

Bord, Janet and Colin, 1976, *The Secret Country: An Interpretation of the Folklore of Ancient Sites in the British Isles.* London: Paul Elek.

Borlase, William, 1769, *Antiquities, Historical and Monumental, of the County of Cornwall.* London: Baker, Leigh, Payne and White.

Borlase, William Copeland, 1872, *Naenia Cornubiae: A Descriptive Essay, Illustrative of the Sepulchres and Funeral Customs of the Early Inhabitants of the County of Cornwall.* Truro: J. R. Netherton, and London: Longmans, Green, Reader and Dyer.

Borlase, William Copeland, 1885, 'Typical Specimens of Cornish Barrows', *Archaeologia* 49, 181–98.

Bowen, E. G., 1971, 'Llandisiliogogo', *Antiquity* 45, 213–15.

Bradley, Richard, 1984, *The Social Foundations of Prehistoric Britain: Themes and Variations in the Archaeology of Power.* Harlow: Longman

Bradley, Richard, 1993, *Altering the Earth: The Origins of Monuments in Britain and Continental Europe.* Edinburgh: Society of Antiquaries of Scotland Monograph Series 8.

Bradley, R., Harding J., and Mathews, M., 1993, 'The Siting of Prehistoric Rock Art in Galloway, South-West Scotland', *Proceedings of the Prehistoric Society* 59, 269–83.

Briggs, Katharine M., 1974, *The Folklore of the Cotswolds.* London: Batsford.

Broadhurst, Paul, and Miller, Hamish, 1989, *The Sun and the Serpent.* Launceston: Pendragon Press.

Broome, J. H., 1869, 'Astronomical Date of Stonehenge', *Astronomical Register* 7, 202–4.

Brown, Peter Lancaster, 1976, *Megaliths, Myths and Men: An Introduction to Astro-Archaeology*. Poole: Blandford.

Brown, Peter Lancaster, 1979, *Megaliths and Masterminds*. London: Robert Hale.

Brushfield, T. N., 1900, 'Arbor Low', *Journal of the British Archaeological Association*, new series 6, 127–39.

Bryce, James, 1862, 'An Account of Excavations within the Stone Circles of Arran', *Proceedings of the Society of Antiquaries of Scotland* 4, 499–524.

Burgess, Colin, 1980, *The Age of Stonehenge*. London: Dent.

Burl, Aubrey, 1976, *The Stone Circles of the British Isles*. London: Yale University Press.

Burl, Aubrey, 1979, *Prehistoric Avebury*. London: Yale University Press.

Burl, Aubrey, 1979, *Rings of Stone: The Prehistoric Stone Circles of Britain and Ireland*. London: Frances Lincoln.

Burl, Aubrey, 1980, 'Science or Symbolism: Problems of Archaeo-Astronomy', *Antiquity* 54, 191–200.

Burl, Aubrey, 1981, *Rites of the Gods*. London: Dent.

Burl, Aubrey, 1981, 'By the Light of the Cinerary Moon: Chambered Tombs and the Astronomy of Death', in C. L. N. Ruggles and A. W. R. Whittle (eds), *Astronomy and Society in Britain during the Period 4000–1500 BC*, 243–74. Oxford: British Archaeological Reports 88.

Burl, Aubrey, 1983, *Prehistoric Stone Circles*. Princes Risborough: Shire Publications.

Burl, Aubrey, 1983, *Prehistoric Astronomy and Ritual*. Princes Risborough: Shire Publications.

Burl, Aubrey, 1987, *The Stonehenge People*. London: Dent.

Burl, Aubrey, 1992, 'Two Early Plans of Avebury', *Wiltshire Archaeological and Natural History Magazine* 85, 163–72.

Burl, Aubrey, 1993, *From Carnac to Callanish: The Prehistoric Stone Rows and Avenues of Britain, Ireland and Brittany*. London: Yale University Press.

Callander, J. Graham, 1927, 'Recent Archaeological Research in Scotland', *Archaeologia* 77, 87–110.

Callender, H., 1857, 'Notice of the Stone Circle at Callernish, in the Island of Lewis', *Proceedings of the Society of Antiquaries of Scotland* 2, 380–84.

Camden, William, 1610, *Britain: or A Chorographicall Description of the Most Flourishing Kingdomes, England, Scotland and Ireland*, translated by Philemon Holland. London: G. Bishop and J. Norton.

Carew, Richard, 1969, *Survey of Cornwall*. London: Adams and Dart.

Case, Humphrey, 1969, 'Neolithic Explanations', *Antiquity* 43, 176–86.

Castleden, Rodney, 1987, *The Stonehenge People: An Exploration of Life in Neolithic Britain, 4700–2000 BC*. London: Routledge.

Charleton, Walter, 1663, *Chorea Gigantum: or The most Famous Antiquity of Great-Britain, Vulgarly called Stone-heng, Standing on Salisbury Plain, Restored to the Danes*. London: H. Herriman.

Childe, V. G., 1925, *The Dawn of European Civilization*. London: Routledge and Kegan Paul.

Childe, V. G., 1930, *The Bronze Age*. Cambridge: Cambridge University Press.

Childe V. G., 1934, 'Final Report on the Excavation of the Stone Circle at Old Keig, Aberdeenshire', *Proceedings of the Society of Antiquaries of Scotland* 68, 372–93.

Childe, V. G., 1940, *Prehistoric Communities of the British Isles*. Edinburgh: Chambers.

Childe, V. G., 1954, *What Happened in History*. Harmondsworth: Penguin.

Chippindale, Christopher, 1994, *Stonehenge Complete*. London: Thames and Hudson.

Chippindale, C., Devereux, P., Fowler, P., Jones, R., and Sebastian, T., 1990, *Who Owns Stonehenge?* London: Batsford.

Clare, T., 1987, 'Towards a Reappraisal of Henge Monuments: Origins, Evolution and Hierarchies', *Proceedings of the Prehistoric Society* 53, 457–77.

Clark, J. G. D., 1936, 'The Timber Monument at Arminghall and its Affinities', *Proceedings of the Prehistoric Society* 2, 1–51.

Clarke, David L., 1972, 'Models and Paradigms in Contemporary Archaeology', in D. L. Clarke (ed.), *Models in Archaeology*, 1–60. London: Methuen.

Clarke, David L., 1973, 'Archaeology: The Loss of Innocence', *Antiquity* 47, 6–18.

Clarke, David L., 1978, *Analytical Archaeology*. London: Methuen.

Clarke, D. V., Cowie, T. G., and Foxon, A., 1985, *Symbols of Power at the Time of Stonehenge*. Edinburgh: HMSO.

Cleal, R., Montague, R., and Walker, K., 1995, *Stonehenge: In its Landscape*. London: English Heritage Archaeological Report 10.

Clifford, Elsie M., 1936, 'Notgrove Long Barrow, Gloucestershire', *Archaeologia* 86, 119–61.

Clifford, Elsie M., 1938, 'The Excavation of Nympsfield Long Barrow, Gloucestershire', *Proceedings of the Prehistoric Society* 4, 188–213.

Coles, Fred, 1901, 'Report on the Stone Circles of the North-East of Scotland, Inverurie District', *Proceedings of the Society of Antiquaries of Scotland* 35, 187–248.

Coles, Fred, 1902, 'Report on Stone Circles in Aberdeenshire', *Proceedings of the Society of Antiquaries of Scotland* 36, 488–581.

Corcoran, J. X. W. P., 1972, 'Multi-Period Construction and the Origins of the Chambered Long Cairn in Western Britain and Ireland', in F. Lynch and C. Burgess (eds), *Prehistoric Man in Wales and the West*, 31–63. Bath: Adams and Dart.

Courtenay, M. A., 1890, *Cornish Feasts and Folklore*. Penzance: Beare and Son.

Crawford, O. G. S., 1953, *Archaeology in the Field*. London: Phoenix House.

Cunnington, M. E., 1929, *Woodhenge*. Devizes: George Simpson.

Cunnington, M. E., 1931, 'The "Sanctuary" on Overton Hill, near Avebury', *Wiltshire Archaeology and Natural History Magazine* 45, 300–35.

Cunnington, R. H., 1975, *From Antiquary to Archaeologist: A Biography of William Cunnington, 1754–1810*. Princes Risborough: Shire Publications.

Dalrymple, Charles, 1884, 'Notes of the Excavation of the Stone Circle at Crichie, Aberdeenshire', *Proceedings of the Society of Antiquaries of Scotland* 18, 319–25.

Dames, Michael, 1976, *The Silbury Treasure: The Great Goddess Rediscovered*. London: Thames and Hudson.

Dames, Michael, 1977, *The Avebury Cycle*. London: Thames and Hudson.

Daniel, Glyn, 1950, *The Prehistoric Chamber Tombs of England and Wales*. Cambridge: Cambridge University Press.

Daniel, Glyn, 1958, *The Megalith Builders of Western Europe*. London: Hutchinson.

Daniel, Glyn, 1966, 'Editorial', *Antiquity* 40, 169–71.

Daniel, Glyn, 1967, 'Edward Lhwyd: Antiquary and Archaeologist', *Welsh History Review* 3, 345–59.

Daniel, Glyn, 1972, *Megaliths in History*. London: Thames and Hudson.

Daniel, Glyn, 1975, *A Hundred and Fifty Years of Archaeology*. London: Duckworth.

Daniel, Glyn, 1981, *A Short History of Archaeology*. London: Thames and Hudson.

Defoe, Daniel, 1974, *A Tour Through the Whole Island of Great Britain*. London: Dent.

Devereux, Paul, 1982, *Earth Lights: Towards an Explanation of the UFO Enigma*. Wellingborough: Turnstone Press.

Devereux, Paul, 1989, *Earth Lights Revelation*. London: Blandford.

Devereux, Paul, 1990, *Places of Power*. London: Blandford.

Devereux, Paul, 1992, *Shamanism and the Mystery Lines*. London: Quantum.

Devereux, Paul, 1992, *Symbolic Landscapes: The Dreamtime Earth and Avebury's Open Secrets*. Glastonbury: Gothic Image.

Devereux, Paul, 1994, *The New Ley Hunter's Guide*. Glastonbury: Gothic Image.

Devereux, Paul, and Thomson, Ian, 1979, *The Ley Hunter's Companion: Aligned Ancient Sites*. London: Thames and Hudson.

Diodorus Siculus, *Histories*, vol. 2, translated by C. H. Oldfather. London: William Heinemann, 1935.

Duke, E., 1846, *The Druidical Temples of the County of Wilts*. London: John Russell Smith.

Dymond, C. W., 1877, 'Notes on the Men-an-tol and Chywoon Quoit, Cornwall', *Journal of the British Archaeological Association* 33, 176–78.

Dymond, C. W., 1877, 'The Megalithic Antiquities at Stanton Drew', *Journal of the British Archaeological Association* 33, 297–307.

Dymond, C. W., 1878, 'A Group of Cumbrian Megaliths', *Journal of the British Archaeological Association* 34, 31–36.

Eitel, E.J., 1873, *Feng-Shui: The Science of Sacred Landscapes in Old China*. London: Trubner & Co (republished by Synergetic Press, London, 1984).

Emery, Frank, 1971, *Edward Lhuyd, 1660–1709*. Cardiff: University of Wales Press.

Evans, A.J., 1891, 'Rollright Stones', *Transactions of the Bristol and Gloucestershire Archaeological Society* 16, 38–40.

Evans, A.J., 1895, 'The Rollright Stones and Their Folk-Lore', *Folklore* 6, 6–51.

Farrer, James, 1868, 'Note of Excavations in Sanday, One of the North Isles of Orkney', *Proceedings of the Society of Antiquaries of Scotland* 6, 398–401.

Fergusson, James, 1872, *Rude Stone Monuments in All Countries: Their Age and Uses*. London: John Murray.

Fleming, Andrew, 1973, 'Tombs for the Living', *Man* new series 8, 177–93.

Fleming, Andrew, 1988, *The Dartmoor Reaves*. London: Batsford.

Fowles, John, and Legg, Rodney (eds), 1980, *Monumenta Britannica, John Aubrey, 1626–97, Parts 1 and 2*. Milborne Port: Dorset Publishing Company.

Fox, C., 1959, *Life and Death in the Bronze Age*. London: Routledge and Kegan Paul.

Fraser, David, 1983, *Land and Society in Neolithic Orkney*. Oxford: British Archaeological Reports 117.

Garden, J., 1766, 'A Copy of a Letter from the Reverend Dr James Garden, Professor of Theology in the King's College, at Aberdeen, to – – Aubrey, Esquire', *Archaeologia* 1, 312–19.

Geoffrey of Monmouth, *The History of the Kings of Britain*, translated by Lewis Thorpe. Harmondsworth: Penguin, 1966.

Gidley, Lewis, 1877, *Stonehenge, Viewed by the Light of Ancient History and Modern Observation*. Salisbury: Brown and Co.

Gowland, William, 1902, 'Recent Excavations at Stonehenge', *Archaeologia* 58, 37–118.

Graves, Tom, 1978, *Needles of Stone*. London: Turnstone.

Gray, Harold St George, 1903, 'On the Excavations at Arbor Low, 1901–1902', *Archaeologia* 58, 461–98.

Gray, Harold St George, 1905, 'A Memoir of General Pitt Rivers', in *Excavations in Cranborne Chase*, index volume (vol. v). Privately published.

Gray, Harold St George, 1908, 'On the Stone Circles of East Cornwall', *Archaeologia* 61, 1–60.

Gray, Harold St George, 1935, 'The Avebury Excavations, 1908–22', *Archaeologia* 84, 99–162.

Greenwell, William, 1865, 'Notices of the Examination of Ancient Grave-Hills in the North Riding of Yorkshire', *Archaeological Journal* 22, 97–117.

Greenwell, William, 1877, *British Barrows: A Record of the Examination of the Sepulchral Mounds in Various Parts of England*. Oxford: Clarendon Press.

Grimes, W. F., 1936, 'The Megalithic Monuments of Wales', *Proceedings of the Prehistoric Society* 2, 106–39.

Grinsell, L. V., 1969, 'A Visit to William Cunnington's Museum at Heytesbury in 1807', *Antiquity* 43, 62–63.

Grinsell, L. V., 1976, *Folklore of Prehistoric Sites in Britain*. Newton Abbot: David and Charles.

Hadingham, Evan, 1978, *Circles and Standing Stones*. London: Abacus.

Hadingham, Evan, 1983, *Early Man and the Cosmos*. London: Heinemann.

Haggarty, Alison, 1988, 'Machrie Moor', *Current Archaeology* 109, 35–37.

Hawkes, C. F. C., 1954, 'Archaeological Theory and Method: Some Suggestions from the Old World', *American Anthropologist* 56, 155–68.

Hawkes, J., 1967, 'God in the Machine', *Antiquity* 41, 174–80.

Hawkes, J., and Hawkes, C. F. C., 1947, *Prehistoric Britain*. London: Chatto and Windus.

Hawkins, Gerald, 1970, *Stonehenge Decoded*. London: Fontana.

Hawkins, Gerald, 1973, *Beyond Stonehenge*. London: Hutchinson.

Headley, Gwyn, and Meulenkamp, Wim, 1990, *Follies*. London: Jonathan Cape.

Hedges, John, 1984, *Tomb of the Eagles: A Window on Stone Age Tribal Britain*. London: John Murray.

Heggie, Douglas, 1981, *Megalithic Science*. London: Thames and Hudson.

Hemp, W. J., 1930, 'The Chambered Cairn of Bryn Celli Ddu', *Archaeologia* 80, 179–214.

Henshall, A. S., 1963 and 1972, *The Chambered Tombs of Scotland*, 2 vols. Edinburgh: Edinburgh University Press.

Henshall, A. S., and Davidson, J. L., 1989, *The Chambered Cairns of Orkney*. Edinburgh: Edinburgh University Press.

Henshall, A. S., and Davidson, J. L., 1991, *The Chambered Cairns of Caithness*. Edinburgh: Edinburgh University Press.

Herbert, Algernon, 1849, *Cyclops Christianus: or An Argument to Disprove the Supposed Antiquity of Stonehenge and Other Megalithic Erections in England and Brittany*. London: John Petheram.

Herodotus, *The Histories*, translated by Aubrey de Selincourt. Harmondsworth: Penguin, 1954.

Hitching, Francis, 1977, *Earth Magic*. London: Picador.

Hitchins, Malachi, 1803, 'Account of Roman Urns Discovered in Cornwall, and of a Cromlech Discovered in the Parish of Madron in the Same County', *Archaeologia* 14, 224–30.

Hoare, Sir Richard Colt, 1812, *The Ancient History of South Wiltshire*. London: William Miller.

Hoare, Sir Richard Colt, 1819, *The Ancient History of North Wiltshire*. London: Lackington, Hughes, Harding, Mavor and Jones.

Hodder, Ian, 1988, 'Material Culture Texts and Social Change: A Theoretical Discussion and Some Archaeological Examples', *Proceedings of the Prehistoric Society* 58, 67–75.

Hodder, Ian, 1991, *Reading the Past: Current Approaches to Interpretation in Archaeology.* Cambridge: Cambridge University Press.

Hoskins, W. G., 1955, *The Making of the English Landscape.* London: Hodder and Stoughton.

Hoyle, Fred, 1966, 'Stonehenge: An Eclipse Predictor', *Nature* 211, 454–56.

Hoyle, Fred, 1966, 'Speculations on Stonehenge', *Antiquity* 40, 262–76.

Hoyle, Fred, 1977, *On Stonehenge.* London: Heinemann.

Hunt, Robert, 1923, *Popular Romances of the West of England.* London: Chatto & Windus.

Hunter, Michael, 1975, *John Aubrey and the Realm of Learning.* London: Duckworth.

Innes, Cosmo, 1860, 'Notice of the Stone Circle of Callernish', *Proceedings of the Society of Antiquaries of Scotland* 3, 110–12.

Ivimy, John, 1974, *The Sphinx and the Megaliths.* London: Turnstone.

Jackson, J. E. (ed.), 1862, *Wiltshire: The Topographical Collections of John Aubrey.* Devizes: Wiltshire Archaeological and Natural History Society.

Jolly, William, 1882, 'On Cup-Marked Stones in the Neighbourhood of Inverness', *Proceedings of the Society of Antiquaries of Scotland* 16, 300–40.

Jones, Barbara, 1974, *Follies and Grottoes.* London: Constable.

Jones, Inigo, 1655, *The Most Notable Antiquity of Great Britain, Vulgarly Called Stone-heng on Salisbury Plain.* London: Daniel Pakeman and Laurence Chapman (facsimile edition The Scolar Press, London, 1972).

Keiller, A., and Piggott, S., 1936, 'The Recent Excavations at Avebury', *Antiquity* 10, 417–27.

Keiller, A., and Piggott, S., 1938, 'Excavation of an Untouched Chamber in the Lanhill Long Barrow', *Proceedings of the Prehistoric Society* 4, 122–50.

Keiller, A., and Piggott, S., 1939, 'The Chambered Tomb in Beowulf', *Antiquity* 13, 360–61.

Kemble, J. M., 1857, 'Notices of Heathen Interment in the Codex Diplomaticus', *Archaeological Journal* 14, 119–39.

Kendrick, T. D., 1927, *The Druids.* London: Methuen.

Kilbride-Jones, H. E., 1935, 'An Account of the Excavation of the Stone Circle at Loanhead of Daviot, and of the Standing Stones of Cullerlie, Echt, both in Aberdeenshire', *Proceedings of the Society of Antiquaries of Scotland* 69, 168–223.

Kinnes, Ian, 1992, *Non-Megalithic Long Barrows and Allied Structures in the British Neolithic.* London: British Museum Occasional Paper 52.

Knight, W. F. J., 1932, 'Maze Symbolism and the Trojan Game', *Antiquity* 6, 445–58.

Lambrick, George, 1988, *The Rollright Stones: Megaliths, Monuments and Settlement in the*

Prehistoric Landscape. London: Historic Buildings and Monuments Commission, Archaeological Report 6.

Lethbridge, T. C., 1972, *The Legend of the Sons of God*. London: Routledge and Kegan Paul.

Lewis, A. L., 1892, 'Stone Circles of Britain', *Archaeological Journal* 49, 136–54.

Lewis, A. L., 1895, 'Prehistoric Remains in Cornwall', *Journal of the Anthropological Institute* 25, 2–16.

Lewis, A. L., 1900, 'The Stone Circles of Scotland', *Journal of the Anthropological Institute* 30 (new series 3), 56–73.

Lockyer, Sir J. Norman, 1909, *Stonehenge and Other British Stone Monuments, Astronomically Considered*. London: Macmillan.

Long, William, 1858, 'Abury', *Wiltshire Archaeological and Natural History Magazine* 4, 309–63.

Lubbock, J., 1865, *Pre-Historic Times, as Illustrated by Ancient Remains and the Manners and Customs of Modern Savages*. London: Williams and Norgate.

Lukis, W. C., 1877, 'On Some Megalithic Monuments in Western Cornwall', *Journal of the British Archaeological Association* 33, 291–96.

Lukis, W. C., 1883, 'Report on the Prehistoric Monuments of Wilts, Somerset, and South Wales', *Proceedings of the Society of Antiquaries of London* 9, 344–55.

MacKie, E. W., 1977, *Science and Society in Prehistoric Britain*. London: Paul Elek.

Marsden, Barry M., 1974, *The Early Barrow Diggers*. Princes Risborough: Shire Publications.

Marsden, Barry M., 1984, *Pioneers of Prehistory: Leaders and Landmarks in English Archaeology, 1500–1900*. Ormskirk: G. W. and A. Hesketh.

Marwick, Ernest, 1975, *The Folklore of Orkney and Shetland*. London: Batsford.

Mercer, Roger, 1980, *Hambledon Hill: A Neolithic Landscape*. Edinburgh: Edinburgh University Press.

Mercer, Roger, 1981, 'The Excavation of a Late Neolithic Henge-Type Enclosure at Balfarg, Markinch, Fife, Scotland', *Proceedings of the Society of Antiquaries of Scotland* 111, 63–171.

Merewether, John, 1851, *Diary of a Dean: Being an Account of the Examination of Silbury Hill*. London: George Bell.

Michell, John, 1969, *The View over Atlantis*. London: Sago Press.

Michell, John, 1970, 'Alfred Watkins: A Note', in Alfred Watkins, *The Old Straight Track*, xv-xvii. London: Garnstone Press.

Michell, John, 1974, *The Old Stones of Land's End: An Enquiry into the Mysteries of Megalithic Science*. London: Garnstone Press.

Michell, John, 1983, *The New View over Atlantis*. London: Thames and Hudson.

Michell, John, 1989, *A Little History of Astro-Archaeology: Stages in the Transformation of a Heresy*. London: Thames and Hudson.

Morgan, Faith de Mallet, 1959, 'The Excavation of a Long Barrow at Nutbane, Hants', *Proceedings of the Prehistoric Society* 25, 15–51.

Morris, Christopher (ed.), 1949, *The Journeys of Celia Fiennes*. London: Cresset.

Morrison, Tony, 1978, *Pathways to the Gods: The Mystery of the Andes Lines*. Salisbury: Michael Russell.

Mortimer, J. R., 1905, *Forty Years' Researches in British and Saxon Burial Mounds of East Yorkshire*. London: Brown and Sons.

Mowl, Tim, and Earnshaw, Brian, 1988, *John Wood: Architect of Obsession*. Bath: Millstream Books.

Muir, Richard, 1981, *Shell Guide to Reading the Landscape*. London: Michael Joseph.

Newall, R. S., 1977, *Stonehenge*. London: HMSO.

Newham, C. A., 1964, *The Enigma of Stonehenge and its Astronomical and Geometrical Significance*. Privately published.

Newham, C. A., 1966, 'Stonehenge: A Neolithic Observatory', *Nature* 211, 456–58.

Newham, C. A., 1972, *The Astronomical Significance of Stonehenge*. Leeds: John Blackburn.

North, John, 1996, *Stonehenge: Neolithic Man and the Cosmos*. London: Harper Collins.

O'Brien, Christian, 1983, *The Megalithic Odyssey*. Wellingborough: Turnstone Press.

O'Kelly, Michael J., 1982, *Newgrange: Archaeology, Art and Legend*. London: Thames and Hudson.

Owen, A. L., 1962, *The Famous Druids*. Oxford: Clarendon Press.

Owen, Tim, and Pilbeam, Elaine, 1992, *Ordnance Survey: Map Makers to Britain since 1791*. Southampton: Ordnance Survey, and Norwich: HMSO.

Parker Pearson, Michael, 1993, *Bronze Age Britain*. London: Batsford.

Patrick, J., 1974, 'Midwinter Sunrise at Newgrange', *Nature* 249, 517–19.

Pegge, Rev., 1785, 'A Disquisition on the Lows or Barrows in the Peak of Derbyshire, Particularly that Capital British Monument called Arbelows', *Archaeologia* 7, 131–48.

Pennick, Nigel, and Devereux, Paul, 1989, *Lines on the Landscape: Leys and Other Linear Enigmas*. London: Robert Hale.

Peter, James, 1885, 'Notice of Stone Circles, in the Parish of Old Deer', *Proceedings of the Society of Antiquaries of Scotland* 19, 370–77.

Petrie, George, 1863, 'The Picts' Houses in the Orkneys', *Archaeological Journal* 20, 32–37.

Petrie, W. M. Flinders, 1880, *Stonehenge: Plans, Descriptions and Theories*. London: Edward Stanford.

Phillips, C. W., 1935, 'The Excavation of Giants' Hills Long Barrow, Skendleby, Lincolnshire', *Archaeologia* 85, 37–106.

Piggott, Stuart, 1938, 'The Early Bronze Age in Wessex', *Proceedings of the Prehistoric Society* 4, 52–106.

Piggott, Stuart, 1940, 'Timber Circles: A Re-Examination', *Archaeological Journal* 96, 193–222.

Piggott, Stuart, 1949, 'The Excavation at Cairnpapple Hill, West Lothian', *Proceedings of the Society of Antiquaries of Scotland* 82, 68–123.

Piggott, Stuart, 1954, *The Neolithic Cultures of the British Isles*. Cambridge: Cambridge University Press.

Piggott, Stuart, 1959, *Approach to Archaeology*. London: A. and C. Black.

Piggott, Stuart, 1959, 'The Radio-Carbon Date from Durrington Walls', *Antiquity* 33, 289–90.

Piggott, Stuart, 1962, *The West Kennet Long Barrow: Excavations, 1955–56*. London: HMSO.

Piggott, Stuart, 1973, 'The Dalladies Long Barrow', *Antiquity* 47, 32–36.

Piggott, Stuart, 1974, *The Druids*. Harmondsworth: Penguin.

Piggott, Stuart, 1985, *William Stukeley: An Eighteenth-Century Antiquary*. London: Thames and Hudson.

Piggott, Stuart, 1989, *Ancient Britons and the Antiquarian Imagination*. London: Thames and Hudson.

Piggott, Stuart, 1993, 'John Thurnam and British Prehistory', *Wiltshire Archaeology and Natural History Magazine* 86, 1–7.

Piggott, S., and Powell, T. G. E., 1950, 'The Excavation of Three Neolithic Chambered Tombs in Galloway', *Proceedings of the Society of Antiquaries of Scotland* 83, 103–61.

Pitt Rivers, A. L. F., 1898, *Excavations in Cranborne Chase*, vol. 4. Privately published.

Pitts, M., and Whittle, A., 1992, 'The Development and Date of Avebury', *Proceedings of the Prehistoric Society* 58, 203–12.

Pollard, J., 1992, 'The Sanctuary, Overton Hill, Wiltshire: A Re-Examination', *Proceedings of the Prehistoric Society* 58, 213–26.

Pool, P. A. S., 1986, *William Borlase*. Truro: Royal Institution of Cornwall.

Powell, Anthony, 1948, *John Aubrey and his Friends*. London: Eyre and Spottiswoode.

Radford, C. A. R., and Rawlins, S. W., 1963, 'Harold St George Gray, 1872–1963', *Proceedings of the Somerset Archaeological and Natural History Society* 107, 111–15.

Renfrew, Colin, 1973, 'Monuments, Mobilization and Social Organisation in Neolithic Wessex', in Colin Renfrew (ed.), *The Explanation of Culture Change: Models in Prehistory*, 539–58. London: Duckworth.

Renfrew, Colin, 1976, *Before Civilization: The Radiocarbon Revolution and Prehistoric Europe*. Harmondsworth: Penguin.

Renfrew, Colin, 1979, *Investigations in Orkney*. London: Society of Antiquaries of London.

Renfrew, Colin (ed.), 1985, *The Prehistory of Orkney*. Edinburgh: Edinburgh University Press.

Renfrew, Colin and Shennan, Stephen (eds), 1982, *Ranking, Resource and Exchange: Aspects of the Archaeology of Early European Society*. Cambridge: Cambridge University Press.

Richards, Julian, 1990, *The Stonehenge Environs Project*. London: Historic Buildings and Monuments Commission for England, Archaeological Report 16.

Richards, Julian, 1991, *The English Heritage Book of Stonehenge*. London: Batsford.

Ritchie, James, 1918, 'Cup-Marks on the Stone Circles and Standing-Stones of Aberdeenshire and Part of Banffshire', *Proceedings of the Society of Antiquaries of Scotland* 52, 86–121.

Ritchie, James, 1927, 'Folklore of the Aberdeenshire Stone Circles and Standing Stones', *Proceedings of the Society of Antiquaries of Scotland* 60, 304–13.

Ritchie, J. N. G., 1976, 'The Stones of Stenness, Orkney', *Proceedings of the Society of Antiquaries of Scotland* 107, 1–60.

Roberts, Anthony, 1975, *Atlantean Traditions in Ancient Britain*. London: Rider.

Roberts, Anthony, 1978, *Sowers of Thunder: Giants in Myth and History*. London: Rider.

Robins, Don, 1985, *Circles of Silence*. London: Souvenir Press.

Rooke, Hayman, 1796, 'An Account of Some Druidical Remains in Derbyshire', *Archaeologia* 12, 41–49.

Rowe, Samuel, 1896, *A Perambulation of the Antient and Royal Forest of Dartmoor* (reprinted Devon Books, Exeter, 1985).

Rowlands, Henry, 1766, *Mona Antiqua Restaurata: An Archaeological Discourse on the Antiquities, Natural and Historical, of the Isle of Anglesey*. London: J. Knox.

Saville, Alan, 1990, *Hazleton North, Gloucestershire, 1979–82*. London: Historic Buildings and Monuments Commission, Archaeological Report 13.

Scott, Sir Walter, 1895, *The Pirate*. London: Macmillan.

Scott, W. L., 1933, 'The Chambered Tomb of Pant-y-Saer, Anglesey', *Archaeologia Cambrensis* 88, 185–228.

Scott, W. L., 1935, 'The Chambered Cairn of Clettraval, North Uist', *Proceedings of the Society of Antiquaries of Scotland* 69, 480–536.

Scott, W. L., 1949, 'The Chamber Tomb of Unival, North Uist', *Proceedings of the Society of Antiquaries of Scotland* 82, 1–49.

Screeton, Paul, 1974, *Quicksilver Heritage: The Mystic Leys: Their Legacy of Ancient Wisdom*. Wellingborough: Thorsons.

Seyer, Samuel, 1821, *Memoirs Historical and Topographical of Bristol and its Neighbourhood*. Bristol: John Mathew Gutch.

Sherratt, A. G., 1972, 'Socio-Economic and Demographic Models for the Neolithic and Bronze Ages of Europe', in David L. Clarke (ed.), *Models in Archaeology*, 477–542. London: Methuen.

Simpson, James, 1867, 'On Ancient Sculpturings of Cups and Concentric Rings &c', *Proceedings of the Society of Antiquaries of Scotland* 6, appendix volume.

Smith, A. C., 1867, 'Excavations at Avebury', *Wiltshire Archaeology and Natural History Magazine* 10, 209–16.

Smith, I. F., 1965, *Windmill Hill and Avebury: Excavations by Alexander Keiller, 1925–1939*. Oxford: Clarendon Press.

Smith, Lucy Toulmin (ed.), 1907–10, *The Itinerary of John Leland in or about the Years 1535–43*, 5 vols. London: George Bell and Sons.

Somerville, Boyle, 1912, 'Prehistoric Monuments in the Outer Hebrides, and Their Astronomical Significance', *Journal of the Royal Anthropological Institute* 42, 23–53.

Somerville, Boyle, 1923, 'Instances of Orientation in Prehistoric Monuments of the British Isles', *Archaeologia* 73, 193–224.

Somerville, Boyle, 1927, 'Orientation', *Antiquity* 1, 31–41.

Spence, Magnus, 1894, *Standing Stones and Maeshowe of Stenness*. Paisley: Gardner.

Stevens, Frank, 1919, *Stonehenge: To-Day and Yesterday*. London: HMSO.

Stone, J. F. S., 1947, 'The Stonehenge Cursus and its Affinities', *Archaeological Journal* 104, 7–19.

Stukeley, William, 1722–24, 'Celtic Religion'. Cardiff Central Library, MS 4.26.

Stukeley, William, 1722–24, 'Stonehenge'. Cardiff Central Library, MS 4.253.

Stukeley, William, 1722–24, 'The History of the Temples of the Antient Celts'. Bodleian Library, MS Eng. Misc. c 323.

Stukeley, William, 1740, *Stonehenge, a Temple Restored to the British Druids*. London: W. Innys and R. Manby.

Stukeley, William, 1743, *Abury, a Temple of the British Druids, with Some Others, Described*. London: W. Innys, R. Manby, B. Dod and J. Brindley.

Stukeley, William, 1887, *The Family Memoirs of the Rev. William Stukeley*, vol. 3. Surtees Society 80, for 1885.

Tacitus, *The Annals of Imperial Rome*, translated by Michael Grant. Harmondsworth: Penguin, 1971.

Taylor, Christopher, 1988, 'Introduction and Commentary', in W. G. Hoskins, *The Making of the English Landscape*. London: Hodder and Stoughton.

Thom, Alexander, 1967, *Megalithic Sites in Britain*. Oxford: Clarendon Press (2nd edition, 1971).

Thom, Alexander, 1971, *Megalithic Lunar Observatories*. Oxford: Clarendon Press.

Thom, A., and Thom, A. S., 1978, *Megalithic Remains in Britain and Brittany*. Oxford: Clarendon Press.

Thomas, F. W. L., 1852, 'Account of Some of the Celtic Antiquities of Orkney', *Archaeologia* 34, 88–117.

Thomas, Julian, 1991, *Rethinking the Neolithic*. Cambridge: Cambridge University Press.

Thomas, J., and Whittle, A., 1986, 'Anatomy of a Tomb: West Kennet Revisited', *Oxford Journal of Archaeology* 5, 129–56.

Thomsen, C. J., 1848, *Guide to Northern Antiquities*, translated by the Earl of Ellesmere. London.

Thurnam, J., 1860, 'On the Examination of a Chambered Long-Barrow at West Kennet, Wiltshire', *Archaeologia* 38, 405–21.

Thurnam, J., 1869, 'On Ancient British Barrows: Part I, Long Barrows', *Archaeologia* 42, 161–244.

Thurnam, J., 1871, 'On Ancient British Barrows: Part II, Round Barrows', *Archaeologia* 43, 285–552.

Tilley, Christopher, 1994, *A Phenomenology of Landscape: Places, Paths and Monuments*. Oxford: Berg.

Toulson, Shirley, 1984, *The Moors of the Southwest*, 2 vols. London: Hutchinson.

Tregelles, G. F., 1906, 'Stone Circles', in W. Page (ed.), *The Victoria History of the County of Cornwall*, vol. 1, 379–406. London: Archibald Constable.

Trotter, A. P., 1927, 'Stonehenge as an Astronomical Instrument', *Antiquity* 1, 42–53.

Twining, Thomas, 1723, *Avebury in Wiltshire: The Remains of a Roman Work, Erected by Vespasian and Julius Agricola, during their Several Commands in Brittany*. London: J. Downing.

Tylden-Wright, David, 1991, *John Aubrey: A Life*. London: Harper Collins.

Ucko, P. J., Hunter, M., Clark, A. J., and David, A., 1991, *Avebury Reconsidered: From the 1660s to the 1990s*. London: Unwin Hyman.

Underwood, Guy, 1969, *The Pattern of the Past*. London: Museum Press.

Virgil, *The Aeneid*, translated by W. F. Jackson Knight. Harmondsworth: Penguin, 1956.

Wainwright, Geoffrey, 1989, *The Henge Monuments*. London: Thames and Hudson.

Warne, Charles, 1866, *The Celtic Tumuli of Dorset*. London: John Russell Smith.

Watkins, Alfred, 1922, *Early British Trackways*. London: Simpkin Marshall.

Watkins, Alfred, 1925, *The Old Straight Track*. London, Methuen (facsimile edition, Garnstone Press, London, 1970).

Watkins, Alfred, 1927, *The Ley Hunter's Manual: A Guide to Early Tracks*, (facsimile edition, Turnstone Press, Wellingborough, 1983).

Weatherhill, Craig, 1981, *Belerion: Ancient Sites of Land's End*. Penzance: Alison Hodge.

Wedd, Tony, 1961, *Skyways and Landmarks*. Privately printed.

Wheeler, R. E. M., 1925, *Prehistoric and Roman Wales*. Oxford: Clarendon Press.

Whitlock, Ralph, 1977, *The Folklore of Devon*. London: Batsford.

Whittle, A., 1991, 'Wayland's Smithy, Oxfordshire: Excavations at the Neolithic Tomb in 1962–63 by R. J. C. Atkinson and S. Piggott', *Proceedings of the Prehistoric Society* 57/2, 61–101.

Whittle, A., 1991, 'A Late Neolithic Complex at West Kennet, Wiltshire, England', *Antiquity* 65, 256–62.

Willey, Basil, 1934, *The Eighteenth-Century Background*. London: Chatto.

Williamson, Tom, and Bellamy, Liz, 1983, *Ley Lines in Question*. Tadworth: World's Work.

Wilson, Daniel, 1851, *The Archaeology and Prehistoric Annals of Scotland*. Edinburgh: Sutherland and Knox.

Wilson, Daniel, 1862, *Prehistoric Man: Researches into the Origin of Civilisation in the Old and New World*. Cambridge: Macmillan.

Wood, John, 1747, *Choir Gaure, Vulgarly Called Stonehenge, on Salisbury Plain, Described, Restored, and Explained*. Oxford.

Wood, John, 1749, *An Essay towards a Description of Bath*, vol. 1. London: C. Hitch, and Bath: J. Leake.

Wood, J. E., 1978, *Sun, Moon and Standing Stones*. Oxford: Oxford University Press.

Woodbridge, Kenneth, 1970, *Landscape and Antiquity: Aspects of English Culture at Stourhead, 1718–1838*. Oxford: Clarendon Press.

Worth, R. H., 1953, *Worth's Dartmoor*. Privately published (republished David and Charles, Newton Abbot, 1967).

Worth, R. N., 1892, 'The Stone Rows of Dartmoor', *Transactions of the Devon Association for the Advancement of Science* 24, 387–417.

Worth, R. N., 1893, 'The Stone Rows of Dartmoor, Part II', *Transactions of the Devon Association for the Advancement of Science* 25, 541–46.

Index